# The Book of
# the Courtier

# The Book of the Courtier

Baldassare Castiglione

Translated by
Leonard Eckstein Opdycke

Dover Publications, Inc.
Mineola, New York

*Bibliographical Note*

This Dover edition, first published in 2003, is an unabridged republication of the edition published by Horace Liveright, New York, in 1929 (originally published in 1901).

*Library of Congress Cataloging-in-Publication Data*

Castiglione, Baldassare, conte, 1478-1529.
   [Libro del cortegiano. English]
   The book of the courtier / Baldassare Castiglione.—Dover ed.
     p. cm.
   Originally published: New York : H. Liveright, c1929.
   Includes bibliographical references and index.
   ISBN 0-486-42702-1 (pbk.)
    1. Courts and courtiers—Early works to 1800. 2. Courtesy—Early works to 1800. I. Title.

BJ1604.C4413 2003
170'.44—dc21
                                          2002041559

Manufactured in the United States of America
Dover Publications, Inc., 31 East 2nd Street, Mineola, N.Y. 11501

# TRANSLATOR'S PREFACE

REASONS for presenting this old book anew were found in the esteem that it long enjoyed, in the rank still held by it in Italian literature, and in the fact that, of three former English versions, the first (recently twice reprinted) is too antiquated to be readily intelligible to the general reader, while the other two (published more than one hundred and fifty years ago) are seldom met in any but large public libraries.

When Castiglione wrote, the sturdy Knight of earlier ages had become the accomplished Courtier. In describing this new hero, the author gave utterance to the finest aspirations of his day. Life was, it is true, sometimes gross and violent, but even if the delicate and gentle beauty of Renaissance art furnished us no evidence, these pages would suffice to show that a loftier standard of thought and conduct had been raised. The book will not lack interest until mankind ceases to be interesting to man, and will reward study so long as the past shall continue to instruct the present and the future.

The only deviations that the translator has consciously made from the letter of the original were deemed necessary to render its meaning clear. The notes that he offers are intended to give further light on obscure passages and to relieve the reader from the tedium of searching in books of reference. No one, perhaps, will take it amiss to be reminded of what all may have known but few are able to remember with precision.

The translator desires to repeat his thanks for the friendly encouragement that he received from Miss Grace Norton, at whose suggestion his task was undertaken. He is indebted to Dr. Luigi Roversi and Signor Leopoldo Jung for patient aid, to Professor Hastings Crossley for revision of the notes, and to Signor Alessandro Luzio and other scholars for the kindness with which they contributed iconographical and bibliographical data. He gratefully acknowledges, also, his constant use of the material contained in Professor Vittorio Cian's admirable edition of the text.

The second issue of the present translation has afforded opportunity for some corrections.

THE BOOK OF THE COURTIER was written, partly at
Urbino and partly at Rome, between the years
1508 and 1516, and was first printed at the Aldine
Press, Venice, in the month of April, 1528.
There have since been published more than one hun-
dred and forty editions. The first Spanish version,
by JUAN BOSCAN ALMOGAVER, was issued at
Barcelona in 1534; the first French version, by
JACQUES COLIN, was issued at Paris in 1537; the
first English version, by THOMAS HOBY, was issued
at London in 1561; the first Latin version, by
HIERONYMUS TURLER, was issued at Wittenberg
in 1561; the first German version, by LORENZ
KRATZER, was issued at Munich in 1566.

# CONTENTS

x CONTENTS

# INTERLOCUTORS

ELISABETTA GONZAGA, wife of Guidobaldo di Montefeltro, Duke of Urbino. Aged 46.

EMILIA PIA, friend and companion of the Duchess, and widow of the Duke's half-brother. Aged about 30.

MARGARITA GONZAGA, young niece and companion of the Duchess.

COSTANZA FREGOSA, young half-niece of the Duke.

FRANCESCO MARIA DELLA ROVERE, nephew and adopted heir of the Duke. Aged 17.

Count LUDOVICO DA CANOSSA, a kinsman of the author, afterwards made Bishop of Bayeux, Aged 31.

FEDERICO FREGOSO, half-nephew of the Duke, afterwards made a cardinal. Aged 27.

GIULIANO DE' MEDICI, an exile from Florence, known at Urbino as "My lord Magnifico," and afterwards made Duke of Nemours. Aged 29.

BERNARDO DOVIZI, better known as BIBBIENA, an adherent of the Medici, afterwards made a cardinal. Aged 37.

OTTAVIANO FREGOSO, elder brother of Costanza and Federico, afterwards Doge of Genoa.

PIETRO BEMBO, a Venetian scholar and poet, afterwards made a cardinal. Aged 37.

CESARE GONZAGA, a kinsman of the Duchess, and cousin as well as close friend of the author. Aged about 32.

BERNARDO ACCOLTI, better known as the UNICO ARETINO, a courtier-poet and popular extemporizer. Aged about 42.

Count GASPAR PALLAVICINO. Aged 21.

GIANCRISTOFORO ROMANO, a sculptor, medallist, etc. Aged about 42.

COLLO VINCENZO CALMETA, a courtier-poet.

LUDOVICO PIO, a brave young soldier, and kinsman of Emilia Pia.

SIGISMONDO MORELLO DA ORTONA, an elderly courtier.

Marquess FEBUS DI CEVA, ⎫
NICCOLO FRISIO, ⎪
PIETRO DA NAPOLI, ⎬ courtiers.
ROBERTO MASSIMO DA BARI, ⎭

Fra SERAFINO, a jester.

Time: March 1507.

Place: The Palace of Urbino.

# THE BOOK OF
# THE COURTIER

## TO THE REVEREND AND ILLUSTRIOUS LORD DOM MIGUEL DE SILVA,[1] BISHOP OF VISEU

HEN MY LORD GUIDOBALDO DI MONTE-FELTRO,[2] Duke of Urbino, passed from this life, I, together with several other cavaliers who had served him, remained in the service of Duke Francesco Maria della Rovere,[3] his heir and successor in the State. And as the recollection of Duke Guido's character was fresh in my mind, and the delight I had during those years in the kind companionship of the notable persons who at that time frequented the Court of Urbino, I was moved by their memory to write these books of the Courtier, which I did in a few days,[4] purposing in time to correct those errors that arose from the wish to pay this debt speedily. But for many years past fortune has burdened me with toil so constant that I never could find leisure to make the book such as would content even my poor judgment.

Now being in Spain,[5] and learning from Italy that my lady Vittoria della Colonna, Marchioness of Pescara,[6] to whom I gave a copy of the book, had against her word caused a large part of it to be transcribed, I could not but feel some annoyance, fearing the many inconveniences that may befall in such cases. Still, I relied upon the wit and good sense of this lady (whose character I have always held in veneration as a thing divine) to prevent any mischief coming to me from having obeyed her wishes. Finally I was informed that this part of the book was in the hands of many people at Naples; and as men are always eager for anything new, it seemed likely that someone might try to have it printed.[7] Alarmed at this peril, then, I resolved to revise the book at once so far as I had time, with intent to publish it; for I thought

I

ﬀﬀﬀﬀﬀﬀﬀﬀﬀﬀﬀﬀﬀﬀﬀﬀﬀﬀﬀﬀﬀﬀﬀﬀﬀﬀﬀﬀﬀﬀﬀﬀﬀﬀﬀﬀﬀﬀﬀﬀﬀﬀﬀﬀﬀ

better to let it be seen imperfectly corrected by my own hand than grievously mutilated by the hand of others.

And so, to carry out this plan, I began to read the book again; and touched at the very outset by the title, I was saddened not a little, and far more so as I went on, by the thought that most of the personages introduced in the discussion were already dead; for besides those mentioned in the proem of the last Book, messer Alfonso Ariosto [8] (to whom the work is dedicated) is also dead, a gracious youth, considerate, of the highest breeding, and apt in everything proper to a man who lives at court. Likewise Duke Giuliano de' Medici,[9] whose kindness and noble courtesy deserved to be enjoyed longer by the world. Messer Bernardo,[10] Cardinal of Santa Maria in Portico, who for his keen and playful readiness of wit was most delightful to all that knew him, he, too, is dead. Dead also is my lord Ottaviano Fregoso,[11] a man very rare in our times: magnanimous, devout, full of kindness, talent, good sense, and courtesy, a true lover of honour and merit, and so worthy of praise that his very enemies were ever forced to praise him; and the misadventures that he bore so bravely were enough to prove that fortune is still, as always, adverse to merit. And of those mentioned in my book many more besides are dead, to whom nature seemed to promise very long life.

But what should not be told without tears is that my lady Duchess,[12] too, is dead. And if my heart mourns the loss of so many friends and patrons, who have left me in this life as in a solitude full of sorrows, it is meet that I grieve more bitterly for the death of my lady Duchess than of all the others; for she was more precious than they, and I more bound to her than to all the others. Not to delay, then, the tribute that I owe the memory of so excellent a Lady and of the others who are no more, and moved also by the danger to my book, I have had it printed and published in such state as the shortness of time permitted.

And since you had no knowledge in their lifetime either of my lady Duchess or of the others who are dead (except Duke Giuliano and the Cardinal of Santa Maria in Portico), in order to give you that knowledge after their death as far as I can, I send you this book as a picture of the Court of Urbino, not by the hand of Raphael [98] or Michelangelo,[99] but of a humble painter, who

knows only how to trace the chief lines, and cannot adorn truth
with bright colouring, or by perspective art make that which is
not seem to be. And although I tried to show forth in their discourse the qualities and character of my personages, I own I failed
to express or even to suggest the excellences of my lady Duchess,
not only because my style is inadequate to describe them, but because my intelligence fails even to conceive of them;[13] and if I be
censured for this or any other matter worthy of censure (for I
well know that my book contains many such), I shall not gainsay the truth.

2.—But as men sometimes so delight in finding fault that
they reprehend even that which does not merit reprehension, to
such as blame me because I did not imitate Boccaccio[14] or conform
to the usages of present Tuscan speech, I shall not refrain from
saying that while, for his time, Boccaccio had a charming faculty
and often wrote with care and diligence, yet he wrote far better
when he followed only the guidance of his natural wit and instinct,
without further thought or care to polish his writings, than when
he strove industriously and laboriously to be more refined and
correct. For this reason even his followers declare that he greatly
erred in judgment concerning his own works, holding cheap
what did him honour[15] and prizing what was worthless. Therefore, if I had imitated that manner of writing which in Boccaccio
is censured by those who elsewise praise him, I should not have
been able to escape those same aspersions that were cast on him
in this regard; and I should have more deserved them, because
he committed his faults thinking he was doing well, while I
should have known I was doing ill. Again, if I had imitated the
style now admired by many but less esteemed by him, it seemed
to me that by such imitation I should show myself at variance
with him whom I was imitating, a thing I deemed unseemly.
And again, if this consideration had not moved me, I was not
able to imitate him in my subject-matter, for he never wrote anything at all in the manner of these books of the Courtier; and I
thought I ought not to imitate him in language, because the
power and true law of good speech consist rather in usage than
in aught else, and it is always a bad habit to employ words not
in use. Therefore it was not meet for me to borrow many of

Boccaccio's words that were used in his day, but are not now used even by the Tuscans themselves.

Nor was I willing to limit myself to the Tuscan usage of to-day, because intercourse between different nations has always had the effect to transport, as it were like merchandise, new forms of speech from one to the other; and these endure or fail according as custom accepts or rejects them. Besides being at-tested by the ancients, this is clearly seen in Boccaccio, who used so many French, Spanish, and Provençal words (some of them perhaps not very intelligible to modern Tuscans) that if they were all omitted his work would be far shorter.

And since, in my opinion, we ought not to despise the idiom of the other noble cities of Italy, whither men resort who are wise, witty, and eloquent, wont to discourse on weighty matters of statecraft, letters, war, and commerce, I think that, of the words used in the speech of these places, I could fitly use in writing such as are graceful in themselves, elegant to pronounce, and commonly deemed good and expressive, although they might not be Tuscan or even of Italian origin. Moreover, in Tuscany, many words are used which are plainly corruptions of the Latin, but which in Lombardy and other parts of Italy have remained pure and unchanged, and are so generally employed by everyone that they are accepted by the gentle and easily understood by the vul-gar. Hence I think I did not err if in writing I used some of these words, or preferred what is whole and true speech of my own country rather than what is corrupt and mutilated from abroad.

Neither do I regard as sound the maxim laid down by many, that our common speech is the more beautiful the less it is like Latin; nor do I understand why one fashion of speech should be accorded so much greater authority than another, that, if the Tuscan tongue can ennoble debased and mutilated Latin words and lend them such grace that, mutilated as they are, they may be used by anyone without reproach (which is not denied), the Lombard or any other tongue may not support these same Latin words, pure, whole, precise, and quite unchanged, so that they be tolerable. And truly, just as to undertake, in spite of usage, to coin new words or to preserve old ones may be called bold presumption, so also, besides being difficult, it seems almost impious to undertake, against the force of that same usage, to suppress and bury alive, as it were, words that have already endured for many centuries, protected by the shield of custom against the envy of time, and have maintained their dignity and splendour through the changes in language, in buildings, in habits and in customs, wrought by the wars and disasters of Italy.

Hence if in writing I have chosen not to use those words of Boccaccio that are no longer used in Tuscany, nor to conform to the rule of those who deem it not permissible to use any words that the Tuscans of to-day do not use, I seem to myself excusable. And I think that both in the matter and in the language of my book (so far as one language can aid another), I have followed authors as worthy of praise as is Boccaccio. Nor do I believe that it ought to be counted against me as a fault that I have elected to make myself known rather as a Lombard speaking Lombard, than as a non-Tuscan speaking Tuscan too precisely, in order that I might not resemble Theophrastus, who was detected as non-Athenian by a simple old woman, because he spoke the Athenian dialect with excess of care.[16]

But as this subject is sufficiently treated of in my first Book,[17] I shall say no more, except that, to prevent all possible discussion, I grant my critics that I do not know this Tuscan dialect of theirs, which is so difficult and recondite. And I declare that I have written in my own dialect, just as I speak and for those who speak as I do; and in this I think I have wronged no man, because it seems to me that no one is forbidden to write and speak in his own language; nor is anyone bound to read or listen to what does not please him. Therefore if these folk do not care to read my Courtier, I shall not hold myself in the least wronged by them.

3.—Others say that since it is so very hard and well nigh impossible to find a man as perfect as I wish the Courtier to be, it was superfluous to write of him, because it is folly to teach what cannot be learned. To these I make answer that I am content to have erred in company with Plato, Xenophon and Marcus Tullius, leaving on one side all discussion about the Intelligible World and Ideals; among which, just as are included (according to those authors) the ideal of the perfect State, of the perfect King and of the perfect Orator,[18] so also is the ideal of the perfect Courtier. And if in my style I have failed to approach the image of this ideal, it will be so much the easier for courtiers to approach in deeds the aim and goal that I have set them by my writing; and even if they fail to attain the perfection, such as it is, that I have tried to express, he that approaches nearest to it will be the most perfect; just as when many archers shoot at a target and none hit the very mark, surely he that comes nearest to it is better than the rest.

Still others say that I thought to paint my own portrait, as if I were convinced that I possessed all the qualities that I attribute to the Courtier.[19] To these I shall not indeed deny having essayed everything that I should wish the Courtier to know; and I think that a man, however learned, who did not know something òf the matters treated of in the book, could not well have written of them; but I am not so lacking in self-discernment as to fancy that I know everything I have the wit to desire.

My defence then against these and perhaps many other accusations, I leave for the present to the verdict of public opinion; for while the many may not perfectly understand, yet oftener than not they scent by natural instinct the savour of good and bad, and without being able to explain why, they relish one thing and like it, and reject another and hate it. Therefore if my book wins general favour, I shall think it must be good and ought to live;[20] but if it fails to please, I shall think it must be bad and soon to be forgot. And if my censors be not satisfied with the common verdict of opinion, let them rest content with that of time, which in the end reveals the hidden defects of everything, and being father of truth and judge without passion, ever passes on men's writings just sentence of life or death.

BALDESAR CASTIGLIONE.

## The First Book

### TO MESSER ALFONSO ARIOSTO

ITHIN MYSELF I HAVE LONG DOUBTED, dearest messer Alfonso, which of two things were the harder for me: to deny you what you have often begged of me so urgently, or to do it. For while it seemed to me very hard to deny anything (and especially a thing in the highest degree laudable) to one whom I love most dearly and by whom I feel myself to be most dearly loved, yet to set about an enterprise that I was not sure of being able to finish, seemed to me ill befitting a man who esteems just censure as it ought to be esteemed. At last, after much thought, I am resolved to try in this matter how much aid my assiduity may gain from that affection and intense desire to please, which in other things are so wont to stimulate the industry of man.

You ask me then to write what is to my thinking the form of Courtiership [21] most befitting a gentleman who lives at the court of princes, by which he may have the ability and knowledge perfectly to serve them in every reasonable thing, winning from them favour, and praise from other men; in short, what manner of man he ought to be who may deserve to be called a perfect Courtier without flaw. Wherefore, considering your request, I say that had it not seemed to me more blameworthy to be reputed somewhat unamiable by you than too conceited by everyone else, I should have avoided this task, for fear of being held over bold by all who know how hard a thing it is, from among such a variety of customs as are in use at the courts of Christendom, to choose the perfect form and as it were the flower of Courtiership. For custom often makes the same thing pleasing and displeasing to us; whence it

7

sometimes follows that customs, habits, ceremonies and fashions that once were prized, become vulgar, and contrariwise the vulgar become prized. Thus it is clearly seen that use rather than reason has power to introduce new things among us, and to do away with the old; and he will often err who seeks to determine which are perfect. Therefore being conscious of this and many other difficulties in the subject set before me to write of, I am constrained to offer some apology, and to testify that this error (if error it may indeed be called) is common to us both, to the end that if I be blamed for it, the blame may be shared by you also; for your offence in setting me a task beyond my powers should not be deemed less than mine in having accepted it.

So now let us make a beginning of our subject, and if possible let us form such a Courtier that any prince worthy to be served by him, although of but small estate,[22] might still be called a very great lord.

In these books we shall follow no fixed order or rule of distinct precepts, such as are usually employed in teaching anything whatever; but after the fashion of many ancient writers, we shall revive a pleasant memory and rehearse certain discussions that were held between men singularly competent in such matters; and although I had no part in them personally, being in England at the time they took place,[23] yet having received them soon after my return, from one who faithfully reported them to me, I will try to recall them as accurately as my memory will permit, so that you may know what was thought and believed on this subject by men who are worthy of highest praise, and to whose judgment implicit faith may be given in all things. Nor will it be amiss to tell the cause of these discussions, so that we may reach in orderly manner the end to which our discourse tends.

2.—On the slopes of the Apennines towards the Adriatic sea, almost in the centre of Italy, there lies (as everyone knows) the little city of Urbino. Although amid mountains, and less pleasing ones than perhaps some others that we see in many places, it has yet enjoyed such favour of heaven that the country round about is very fertile and rich in crops; so that besides the wholesomeness of the air, there is great abundance of everything needful for human life. But among the greatest blessings that can be

attributed to it, this I believe to be the chief, that for a long time
it has ever been ruled by the best of lords; [24] although in the
calamities of the universal wars of Italy, it was for a season deprived of them.[25] But without seeking further, we can give good
proof of this by the glorious memory of Duke Federico,[26] who in
his day was the light of Italy; nor is there lack of credible and
abundant witnesses, who are still living, to his prudence, humanity,
justice, liberality, unconquered courage,—and to his military discipline, which is conspicuously attested by his numerous victories,
his capture of impregnable places, the sudden swiftness of his expeditions, the frequency with which he put to flight large and
formidable armies by means of a very small force, and by his loss
of no single battle whatever; [27] so that we may not unreasonably
compare him to many famous men of old.

Among his other praiseworthy deeds, he built on the rugged
site of Urbino a palace regarded by many as the most beautiful
to be found in all Italy; and he so well furnished it with everything suitable that it seemed not a palace but a city in the form of
a palace; and not merely with what is ordinarily used,—such as
silver vases, hangings of richest cloth-of-gold and silk, and other
similar things,—but for ornament he added countless antique
statues in marble and bronze, pictures most choice, and musical
instruments of every sort, nor would he admit anything there
that was not very rare and excellent. Then at very great cost he
collected a goodly number of most excellent and rare books in
Greek, Latin and Hebrew, all of which he adorned with gold
and with silver, esteeming this to be the chiefest excellence of his
great palace.[28]

3.—Following then the course of nature, and already sixty-
five years old,[29] he died gloriously, as he had lived; and he left as
his successor a motherless little boy of ten years, his only son
Guidobaldo. Heir to the State, he seemed to be heir also to all his
father's virtues, and soon his noble nature gave such promise as
seemed not permissible to hope for from mortal man; so that men
esteemed none among the notable deeds of Duke Federico to be
greater than to have begotten such a son. But envious of so much
virtue, fortune thwarted this glorious beginning with all her
power; so that before Duke Guido reached the age of twenty

years, he fell ill of the gout,[30] which grew upon him with grievous
pain, and in a short space of time so crippled all his members that
he could neither stand upon his feet nor move; and thus one of
the fairest and most promising forms in the world was distorted
and spoiled in tender youth.

And not content even with this, fortune was so contrary to
him in all his purposes, that he could seldom carry into effect anything that he desired; and although he was very wise of counsel
and unconquered in spirit, it seemed that what he undertook, both
in war and in everything else whether small or great, always
ended ill for him. And proof of this is found in his many and diverse calamities, which he ever bore with such strength of mind,
that his spirit was never vanquished by fortune; nay, scorning her
assaults with unbroken courage, he lived in illness as if in health
and in adversity as if fortunate, with perfect dignity and universal esteem; so that although he was thus infirm of body, he
fought with most honourable rank in the service of their Serene
Highnesses the Kings of Naples, Alfonso [31] and Ferdinand the
Younger; [32] later with Pope Alexander VI,[33] and with the Venetian and Florentine signories.

Upon the accession of Julius II [34] to the pontificate, he was
made Captain of the Church; at which time, following his accustomed habit, above all else he took care to fill his household with
very noble and valiant gentlemen, with whom he lived most
familiarly, delighting in their intercourse: wherein the pleasure
he gave to others was not less than that he received from others,
he being well versed in both the [learned] [35] languages, and uniting affability and pleasantness [36] to a knowledge of things without
number. And besides this, the greatness of his spirit so set him on,
that although he could not practise in person the exercises of
chivalry, as he once had done, yet he took the utmost pleasure in
witnessing them in others; and by his words, now correcting now
praising every man according to desert, he clearly showed his
judgment in those matters; wherefore, in jousts and tournaments,
in riding, in the handling of every sort of weapon, as well as in
pastimes, games, music,—in short, in all the exercises proper to
noble cavaliers,—everyone strove so to show himself, as to merit
being deemed worthy of such noble fellowship.

44

4.—Thus all the hours of the day were assigned to honourable and pleasant exercises as well for the body as for the mind;
but since my lord Duke was always wont by reason of his infirmity
to retire to sleep very early after supper, everyone usually betook
himself at that hour to the presence of my lady Duchess, Elisabetta Gonzaga; where also was ever to be found my lady Emilia
Pia,[37] who was endowed with such lively wit and judgment that,
as you know, it seemed as if she were the Mistress of us all, and as
if everyone gained wisdom and worth from her. Here then, gentle
discussions and innocent pleasantries were heard, and on the face
of everyone a jocund gaiety was seen depicted, so that the house
could truly be called the very abode of mirth: nor ever elsewhere,
I think, was so relished, as once was here, how great sweetness
may flow from dear and cherished companionship; for not to
speak of the honour it was to each of us to serve such a lord as he
of whom I have just spoken, there was born in the hearts of all a
supreme contentment every time we came into the presence of my
lady Duchess; and it seemed as if this were a chain that held us
all linked in love, so that never was concord of will or cordial love
between brothers greater than that which here was between us all.

The same was it among the ladies, with whom there was intercourse most free and honourable; for everyone was permitted
to talk, sit, jest and laugh with whom he pleased; but such was
the reverence paid to the wish of my lady Duchess, that this same
liberty was a very great check; [38] nor was there anyone who did
not esteem it the utmost pleasure he could have in the world, to
please her, and the utmost pain to displease her. And thus, most
decorous manners were here joined with greatest liberty, and
games and laughter in her presence were seasoned not only with
witty jests, but with gracious and sober dignity; for that modesty
and loftiness which governed all the acts, words and gestures of
my lady Duchess, bantering and laughing, were such that she
would have been known for a lady of noblest rank by anyone who
saw her even but once. And impressing herself thus upon those
about her, she seemed to attune us all to her own quality and
tone; accordingly every man strove to follow this pattern, taking
as it were a rule of beautiful behaviour from the presence of so
great and virtuous a lady; whose highest qualities I do not now

purpose to recount, they not being my theme and being well known to all the world, and far more because I could not express them with either tongue or pen; and those that perhaps might have been somewhat hid, fortune, as if wondering at such rare virtue, chose to reveal through many adversities and stings of calamity, so as to give proof that in the tender breast of woman, in company with singular beauty, there may abide prudence and strength of soul, and all those virtues that even among stern men are very rare.[39]

5.—But leaving this aside, I say that the custom of all the gentlemen of the house was to betake themselves straightway after supper to my lady Duchess; where, among the other pleasant pastimes and music and dancing that continually were practised, sometimes neat questions were proposed, sometimes ingenious games were devised at the choice of one or another, in which under various disguises the company disclosed their thoughts figuratively to whom they liked best. Sometimes other discussions arose about different matters, or biting retorts passed lightly back and forth. Often "devices" (*imprese*), as we now call them, were displayed; [40] in discussing which there was wonderful diversion, the house being (as I have said) full of very noble talents; among whom (as you know) the most famous were my lord Ottaviano Fregoso, his brother messer Federico,[41] the Magnifico Giuliano de' Medici, messer Pietro Bembo,[42] messer Cesare Gonzaga,[43] Count Ludovico da Canossa,[44] my lord Gaspar Pallavicino,[45] my lord Ludovico Pio,[46] my lord Morello da Ortona,[47] Pietro da Napoli, messer Roberto da Bari,[48] and countless other very noble cavaliers. Moreover there were many, who, although usually they did not dwell there constantly, yet spent most of the time there: like messer Bernardo Bibbiena, the Unico Aretino,[49] Giancristoforo Romano,[50] Pietro Monte,[51] Terpandro,[52] messer Niccolò Frisio; [53] so that there always flocked thither poets, musicians and all sorts of agreeable [54] men, and in every walk the most excellent that were to be found in Italy.

6.—Now Pope Julius II, having by his presence and the aid of the French brought Bologna under subjection to the apostolic see in the year 1506, and being on his way back to Rome, passed through Urbino; where he was received with all possible honour

and with as magnificent and splendid state as could have been
proposed in any other noble city of Italy. so that besides the pope,
all the lord cardinals and other courtiers were most highly grati-
fied. And some there were, attracted by the charm of this society,
who tarried at Urbino many days after the departure of the pope
and his court; during which time not only were the ordinary
pastimes and diversions continued in the usual manner, but every
man strove to contribute something new, and especially in the
games, to which almost every evening was devoted. And the order
of them was such that immediately after reaching the presence of
my lady Duchess, everyone sat down in a circle as he pleased or
as chance decided; and in sitting they were arranged alternately,
a man and a woman, as long as there were women, for nearly
always the number of men was by far the greater; then they were
governed as seemed best to my lady Duchess, who for the most
part left this charge to my lady Emilia.

So, the day after the pope's departure,[55] the company being
assembled at the wonted hour and place, after much pleasant talk,
my lady Duchess desired my lady Emilia to begin the games;
and she, after having for a time refused the task, spoke thus:

"My Lady, since it pleases you that I shall be the one to
begin the games this evening, not being able in reason to fail to
obey you, I will propose a game in which I think I ought to have
little blame and less labour; and this shall be for everyone to
propose after his liking a game that has never been given; and
then we will choose the one that seems best worthy to be played
in this company."

And so saying, she turned to my lord Gaspar Pallavicino, requiring him to tell his choice; and he at once replied:

"It is for you, my Lady, first to tell your own."

"But I have already told it," said my lady Emilia; "now do
you, my lady Duchess, bid him be obedient."[56]

Then my lady Duchess said, smiling:

"To the end that everyone may be bound to obey you, I
make you my deputy and give you all my authority."

7.—"It is a remarkable thing," replied my lord Gaspar, "that
women should always be allowed this exemption from toil, and it
certainly would not be unreasonable to wish in some way to learn

the reason why; but not to be the first to disobey, I will leave this for another time, and will tell what is required of me;" and he began: "It seems to me that in love, as in everything else, our minds judge diversely and thus it often happens that what is very delightful to one man, is very hateful to another; but none the less we all are ever alike in this, that every man holds his beloved very dear; so that the over fondness of lovers often cheats their judgment to such a degree, that they esteem the person whom they love to be the only one in the world adorned with every excellent virtue and wholly without defect; but since human nature does not admit such complete perfection, and since there is no one to be found who does not lack something, it cannot be said that such men do not cheat themselves, and that the lover does not become blind concerning the beloved. I would therefore that this evening our game might be that each of us should tell what virtue above others he would have the person whom he loves adorned with; and then, as all must have some blemish, what fault he would have in her; in order that we may see who can find the most praiseworthy and useful virtues, and the most excusable faults and least harmful to lover and beloved."

My lord Gaspar having spoken thus, my lady Emilia made sign to madonna Costanza Fregosa [57] to follow after, because she sat next in order, and she was preparing to speak; but my lady Duchess said quickly:

"Since my lady Emilia will not make the effort to invent a game, it were only fair that the other ladies share this ease and that they too be exempt from such exertion for this evening, especially as there are here so many men that there is no danger of lack of games."

"So be it," replied my lady Emilia; and imposing silence on madonna Costanza, she turned to messer Cesare Gonzaga, who sat next, and bade him speak; and he began thus:

8.—"Whoso will carefully consider all our actions, will ever find various defects in them; the reason whereof is that nature, variable in this as in other things, has given to one man the light of reason in one thing, to another man in another thing; and so it happens that, the one knowing what the other does not know and being ignorant of what the other understands, each readily perceives his neighbour's fault and not his own, and we all seem to ourselves very wise and perhaps most of all in that wherein we most are foolish. Thus we have seen it happen in this house that many, at first accounted very wise, were in course of time recognized as very foolish, which came about from nothing else but our own watchfulness. For, as they say that in Apulia musical instruments are used for those bitten by the tarantula,[58] and various tunes are tried until the humour that causes the malady (through a certain affinity it has for some one of those tunes) is suddenly stirred by the sound, and so excites the sick man that he is restored to health by virtue of that excitement: so when we have perceived a hidden touch of folly, we have stimulated it so artfully and with such various persuasions and diverse means, that at length we have learned whither it tended; then, the humour once recognized, so well have we excited it that it has always reached the perfection of open folly. Thus one man has waxed foolish over poetry, another over music, another over love, another over dancing, another over inventing mimes,[59] another over riding, another over fencing,—each according to the native quality of his metal; whence, as you know, great amusement has been derived. I hold it then as certain that there is some grain of folly in each of us, which being quickened can multiply almost infinitely.

"Therefore I would that this evening our game might be a discussion upon this subject, and that each one tell with what kind of folly, and about what thing, he thinks I should make a fool of myself if I had to make a fool of myself openly, judging of this outburst by the sparks of folly that are daily seen to issue from me. Let the same be told of all the rest, keeping to the order of our games, and let each one try to found his opinion upon some actual sign and argument. And thus we shall each derive from our game the advantage of learning our defects, and so shall be better able to guard against them; and if the vein of folly that is discovered proves so rich that it seems incurable, we will assist it, and according to fra Mariano's [60] teaching, we shall have saved a soul, which will be no small gain."

There was much laughter at this game, nor were there any who could keep from talking; one said, "I should make a fool of myself over thinking;" another, "Over looking;" another said, "I have already made a fool of myself over loving;" and the like.

9.—Then fra Serafino [61] said, laughing after his manner:

"That would take too long; but if you want a fine game, let everyone give his opinion why it is that nearly all women hold rats in hatred, and are fond of snakes; and you will see that no one will guess the reason except myself, who learned this secret in a strange way." And he began to tell his stories; but my lady Emilia bade him be silent, and passing over the lady who sat next, made sign to the Unico Aretino whose turn it was; and he, without waiting for further command, said:

"I would I were a judge with power to search the heart of evil-doers by every sort of torture; and this that I might fathom the deceits of an ingrate with angel eyes and serpent heart, who never lets her tongue reveal her soul, and with deceitful pity feigned has no thought but of dissecting hearts. Nor is there in sandy Libya to be found a serpent so venomous and eager for human blood as is this false one; who not only in the sweetness of her voice and honeyed words, but in her eyes, her smiles, her aspect and in all her ways, is a very siren.

"But since I am not suffered, as I would I were, to use chains, rope and fire to learn a certain truth, I fain would learn it by a game,—which is this: let each one tell what he believes to be the meaning of that letter S which my lady Duchess wears upon her brow; for, although this too is surely an artful veil to aid deceit, perchance there will be given it some interpretation unthought of by her perhaps, and it will be found that fortune, compassionate spectatress of men's martyrdoms, has led her against her will to disclose by this small token her secret wish to slay and bury alive in calamity everyone who beholds her or serves her."

My lady Duchess laughed, and the Unico, seeing that she wished to defend herself against this imputation, said:

"Nay, my Lady, do not speak, for it is not now your turn to speak."

My lady Emilia then turned and said:

"Sir Unico, there is no one of us here who does not yield to you in everything, but above all in knowledge of my lady

ↆↆↆↆↆↆↆↆↆↆↆↆↆↆↆↆↆↆↆↆↆↆↆↆↆↆↆↆↆↆↆↆↆↆↆↆↆↆↆↆↆↆↆↆↆↆↆↆↆↆↆↆↆↆↆↆↆↆ

Duchess's mind; and since you know it better than the others
(thanks to your divine genius), you love it better than the others,
who like those weak-sighted birds that fix not their eyes upon the
sun's orb, cannot so justly know how perfect it is; wherefore every
effort to clear this doubt would be vain, save your own judgment.
To you alone then be left this task, as to him who alone can perform it."

The Unico remained silent for awhile, then being urged to
speak, at last recited a sonnet upon the aforesaid subject, declaring what that letter S meant; which was by many believed to be
done impromptu, but as it was more ingenious and finished than
seemed to accord with the shortness of the time, it was thought
rather to have been prepared.[62]

10.—Then having bestowed a merry plaudit in praise of the
sonnet, and talked of it awhile, my lord Ottaviano Fregoso, whose
turn it was, smilingly began as follows:

"My Lords, if I were to affirm that I had never felt the passion of love, I am sure that my lady Duchess and my lady Emilia
would feign to believe it even though they believed it not, and
would say that it was because I mistrusted ever being able to pre-
vail upon any woman to love me; whereof indeed I have not
made trial hitherto with such persistence as reasonably to despair
of being able sometime to succeed. But yet I have not refrained
because I rate myself so high, or women so low, that I do not
deem many of them worthy to be loved and served by me; but
made timorous rather by the continual laments of some lovers,
who—pallid, gloomy and taciturn—seem always to wear their
unhappiness depicted in their eyes; and if they speak, they accompany every word with triple sighs, and discourse of nothing
but tears, torments, despairings and longings for death; so that if
an amourous spark has sometimes kindled in my heart, I have at
once striven with all my might to quench it, not from any hate I
bear to women as these ladies think, but for my own good.

"I have also known some others quite different from these
dolorous souls,—lovers who not only give thanks and praise for
the kind looks, tender words and gentle bearing of their mis-
tresses, but flavour all evils with sweetness, so that they call their
ladies' warrings, anger and disdain, most sweet. Wherefore such

as these seem to me far more than happy. For if they find such sweetness in lovers' quarrels, which those others deem far more bitter than death, I think that in loving endearments they must enjoy that supreme beatitude which we vainly seek in this world. So I would that this evening our game might be, that each man tell, if she whom he loves must needs be angry with him, by what cause he would have her anger roused. Because if there be any here who have enjoyed this sweet anger, I am sure that out of courtesy they will choose one of those causes that make it so sweet; and perhaps I shall take courage to advance a little farther in love, hoping that I too may find this sweetness where some find bitterness; and then these ladies will be no longer able to cast shame upon me because I do not love."

11.—This game found much favour and everyone made ready to speak upon the subject, but as my lady Emilia made no further mention of it, messer Pietro Bembo, who sat next in order, spoke thus:

"My Lords, no small uncertainty has been awakened in my mind by the game proposed by my lord Ottaviano in his discourse about love's anger: the which, however varied it be, has in my case always been most bitter, nor do I believe that any seasoning could be learned from me that would avail to sweeten it; but perhaps it is more or less bitter according to the cause from which it springs.[63] For I remember once to have seen the lady whom I served wrought up against me, either by some idle suspicion that she had herself conceived as to my loyalty, or by some other false notion awakened in her by what others had said to my injury; insomuch that I believed no pain could equal mine, and it seemed to me that the greatest suffering I felt was to endure that which I had not deserved, and to have this affliction come upon me not from my fault but from her lack of love. At other times I saw her angered by some error of mine, and knew her ire to proceed from my fault; and then I deemed that my former woe was very light compared with that which now I felt; and it seemed to me that to have displeased, and through my own guilt, the person whom alone I desired and so zealously strove to please, was the greatest torment and above all others. I would therefore that our game might be that each man tell, if she whom he loves must needs be angry with him, from which of the two he would have her anger spring, from her or from himself; so that we may know which is the greater suffering, to give displeasure to her who is loved, or to receive it from her who is loved."

12.—Everyone waited for my lady Emilia to reply; but she, saying nothing more to Bembo, turned and made sign to messer Federico Fregoso that he should tell his game; and he at once began as follows:

"My Lady, I would it were permitted me, as it sometimes is, to assent to another's proposal; since for my part I would readily approve any of the games proposed by these gentlemen, for I really think that all of them would be amusing. But not to break our rule, I say that anyone who wished to praise our court,—laying aside the merit of our lady Duchess, which with her divine virtue would suffice to lift from earth to heaven the meanest souls that are in the world,—might well say without suspicion of flattery, that in all Italy it would perhaps be hard to find so many cavaliers so singularly admirable and so excellent in divers other matters besides the chief concerns of chivalry, as are now to be found here: wherefore if anywhere there be men who deserve to be called good Courtiers and who are able to judge of what pertains to the perfection of Courtiership, it is reasonable to believe that they are here. So, to repress the many fools who by impudence and folly think to win the name of good Courtier, I would that this evening's game might be, that we select some one of the company and give him the task of portraying a perfect Courtier, explaining all the conditions and special qualities requisite in one who deserves this title; and as to those things that shall not appear sound, let everyone be allowed to contradict, as in the schools of the philosophers it is allowed to contradict anyone who proposes a thesis."

Messer Federico was continuing his discourse still further, when my lady Emilia interrupted him and said:

"This, if it pleases my lady Duchess, shall for the present be our game."

My lady Duchess answered:

"It does please me."

Then nearly all those present began to say, both to my lady

Duchess and among themselves, that this was the finest game that could possibly be; and without waiting for each other's answer, they entreated my lady Emilia to decide who should begin. She turned to my lady Duchess and said:

"Command, my Lady, him who it best pleases you should have this task; for I do not wish, by selecting one rather than another, to seem to decide whom I think more competent in this matter than the rest, and so do wrong to anyone."

My lady Duchess replied:

"Nay, make this choice yourself, and take heed lest by not obeying you give an example to the others, so that they too prove disobedient in their turn."

13.—At this my lady Emilia laughed and said to Count Ludovico da Canossa:

"Then not to lose more time, you, Count, shall be the one to take this enterprise after the manner that messer Federico has described; not indeed because we account you so good a Courtier that you know what befits one, but because, if you say everything wrong as we hope you will, the game will be more lively, for everyone will then have something to answer you; while if someone else had this task who knew more than you, it would be impossible to contradict him in anything, because he would tell the truth, and so the game would be tedious."

The Count answered quickly:

"Whoever told the truth, my Lady, would run no risk of lacking contradiction, so long as you were present;" and after some laughter at this retort, he continued: "But truly I would fain escape this burden, it seeming to me too heavy, and I being conscious that what you said in jest is very true; that is, that I do not know what befits a good Courtier: and I do not seek to prove this with further argument, because, as I do not practise the rules of Courtiership, one may judge that I do not know them; and I think my blame may be the less, for sure it is worse not to wish to do well than not to know how. Yet, since it so happens that you are pleased to have me bear this burden, I neither can nor will refuse it, in order not to contravene our rule and your judgment, which I rate far higher than my own."

Then messer Cesare Gonzaga said:

"As the early evening is now spent and many other kinds of
entertainment are ready, perhaps it will be well to put off this
discussion until to-morrow and give the Count time to think of
what he has to say; for it is difficult indeed to speak unprepared
on such a subject."

The Count replied:

"I do not wish to be like the fellow who, when stripped to his
shirt, vaulted less well than he had done in his doublet; hence it
seems to me good fortune that the hour is late, for I shall be
obliged by the shortness of time to say but little, and my not having taken thought will excuse me, so that I shall be allowed to say
without blame whatever first comes to my lips.

"Therefore, not to carry this burden of duty longer on my
shoulders, I say that in everything it is so hard to know the true
perfection as to be well nigh impossible; and this because of the
variety of opinions. Thus there are many that will like a man who
speaks much, and will call him pleasing; some will prefer modesty; some others, an active and restless man; still others, one
who shows calmness and deliberation in everything; and so every
man praises or decries according to his mind, always clothing vice
with the name of its kindred virtue, or virtue with the name of
its kindred vice; for example, calling an impudent man frank, a
modest man dull, an ignorant man good, a knave discreet; and so
in all things else. Yet I believe that there exists in everything its
own perfection, although concealed; and that this can be determined through rational discussion by any having knowledge of
the thing in hand. And since, as I have said, the truth often lies
concealed, and I do not profess to have this knowledge, I can only
praise the kind of Courtier that I most esteem, and approve him
who seems to me nearest right, according to my poor judgment;
the which you will follow if you find it good, or you will hold to
your own if it differs from mine. Nor shall I at all insist that mine
is better than yours; not only because you may think one thing
and I another, but I myself may sometimes think one thing, and
sometimes another.

14.—"I wish, then, that this Courtier of ours should be nobly
born and of gentle race; because it is far less unseemly for one of
ignoble birth to fail in worthy deeds, than for one of noble birth,

who, if he strays from the path of his predecessors, stains his family name, and not only fails to achieve but loses what has been achieved already; for noble birth is like a bright lamp that manifests and makes visible good and evil deeds, and kindles and stimulates to virtue both by fear of shame and by hope of praise. And since this splendour of nobility does not illumine the deeds of the humbly born, they lack that stimulus and fear of shame, nor do they feel any obligation to advance beyond what their predecessors have done; while to the nobly born it seems a reproach not to reach at least the goal set them by their ancestors. And thus it nearly always happens that both in the profession of arms and in other worthy pursuits the most famous men have been of noble birth, because nature has implanted in everything that hidden seed which gives a certain force and quality of its own essence to all things that are derived from it, and makes them like itself: as we see not only in the breeds of horses and of other animals, but also in trees, the shoots of which nearly always resemble the trunk; and if they sometimes degenerate, it arises from poor cultivation. And so it is with men, who if rightly trained are nearly always like those from whom they spring, and often better; but if there be no one to give them proper care, they become like savages and never reach perfection.

"It is true that, by favour of the stars or of nature, some men are endowed at birth with such graces that they seem not to have been born, but rather as if some god had formed them with his very hands and adorned them with every excellence of mind and body. So too there are many men so foolish and rude that one cannot but think that nature brought them into the world out of contempt or mockery. Just as these can usually accomplish little even with constant diligence and good training, so with slight pains those others reach the highest summit of excellence. And to give you an instance: you see my lord Don Ippolito d'Este,[64] Cardinal of Ferrara, who has enjoyed such fortune from his birth, that his person, his aspect, his words and all his movements are so disposed and imbued with this grace, that—although he is young—he exhibits among the most aged prelates such weight of character that he seems fitter to teach than to be taught; likewise in conversation with men and women of every rank, in games, in pleasantry and in banter, he has a certain sweetness and manners so gracious, that whoso speaks with him or even sees him, must needs remain attached to him forever.

"But to return to our subject: I say that there is a middle state between perfect grace on the one hand and senseless folly on the other; and those who are not thus perfectly endowed by nature, with study and toil can in great part polish and amend their natural defects. Besides his noble birth, then, I would have the Courtier favoured in this regard also, and endowed by nature not only with talent and beauty of person and feature, but with a certain grace and (as we say) air that shall make him at first sight pleasing and agreeable to all who see him; and I would have this an ornament that should dispose and unite all his actions, and in his outward aspect give promise of whatever is worthy the society and favour of every great lord."

15.—Here, without waiting longer, my lord Gaspar Pallavicino said:

"In order that our game may have the form prescribed, and that we may not seem to slight the privilege given us to contradict, I say that this nobility of birth does not appear to me so essential in the Courtier; and if I thought I were saying what was new to any of us, I should cite instances of many men born of the noblest blood who have been full of vices; and on the other hand, of many men among the humbly born who by their virtue have made their posterity illustrious. And if what you just said be true, namely that there is in everything this occult influence of the original seed, then we should all be in the same case, because we had the same origin, nor would any man be more noble than another. But as to our differences and grades of eminence and obscurity, I believe there are many other causes: among which I rate fortune to be chief; for we see her holding sway in all mundane affairs, often amusing herself by lifting to heaven whom she pleases (although wholly without merit), and burying in the depths those most worthy to be exalted.

"I quite agree with what you say as to the good fortune of those endowed from birth with advantages of mind and body: but this is seen as well among the humbly born as among the nobly born, since nature has no such subtle distinctions as these;

and often, as I said, the highest gifts of nature are found among the most obscure. Therefore, since this nobility of birth is won neither by talent nor by strength nor by craft, and is rather the merit of our predecessors than our own, it seems to me too extravagant to maintain that if our Courtier's parents be humbly born, all his good qualities are spoiled, and that all those other qualifications that you mentioned do not avail to raise him to the summit of perfection; I mean talent, beauty of feature, comeliness of person, and that grace which makes him always charming to everyone at first sight."

16.—Then Count Ludovico replied:

"I do not deny that the same virtues may rule the low-born and the noble: but (not to repeat what we have said already or the many other arguments that could be adduced in praise of noble birth, which is honoured always and by everyone, it being reasonable that good should beget good), since we have to form a Courtier without flaw and endowed with every praiseworthy quality, it seems to me necessary to make him nobly born, as well for many other reasons as for universal opinion, which is at once disposed in favour of noble birth. For if there be two Courtiers who have as yet given no impression of themselves by good or evil acts, as soon as the one is known to have been born a gentleman and the other not, he who is low-born will be far less esteemed by everyone than he who is high-born, and will need much effort and time to make upon men's minds that good impression which the other will have achieved in a moment and merely by being a gentleman. And how important these impressions are, everyone can easily understand: for in our own case we have seen men present themselves in this house, who, being silly and awkward in the extreme, yet had throughout Italy the reputation of very great Courtiers; and although they were detected and recognized at last, still they imposed upon us for many days, and maintained in our minds that opinion of them which they first found impressed there, although they conducted themselves after the slightness of their worth. We have seen others, held at first in small esteem, then admirably successful at the last.

"And of these mistakes there are various causes: and among others, the regard of princes, who in their wish to perform mira-

also sometimes undertake to bestow favour on a man who seems
to them to merit disfavour. And often too they are themselves
deceived; but since they always have a host of imitators, their
favour begets very great fame, which chiefly guides our judgments: and if we find anything that seems contrary to common
opinion, we suspect that it is we ourselves who are wrong, and
always seek for something hidden: because it seems that these
universal opinions must after all be founded on fact and spring
from rational causes; and because our minds are very prone to
love and hate, as is seen in battle-shows and games and every
other sort of contest, wherein the spectators without apparent
cause become partisans of one side, with eager wish that it may win
and the other lose. In our opinion of men's character also, good
or evil fame sways our minds to one of these two passions from
the start; and thus it happens that we usually judge with love or
hate. You see then how important this first impression is, and how
he ought to strive to make a good one at the outset, who thinks
to hold the rank and name of good Courtier.

17.—"But to come to some details, I am of opinion that the
principal and true profession of the Courtier ought to be that of
arms; which I would have him follow actively above all else, and
be known among others as bold and strong, and loyal to whomsoever he serves. And he will win a reputation for these good qualities by exercising them at all times and in all places, since one may
never fail in this without severest censure. And just as among
women, their fair fame once sullied never recovers its first lustre,
so the reputation of a gentleman who bears arms, if once it be in
the least tarnished with cowardice or other disgrace, remains forever infamous before the world and full of ignominy. Therefore
the more our Courtier excels in this art, the more he will be
worthy of praise; and yet I do not deem essential in him that
perfect knowledge of things and those other qualities that befit a
commander; since this would be too wide a sea, let us be content,
as we have said, with perfect loyalty and unconquered courage,
and that he be always seen to possess them. For the courageous
are often recognized even more in small things than in great;
and frequently in perils of importance and where there are
many spectators, some men are to be found, who, although their

hearts be dead within them, yet, moved by shame or by the presence of others, press forward almost with their eyes shut, and do
their duty God knows how. While on occasions of little moment,
when they think they can avoid putting themselves in danger
without being detected, they are glad to keep safe. But those who,
even when they do not expect to be observed or seen or recognized by anyone, show their ardour and neglect nothing, however
paltry, that may be laid to their charge,—they have that strength
of mind which we seek in our Courtier.

"Not that we would have him look so fierce, or go about
blustering, or say that he has taken his cuirass to wife, or threaten
with those grim scowls that we have often seen in Berto; [65] because to such men as this, one might justly say that which a brave
lady jestingly said in gentle company to one whom I will not
name at present; [66] who, being invited by her out of compliment
to dance, refused not only that, but to listen to the music, and
many other entertainments proposed to him,—saying always that
such silly trifles were not his business; so that at last the lady said,
'What is your business, then?' He replied with a sour look, 'To
fight.' Then the lady at once said, 'Now that you are in no war
and out of fighting trim, I should think it were a good thing to
have yourself well oiled, and to stow yourself with all your battle
harness in a closet until you be needed, lest you grow more rusty
than you are;' and so, amid much laughter from the bystanders,
she left the discomfited fellow to his silly presumption.

"Therefore let the man we are seeking, be very bold, stern,
and always among the first, where the enemy are to be seen; and
in every other place, gentle, modest, reserved, above all things
avoiding ostentation and that impudent self-praise by which men
ever excite hatred and disgust in all who hear them."

18.—Then my lord Gaspar replied:

"As for me, I have known few men excellent in anything whatever, who do not praise themselves; and it seems to me
that this may well be permitted them; for when anyone who feels
himself to be of worth, sees that he is not known to the ignorant
by his works, he is offended that his worth should lie buried, and
needs must in some way hold it up to view, in order that he may
not be cheated of the fame that is the true reward of worthy effort.

Thus among the ancient authors, whoever carries weight seldom fails to praise himself. They indeed are insufferable who do this without desert, but such we do not presume our Courtier to be."

The Count then said:

"If you heard what I said, it was impudent and indiscriminate self-praise that I censured: and as you say, we surely ought not to form a bad opinion of a brave man who praises himself modestly, nay we ought rather to regard such praise as better evidence than if it came from the mouth of others. I say, however, that he, who in praising himself runs into no error and incurs no annoyance or envy at the hands of those that hear him, is a very discreet man indeed and merits praise from others in addition to that which he bestows upon himself; because it is a very difficult matter."

Then my lord Gaspar said:

"You must teach us that."

The Count replied:

"Among the ancient authors there is no lack of those who have taught it; but to my thinking, the whole art consists in saying things in such a way that they shall not seem to be said to that end, but let fall so naturally that it was impossible not to say them, and while seeming always to avoid self-praise, yet to achieve it; but not after the manner of those boasters, who open their mouths and let the words come forth haphazard. Like one of our friends a few days ago, who, being quite run through the thigh with a spear at Pisa, said he thought it was a fly that had stung him; and another man said he kept no mirror in his room because, when angry, he became so terrible to look at, that the sight of himself would have frightened him too much."

Everyone laughed at this, but messer Cesare Gonzaga added:

"Why do you laugh? Do you not know that Alexander the Great, on hearing the opinion of a philosopher [67] to be that there was an infinite number of worlds, began to weep, and being asked why he wept, replied, 'Because I have not yet conquered one of them;' as if he would fain have vanquished all? Does not this seem to you a greater boast than that about the fly-sting?"

Then the Count said:

"Yes, and Alexander was a greater man than he who made

the other speech. But extraordinary men are surely to be pardoned
when they assume much; for he who has great things to do must
needs have daring to do them, and confidence in himself, and
must not be abject or mean in spirit, yet very modest in speech,
showing less confidence in himself that he has, lest his self-
confidence lead to rashness."

19.—The Count now paused a little, and messer Bernardo
Bibbiena said, laughing:

"I remember what you said earlier, that this Courtier of ours
must be endowed by nature with beauty of countenance and person, and with a grace that shall make him so agreeable. Grace
and beauty of countenance I think I certainly possess, and this is
the reason why so many ladies are ardently in love with me, as
you know; but I am rather doubtful as to the beauty of my person, especially as regards these legs of mine, which seem to me
decidedly less well proportioned than I should wish: as to my
bust and other members however, I am quite content. Pray, now,
describe a little more in particular the sort of body that the
Courtier is to have, so that I may dismiss this doubt and set my
mind at rest."

After some laughter at this, the Count continued:

"Of a certainty that grace of countenance can be truly said to
be yours, nor need I cite further example than this to show what
manner of thing it is, for we unquestionably perceive your aspect
to be most agreeable and pleasing to everyone, albeit the linea-
ments of it are not very delicate. Still it is of a manly cast and
at the same time full of grace; and this characteristic is to be
found in many different types of countenance. And of such sort
I would have our Courtier's aspect; not so soft and effeminate
as is sought by many, who not only curl their hair and pluck their
brows, but gloss their faces with all those arts employed by the
most wanton and unchaste women in the world; and in their
walk, posture and every act, they seem so limp and languid that
their limbs are like to fall apart; and they pronounce their words
so mournfully that they appear about to expire upon the spot:
and the more they find themselves with men of rank, the more
they affect such tricks. Since nature has not made them women,
as they seem to wish to appear and be, they should be treated

not as good women but as public harlots, and driven not merely from the courts of great lords but from the society of honest men.

20.—"Then coming to the bodily frame, I say it is enough if this be neither extremely short nor tall, for both of these conditions excite a certain contemptuous surprise, and men of either sort are gazed upon in much the same way that we gaze on monsters. Yet if we must offend in one of the two extremes, it is preferable to fall a little short of the just measure of height than to exceed it, for besides often being dull of intellect, men thus huge of body are also unfit for every exercise of agility, which thing I should much wish in the Courtier. And so I would have him well built and shapely of limb, and would have him show strength and lightness and suppleness, and know all bodily exercises that befit a man of war; whereof I think the first should be to handle every sort of weapon well on foot and on horse, to understand the advantages of each, and especially to be familiar with those weapons that are ordinarily used among gentlemen; for besides the use of them in war, where such subtlety in contrivance is perhaps not needful, there frequently arise differences between one gentleman and another, which afterwards result in duels often fought with such weapons as happen at the moment to be within reach: thus knowledge of this kind is a very safe thing. Nor am I one of those who say that skill is forgotten in the hour of need; for he whose skill forsakes him at such a time, indeed gives token that he has already lost heart and head through fear.

21.—"Moreover I deem it very important to know how to wrestle, for it is a great help in the use of all kinds of weapons on foot. Then, both for his own sake and for that of his friends, he must understand the quarrels and differences that may arise, and must be quick to seize an advantage, always showing courage and prudence in all things.[68] Nor should he be too ready to fight except when honour demands it; for besides the great danger that the uncertainty of fate entails, he who rushes into such affairs recklessly and without urgent cause, merits the severest censure even though he be successful. But when he finds himself so far engaged that he cannot withdraw without reproach, he ought to be most deliberate, both in the preliminaries to the duel and in the duel itself, and always show readiness and daring. Nor must he act like some, who fritter the affair away in disputes and controversies, and who, having the choice of weapons, select those that neither cut nor pierce, and arm themselves as if they were expecting a cannonade; and thinking it enough not to be defeated, stand ever on the defensive and retreat,—showing therein their utter cowardice. And thus they make themselves a laughing-stock for boys, like those two men of Ancona who fought at Perugia not long since, and made everyone laugh who saw them."

"And who were they?" asked my lord Gaspar Pallavicino.

"Two cousins," replied messer Cesare.

Then the Count said:

"In their fighting they were as like as two brothers;" and soon continued: "Even in time of peace weapons are often used in various exercises, and gentlemen appear in public shows before the people and ladies and great lords. For this reason I would have our Courtier a perfect horseman in every kind of seat; and besides understanding horses and what pertains to riding, I would have him use all possible care and diligence to lift himself a little beyond the rest in everything, so that he may be ever recognized as eminent above all others. And as we read of Alcibiades that he surpassed all the nations with whom he lived, each in their particular province, so I would have this Courtier of ours excel all others, and each in that which is most their profession. And as it is the especial pride of the Italians to ride well with the rein, to govern wild horses with consummate skill, and to play at tilting and jousting,—in these things let him be among the best of the Italians. In tourneys and in the arts of defence and attack, let him shine among the best in France.[69] In stick-throwing, bull-fighting, and in casting spears and darts, let him excel among the Spaniards. But above everything he should temper all his movements with a certain good judgment and grace, if he wishes to merit that universal favour which is too greatly prized.

22.—"There are also many other exercises, which although not immediately dependent upon arms, yet are closely connected therewith, and greatly foster manly sturdiness; and one of the chief among these seems to me to be the chase, because it bears a certain likeness to war: and truly it is an amusement for great lords and befitting a man at court, and furthermore it is seen to have been much cultivated among the ancients. It is fitting also to know how to swim, to leap, to run, to throw stones, for besides the use that may be made of this in war, a man often has occasion to show what he can do in such matters; whence good esteem is to be won, especially with the multitude, who must be taken into account withal. Another admirable exercise, and one very befitting a man at court, is the game of tennis, in which are well shown the disposition of the body, the quickness and suppleness of every member, and all those qualities that are seen in nearly every other exercise. Nor less highly do I esteem vaulting on horse, which although it be fatiguing and difficult, makes a man very light and dexterous more than any other thing; and besides its utility, if this lightness is accompanied by grace, it is to my thinking a finer show than any of the others."⁷⁰

"Our Courtier having once become more than fairly expert in these exercises, I think he should leave the others on one side: such as turning summersaults, rope-walking, and the like, which savour of the mountebank and little befit a gentleman.

"But since one cannot devote himself to such fatiguing exercises continually, and since repetition becomes very tiresome and abates the admiration felt for what is rare, we must always diversify our life with various occupations. For this reason I would have our Courtier sometimes descend to quieter and more tranquil exercises, and in order to escape envy and to entertain himself agreeably with everyone, let him do whatever others do, yet never departing from praiseworthy deeds, and governing himself with that good judgment which will keep him from all folly; but let him laugh, jest, banter, frolic and dance, yet in such fashion that he shall always appear genial and discreet, and that everything he may do or say shall be stamped with grace."

23.—Then messer Cesare Gonzaga said:

"We certainly ought on no account to hinder the course of this discussion; but if I were to keep silence, I should be neglectful both of the right I have to speak and of my desire to know one thing: and let me be pardoned if I ask a question instead of contradicting; for this I think may be permitted me, after the prece-

dent of messer Bernardo here, who in his over desire to be held
comely, broke the rules of our game by asking a question instead
of contradicting."

Then my lady Duchess said:

"You see how one error begets many. Therefore he who
transgresses and sets a bad example, like messer Bernardo, deserves to be punished not only for his own transgression but also
for the others'."

Then messer Cesare replied:

"In that case, my Lady, I shall be exempt from penalty,
since messer Bernardo is to be punished for his own fault as well
as mine."

"Nay," said my lady Duchess, "you both ought to have
double punishment: he for his own transgression and for leading
you to transgress; you for your own transgression and for imitating him."

"My Lady," replied messer Cesare, "as yet I have not transgressed; so, to leave all this punishment to messer Bernardo alone,
I will keep silence."

And indeed he remained silent; when my lady Emilia
laughed and said:

"Say whatever you like, for under leave of my lady Duchess
I pardon him that has transgressed and him that shall transgress,
in so small a degree."

"I consent," continued my lady Duchess. "But take care lest
perchance you fall into the mistake of thinking to gain more by
being merciful than by being just; for to pardon him too easily
that has transgressed is to wrong him that transgresses not. Yet
I would not have my severity reproach your indulgence, and thus
be the cause of our not hearing this question of messer Cesare."

And so, being given the signal by my lady Duchess and by
my lady Emilia, he at once said:

24.—"If I remember rightly, Sir Count, I think you have
repeated several times this evening that the Courtier must accompany his actions, gestures, habits, in short his every movement, with grace; and this you seem to regard as an universal
seasoning, without which all other properties and good qualities
are of little worth. And indeed I think that in this everyone

would allow himself to be persuaded easily, since from the very
force of the word, it may be said that he who has grace finds
grace.[71] But since you said that this is oftentimes the gift of nature and of heaven and, even when not thus perfect, can with care
and pains be made much greater,—those men who are born so
fortunate and so rich in this treasure as are some we see, seem to
me in this to have little need of other master; because that benign
favour of heaven almost in despite of themselves leads them
higher than they will, and makes them not only pleasing but admirable to all the world. Therefore I do not discuss this, it not
being in our power to acquire it of ourselves. But they who have
received from nature only so much, that they are capable of becoming graceful by pains, industry and care,—I long to know
by what art, by what training, by what method, they can acquire
this grace, as well in bodily exercises (in which you esteem it to
be so necessary) as also in everything else that they may do or
say. Therefore, since by much praise of this quality you have
aroused in all of us, I think, an ardent thirst to pursue it, you are
further bound, by the charge that my lady Emilia laid upon you,
to satisfy that thirst by teaching us how to attain it."

25.—"I am not bound," said the Count, "to teach you how to
become graceful, or anything else; but only to show you what
manner of man a perfect Courtier ought to be. Nor would I in
any case undertake the task of teaching you this perfection; especially having said a little while ago that the Courtier must know
how to wrestle, vault, and do many other things, which I am sure
you all know quite as well as if I, who have never learned them,
were to teach you. For just as a good soldier knows how to tell
the smith what fashion, shape and quality his armour ought to
have, but cannot show how it is to be made or forged or tempered; so I perhaps may be able to tell you what manner of man
a perfect Courtier ought to be, but cannot teach you what you
must do to become one.

"Yet to comply with your request as far as is within my
power,—although it is almost a proverb that grace is not to be
learned,—I say that whoever would acquire grace in bodily exercises (assuming first that he be by nature not incapable), ought
to begin early and learn the rudiments from the best masters.

And how important this seemed to King Philip of Macedon, may be seen from the fact that he chose Aristotle, the famous philosopher and perhaps the greatest that has ever been in the world, to teach his son Alexander the first elements of letters. And of the men whom we know at the present day, consider how well and how gracefully my lord Galeazzo Sanseverino,[72] Grand Equerry of France, performs all bodily exercises; and this because in addition to the natural aptitude of person that he possesses, he has taken the utmost pains to study with good masters, and always to have about him men who excel and to select from each the best of what they know: for just as in wrestling, vaulting and in the use of many sorts of weapons, he has taken for his guide our friend messer Pietro Monte, who (as you know) is the true and only master of every form of trained strength and agility,—so in riding, jousting and all else, he has ever had before his eyes the most proficient men that were known in those matters.

26.—"Therefore he who wishes to be a good pupil, besides performing his tasks well, must put forth every effort to resemble his master, and, if it were possible, to transform himself into his master. And when he feels that he has made some progress, it will be very profitable to observe different men of the same calling, and governing himself with that good judgment which must ever be his guide, to go about selecting now this thing from one and that thing from another. And as the bee in the green meadows is ever wont to rob the flowers among the grass, so our Courtier must steal this grace from all who seem to possess it, taking from each that part which shall most be worthy praise; and not act like a friend of ours whom you all know, who thought he greatly resembled King Ferdinand the Younger [32] of Aragon, and made it his care to imitate the latter in nothing but a certain trick of continually raising the head and twisting one side of the mouth, which the king had contracted from some infirmity. And there are many such, who think they gain a point if only they be like a great man in some thing; and frequently they devote themselves to that which is his only fault.

"But having before now often considered whence this grace springs, laying aside those men who have it by nature, I find one universal rule concerning it, which seems to me worth more in

this matter than any other in all things human that are done or
said: and that is to avoid affectation to the uttermost and as it
were a very sharp and dangerous rock; and, to use possibly a new
word, to practise in everything a certain nonchalance [73] that shall
conceal design and show that what is done and said is done without effort and almost without thought. From this I believe grace
is in large measure derived, because everyone knows the difficulty
of those things that are rare and well done, and therefore facility
in them excites the highest admiration; while on the other hand,
to strive and as the saying is to drag by the hair, is extremely ungraceful, and makes us esteem everything slightly, however great
it be.

"Accordingly we may affirm that to be true art which does
not appear to be art; nor to anything must we give greater care
than to conceal art, for if it is discovered, it quite destroys our
credit and brings us into small esteem. And I remember having
once read that there were several very excellent orators of antiquity, who among their other devices strove to make everyone
believe that they had no knowledge of letters; and hiding their
knowledge they pretended that their orations were composed very
simply and as if springing rather from nature and truth than
from study and art; the which, if it had been detected, would
have made men wary of being duped by it.

"Thus you see how the exhibition of art and study so intense
destroys the grace in everything. Which of you is there who does
not laugh when our friend messer Pierpaolo dances in his peculiar
way, with those capers of his,—legs stiff to the toe and head motionless, as if he were a stick, and with such intentness that he
actually seems to be counting the steps? What eye so blind as
not to see in this the ungracefulness of affectation,—and in many
men and women who are here present, the grace of that nonchalant ease (for in the case of bodily movements many call it
thus), showing by word or laugh or gesture that they have no
care and are thinking more of everything else than of that, to
make the onlooker think they can hardly go amiss?"

27.—Messer Bernardo Bibbiena here said, without waiting:
"Now at last our friend messer Roberto [48] has found someone
to praise the manner of his dancing, as all the rest of you seem to

ファファファファファファファファファファファファファファファファファファ

value it lightly; because if this merit consists in nonchalance, and in appearing to take no heed and to be thinking more of everything else than of what you are doing, messer Roberto in dancing has no peer on earth; for to show plainly that he is not thinking about it, he often lets the cloak drop from his shoulders and the slippers from his feet, and still goes on dancing without picking up either the one or the other."

Then the Count replied:

"Since you insist on my talking, I will speak further of our faults. Do you not perceive that what you call nonchalance in messer Roberto, is really affectation? For it is clearly seen that he is striving with all his might to seem to be taking no thought, and this is taking too much thought; and since it passes the true limits of moderation, his nonchalance is affected and unbecoming; and it is a thing that works precisely the reverse of the effect intended, that is the concealment of art. Thus in nonchalance (which is praiseworthy in itself), I do not think that it is less a vice of affectation to let the clothes fall from one's back, than in care of dress (which also is praiseworthy in itself), to hold the head stiff for fear of disarranging one's locks, or to carry a mirror in the peak of one's cap and a comb in one's sleeve, and to have a valet follow one about the streets with sponge and brush: for such care in dress and such nonchalance both touch upon excess, which is always offensive and contrary to that pure and charming simplicity which is so pleasing to the human mind.

"You see how ungraceful a rider is who strives to sit bolt upright in the saddle after the manner we are wont to call Venetian,[74]—as compared with another who seems not to be thinking about it, and sits his horse as free and steady as if he were afoot. How much more pleasing and how much more praised is a gentleman who carries arms, if he be modest, speak little and boast little, than another who is forever sounding his own praises, and with blasphemy and bluster seems to be hurling defiance at the world! This too is naught but affectation of wishing to appear bold. And so it is with every exercise, nay with everything that can be done or said in the world."

28.—Then my lord Magnifico [9] said:

"This is true also with music, wherein it is a very great fault to place two perfect consonances one after the other, so that our very sense of hearing abhors it and often enjoys a second or seventh, which in itself is a harsh and intolerable discord. And the reason is that repetition of perfect consonances begets satiety and exhibits a too affected harmony; which is avoided by introducing imperfect consonances, and thus a kind of contrast is given, whereby our ears are held more in suspense, and more eagerly await and enjoy the perfect consonances, and sometimes delight in that discord of the second or seventh, as in something unpremeditated."

"You see then," replied the Count, "the harmful effect of affectation in this as in other things. It is said also to have been proverbial among some very excellent painters of antiquity, that over diligence is harmful, and Protogenes is said to have been censured by Apelles because he did not know when to take his hand from the tablet." [75]

Then messer Cesare said:

"Methinks our friend fra Serafino has this same fault, or not knowing when to take his hands from the table, at least until all the food has been taken from it too." [76]

The Count laughed, and continued:

"Apelles meant that in his painting Protogenes did not know when he had finished, which was the same thing as reproving him for being affected in his work. Thus this excellence, which is the opposite of affectation and which for the present we call nonchalance, besides being the true fountain from which grace springs, carries with it another ornament, which, in accompanying any human action whatever and however trifling it be, not only at once reveals the knowledge of him who performs it, but often leads us to rate his knowledge as much greater than in fact it is; because it impresses upon the minds of the bystanders the idea that he who does well so easily, knows much more than he does, and that if he were to use care and effort in what he did, he could do it far better.

"And to multiply like examples, here is a man who handles weapons, either about to throw a dart or holding a sword in his hand or other weapon; if he nimbly and without thinking puts himself in an attitude of readiness, with such ease that his body

ꜰꜰꜰꜰꜰꜰꜰꜰꜰꜰꜰꜰꜰꜰꜰꜰꜰꜰꜰꜰꜰꜰꜰꜰꜰꜰꜰꜰꜰꜰꜰꜰꜰꜰꜰꜰꜰꜰꜰꜰꜰꜰꜰꜰꜰꜰꜰꜰꜰꜰꜰꜰꜰꜰꜰꜰꜰꜰꜰꜰꜰꜰ

and all his members seem to fall into that posture naturally and quite without effort,—although he do not more, he will prove himself to everyone to be perfect in that exercise. Likewise in dancing, a single step, a single movement of the person that is graceful and not forced, soon shows the knowledge of the dancer. A musician who in singing utters a single note ending with sweet tone in a little group of four notes with such ease as to seem spontaneous, shows by that single touch that he can do much more than he is doing. Often too in painting, a single line not laboured, a single brush-stroke easily drawn, so that it seems as if the hand moves unbidden to its aim according to the painter's wish, without being guided by care or any skill, clearly reveals the excellence of the craftsman, which every man appreciates according to his capacity for judging. And the same is true of nearly everything else.

"Our Courtier then will be esteemed excellent and will attain grace in everything, particularly in speaking, if he avoids affectation; into which fault many fall, and often more than others, some of us Lombards; who, if they have been a year away from home, on their return at once begin to speak Roman, sometimes Spanish or French, and God knows how. And all this comes from over zeal to appear widely informed; in such fashion do men devote care and assiduity to acquiring a very odious fault. And truly it would be no light task for me, if I were to try in these discussions of ours to use those antique Tuscan words that are quite rejected by the usage of the Tuscans of to-day; and besides I think everyone would laugh at me."

29.—Then messer Federico said:

"Of course in discussing among ourselves as we now are doing, perhaps it would be amiss to use those antique Tuscan words, since (as you say) they would be fatiguing to him who uttered them and to him who listened to them, and by many would not be understood without difficulty. But if one were writing, I should certainly think he would be wrong not to use them, because they add much grace and authority to writing, and from them there results a style more grave and full of majesty than from modern words."

"I do not know," replied the Count, "that writings can gain

grace and authority from those words that ought to be avoided, not merely in such talk as we are now engaged in (which you yourself admit), but also under every other circumstance that can be imagined. For if any man of good judgment should chance to make a speech on serious matters before the very senate of Florence, which is the capital of Tuscany, or even to converse privately with a person of weight in that city about important business, or with his closest friend about affairs of pleasure, with ladies or gentlemen about love, or joking or jesting at feasts, games, and where you will,—or whatever the time, place or matter,—I am sure he would avoid using those antique Tuscan words; and if he did use them, besides exciting ridicule, he would give no little annoyance to everyone who listened to him.

"It seems to me then a very strange thing to use as good in writing those words that are avoided as faulty in every sort of speaking, and to insist that what is never proper in speaking, is the most proper style that can be used in writing. For in my opinion writing is really nothing but a form of speech, which still remains after we have spoken, as it were an image or rather the life of our words: and thus in speech, which is lost as soon as the sound has gone forth, some things are bearable perhaps that are not in writing, because writing preserves the words and subjects them to the judgment of the reader and gives time to consider them advisedly. Hence in writing it is reasonable to take greater pains to make it more refined and correct; not however in such wise that the written words may be unlike the spoken, but that, in writing, choice be made of the most beautiful that are used in speaking. And if that were allowed in writing which is not allowed in speaking, I think a very great inconvenience would arise: which is that greater license could be taken in that respect wherein greater care ought to be taken; and the industry bestowed on writing would work harm instead of good.

"Therefore it is certain that what is proper in writing, is proper also in speaking, and that manner of speaking is most beautiful which is like beautiful writing. Moreover I think it is far more necessary to be understood in writing than in speaking, because those who write are not always present before those who read, as those who speak are present before those who speak."

But I should praise him, who besides avoiding many antique Tuscan words, acquired facility, both writing and speaking, in the use of those that are to-day familiar in Tuscany and in the other parts of Italy, and that have comeliness of sound. And I think that whoever imposes other rule upon himself, is not very sure of escaping that affectation which is so much censured and of which we were speaking earlier."

30.—Then messer Federico said:

"Sir Count, I cannot gainsay you that writing is a kind of speech. Indeed, I say that if words that are spoken have any obscurity in them, the meaning does not penetrate the mind of him who hears, and passing without being understood, comes to naught: which does not occur in writing, because if the words that the writer uses carry with them a little, I will not say difficulty, but subtlety that is recondite and thus not so familiar as are the words that are commonly used in speaking,—they give a certain greater authority to the writing, and cause the reader to proceed more cautiously and collectedly, to consider more, and to enjoy the genius and learning of him who writes; and by judiciously exerting himself a little, he tastes that delight which is found in the pursuit of difficult things. And if the ignorance of him who reads is so great that he cannot overcome those difficulties, it is not the fault of the writer, nor on this account ought that style to be deemed unbeautiful.

"Therefore in writing, I believe it is proper to use Tuscan words used only by the ancient Tuscans, because that is great proof and tested by time, that they are good and effective to express the sense in which they are used. And besides this, they have that grace and venerableness which age lends not only to words, but to buildings, to statues, to pictures, and to everything that is able to attain it, and often merely by their splendour and dignity they make diction beautiful, by virtue whereof (and of grace) every theme, however mean it be, can be so adorned as to merit very high praise. But this custom of yours, by which you set such store, seems to me very dangerous, and often it may be bad; and if some fault of speech is found widely prevalent among the ignorant many, methinks it ought not on this account to be taken as a rule and followed by other men. Moreover customs are very diverse, nor is there a noble city of Italy that has not a different manner of speaking from all the others. But as you do not limit yourself to declaring which is the best, a man might as well adopt the Bergamasque as the Florentine, and according to you it would be no error.[78]

"Therefore I think that whoever wishes to avoid all doubt and be quite safe, must needs select as model someone who by consent of all is rated good, and must take him as a constant guide and shield against any possible adverse critic. And this model (in the vernacular, I mean) I do not think should be other than Petrarch [79] and Boccaccio; and whoever departs from these two, gropes like one who walks in the dark without a light and thus often mistakes the road. But we are so daring that we do not deign to do that which the good writers of old did,—that is, devote themselves to imitation, without which I think a man cannot write well.[80] And methinks good proof of this is shown us by Virgil, who by his genius and judgment so divine took from all posterity the hope of ever being able to imitate him well, yet fain would imitate Homer."

31.—Then my lord Gaspar Pallavicino said:

"This discussion about writing is certainly well worth listening to: still it would be more to our purpose if you were to teach us in what manner the Courtier ought to speak, for I think he has greater need of it and more often has occasion to employ speaking than writing."

The Magnifico replied:

"Nay, for a Courtier so excellent and so perfect there is no doubt but it is necessary to know both the one and the other, and that without these two accomplishments perhaps all the rest would not be very worthy of praise. So if the Count wishes to perform his duty, he will teach the Courtier not only how to speak, but also how to write well."

Then the Count said:

"My lord Magnifico, that task I will on no account accept; for great folly would be mine to pretend to teach others that which I do not myself know, and (even if I did know it) to think myself able to do in only a few words that which with so much care and pains has hardly been done by most learned men,—to whose works I should refer our Courtier, if I were indeed bound to teach him how to write and speak."

Messer Cesare said:

"My lord Magnifico means speaking and writing the vernacular [Italian], and not Latin; so those works by learned men are not to our purpose. But in this matter there is need for you to tell us what you know about it, because for the rest we will hold you excused."

The Count replied:

"I have told you that already; but as we are speaking of the Tuscan tongue, perhaps it would be, more than any other man's, my lord Magnifico's office to give an opinion on it."

The Magnifico said:

"I cannot and in reason ought not to contradict any man who says that the Tuscan tongue is more beautiful than the others.[81] It is very true that in Petrarch and in Boccaccio are found many words that are now discarded by the custom of to-day; and these I for my part would never use either in speaking or in writing; and I believe that they themselves, if they had survived until now, would no longer use those words."

Then messer Federico said:

"Indeed they would. And you Tuscan gentlemen ought to keep up your mother tongue, and not suffer it to decay, as you do,—so that now one may say that there is less knowledge of it in Florence than in many other parts of Italy."

Then messer Bernardo said:

"These words that are no longer used in Florence have survived among the country folk, and are rejected by the gentle as corrupt and spoiled with age."

32.—Then my lady Duchess said:

"Let us not wander from our main purpose, but have Count Ludovico teach the Courtier how to speak and write well, whether it be in the Tuscan or any other dialect."

"My Lady," replied the Count, "I have already told what I know about it; and I hold that the same rules which serve to teach the one, serve also to teach the other. But since you require it of me, I will make such response as I may to messer Federico, who has a different opinion from mine; and perhaps I shall have need to discuss the matter somewhat more diffusely than is right. However, it shall be all I can tell.

"And first I say that in my judgment this language of ours, which we call vulgar, is still tender and new, although it be already long in use. For since Italy was not only vexed and ravaged but long inhabited by the barbarians, the Latin language was corrupted and spoiled by contact with those nations, and from that corruption other languages were born: and like rivers that from the crest of the Apennines separate and flow down into the two seas, so also these languages divided, and some of them tinged with Latinity reached by diverse paths, one this country and one that; and one of them remained in Italy tinged with barbarism. Thus our language was long unformed and various, from having had no one to bestow care upon it or write in it or try to give it splendour or grace: but afterwards it was somewhat more cultivated in Tuscany than in the other parts of Italy. And so its flower seems to have remained there even from those early times, because that nation more than the others preserved a sweet accent and a proper grammatical order, and have had three noble writers [82] who expressed their thoughts ingeniously and in those words and terms that the custom of their times permitted: wherein I think Petrarch succeeded more happily than the others in amorous subjects.

"Afterwards from time to time, not only in Tuscany but in all Italy, among noble men and those well versed in courts and arms and letters, there arose some desire to speak and write more elegantly than had been done in that rude and uncultivated age, when the blaze of the calamities inflicted by the barbarians was not yet quenched. Many words were laid aside, as well in the city of Florence itself and in all Tuscany as in the rest of Italy, and instead of them others were taken up; and herein there thus occurred that change which takes place in all human affairs and has always happened in the case of the other languages also. For if those earliest writings in ancient Latin had survived until now, we should see that Evander and Turnus [83] and the other Latins of that age spoke differently from the last Roman kings and the first consuls. See how the verses that the Salian priests chaunted were hardly understood by posterity; [84] but being established in that form by the first founders, out of religious reverence they were not changed. Likewise the orators and poets continued one after another to lay aside many words used by their predecessors: thus Antonius, Crassus, Hortensius and Cicero avoided many of Cato's words, and Virgil avoided many of Ennius's;[85] and the others did the same. For although they had reverence for antiquity, yet they did not esteem it so highly as to consent to be bound by it in the way you would have us bound by it now. Nay they criticised it where they saw fit, as did Horace, who says that his forefathers lauded Plautus foolishly, and thinks he has a right to gather in new words.[86] And in sundry places Cicero reprehends many of his predecessors, and slightingly affirms that Sergius Galba's orations had an antique flavour,[87] and says that Ennius himself disprized his predecessors in certain things: so that if we would imitate the ancients, in doing so we shall not imitate them. And Virgil, who (you say) imitated Homer, did not imitate him in language.

33.—"Therefore I for my part should always avoid using these antique words, save however in certain places, and seldom even there; and it seems to me that whoever uses them otherwise makes a mistake, not less than he who, in order to imitate the ancients, should wish to feed on acorns when wheat had been discovered in plenty. And since you say that by their mere splendour of antiquity, antique words so adorn every subject, however mean it be, that they can make it worthy of much praise,—I say that I do not set such store, not only by these antique words but even by good ones, as to think that they ought in reason to be prized without the pith of beautiful thoughts; for to divide thought from words is to divide soul from body, which can be done in neither case without destruction.

"So I think that what is chiefly important and necessary for the Courtier, in order to speak and write well, is knowledge; for he who is ignorant and has nothing in his mind that merits being heard, can neither say it nor write it.

"Next he must arrange in good order what he has to say or write; then express it well in words, which (if I do not err) ought to be precise, choice, rich and rightly formed, but above all, in use even among the masses; because such words as these make

the grandeur and pomp of speech, if the speaker has good sense
and carefulness, and knows how to choose the words most expressive of his meaning, and to exalt them, to mould them like
wax to his will, and to arrange them in such position and order
that they shall at a glance show and make known their dignity
and splendour, like pictures placed in good and proper light.

"And this I say as well of writing as of speaking: in which
however some things are required that are not needful in writing,—such as a good voice, not too thin and soft like a woman's,
nor yet so stern and rough as to smack of the rustic's,—but sono-
rous, clear, sweet and well sounding, with distinct enunciation, and
with proper bearing and gestures; which I think consist in certain movements of the whole body, not affected or violent, but
tempered by a calm face and with a play of the eyes that shall
give an effect of grace, accord with the words, and as far as possible express also, together with the gestures, the speaker's intent
and feeling.

"But all these things would be vain and of small moment, if
the thoughts expressed by the words were not beautiful, ingenious,
acute, elegant and grave,—according to the need."

34.—Then my lord Morello said:

"If this Courtier speaks with so much elegance and grace, I
doubt if anyone will be found among us who will understand
him."

"Nay, he will be understood by everyone," replied the Count,
"because facility is no impediment to elegance.

"Nor would I have him speak always of grave matters, but
of amusing things, of games, jests and waggery, according to the
occasion; but sensibly of everything, and with readiness and lucid
fullness; and in no place let him show vanity or childish folly.
And again when he is speaking on an obscure or difficult subject,
I would have him carefully explain his meaning with precision
of both word and thought, and make every ambiguity clear and
plain with a certain touch of unpedantic care. Likewise, where
there is occasion, let him know how to speak with dignity and
force, to arouse those emotions that are part of our nature, and
to kindle them or to move them according to the need. Sometimes,
with that simple candour that makes it seem as if nature herself

were speaking, let him know how to soften them, and as it were to intoxicate them with sweetness, and so easily withal that the listener shall think that with very little effort he too could reach that excellence, and when he tries, shall find himself very far behind.

"In such fashion would I have our Courtier speak and write; and not only choose rich and elegant words from every part of Italy, but I should even praise him for sometimes using some of those French and Spanish terms that are already accepted by our custom.[88] Thus it would not displease me if on occasion he were to say, *primor* (excellence); or *acertare* (to succeed), *aventurare* (to run a risk successfully); or *ripassare una persona con ragionamento*, meaning to sound a person and to talk with him in order to gain perfect knowledge of him; or *un cavalier senza rimproccio* (a cavalier without reproach), *attilato* (elegant), *creato d'un principe* (a prince's creature), and other like terms, provided he might hope to be understood.[89]

"Sometimes I would have him use a few words in a sense other than that proper to them, to transpose them aptly, and as it were to graft them, like the branch of a tree, upon a more appropriate trunk,—so as to make them more attractive and beautiful, and as it were to bring things within the range of our vision, and within hand-touch as we say, to the delight of him who hears or reads. Nor would I have him scruple to form new words and in new figures of speech, deriving them tastefully from the Latins, as of old the Latins derived them from the Greeks.

35.—"Now if among the lettered men of good talent and judgment who to-day are found in our midst, there were a few who would take care to write in this language (as I have described) things worthy of being read, we should soon see it studied and abounding in beautiful terms and figures, and capable of being written in as well as is any other whatsoever; and if it were not pure old Tuscan, it would be Italian,—universal, copious and varied, and in a way like a delightful garden full of various flowers and fruits. Nor would this be a novel thing; for from the four dialects that the Greek writers had in use,[90] they culled words, forms and figures from each as they saw fit, and thence they brought forth another dialect which was called 'common,' and later they called all five by the single name Greek. And although the Attic dialect was more elegant, pure and copious than the others, good writers who were not Athenians by birth did not so affect it as to be unrecognizable by their style and by the perfume (as it were) and essence of their native speech. Nor yet were they disprized for this; on the contrary those who tried to seem too Athenian, were censured for it. Among the Latin writers too, many non-Romans were highly esteemed in their day, although there was not found in them that typical purity of the Roman tongue which men of other race can rarely acquire. Thus Titus Livius was not at all discarded, although someone professed to have detected a Paduan flavour in him; [91] nor was Virgil, albeit reproached with not speaking Roman. Moreover, as you know, many writers of barbarian race were read and esteemed at Rome.

"We, on the contrary, much more strict than the ancients, needlessly impose certain new laws upon ourselves, and with the beaten highways before our eyes, we seek to go along the by-paths; for in our own language,—of which, as of all others, the office is to express thought well and clearly,—we delight ourselves with obscurity; and calling it the vulgar tongue, we try in speaking it to use words that are understood neither by the vulgar nor yet by the gentle and lettered, and are no longer used in any place; unmindful that all the good writers of old disapproved words discarded by custom. Which to my thinking, you do not rightly understand; since you say that if some fault of speech is widely prevalent among the ignorant, it ought not for that reason to be called custom or accepted as a rule of speech, and from what I have heard you sometimes say, you would have us use *Campidoglio* in place of *Capitolio; Girolamo* for *Hieronymo; aldace* for *audace;* and *padrone* for *patrone*, and other words corrupt and spoiled like these; because they are found written thus by some ignorant old Tuscan, and because the Tuscan country folk speak thus to-day.[92]

"Hence I believe that good custom in speech springs from men who have talent and who have gained good judgment from study and experience, and who therefore agree and consent to accept the words that to them seem good, which are recognized by a certain innate judgment and not by any art or rule. Do you not know that figures of speech, which give so much grace and splendour to an oration, are all infringements of grammatical rules, yet accepted and confirmed by usage, because, although unable to offer other reason, they give pleasure and seem to carry suavity and sweetness to our very sense of hearing? And this I believe to be good custom,—of which the Romans, the Neapolitans, the Lombards and the rest, may be as capable as the Tuscans are.

36.—"It is very true that in every language certain things are always good, such as ease, good order, richness, beautiful sentences, harmonious periods; and on the contrary affectation and other things opposed to these, are bad. But among words there are some that remain good for a time, then grow antiquated and wholly lose their grace; others gain strength and come to be esteemed. For as the seasons of the year despoil the earth of flowers and fruits and then clothe it anew with others, so time causes those primal words to decay, and use makes others to be born again and gives them grace and dignity, until they in their turn meet their death, consumed by the envious gnawing of time; for in the end both we and all our concerns are mortal. Consider that we no longer have any knowledge of the Oscan tongue.[93] The Provençal, although it may be said to have been but lately celebrated by noble writers, is not now understood by the inhabitants of that country. Hence I think, as my lord Magnifico has well said, that if Petrarch and Boccaccio were alive at this time, they would not use many words that we find in their writings: therefore it does not seem to me well for us to copy these words. I applaud very highly those who know how to imitate that which ought to be imitated, but I do not at all believe that it is impossible to write well without imitating,—and particularly in this language of ours, wherein we may be aided by usage: which I should not dare say of Latin."

37.—The messer Federico said:

"Why would you have usage more esteemed in the vernacular than in Latin?"

"Nay," replied the Count, "I esteem usage as mistress of both the one and the other. But since those men to whom the Latin tongue was as natural as the vernacular now is to us, are no

ˊˊˊˊˊˊˊˊˊˊˊˊˊˊˊˊˊˊˊˊˊˊˊˊˊˊˊˊˊˊˊˊˊˊˊˊˊˊˊˊˊˊˊˊˊˊˊˊˊˊˊˊˊˊˊˊ

longer on earth, we must needs learn from their writings that which they learned from usage. Nor does ancient speech mean anything more than ancient usage of speech, and it would be a silly business to like ancient speech for no other reason than a wish to speak as men used to speak rather than as they now speak."

"Then," replied messer Federico, "the ancients did not imitate?"

"I believe," said the Count, "that many of them did, but not in everything. And if Virgil had imitated Hesiod in everything, he would not have surpassed his master; nor Cicero, Crassus; nor Ennius, his predecessors. You know Homer is so ancient that many believe he is the first heroic poet in time as he is also in excellence of diction: and whom would you think he imitated?"

"Some other poet," replied messer Federico, "more ancient than he, of whom we have no knowledge because of excessive antiquity."

"Then whom," said the Count, "would you say Petrarch and Boccaccio imitated, who were on earth only three days since, one may say?"

"I know not," replied messer Federico; "but we may believe that even their minds were directed to imitation, although we do not know of whom."

The Count replied:

"We may believe that they who were imitated, surpassed those who imitated them; and if they were admirable, it would be too great a marvel that their name and fame should be so soon extinguished. But I believe that their real master was aptitude and their own native judgment; and at this there is no one who ought to wonder, since nearly always the summit of every excellence may be approached by diverse roads. Nor is there anything that has not in it many things of the same sort which are dissimilar and yet intrinsically deserving of equal praise.

"Consider music, the harmonies of which are now grave and slow, now very fast and of novel moods and means; yet all give pleasure, albeit for different reasons: as is seen in Bidon's [94] manner of singing, which is so skilful, ready, vehement, fervid, and of such varied melodies, that the listener's spirits are moved and inflamed, and thus entranced seem to be lifted up to heaven. Nor does our friend Marchetto Cara [95] move us less by his singing, but with a gentler harmony; because he softens and penetrates our souls by placid means and full of plaintive sweetness, gently stirring them to sweet emotion.

"Again, various things give equal pleasure to our eyes, so that we can with difficulty decide which are more pleasing to them. You know that in painting Leonardo da Vinci,[96] Mantegna,[97] Raphael,[98] Michelangelo,[99] Giorgio da Castelfranco,[100] are very excellent, yet they are all unlike in their work; so that no one of them seems to lack anything in his own manner, since each is known as most perfect in his style.

"It is the same with many Greek and Latin poets, who, although different in their writing, are equal in their fame. The orators, too, have always had so much diversity among themselves, that almost every age has produced and prized a type of orator peculiar to its own time; and these have been different not only from their predecessors and successors, but from one another: as it is written of Isocrates, Lysias, Æschines,[101] and many others among the Greeks,—all excellent, yet each resembling no one but himself. So, among the Latins, Carbo, Lælius, Scipio Africanus, Galba, Sulpicius, Cotta, Gracchus, Marcus Antonius, Crassus,[102] and so many others that it would be tedious to name them,—all good and very different one from another; so that if a man were able to consider all the orators that have been in the world, he would find as many kinds of oratory as of orators. I think I remember too that Cicero in a certain place [103] makes Marcus Antonius say to Sulpicius that there are many who imitate no man and yet arrive at the highest pitch of excellence; and he speaks of certain ones who had introduced a new form and figure of speech, beautiful but not usual among the orators of that time, wherein they imitated no one but themselves. For that reason he affirms also that masters ought to consider the pupils' nature, and taking this as guide ought to direct and aid them to the path towards which their aptitude and natural disposition incline them. Hence I believe, dear messer Federico, that if a man has no innate affinity for any particular author, it is not well to force him to imitate, because the vigour [104] of his faculty languishes and is impeded when turned from the channel in which it would have made progress had that channel not been barred.

"Therefore I do not see how it can be well, instead of enriching this language of ours and giving it spirit and grandeur and light, to make it poor, thin, humble and obscure, and to try to restrict it in such narrow bounds that everyone shall be forced to imitate Petrarch and Boccaccio alone; and how, in respect of language, we ought not also to give credence to Poliziano,[105] to Lorenzo de' Medici,[106] to Francesco Diacceto,[107] and to some others who are also Tuscans and perhaps of no less learning and judgment than were Petrarch and Boccaccio. And great pity would it be indeed to set a limit, and not to surpass that which almost the earliest writers achieved, and to deny that so many men of such noble genius can ever find more than one beautiful form of expression in this language which is proper and natural to them. But to-day there are certain scrupulous souls, who so frighten the listener with the cult and ineffable mysteries of this Tuscan tongue of theirs, as to put even many a noble and learned man in such fear, that he dare not open his mouth and confesses that he does not know how to speak the very language which he learned in swaddling clothes from his nurse.

"However I think we have said only too much of this; so now let us go on with our discussion about the Courtier."

38.—Then messer Federico replied:

"I should first like to say one thing more, which is that I do not deny men's opinions and aptitudes to be different among themselves. Nor do I believe that it would be well for a naturally vehement and excitable man to set himself to write of placid themes, or for another, being severe and grave, to write jests; for in this matter it seems to me reasonable that everyone should adapt himself to his own proper instinct. And I think Cicero was speaking of this when he said that masters ought to have regard to their pupils' nature, in order not to act like bad husbandmen, who will sometimes sow grain in land that is fruitful only for the vine.

"Still I cannot get it into my head why, in the case of a particular language,—which is not proper to all men equally, like speech and thought and many other functions, but an invention of limited use,—it is not more rational to imitate those who speak better, than to speak at random; or why, just as in Latin we ought to try to approach the language of Virgil and Cicero rather than that of Silius or Cornelius Tacitus,[108] it is not better in the vernacular also to imitate the language of Petrarch and Boccaccio than any other's; yet to express our thoughts in it well, and thus to give heed to our own natural instinct, as Cicero teaches. And in this way it will be found that the difference which you say there is among good orators, consists in sense and not in language."

Then the Count said:

"I fear we shall be entering on a wide sea, and shall be leaving our first subject of the Courtier. However, I ask you in what consists the excellence of this language?"

Messer Federico replied:

"In preserving strictly its proprieties, in giving it that sense, and in using that style and those rhythms, which have been used by all who have written well."

"I should like to know," said the Count, "whether this style and these rhythms of which you speak, arise from the thought or from the words."

"From the words," replied messer Federico.

"Then," said the Count, "do not the words of Silius and Cornelius Tacitus seem to you the same that Virgil and Cicero use? and employed in the same sense?"

"Certainly they are the same," replied messer Federico, "but some of them wrongly applied and turned awry."

The Count replied:

"And if from a book of Cornelius and from one of Silius, all those words were removed that are used in a sense different from that of Virgil and Cicero, which would be very few,—would you not then say that Cornelius was the equal of Cicero in language, and Silius of Virgil, and that it would be well to imitate their manner of speech?"

39.—Then my lady Emilia said:

"Methinks this debate of yours is far too long and tedious; therefore it were well to postpone it to another time."

Messer Federico was about to reply none the less, but my lady Emilia always interrupted him. At last the Count said:

"Many men like to pass judgment upon style and to talk

ʄʄʄʄʄʄʄʄʄʄʄʄʄʄʄʄʄʄʄʄʄʄʄʄʄʄʄʄʄʄʄʄʄʄʄʄʄʄʄʄʄʄʄʄʄʄʄʄʄʄʄʄʄʄ

about rhythms and imitation; but they cannot make it at all clear to me what manner of thing style or rhythm is, or in what imitation consists, or why things taken from Homer or from someone else are so becoming in Virgil that they seem illumined rather than imitated. Perhaps this is because I am not capable of understanding them; but since a good sign that a man knows a thing, is his ability to teach it, I suspect that they too understand it but little, and that they praise both Virgil and Cicero because they hear such praise from many, not because they perceive the difference that exists between these two and others: for in truth it does not consist in preserving two or three or ten words used in a way different from the others.

"In Sallust, Cæsar, Varro [109] and the other good writers, some terms are found used differently from the way Cicero uses them; and yet both ways are proper, for the excellence and force of a language lie in no such trifling matter: as Demosthenes well said to Æschines, who tauntingly asked him whether certain words that he had used (although not Attic) were prodigies or portents; and Demosthenes laughed and replied that the fortunes of Greece did not hang on such a trifle. So I too should care little if I were reproved by a Tuscan for having said *satisfatto* rather than *sodisfatto, honorevole* for *horrevole, causa* for *cagione, populo* for *popolo,* and the like."

Then messer Federico rose to his feet and said:

"Hear me these few words, I pray."

"The pain of my displeasure," replied my lady Emilia, laughing, "be upon him who speaks more of this matter now, for I wish to postpone it to another evening. But do you, Count, go on with the discussion about the Courtier,—and show us what a fine memory you have, which I think you will do in no small measure, if you are able to take up the discussion where you left it."

40.—"My Lady," replied the Count, "I fear the thread is broken; yet if I am not wrong, methinks we were saying that the pest of affectation imparts extreme ungracefulness to everything, while on the other hand simplicity and nonchalance produce the height of grace: in praise of which, and in blame of affectation, we might cite many other arguments; but of these I wish to add only one, and no more. Women are always very eager to be—and when they cannot be, at least to seem—beautiful. So where nature is somewhat at fault in this regard, they try to piece it out by artifice; whence arise that painting of the face with so much care and sometimes pains, that plucking of the eyebrows and forehead, and the use of all those devices and the endurance of that trouble, which you ladies think to keep very secret from men, but which are all well known."

Here madonna Costanza Fregosa laughed and said:

"It would be far more courteous for you to keep to your discussion, and tell us of what grace is born, and talk about Courtiership,—than to try to unveil the weaknesses of women, which are not to the purpose."

"Nay, much to the purpose," replied the Count: "for these weaknesses of yours I am speaking of, deprive you of grace because they spring from nothing but affectation, wherein you openly make known to everyone your over-eagerness to be beautiful.

"Do you not see how much more grace a lady has who paints (if at all) so sparingly and so little, that whoever sees her is in doubt whether she be painted or not; than another lady so plastered that she seems to have put a mask upon her face and dares not laugh for fear of cracking it, nor ever changes colour but when she dresses in the morning, and then stands motionless all the rest of the day like a wooden image, showing herself only by candle-light, like wily merchants who display their cloths in a dark place? Again, how much more pleasing than all others is one (I mean not ill-favoured) who is plainly seen to have nothing on her face, although it be neither very white nor very red, but by nature a little pale and sometimes tinged with an honest flush from shame or other accident,—with hair artlessly unadorned and hardly confined, her gestures simple and free, without showing care or wish to be beautiful! This is that nonchalant simplicity most pleasing to the eyes and minds of men, who are ever fearful of being deceived by art.

"Beautiful teeth are very charming in a woman, for since they are not so much in view as the face is, but lie hidden most of the time, we may believe that less care is taken to make them beautiful than with the face. Yet if one were to laugh without cause and solely to display the teeth, he would betray his art, and however beautiful they were, would seem most ungraceful to all, like Catullus's Egnatius.[110] It is the same with the hands; which, if they are delicate and beautiful, and occasionally left bare when there is need to use them, and not in order to display their beauty, they leave a very great desire to see more of them, and especially if covered with gloves again; for whoever covers them seems to have little care or thought whether they be seen or not, and to have them thus beautiful more by nature than by any effort or pains.

"Have you ever noticed when a woman, in passing through the street to church or elsewhere, thoughtlessly happens (either in frolic or from other cause) to lift her dress high enough to show the foot and often a little of the leg? Does this not seem to you full of grace, when you see her tricked out with a touch of feminine daintiness in velvet shoes and neat stockings? I for one delight in it and believe you all do, for everyone is persuaded that elegance, in matters thus hidden and rarely seen, is natural and instinctive to the lady rather than forced, and that she does not think to win any praise by it.

41.—"In this way we avoid and hide affectation, and you can now see how opposed and destructive it is to grace in every office as well of the body as the mind: whereof we have thus far spoken little, and yet we must not omit it, for since the mind is of far more worth than the body, it deserves to be more cultivated and adorned. And as to what ought to be done in the case of our Courtier, we will lay aside the precepts of the many sage philosophers who write of this matter and define the properties of the mind and discuss so subtly about their rank,—and keeping to our subject, we will in a few words declare it to be enough that he be (as we say) an honest and upright man; for in this are included prudence, goodness, strength and temperance of mind, and all the other qualities that are proper to a name so honoured. And I esteem him alone to be a true moral philosopher, who wishes to be good; and in this regard he needs few other precepts than that wish. And therefore Socrates was right in saying that he thought his teachings bore good fruit indeed whenever they incited anyone to understand and teach virtue: for they who have reached the goal of desiring nothing more ardently than to be good, easily acquire knowledge of everything needful therefor; so we will discuss this no further.

42.—"Yet besides goodness, I think that letters are for everyone the true and principal ornament of the mind: although the French recognize only the nobility of arms and esteem all else as naught. Thus they not only fail to prize but they abhor letters, and hold all men of letters most base, and think they speak very basely of any man when they call him a clerk."

Then the Magnifico Giuliano replied:

"You say truly, that this fault has long been prevalent among the French. But if kind fate decrees that Monseigneur d'Angoulême [111] shall succeed to the crown, as is hoped, I think that just as the glory of arms flourishes and shines in France, so too ought that of letters to flourish in highest state; for it is not long since I, being at the court, saw this prince, and it seemed to me that besides the grace of his person and the beauty of his face, he had in his aspect such loftiness, joined however with a certain gracious humanity, that the realm of France must always seem small for him. I heard afterwards from many gentlemen, both French and Italian, of his very noble manner of life, of his loftiness of mind, of his valour and liberality. And among other things I was told that he loved and esteemed letters especially and held all men of letters in greatest honour; and he condemned the French themselves for being so hostile to this profession, especially as they have within their borders such a noble school as that of Paris, frequented by all the world." [112]

Then the Count said:

"It is a great marvel that in such tender youth, solely by natural instinct and against the usage of his country, he has of himself chosen so worthy a path. And as subjects always copy the customs of their superiors, it may be that, as you say, the French will yet come to esteem letters at their true worth: whereto they may easily be persuaded, if they will but listen to reason; since nothing is by nature more desirable for men, or more proper to them, than knowledge, which it is great folly to say or believe is not always a good thing.

43.—"And if I were speaking with them, or with others

who had an opinion contrary to mine, I should strive to show them how useful and necessary letters are to our life and dignity, having indeed been granted by God to men as a crowning gift. Nor should I lack instances of many excellent commanders of antiquity, who all added the ornament of letters to the valour of their arms.

"Thus you know Alexander held Homer in such veneration that he always kept the Iliad by his bedside; and he devoted the greatest attention not only to these studies but to philosophical speculation under Aristotle's guidance. Alcibiades enlarged his natural aptitudes and made them greater by means of letters and the teachings of Socrates. The care that Cæsar gave to study is also attested by the surviving works that he divinely wrote. It is said that Scipio Africanus always kept in his hand the works of Xenophon, wherein the perfect king is portrayed under the name of Cyrus. I could tell you of Lucullus, Sulla, Pompey, Brutus,[113] and many other Romans and Greeks; but I will merely remind you that Hannibal, the illustrious commander,—although fierce by nature and a stranger to all humanity, faithless and a despiser of both men and gods,—yet had knowledge of letters and was conversant with the Greek language; and if I mistake not, I once read that he even left a book composed by him in Greek.

"However it is superfluous to tell you this, for I well know that you all see how wrong the French are in thinking that letters are injurious to arms. You know that glory is the true stimulus to great and hazardous deeds of war, and whoso is moved thereto by gain or other motive, besides doing nothing good, deserves not to be called a gentleman, but a base trafficker. And true glory is that which is preserved in the sacred treasure-house of letters, as everyone may understand except those unfortunates who have never enjoyed them.

"What soul is there so abject, timid and humble, that when he reads of the deeds of Cæsar, Alexander, Scipio, Hannibal, and many others, is not inflamed by an ardent desire to be like them, and does not make small account of this frail two days' life, in order to win the almost eternal life of fame, which in spite of death makes him live in far greater glory than before?

But he who does not feel the delight of letters, cannot either know how great is the glory they so long preserve, and measures it by the life of one man or two, because his memory runs no further. Hence he cannot esteem this short-lived glory so much as he would that almost eternal glory if knowledge of it were unhappily not denied him, and as he does not esteem it so much, we may reasonably believe that he will not run such danger to pursue it as one who knew it would.

"I should be far from willing to have an antagonist cite instances to the contrary in refutation of my view, and urge upon me that with all their knowledge of letters the Italians have for some time since shown little martial valour,—which is alas only too true.[114] But it very certainly might be said that the fault of a few has brought not only grievous harm but eternal obloquy upon all the rest; and from them was derived the true cause of our ruin and of the decadence if not the death of valour in our souls: yet it would be far more shameful in us to publish it, than for the French to be ignorant of letters. Therefore it is better to pass over in silence that which cannot be recalled without pain: and avoiding this subject (upon which I entered against my will) to return to our Courtier.

44.—"I would have him more than passably accomplished in letters, at least in those studies that are called the humanities, and conversant not only with the Latin language but with the Greek, for the sake of the many different things that have been admirably written therein.[115] Let him be well versed in the poets, and not less in the orators and historians, and also proficient in writing verse and prose, especially in this vulgar tongue of ours; [116] for besides the enjoyment he will find in it, he will by this means never lack agreeable entertainment with ladies,[117] who are usually fond of such things. And if other occupations or want of study prevent his reaching such perfection as to render his writings worthy of great praise, let him be careful to suppress them so that others may not laugh at him, and let him show them only to a friend whom he can trust: because they will at least be of this service to him, that the exercise will enable him to judge the work of others. For it very rarely happens that a man who is not accustomed to write, however learned he may

*᛭᛭᛭᛭᛭᛭᛭᛭᛭᛭᛭᛭᛭᛭᛭᛭᛭᛭᛭᛭᛭᛭᛭᛭᛭᛭᛭᛭᛭᛭᛭᛭᛭᛭᛭᛭᛭᛭᛭᛭᛭᛭᛭᛭᛭᛭᛭᛭᛭᛭᛭᛭᛭᛭᛭*

be, can ever quite appreciate the toil and industry of writers, or taste the sweetness and excellence of style, and those latent niceties that are often found in the ancients.

"Moreover these studies will also make him fluent, and as Aristippus said to the tyrant, confident and assured in speaking with everyone.[118] Hence I would have our Courtier keep one precept fixed in mind; which is that in this and everything else he should be always on his guard, and diffident rather than forward, and that he should keep from falsely persuading himself that he knows that which he does not know. For by nature we are all fonder of praise than we ought to be, and our ears love the melody of words that praise us more than any other sweet song or sound; and thus, like sirens' voices, they are often the cause of shipwreck to him who does not close his ears to such deceptive harmony. Among the ancient sages this danger was recognized, and books were written showing in what way the true friend may be distinguished from the flatterer.[119] But what does this avail, if there be many, nay a host, of those who clearly perceive that they are flattered, yet love him who flatters them, and hold him in hatred who tells them the truth? And often when they find him who praises them too sparing in his words, they even help him and say such things of themselves, that the flatterer is put to shame, most impudent though he be.

"Let us leave these blind ones to their error, and have our Courtier of such good judgment that he will not take black for white, or have more self-confidence than he clearly knows to be well founded; and especially in those peculiarities which (if you remember) messer Cesare in his game said we had often used as an instrument to bring men's folly to light. On the contrary, even if he well knows the praises bestowed upon him to be true, let him not err by accepting them too openly or confirming them without some protest; but rather let him as it were disclaim them modestly, always showing and really esteeming arms as his chief profession, and all other good accomplishments as an ornament thereto. And particularly among soldiers let him not act like those who insist on seeming soldiers in learning, and learned men among soldiers. In this way, for the reasons we have alleged, he will avoid affectation, and even the middling things that he does, shall seem very great."

45.—Messer Pietro Bembo here replied:

"Count, I do not see why you insist that this Courtier, being lettered and endowed with so many other admirable accomplishments, should hold everything as an ornament of arms, and not arms and the rest as an ornament of letters; which without other accompaniment are as superior in dignity to arms, as the mind is to the body, for the practice of them properly pertains to the mind, as that of arms does to the body."

Then the Count replied:

"Nay, the practice of arms pertains to both mind and body. But I would not have you judge in such a cause, messer Pietro, for you would be too much suspected of bias by one of the two sides: and as the controversy has already been long waged by very wise men, there is no need to renew it; but I regard it as settled in favour of arms, and would have our Courtier so regard it too, since I may form him as I wish. And if you are of contrary mind, wait till you hear of a contest wherein he who defends the cause of arms is allowed to use arms, just as those who defend letters make use of letters in their defence; for if everyone avails himself of his proper weapons, you shall see that men of letters will be worsted."

"Ah," said messer Pietro, "a while ago you blamed the French for prizing letters little, and told what glorious lustre is shed on man by letters and how they make him immortal; and now it seems you have changed your mind. Do you not remember that

> Before the famous tomb of brave Achilles
> Thus spake the mighty Alexander, sighing:
> 'O happy youth, who found so clear a trumpet,
> And lofty bard to make thy deeds undying!' [120]

And if Alexander envied Achilles not for his deeds, but for the fortune that had granted him the happiness of having his exploits celebrated by Homer, we may conclude that Alexander esteemed Homer's poems above Achilles's arms. For what other judge do you wait then, or for what other sentence upon the dignity of arms and letters, than that pronounced by one of the greatest commanders that have ever been?"

46.—Then the Count replied:

"I blame the French for thinking that letters are a hindrance to the profession of arms, and I hold that learning is more proper to no one than to a warrior; and in our Courtier I would have these two accomplishments joined and each aided by the other, as is most proper: nor do I think I have changed my mind in this. But as I said, I do not wish to discuss which of the two is more worthy of praise. It is enough that men of letters almost never select for praise any but great men and glorious deeds, which in themselves merit praise for the mere essential quality from which they spring; besides this they are very noble material for writers: which is a great ornament, and in part the cause of perpetuating writings, which perhaps would not be so much read and appreciated if they lacked their noble theme, but vain and of little moment.

"And if Alexander was envious that Achilles should be praised by Homer, it does not therefore follow that he esteemed letters above arms; wherein if he had felt himself as far behind Achilles as he deemed all those who wrote of him were behind Homer, I am sure he would far rather have desired fine acts on his part than fine speeches on the part of others. Hence I believe that saying of his to have been a tacit eulogy of himself, and that he was expressing a desire for what he thought he did not possess (that is, the supreme excellence of a writer), and not for what he believed he already had attained (that is, prowess in arms, wherein he did not deem Achilles at all his superior). Thus he called Achilles happy, as if hinting that although his own fame had hitherto not been so celebrated in the world as Achilles's, which was made bright and illustrious by that poem so divine,—it was not because his valour and merits were less or deserving of less praise, but because fortune bestowed upon Achilles that miracle of nature as a glorious trumpet for his achievements. Perhaps also he wished to incite some noble genius to write about him, by showing that this must be as pleasing to him as were his love and veneration for the sacred monuments of letters: whereof we have spoken long enough for the present."

"Nay, too long," replied my lord Ludovico Pio; "for I believe that in the whole world it would be impossible to find a receptacle large enough to hold all the things you would have in our Courtier."

Then the Count said:

"Wait a little, for there are many more that he must have."

"In that case," replied Pietro da Napoli, "Grasso de' Medici would have a great advantage over messer Pietro Bembo." [121]

47.—Here everyone laughed, and the Count began anew and said:

"My lords, you must know that I am not content with the Courtier unless he be also a musician and unless, besides understanding and being able to read notes, he can play upon divers instruments. For if we consider rightly, there is to be found no rest from toil or medicine for the troubled spirit more becoming and praiseworthy in time of leisure, than this; and especially in courts, where besides the relief from tedium that music affords us all, many things are done to please the ladies, whose tender and gentle spirit is easily penetrated by harmony and filled with sweetness. Thus it is no marvel that in both ancient and modern times they have always been inclined to favour musicians, and have found refreshing spiritual food in music."

Then my lord Gaspar said:

"I admit that music as well as many other vanities may be proper to women and perhaps to some that have the semblance of men, but not to those who really are men; for these ought not to enervate their mind with delights and thus induce therein a fear of death."

"Say not so," replied the Count; "for I shall enter upon a vast sea in praise of music. And I shall call to mind how it was always celebrated and held sacred among the ancients, and how very sage philosophers were of opinion that the world is composed of music, that the heavens make harmony in their moving, and that the soul, being ordered in like fashion, awakes and as it were revives its powers through music.

"Thus it is written that Alexander was sometimes excited by it so passionately, that he was forced almost against his will to leave the banquet table and rush to arms; and when the musician changed the temper of the tune, he grew calm again, lay aside his arms, and returned to the banquet table. Moreover I will tell you that grave Socrates learned to play the cithern [122] at a very advanced age. And I remember having once heard that Plato and Aristotle would have the man of culture a musician also; and they show by a host of arguments that the power of music over us is very great, and (for many reasons which would be too long to tell now) that it must needs be taught from childhood, not so much for the mere melody that we hear, but for the power it has to induce in us a fresh and good habit of mind and an habitual tendency to virtue, which renders the soul more capable of happiness, just as bodily exercise renders the body more robust;[123] and that music is not only no hindrance in the pursuits of peace and war, but is very helpful therein.

"Again, Lycurgus [124] approved of music in his harsh laws. And we read that in their battles the very warlike Lacedemonians and Cretans used the cithern and other dulcet instruments; that many very excellent commanders of antiquity, like Epaminondas,[125] practised music; and that those who were ignorant of it, like Themistocles,[126] were far less esteemed. Have you not read that music was among the first accomplishments which the worthy old Chiron taught Achilles in tender youth,[127] whom he reared from the age of nurse and cradle? and that the sage preceptor insisted that the hands which were to shed so much Trojan blood, should be often busied with the cithern? Where is the soldier who would be ashamed to imitate Achilles,—to say nothing of many other famous commanders whom I could cite?

"Therefore seek not to deprive our Courtier of music, which not only soothes men's minds, but often tames wild beasts;[128] and he who enjoys it not, may be sure that his spirit is ill attuned. See what power it has, to make (as once it did) a fish submit to be ridden by a man upon the boisterous sea.[129] We find it used in holy temples to render praise and thanks to God; and we must believe that it is pleasing to Him and that He has given it to us as most sweet alleviation for our fatigues and troubles. Wherefore rough toilers of the field under a burning sun often cheat their weariness with crude and rustic song. With music the rude peasant lass, who is up before the day to spin or weave, wards off her drowsiness and makes her toil a pleasure; music is very cheering pastime for poor sailors after rain, wind and tempest: a solace to tired pilgrims on their long and weary journeys, and often to sorrowing captives in their chains and fetters. Thus, as stronger proof that melody even if rude is very great relief from every human toil and care, nature seems to have taught it to the nurse as chief remedy for the continual wailing of frail children, who by the sound of her voice are brought restful and placid sleep, forgetful of the tears so proper to them and given us in that age by nature as a presage of our after life."

48.—As the Count now remained silent for a little, the Magnifico Giuliano said:

"I do not at all agree with my lord Gaspar. Nay I think, for the reasons you give and for many others, that music is not only an ornament but a necessity to the Courtier. Yet I would have you declare in what way this and the other accomplishments that you prescribe for him, are to be practised, and at what time and in what manner.[130] For many things that are praiseworthy in themselves often become very inappropriate when practised out of season, and on the other hand, some that seem of little moment are highly esteemed when made use of opportunely."

49.—Then the Count said:

"Before we enter upon that subject, I wish to discuss another matter, which I deem of great importance and therefore think our Courtier ought by no means to omit: and this is to know how to draw and to have acquaintance with the very art of painting.

"And do not marvel that I desire this art, which to-day may seem to savour of the artisan and little to befit a gentleman; for I remember having read that the ancients, especially throughout Greece, had their boys of gentle birth study painting in school as an honourable and necessary thing, and it was admitted to the first rank of liberal arts; while by public edict they forbade that it be taught to slaves. Among the Romans too, it was held in highest honour, and the very noble family of the Fabii took their name from it; for the first Fabius was given the name *Pictor*, because,—being indeed a most excellent painter, and so

devoted to painting that when he painted the walls of the temple
of Health,—he inscribed his own name thereon;[131] for although
he was born of a family thus renowned and honoured with so
many consular titles, triumphs and other dignities, and although
he was a man of letters and learned in the law, and numbered
among the orators,—yet he thought to add splendour and ornament to his fame by leaving a memorial that he had been a
painter. Nor is there lack of many other men of illustrious
family, celebrated in this art; which besides being very noble
and worthy in itself, is of great utility, and especially in war for
drawing places, sites, rivers, bridges, rocks, fortresses, and the
like; since however well we may keep them in memory (which
is very difficult), we cannot show them to others.

"And truly he who does not esteem this art, seems to me
very unreasonable; for this universal fabric that we see,—with
the vast heaven so rightly adorned with shining stars, and in the
midst the earth girdled by the seas, varied with mountains,
valleys and rivers, and bedecked with so many divers trees,
beautiful flowers and grasses,—may be said to be a great and
noble picture, composed by the hand of nature and of God; and
whoever is able to imitate it, seems to me deserving of great
praise: nor can it be imitated without knowledge of many things,
as he knows well who tries. Hence the ancients greatly prized
both the art and the artist, which thus attained the summit of
highest excellence; very sure proof of which may be found in
the antique marble and bronze statues that yet are seen.[132] And
although painting is different from sculpture, both the one and
the other spring from the same source, which is good design.
Therefore, as the statues are divine, so we may believe the pictures were also; the more indeed because they are susceptible of
greater skill."

50.—Then my lady Emilia turned to Giancristoforo Romano, who was sitting with the others there, and said:

"What think you of this opinion? Do you admit that painting is susceptible of greater skill than sculpture?"[133]

Giancristoforo replied:

"I, my Lady, think that sculpture needs more pains, more
skill, and is of greater dignity than painting."

The Count rejoined:

"In that statues are more enduring, perhaps we might say they are of greater dignity; for being made as memorials, they fulfil better than painting the purpose for which they are made. But besides serving as memorials, both painting and sculpture serve also to beautify, and in this respect painting is much superior; for if less diuturnal (so to speak) than sculpture, yet it is of very long life, and is far more charming so long as it endures."

Then Giancristoforo replied:

"I really think that you are speaking against your convictions and that you are doing so solely for the sake of your friend Raphael; and perhaps too the excellence you find in his painting seems to you so consummate that sculpture cannot rival it: but consider that this is praise of an artist and not of his art."

Then he continued:

"It seems clear to me that both the one and the other are artificial imitations of nature; but I do not see how you can say that truth, such as nature makes it, is not better imitated in a marble or bronze statue,—wherein the members are round, formed and measured, as nature makes them,—than in a painting, where we see nothing but the surface and those colours that cheat the eyes; nor will you tell me, surely, that being is not nearer truth than seeming. Moreover I think sculpture is more difficult, because if a slip is made, it cannot be corrected (since marble cannot be patched again), but another statue must be made anew; which does not happen with painting, for one may change a thousand times, and add and take away, improving always."

51.—The Count said, laughing:

"I am not speaking for Raphael's sake; nor ought you to repute me so ignorant as not to know the excellence of Michelangelo in sculpture, your own, and others'. But I am speaking of the art, and not of the artists.

"You say very truly that both the one and the other are imitations of nature; but it is not true that painting seems, and sculpture is. For while statues are round as in life and painting is seen only on the surface, statues lack many things that paintings do not lack, and especially light and shade. Thus flesh has one tone and marble another; and this the painter imitates to the life by chiaroscuro, greater or less according to the need,— which the sculptor cannot do. And although the painter does not make his figure round, he presents the muscles and members rounded in such fashion as so to join the parts which are not seen, that we can discern very well that the painter knows and understands these also. And in this, another and greater skill is needed to represent those members that are foreshortened and grow smaller in proportion to the distance by reason of perspective; which, by means of measured lines, colours, lights and shades, shows you foreground and distance all on the single surface of an upright wall, in such proportion as he chooses.[134] Do you really think it of small moment to imitate the natural colours, in representing flesh or stuffs or any other coloured thing? The sculptor certainly cannot do this, or express the grace of black eyes or blue, with the splendour of their amorous beams. He cannot show the colour of fair hair, or the gleam of weapons, or a dark night, or a storm at sea, or its lightnings and thunderbolts, or the burning of a city, or the birth of rosy dawn with its rays of gold and purple. In short, he cannot show sky, sea, earth, mountains, woods, meadows, gardens, rivers, cities, or houses,— all of which the painter shows.

52.—"Therefore painting seems to me nobler and more susceptible of skill, than sculpture. And I think that it, like other things, reached the summit of excellence among the ancients: which still is seen in the few slight remains that are left, especially in the grottoes of Rome;[135] but much more clearly may it be perceived in the ancient authors, wherein is such honoured and frequent mention both of works and of masters, and whereby we learn how highly they were always honoured by great lords and by commonwealths.

"Thus we read that Alexander loved Apelles of Ephesus dearly,—so dearly, that having caused the artist to paint a portrait of his favourite slave undraped, and hearing that the worthy painter had become most ardently enamoured of her by reason of her marvellous beauty, he gave her to Apelles without hesitation:—munificence truly worthy of Alexander, to sacrifice not only treasure and states but his very affections and desires; and

✓✓✓✓✓✓✓✓✓✓✓✓✓✓✓✓✓✓✓✓✓✓✓✓✓✓✓✓✓✓✓✓✓✓✓✓✓✓✓✓✓✓✓✓✓✓✓✓✓✓✓

sign of exceeding love for Apelles, in order to please the artist,
not to hesitate at displeasing the woman he dearly loved, who
(we may believe) was sorely grieved to change so great a king
for a painter. Many other signs also are told of Alexander's
favour to Apelles; but he very clearly showed how highly he
esteemed the painter, in commanding by public edict that none
other should presume to paint his portrait.

"Here I could tell you of the rivalries of many noble
painters, which filled nearly the whole world with praise and
wonderment. I could tell you with what solemnity ancient emperors adorned their triumphs with pictures, and set them up in
public places, and how dearly bought them; and that there were
some painters who gave their works as gifts, esteeming gold and
silver inadequate to pay for them; and how a painting by Protogenes was prized so highly, that when Demetrius [136] laid siege
to Rhodes and could have gained an entrance by setting fire to
the quarter where he knew the painting was, he refrained from
giving battle so that it might not be burned, and thus did not
capture the place; and that Metrodorus,[137] a philosopher and very
excellent painter, was sent by the Athenians to Lucius Paulus [138]
to teach his children and to adorn the triumph that he was about
to receive. Moreover many noble authors have written about
this art, which is a great sign of the esteem in which it was held;
but I do not wish to enlarge further upon it in this discussion.

"So let it be enough to say that it is fitting for our Courtier
to have knowledge of painting also, as being honourable and
useful and highly prized in those times when men were of far
greater worth than now they are. And if he should never derive
from it other use or pleasure than the help it affords in judging
the merit of statues ancient and modern, of vases, buildings,
medals, cameos, intaglios, and the like,—it also enables him to
appreciate the beauty of living bodies, not only as to delicacy
of face but as to symmetry of all the other parts, both in men
and in every other creature. Thus you see how a knowledge of
painting is a source of very great pleasure. And let those think
of this, who so delight in contemplating a woman's beauty that
they seem to be in paradise, and yet cannot paint; which if they
could do, they would have much greater pleasure, because they

would more perfectly appreciate that beauty which engenders
such satisfaction in their hearts."

53.—Here messer Cesare Gonzaga laughed, and said:

"Certainly I am no painter; yet I am sure I have greater
pleasure in looking upon a woman than that admirable Apelles,
whom you just mentioned, would have if he were now come back
to life."

The Count replied:

"This pleasure of yours is not derived wholly from her
beauty, but from the affection that perhaps you bear her; and if
you will say the truth, the first time you saw that woman you
did not feel a thousandth part of the pleasure that you did afterwards, although her beauty was the same. Thus you may see how
much more affection had to do with your pleasure, than beauty
had."

"I do not deny this," said messer Cesare; "but just as my
pleasure is born of affection, so is affection born of beauty. Thus
it may still be said that beauty is the cause of my pleasure."

The Count replied:

"Many other causes also inflame our minds, besides beauty:
such as manners, knowledge, speech, gesture, and a thousand
other things which in a way perhaps might also be called beauties; but above all, the consciousness of being loved. So it is
possible to love very ardently even without that beauty you
speak of; but the love that springs from the outward bodily
beauty which we see, will doubtless give far greater pleasure
to him who appreciates it more than to him who appreciates it
less. Therefore, to return to our subject, I think that Apelles
enjoyed the contemplation of Campaspe's beauty far more than
Alexander did:[109] for we may easily believe that both men's love
sprang only from her beauty; and perhaps it was partly on this
account that Alexander resolved to give her to him who seemed
fitted to appreciate her most perfectly.

"Have you not read that those five maidens of Crotona,
whom the painter Zeuxis chose above the others of that city for
the purpose of forming from them all a single type of surpassing
beauty, were celebrated by many poets as having been adjudged

beautiful by one who must have been a consummate judge of beauty?" [140]

54.—Messer Cesare here seemed ill satisfied and unwilling to admit for a moment that anyone but himself could taste that pleasure which he felt in contemplating a woman's beauty, and he began to speak. But just then a great tramping of feet was heard, and the sound of loud talking; whereupon everyone turned, and a glare of torches was seen at the door of the room, and soon there arrived, with a numerous and noble company, my lord Prefect,[3] who returned from attending the pope part way on the journey. At once on entering the palace he had asked what my lady Duchess was doing, and had learned of what manner the game was that evening, and the charge imposed on Count Ludovico to speak about Courtiership. Therefore he came as fast as he could, so as to arrive in season to hear something. Then, immediately after having made his reverence to my lady Duchess and bidden the others to be seated (for everyone had risen when he came in),—he too sat down in the circle with some of his gentlemen; among whom were the Marquess Febus di Ceva and his brother Gerardino,[141] messer Ettore Romano,[142] Vincenzo Calmeta,[143] Orazio Florido,[144] and many others; and as everyone remained silent, my lord Prefect said:

"Gentlemen, my coming here would be indeed a pity, if I were to interrupt such a fine discussion as I think you were just now engaged in; so do me not this wrong of depriving yourselves and me of such a pleasure."

Then Count Ludovico said:

"Nay, my Lord, I think we all must be far better pleased to be silent than to speak; for this burden having fallen more to me than to the others this evening, I have at last grown weary of speaking, and I think all the others are weary of listening, for my talk has not been worthy of this company or adequate to the lofty theme that I was charged with; in which, having little satisfied myself, I think I have satisfied the others still less. So you were fortunate, my Lord, to come in at the end. And for the rest of the discussion, it would indeed be well to appoint someone else to take my place, because whoever he may be, I know he will fill it far better than I should even if I were willing to go on, being now tired as I am."

The Magnifico Giuliano replied:

55.—"I certainly shall not submit to be cheated of the promise that you made me, and am sure my lord Prefect too will not be sorry to hear that part of our discussion."

"And what promise was it?" said the Count.

"To tell us in what way the Courtier must make use of those good qualities that you have said befit him," replied the Magnifico.

Although but a boy, my lord Prefect was wise and sensible beyond what seemed natural to his tender years, and in his every movement he showed a loftiness of mind and a certain vivacity of temper that gave true presage of the high pitch of manliness that he was to attain. So he said quickly:

"If all this is to be told, I think I have come just in time; for by hearing in what way the Courtier must use his good qualities, I shall hear also what they are, and thus shall come to learn everything that has been said before. So do not refuse, Count, to fulfil the obligation of which you have already performed a part."

"I should not have so heavy an obligation to fulfil," replied the Count, "if the labour were more evenly divided; but the mistake was made of giving the right of command to a too partial lady;" and then laughing he turned to my lady Emilia, who quickly said:

"It is not you who ought to complain of my partiality; but since you do so without reason, we will give someone else a share of this honour, which you call labour;" and turning to messer Federico Fregoso, she said: "You proposed the game of the Courtier, hence it is right that you should bear some share in it; and this shall be to comply with my lord Magnifico's request, by declaring in what way, manner and time, the Courtier ought to make use of his good qualities and practise those things which the Count has said it is fitting he should know."

Then messer Federico said:

"My Lady, in trying to separate the way and the time and the manner of the Courtier's good qualities and good practice, you try to separate that which cannot be separated, because these are the very things that make his qualities good, and his practice good. Therefore, since the Count has spoken so much and so well, and has touched somewhat upon these matters and arranged in his mind the rest of what he has to say, it was only right that he should continue to the end."

"Account yourself to be the Count," said my lady Emilia, "and say what you think he would say; and thus all will be right."

56.—Then Calmeta said:

"My Lords, since the hour is late, and in order that messer Federico may have no excuse for not telling what he knows, I think it would be well to postpone the rest of the discussion until to-morrow, and let the little time we have left, be spent in some other quiet diversion."

As everyone approved, my lady Duchess desired madonna Margarita [145] and madonna Costanza Fregosa [57] to dance. Whereupon Barletta,[146] a very charming musician and excellent dancer, who always kept the whole court in good humour, began to play upon his instruments; and joining hands, the two ladies danced first a basset and then a *roegarze*,[147] with consummate grace and to the great delight of those who saw them. Then the night being already far spent, my lady Duchess rose to her feet, and so everyone reverently took leave and retired to sleep.

## *The Second Book*

### TO MESSER ALFONSO ARIOSTO

HAVE OFTEN CONSIDERED NOT WITHOUT wonder whence arises a fault, which, as it is universally found among old people, may be believed to be proper and natural to them. And this is, that they nearly all praise bygone times and censure the present, inveighing against our acts and ways and everything which they in their youth did not do; affirming too that every good custom and good manner of living, every virtue, in short every thing, is always going from bad to worse.

And verily it seems quite contrary to reason and worthy to be wondered at, that ripe age, which in other matters is wont to make men's judgment more perfect with long experience, should in this matter so corrupt it that they do not perceive that if the world were always growing worse, and if fathers were generally better than children, we should long since have reached that last grade of badness beyond which it is impossible to grow worse. And yet we see that not only in our days but in bygone times this failing has always been peculiar to old age, which is clearly gathered from the works of many ancient authors, and especially of the comic writers, who better than the others set forth the image of human life.

Now the cause of this wrong judgment among old people I for my part take to be, that the fleeting years despoil them of many good things, and among others in great part rob the blood of vital spirits; whence the complexion changes, and those organs become weak through which the soul exerts its powers.[148] Thus in old age the sweet flowers of contentment fall from our hearts,

73

like leaves from a tree in autumn, and in place of serene and sunny thoughts, comes cloudy and turbid sadness with its train of thousand ills. So that not the body only but the mind also is infirm; of bygone pleasures naught is left but a lingering memory and the image of that precious time of tender youth, in which (when it is with us) sky and earth and all things seem to us ever making merry and laughing before our eyes, and the sweet springtide of happiness seems to blossom in our thought. as in a delightful and lovely garden.

Therefore in the evening chill of life, when our sun begins to sink to its setting and steals away those pleasures, we should fare better if in losing them, we could lose the memory of them also, and as Themistocles said, find an art that shall teach us to forget. For so deceitful are our bodily senses, that they often cheat even the judgment of our minds. Thus it seems to me that old people are in like case with those who keep their eyes fixed upon the land as they leave port, and think their ship is standing still and the shore recedes, although it is the other way. For both the port and also time and its pleasures remain the same, and one after another we take flight in the ship of mortality upon that boisterous sea which absorbs and devours everything, and are never suffered to touch shore again, but always tossed by adverse winds we are wrecked upon some rock at last.

Since therefore the senile mind is an unfit subject for many pleasures, it cannot enjoy them; and just as to men in fever, when the palate is spoiled by corrupt vapours, all wines seem bitter, however precious and delicate they be,—so old men, because of their infirmity (which yet does not deprive them of appetite), find pleasures flat and cold and very different from those which they remember tasting of old, although the pleasures are intrinsically the same. Thus they feel themselves despoiled, and they lament and call the present times bad, not perceiving that the change lies in themselves and not in the times; and on the other hand they call to mind their bygone pleasures, and bring back the time when these were enjoyed and praise it as good, because it seems to carry with it a savour of what they felt when it was present. For in truth our minds hold all things hateful that have been with us in our sorrows, and love those that have been with us in our joys.

This is why it is sometimes highest bliss for a lover to look at a window although closed, because he there had once the happiness to gaze upon the lady of his love; and in the same way to look at a ring, a letter, a garden or other place, or what you will, which seems to him a conscious witness of his joys. And on the contrary, a gorgeous and beautiful room will often be irksome to a man who has been prisoner or has suffered some other sorrow there. And I once knew some who would not drink from a cup like that from which in illness they had taken medicine. For just as to the one the window or ring or letter recalls the sweet memory that gives him such delight and seems part of his bygone joy,—so to the other, the room or cup brings his illness or imprisonment to mind. I believe that the same cause leads old people to praise bygone times and to censure the present.

2.—Therefore as they speak of other things, so do they also of courts, affirming those which they remember, to have been far more excellent and full of eminent men than those which we see to-day. And as soon as such discussions are started, they begin to extol with boundless praise the courtiers of Duke Filippo or Duke Borso;[149] and they narrate the sayings of Niccolò Piccinino;[150] and they remind us that there were no murders in those days (or very few at most), no brawls, no ambushes, no deceits, but a certain frank and kindly good will among all men, a loyal confidence; and that in the courts of that time such good behaviour and decorum prevailed, that courtiers were all like monks, and woe to him who should have spoken insultingly to another, or so much as made a less than decorous gesture to a woman. And on the other hand they say everything is the reverse in these days, and that not only have courtiers lost their fraternal love and gentle mode of life, but that nothing prevails in courts but envy, malice, immorality and very dissolute living, with every sort of vice,—the women lascivious without shame, the men effeminate. They condemn our dress also as indecorous and too womanish.

In short they censure an infinity of things, among which many indeed merit censure, for it cannot be denied that there are many bad and wicked men among us, or that this age of ours is much fuller of vice than that which they praise.[151] Yet it seems to me that they ill discern the cause of this difference, and that they are foolish. For they would have the world contain all good and no evil, which is impossible; because, since evil is opposed to good and good to evil, it is almost necessary, by force of opposition and counterpoise as it were, that the one should sustain and fortify the other, and that if either wanes or waxes, so must the other also, since there is no contrary without its contrary.

Who does not know that there would be no justice in the world, if there were no wrongs? No courage, if there were no cowards? No continence, if there were no incontinence? No health, if there were no infirmity? No truth, if there were no lying? No good fortune, if there were no misfortunes? Thus, according to Plato,[152] Socrates well says it is surprising that Æsop did not write a fable showing that as God had never been able to join pleasure and pain together, He joined them by their extremities, so that the beginning of the one should be the end of the other; for we see that no joy can give us pleasure, unless sorrow precedes it. Who can hold rest dear, unless he has first felt the hardship of fatigue? Who enjoys food, drink and sleep, unless he has first endured hunger, thirst and wakefulness? Hence I believe that sufferings and diseases were given man by nature not chiefly to make him subject to them (since it does not seem fitting that she who is mother of every good should give us such evils of her own determined purpose), but as nature created health, joy and other blessings,—diseases, sorrows and other ills followed after them as a consequence. In like manner, the virtues having been bestowed upon the world by grace and gift of nature, at once by force of that same bounden opposition, the vices became their fellows by necessity; so that always as the one waxes or wanes, thus likewise must needs the other wax or wane.

3.—So when our old men praise bygone courts for not containing such vicious men as some that our courts contain, they do not perceive that their courts did not contain such virtuous men as some that ours contain which is no marvel, for no evil is so bad as that which springs from the corrupted seed of good, and hence, as nature now puts forth far better wits than she did then, those who devote themselves to good, do far better than was formerly done, and likewise those who devote themselves to evil, do far worse. Therefore we must not on that account say that those who refrained from evil because they did not know how to do evil, deserved any praise for it; for although they did little harm, they did the worst they could. And that the wits of those times were generally inferior to those of our time, can be well enough perceived in all that we see of those times, both in letters and in pictures, statues, buildings, and every other thing.

These old men censure us also for many a thing that in itself is neither good nor evil, simply because they did not do it. And they say it is not seemly for young men to ride through the city on horse, still less in pumps, to wear fur linings or long skirts in winter, or to wear a cap before reaching at least the age of eighteen years, and the like; wherein they certainly are wrong, for besides being convenient and useful, these customs have been introduced by usage and meet universal favour, just as formerly it was to go about in gala dress with open breeches and polished pumps, and for greater elegance to carry a sparrow-hawk on the wrist all day without reason, to dance without touching the lady's hand, and to follow many other fashions that now would be as very clumsy as they then were highly prized.

Therefore let it be allowed us also to follow the custom of our time without being slandered by these old men, who in their wish to praise themselves, often say: "When I was twenty years old, I still slept with my mother and sisters, nor did I for a long time afterwards know what women are; while now, boys hardly have hair on their heads before they know more tricks than grown men did in our time." Nor do they perceive that in saying this they acknowledge that our boys have more mind than their old men had.

Let them cease then to censure our time as full of vices, for in removing the vices they would remove the virtues too; and let them remember that among the worthies of old, in the ages when there lived those spirits who were glorious and truly divine in every virtue, and those more than human minds,—there were also to be found many very bad men; who (if they were living) would be as eminently bad among our bad men, as the good men of that time would be eminently good. And of this, all history gives ample proof.

4.—But I think these old men have now sufficient answer. So we will end this homily, perhaps already too diffuse but not wholly irrelevant to our subject; and as it is enough for us to have shown that the courts of our time were worthy of no less praise than those which old men praise so highly,—we will pursue the discussion about the Courtier, from which we may easily understand what rank the court of Urbino held among other courts, and of what quality were the Prince and Lady to whom such noble spirits did service, and how fortunate they might hold themselves who lived in such companionship.

5.—Now the following day having arrived, there were many and diverse discussions among the cavaliers and ladies of the court concerning the debate of the evening before; which in great part arose because my lord Prefect, eager to know what had been said, questioned nearly everyone about it, and (as is always wont to be the case) he received different answers; for some praised one thing and some another, and among many too there was disagreement as to the Count's real opinion, since everyone's memory did not quite fully retain the things that were said.

Thus the matter was discussed nearly all day; and as soon as night set in, my lord Prefect desired that food be served and took all the gentlemen away to supper. When they had done eating, he repaired to the room of my lady Duchess, who, on seeing such a numerous company and earlier than the custom was, said:

"Methinks, messer Federico, it is a heavy burden that is placed upon your shoulders, and great the expectation you must satisfy."

Then without waiting for messer Federico to reply, the Unico Aretino said:

"And what, forsooth, is this great burden? Who is so foolish that when he knows how to do a thing, does not do it in proper season?"

So, discoursing of this, everyone sat down in the usual place and order, with eager expectation for the debate appointed.

6.—Then messer Federico turned to the Unico, and said:

"So, my lord Unico, you do not think that a laborious part and a great burden are imposed on me this evening, having to show in what way, manner and time the Courtier ought to employ his good accomplishments and practise those things that have been said to befit him?"

"It seems to me no great matter," replied the Unico; "and I think it is quite enough to say that the Courtier should have good judgment, as the Count last evening rightly said he must; and this being so, I think that without other precepts he ought to be able to use what he knows seasonably and in a well bred way. To try to reduce this to more exact rules would be too difficult and perhaps superfluous. For I know no man so stupid as to wish to fence when others are intent on dancing; or to go through the street dancing a morris-dance, however admirably he might know how; or in trying to comfort a mother whose child has died, to begin with pleasantries and witticism. Surely methinks no gentleman would do this, who was not altogether a fool."

Then messer Federico said:

"It seems to me, my lord Unico, that you run too much to extremes. For one may sometimes be silly in a way that is not so easily seen, and faults are not always of the same degree: and it may be that a man will refrain from public and too patent folly,—such as that would be of which you tell, to dance a morris-dance about the piazza,—and yet cannot refrain from praising himself out of season, from displaying a tiresome conceit, from occasionally saying something to cause laughter, which falls cold and wholly flat from being said inopportunely. And these faults are often covered by a kind of veil that does not suffer them to be seen by him who commits them, unless he searches for them with care; and although our eyes see little for many reasons, they most of all are clouded by conceit, since everyone likes to make a show in that wherein he believes himself proficient, whether his belief be true or false.

"Therefore it seems to me that the right course in this regard lies in a certain prudent and judicious choice, and in discerning the more or less which all things gain or lose by being done opportunely or out of season. And although the Courtier may possess good enough judgment to perceive these distinctions, yet I think it would surely be easier for him to attain what he is seeking, if we were to broaden his mind by a few precepts, and show him the way and as it were the foundations upon which he must build,—than if he were to follow generalities only.

7.—"Last evening the Count spoke about Courtiership so fully and so beautifully, that he has aroused in me no little fear and doubt whether I shall be able to satisfy this noble company so well in what I have to say, as he did in what it fell to him to say. Yet to make myself a sharer in his fame as far as I can, and to be sure of avoiding this one mistake at least, I shall contradict him in nothing.

"Accepting his opinions then, and among others his opinion as to the Courtier's noble birth, capacities, bodily form and grace of feature,—I say that to win praise justly and good opinion from everyone and favour from the princes whom he serves, I deem it necessary for the Courtier to know how to dispose his whole life, and to make the most of his good qualities in intercourse with all men everywhere, without exciting envy thereby. And how difficult this in itself is, we may infer from the fewness of those who are seen to reach the goal; for by nature we all are more ready to censure mistakes than to praise things well done, and many men, from a kind of innate malignity and although they clearly see the good, seem to strive with every effort and pains to find either some hidden fault in us or at least some semblance of fault.

"Thus it is needful for our Courtier to be cautious in his every action, and always to mingle good sense with what he says or does. And let him not only take care that his separate parts and qualities are excellent, but let him order the tenour of his life in such fashion, that the whole may be in keeping with these parts and be seen to be always and in everything accordant with his own self and form one single body of all these good qualities; so that his every act may be the result and compound of all his faculties, as the Stoics say is the duty of him who is wise.

"Still, although in every action one faculty is always chief, yet all are so enlinked together, that they make for one end and may all further and serve every purpose. Hence he must know how to make the most of them, and by means of contrast and as it were foil to the one, he must make the other more clearly seen;—like good painters, who display and show forth the lights of projecting objects by the use of shadow, and likewise deepen the shadows of flat objects by means of light, and so assemble their divers colours that both the one and the other are better displayed by reason of that diversity, and the placing of figures in opposition one to another aids them to perform that office which is the painter's aim.

"Thus gentleness is very admirable in a man of noble birth who is valiant and strong. And as his boldness seems greater when accompanied by modesty, so his modesty is enhanced and set off by his boldness.[153] Hence to speak little, to do much, and not to boast of praiseworthy deeds but to conceal them tactfully,—enhances both these attributes in the case of one who knows how to employ this method of discretion; and so it is with all other good qualities.

"Therefore in what our Courtier does or says I would have him follow a few universal rules, which I think comprise briefly all that I have to say. And for the first and most important let him above all avoid affectation, as the Count rightly advised last evening. Next let him consider well what thing it is that he is doing or saying, the place where he is doing it, in whose presence, the cause that impels him, his age, his profession, the object he has in view, and the means that may conduce thereto; and so, with these precautions let him apply himself discreetly to whatever he has a mind to do or say."

8.—After messer Federico had spoken thus, he seemed to pause a little. Whereupon my lord Morello da Ortona at once said:

"These rules of yours teach little, it seems to me; and for my part I know as much about it now, as I did before you propounded them. Still I remember having heard them several times before also from the friars to whom I made confession, and who called them 'the circumstances,' I think."

Then messer Federico laughed and said:

"If you remember rightly, the Count declared last evening that the Courtier's chief business should be that of arms, and spoke at length about the way in which he ought to practise it;

therefore we will not repeat this. Yet among our rules we may also lay it down that when our Courtier finds himself in a skirmish or action or battle, or in other such affairs, he ought to arrange discreetly to withdraw from the crowd, and to perform those glorious and brave deeds that he has to do, with as little company as he can, and in sight of all the noblest and most respected men in the army, and especially in the presence and (if it is possible) before the very eyes of his king or of the prince whom he serves; for in truth it is very proper to make the most of one's good deeds. And I think that just as it is wrong to seek false and unmerited renown, so it is wrong also to defraud oneself of the honour that is one's due, and not to seek that praise which alone is the true reward of worthy effort.

"And I remember having in my time known some men who were very stupid in this regard, although valiant, and who put their lives as much in danger to capture a flock of sheep, as to be the first to scale the walls of a beleaguered town; which our Courtier will not do if he bears in mind the motive that leads him into war, which should be honour only. And again if he happens to be playing at arms in public shows,—such as jousts, tourneys, stick-throwing, or any other bodily exercise,—mindful of the place and presence in which he is, he will contrive to be not less elegant and graceful than unerring with his weapons, and to feast the spectators' eyes with all those things which he thinks may give him an added grace. He will take care that his horse is bravely caparisoned, that his attire becomes him, that his mottoes are appropriate and his devices clever, so that they may attract the eyes of the bystanders as the loadstone attracts iron. He will never be among the last to show themselves, knowing that the crowd and especially women gaze much more attentively upon the first than upon the last; for their eyes and minds, which at the start are eager for novelty and observe and are impressed by every trifle, are afterwards not only sated by repetition but even grow weary. Thus there was an excellent actor of ancient times, who for this reason always wished to be the first to perform his part in the play.

"So too, even in speaking of arms, our Courtier will have regard to the profession of those with whom he converses, and will govern himself accordingly,—speaking in one way with men and in another way with women. And if he wishes to touch on something that is to his credit, he will do so covertly, as if by chance in passing, and with the discreetness and caution that Count Ludovico expounded to us yesterday.

9.—"Does it not seem to you now, my lord Morello, that our rules may teach something? Does it not seem to you that our friend, of whom I was telling you a few days since, quite forgot with whom and why he was speaking, when to entertain a lady he had never seen before, he began his talk by telling her that he had slain so many men, and that he was a terrible fellow and knew how to handle a sword with both hands? Nor did he leave her until he had tried to explain to her how certain blows of the battle-axe ought to be parried when one is armed and how when unarmed, and to show the different ways of grasping the handle; so that the poor soul was on the rack, and thought the hour seemed a thousand years before she could send him off, almost fearing that he would slay her like the others. Such are the mistakes committed by those who pay no regard to the 'circumstances,' of which you say you heard from the friars.

"Next I say that of bodily exercises there are some that are almost never practised except in public,—such as jousts, tourneys, stick-throwing, and all the rest that have to do with arms. Hence when our Courtier has to take part in these, he must first contrive to be so well equipped in point of horses, weapons and dress, that he lacks nothing. And if he does not feel himself well provided with everything, let him on no account engage, for if he fails to do well, the excuse cannot be made that these things are not his business. Then he must carefully consider in whose presence he is seen and of what sort the company is, for it would not be seemly for a gentleman to honour a rustic festival with his presence, where the spectators and the company are of low degree."

10.—Then my lord Gaspar Pallavicino said:

"In our Lombard country we do not make these distinctions. On the contrary, there are many young gentlemen who dance all day with peasants in the sun on holidays, and play with them at throwing the bar, wrestling, running and leaping. And I do not think it amiss, for there the rivalry is not of birth, but of strength and agility, wherein villagers are often quite a match for nobles; and this condescension seems to have in it a pleasant touch of generosity."

Messer Federico replied:

"This dancing of yours in the sun pleases me not in any way, nor do I see what gain there is in it. But in my opinion whoever cares to wrestle or run or leap with peasants, ought to do so as a matter of practice and out of courtesy as we say, not in rivalry with them. And a man ought to be almost sure of winning; else let him not engage, because it is too unseemly and shameful a thing, and beneath his dignity, to see a gentleman vanquished by a peasant, and especially at wrestling. Hence I think it is well to abstain, at least in the presence of many, for the gain of beating is very small and the loss of being beaten is very great.

"The game of tennis also is nearly always played in public, and is one of those sports to which a crowd lends much distinction. Therefore I would have our Courtier practise this, and all the others except the handling of arms, as something that is not his profession, and let him show that he does not seek or expect praise for it, nor let him seem to devote much care or time to it, although he may do it admirably. Nor let him be like some men who delight in music, and in speaking with anyone always begin to sing under their breath whenever there is a pause in the conversation. Others always go dancing as they pass through streets and churches. Others, when they meet a friend in the piazza or anywhere else, at once put themselves in posture as if for fencing or wrestling, according to their favourite humour."

Here messer Cesare Gonzaga said:

"A young cardinal we have in Rome does better than that; for out of pride in his fine bodily frame, he conducts into his garden all who come to visit him (even although he has never seen them before), and urgently presses them to strip to the doublet and try a turn with him at leaping."

11.—Messer Federico laughed; then he went on:

"There are certain other exercises that can be practised in public and in private, like dancing; and in this I think the

Courtier ought to have a care, for when dancing in the presence of many and in a place full of people, it seems to me that he should preserve a certain dignity, albeit tempered with a lithe and airy grace of movement; and although he may feel himself to be very nimble and a master of time and measure, let him not attempt those agilities of foot and double steps which we find very becoming in our friend Barletta, but which perhaps would be little suited to a gentleman. Yet in a room privately, as we are now, I think he may try both, and may dance morris-dances and brawls;[164] but not in public unless he be masked, when it is not displeasing even though he be recognized by all.

"Indeed there is no better way of displaying oneself in such matters at public sports, either armed or unarmed; because disguise carries with it a certain freedom and licence, which among other things enable a man to choose a part for which he feels himself qualified, and to use care and elaboration upon the chief point of the thing wherein he would display himself, and a certain nonchalance as to that which does not count,—which greatly enhances the charm: as for a youth to array himself like an old man, yet in easy dress so as to be able to show his vigour; a cavalier in the guise of a rustic shepherd or some other like costume, but with a perfect horse and gracefully bedecked in character;—because the mind of the spectators is quick to fill out the image of that which is presented to the eyes at first glance; and then seeing the thing turn out much better than the costume promised, they are amused and delighted.

"But in these sports and shows where masks are worn, it would not be seemly for a prince to try to enact the part of a prince, because that pleasure which the spectators find in novelty would be in great measure lacking, since it is news to no one that the prince is the prince; and he, conscious that besides being the prince he is trying to play the prince, loses the freedom to do all those things that are beneath a prince's dignity. And if there were any contest in these sports, especially with arms, he might even make men think that he chose to impersonate a prince in order not to be beaten but spared by others; moreover were he to do in sport the same that it behooves him to do in earnest upon occasion, he would deprive his own proper action of dignity, and make it almost seem as if that too were sport. But at such times, if the prince lays aside his character of prince, and mingles equally with his inferiors yet in such fashion as to be recognizable, by renouncing his own rank he attains a higher one, in that he prefers to excel the rest not by authority but by merit, and to show that his worth is not enhanced by the fact that he is a prince.

12.—"I say then that in these martial sports the Courtier ought to use the like discretion, according to his rank. In horseback vaulting too, in wrestling, running and leaping, I should be well pleased to have him shun the vulgar crowd, or at most let himself be very rarely seen; for there is not on earth a thing so excellent but the ignorant will tire of it and hold it of small account, if they see it often.

"As to music I hold the same opinion: hence I would not have our Courtier behave like many, who are no sooner come anywhere (even into the presence of gentlemen with whom they have no acquaintance), than without waiting to be urged they set about doing what they know and often what they do not know; so that it seems as if they had come only for the purpose of showing themselves, and had that for their chief profession. Therefore let the Courtier resort to music as a pastime and almost unwillingly, and not before vulgar people nor very many. And although he may know and understand that which he is doing, in this too I would have him hide the study and pains that are necessary in everything one would do well, and seem to value this accomplishment lightly in himself, but by practising it admirably make others value it highly."

13.—Then my lord Gaspar Pallavicino said:

"There are many kinds of music, vocal as well as instrumental: therefore I should like to hear which is the best of all, and at what time the Courtier ought to perform it." [155]

Messer Federico replied:

"I regard as beautiful music, to sing well by note, with ease and in beautiful style; but as even far more beautiful, to sing to the accompaniment of the viol,[156] because nearly all the sweetness lies in the solo part, and we note and observe the fine manner and the melody with much greater attention when our ears are not occupied with more than a single voice, and moreover

ʔʔʔʔʔʔʔʔʔʔʔʔʔʔʔʔʔʔʔʔʔʔʔʔʔʔʔʔʔʔʔʔʔʔʔʔʔʔʔʔʔʔʔʔʔʔʔʔʔʔʔʔ

every little fault is more clearly discerned,—which is not the case when several sing together, because each singer helps his neighbour. But above all, singing to the viol by way of recitative seems to me most delightful, which adds to the words a charm and grace that are very admirable.

"All keyed instruments also are pleasing to the ear, because they produce very perfect consonances, and upon them one can play many things that fill the mind with musical delight. And not less charming is the music of the stringed quartet, which is most sweet and exquisite. The human voice lends much ornament and grace to all these instruments, with which I would have our Courtier at least to some degree acquainted, albeit the more he excels with them, the better,—without troubling himself much with those that Minerva forbade to Alcibiades, because it seems that they are ungraceful.[157]

"Then, as to the time for enjoying these various kinds of music, I think it is whenever a man finds himself in familiar and beloved companionship and there are not other occupations. But above all it is fitting where ladies are present, because their aspect fills the listener's heart with sweetness, renders it more sensitive to the tenderness of the music, and quickens the musician's soul.

"As I have already said, it pleases me well that we should avoid the crowd, and especially the ignoble crowd. But discretion must needs be the spice of everything, for it would be quite impossible to foresee all the cases that occur; and if the Courtier rightly understands himself, he will adapt himself to the occasion and will perceive when the minds of his hearers are disposed to listen and when not. He will take his own age into account: for it is indeed unseemly and unlovely in the extreme to see a man of any quality,—old, hoary and toothless, full of wrinkles,—playing on a viol and singing in the midst of a company of ladies, even though he be a passable performer. And the reason of this is that in singing the words are usually amorous, and love is a ridiculous thing in old men,—albeit it is sometimes pleased among its other miracles to kindle frozen hearts in spite of years."

14.—Then the Magnifico replied:

"Do not deprive old men of this pleasure, messer Federico;

for in my time I have known old men who had right perfect voices and hands very dexterous upon their instruments, far more than some young men."

"I do not wish," said messer Federico, "to deprive old men of this pleasure, but I do wish to deprive you and these ladies of the pleasure of laughing at such folly. And if old men wish to sing to the viol, let them do so in secret and only to drive from their minds those painful thoughts and grievous troubles with which our life is filled, and to taste that rapture which I believe Pythagoras and Socrates found in music.[158] And even although they practise it not, by somewhat accustoming their minds to it they will enjoy it far more when they hear it than a man who knows nothing of it. For just as the arms of a smith, who is weak in his other members, become stronger by exercise than those of another man who is more robust but unaccustomed to use his arms,—in like manner ears practised in harmony will perceive it better and more speedily and will appreciate it with far greater pleasure, than others, however good and sharp they be, that are not versed in the varieties of musical consonance; because these modulations do not penetrate ears unused to hearing them, but pass aside without leaving any savour of themselves; albeit even the beasts have some enjoyment in melody.

"This then is the pleasure it is fitting old men should take in music. I say the like of dancing, for in truth we ought to give up these exercises before our age forces us to give them up against our will."

Here my lord Morello replied with a little heat:

"So it is better to exclude all old men, and to say that only young men have a right to be called Courtiers."

Then messer Federico laughed, and said:

"You see, my lord Morello, that they who like these things strive to seem young when they are not, and hence they dye their hair and shave twice a week.[159] And this is because nature silently tells them that such things are proper only to the young."

All the ladies laughed, for each one of them felt that these words fitted my lord Morello; and he seemed rather stung by them. Messer Federico soon continued:

15.—"But there are many other ways of entertaining ladies that are proper to old men."

"What are they?" said my lord Morello. "Telling stories?"

"That is one," replied messer Federico. "But as you know, every age brings its own thoughts with it, and has some peculiar virtue and some peculiar vice. Thus, while old men are ordinarily more prudent than young men, more continent and wiser, so too they are more garrulous, miserly, querulous and timid; they are always scolding about the house, harsh to their children, and wish everyone to follow their way. And on the contrary young men are spirited, generous, frank, but prone to quarrel, voluble, loving and hating in an instant, eager in all their pleasures, unfriendly to him who counsels well.

"But of all ages, that of manhood is the most temperate, because it has left the faults of youth behind and has not yet reached those of old age. Being placed then at the two extremes, young and old must needs learn from reason how to correct the faults that nature implants in them. Thus, old men ought to guard against much self-praise and the other evil habits that we have said are peculiar to them, and to use that prudence and knowledge which they have gained from long experience, and to be like oracles consulted of all men; and in telling what they know, they ought to have the grace to speak to the point and temper the gravity of their years with a certain mild and sportive humour. In this way they will be good Courtiers, enjoy their intercourse with men and with ladies, and be always welcome,—without singing or dancing; and when need arises they will display their worth in affairs of importance.

16.—"Let young men use this same care and judgment, not indeed in copying old men's ways,—for that which befits the one would not at all befit the other, and we are wont to say that over wisdom is a bad sign in the young,—but in correcting their own natural faults. Hence I greatly like to see a youth, and especially when handling weapons, who has a touch of the grave and taciturn; who is master of himself, without those restless manners which are often seen at that age; because such youths seem to have a certain something in them above the rest. Moreover this quietness of manner has in it a kind of impressive boldness, because it seems the result not of anger but of judgment, and governed more by reason than by passion. This is nearly always found in all men of high courage, and we see it also among those brute animals that have more nobility and strength than their fellows,—as in the lion and the eagle.

"Nor is this strange; for an impetuous and sudden movement,—which without words or other signs of wrath abruptly bursts with all its force at once from the quiet that is its contrary, as it were like the discharge of a cannon,—is far more violent and furious than that which increases by degrees and grows hotter little by little. Therefore they who talk much and move about and cannot stand still, when they have an enterprise on foot, seem thus to exhaust their powers; and as our friend messer Pietro Monte well says, they act like boys who sing from fear when they walk at night, as if to keep up their courage by their singing.

"Again, just as calm and thoughtful youthfulness is very praiseworthy in a young man, because the levity which is the fault peculiar to his age seems to be tempered and corrected,—so in an old man a green and lively old age is to be highly esteemed, because his stoutness of heart seems to be so great as to warm and strengthen his feeble and chill years, and to keep him in that middle state which is the best part of our life.

17.—"But in brief not even all these qualities in our Courtier will suffice to win universal favour of lords, cavaliers and ladies, unless he has also a gentle and amiable manner in daily talk. And I verily believe it to be difficult to give any rule for this, because of the infinite variety of things that arise in conversation, and because among all the men on earth no two are found who have minds quite alike. So whoever has to prepare himself for conversation with many, must needs be guided by his own judgment, and distinguishing the differences between one man and another, must daily change his style and method according to the character of the person with whom he has to converse. Nor could I for my part give other rules in this matter than those already given, which our friend my lord Morello has learned at the confessional from his youth up."

Here my lady Emilia laughed, and said:

᚛᚛᚛᚛᚛᚛᚛᚛᚛᚛᚛᚛᚛᚛᚛᚛᚛᚛᚛᚛᚛᚛᚛᚛᚛᚛᚛᚛᚛᚛᚛᚛᚛᚛᚛᚛᚛᚛

"You shirk labour too much, messer Federico. But you shall not succeed, for you must talk on until it is time to go to bed."

"And what, my Lady, if I have nothing to say?" replied messer Federico.

"There you shall show your wit," said my lady Emilia. "And if what I once heard be true, that there was a man so clever and eloquent that he did not lack material to write a book in praise of a fly, others in praise of the fourth day ague, and another in praise of baldness,—will you also not have the courage to find something to say about Courtiership for one evening?" [160]

"We have already said enough about it to make two books," replied messer Federico. "But since my excuse is of no avail, I will talk until you think I have fulfilled, if not my duty, at least the limit of my powers.

18.—"I think that the conversation which the Courtier ought most to try in every way to make acceptable, is that which he holds with his prince; and although this word 'conversation' implies a certain equality that seems impossible between a lord and his inferior, yet we will call it so for the present. Therefore, besides daily showing everyone that he possesses the worth we have already described, I would have the Courtier strive, with all the thoughts and forces of his mind, to love and almost to adore the prince whom he serves, above every other thing, and mould his wishes, habits and all his ways to his prince's liking."

Without waiting for more, Pietro da Napoli here said:

"We already have enough Courtiers of this kind, for methinks you have in a few words described for us a noble flatterer."

"You are much in error," replied messer Federico; "for flatterers love neither their prince nor their friends, which I tell you I wish chiefly in our Courtier.

"Moreover it is possible without flattery to obey and further the wishes of him we serve, for I am speaking of those wishes that are reasonable and right, or of those that in themselves are neither good nor evil, such as would be a liking for play or a devotion to one kind of exercise above another. And I would have the Courtier bend himself to this even if he be by nature alien to it, so that on seeing him his lord shall always feel that he will have something agreeable to say; which will come about if he has the good judgment to perceive what his prince likes, and the wit and prudence to bend himself thereto, and a deliberate purpose to like that which perhaps he by nature dislikes. And adopting these precautions, he will never be out of humour or melancholy before his prince, nor so taciturn as many are who seem to bear a grudge against their patrons, which is a truly odious thing. He will not be given to evil speaking, especially against his own lords; which often happens, for in courts there seems to rage a fury [161] of such sort that those who have been most favoured by their lord and have been raised to eminence from the lowest state, are always complaining and speaking ill of him; which is unseemly not only in such as these, but even in those who chance to have been ill used.

"Our Courtier will show no foolish presumption; he will not be a bearer of evil tidings; he will not be thoughtless in sometimes saying things that offend instead of pleasing as he intends. He will not be obstinate and disputatious, as some are who seem to delight in nothing but to be troublesome and disagreeable like flies, and who make a point of spitefully contradicting everyone without discrimination. He will not be an idle or untruthful tattler, nor a boaster nor pointless flatterer, but modest and reserved, always and especially in public showing that reverence and respect which befit the servant towards the master; and he will not behave like many, who on meeting any great prince, with whom if only they have spoken but once, press forward with a certain smiling and friendly look, as if they wished to caress an equal or show favour to an inferior.

"He will very rarely or almost never ask anything of his lord for himself, lest his lord, being reluctant to deny it to him directly, may sometimes grant it with an ill grace, which is much worse. Even in asking for others he will choose his time discreetly and ask proper and reasonable things; and he will so frame his request, by omitting what he knows may displease and by skilfully doing away with difficulties, that his lord shall always grant it, or shall not think him offended by refusal even if it be denied; for when lords have denied a favour to an importunate suitor, they often reflect that he who asked it with such eagerness, must have desired it greatly, and so having failed to obtain it, must feel ill will towards him who denied it; and believing this, they begin to hate the man and can never more look upon him with favour.

19.—"He will not seek to intrude unasked into his master's chamber or private retreats, even though he be of great consequence; for when great lords are in private, they often like a little liberty to say and do what they please, and do not wish to be seen or heard by any who may criticise them; and it is very proper. Hence I think those men do ill who blame great lords for consorting privately with persons who are of little worth save in matters of personal service, for I do not see why lords should not have the same freedom to relax their minds that we fain would have to relax ours. But if a Courtier accustomed to deal with important matters, chances to find himself in private with his lord, he must put on another face, postpone grave concerns to another place and time, and give the conversation a cast that shall amuse and please his lord, so as not to disturb that repose of mind of which I speak.

"In this however, as in everything else, let him above all take care not to weary his lord, and let him wait for favours to be offered him rather than angle for them so openly as many do, who are so greedy that it seems as if they must die if they do not get what they seek; and if they happen to meet any disfavour or to see others favoured, they suffer such anguish that they can in no wise hide their envy. Thus they make everyone laugh at them, and often are the cause that leads their master to bestow favour on the first comer simply to spite them. Then again, if they find themselves in at all more than common favour, they become so intoxicated by it that they stand palsied [162] with joy, and seem not to know what to do with their hands and feet, and they can hardly keep from calling on the company to come and see and congratulate them as upon something to which they are quite unused.

"Of such sort I would not have our Courtier. I am quite willing that he should like favours, but not that he should value them so highly as to seem unable to do without them. And when he receives them, let him not seem unused or strange to them, or marvel that they are offered him; nor let him refuse them, as some do who refrain from accepting them out of mere ignorance, and thus seem to the bystanders to be conscious of not deserving them.

"Yet a man ought always to be a little more backward than his rank warrants; to accept not too readily the favours and honours that are offered him; and to refuse them modestly, showing that he values them highly, yet in such fashion as to give the donor cause to offer them again with far more urgency. For the greater the reluctance with which they are accepted, the more highly will the prince who gives them think himself esteemed, and the benefit that he bestows will seem the greater, the more the recipient seems to prize it and to hold himself honoured by it. Moreover these are the true and solid favours that make a man esteemed by those who see him from without; for, being unsought, they are assumed by everyone to be the reward of true worth, the more so when they are accompanied by modesty."

20.—Then messer Cesare Gonzaga said:

"Methinks you have stolen this passage from the Evangelist, where he says: 'When thou art bidden to a wedding, go and sit down in the lowest room; that when he that bade thee cometh, he may say: Friend, go up higher: and thus shalt thou have honour in the presence of them that sit at meat with thee.'" [163]

Messer Federico laughed, and said:

"It were too great sacrilege to steal from the Evangelist; but you are more learned in Holy Writ than I thought;" then he went on: "You see what great danger those men sometimes run who boldly begin conversation before a lord without being invited; and to put them down, the lord often makes no reply and turns his head another way, and even if he replies to them, everyone sees that he does it with an ill grace.

"To have the favour of princes, then, there is no better way than to deserve it. And when we see another man who is pleasing to a prince for any reason, we must not think to reach the same height ourselves by imitating him, for all things are not proper to all men. Thus there will sometimes be found a man who by nature is so ready at jesting that whatever he may say carries laughter with it, and he seems to have been born solely for that; and if another man, who has a sober habit of mind (however ex-

cellently endowed) tries to do the like, it will fall so cold and flat
as to disgust those who hear him, and he will prove exactly like
that ass who tried to copy the dogs by frolicking with their master.[164] Hence every man must understand himself and his own
powers, and govern himself accordingly, and consider what things
he ought to imitate, and what things he ought not."

21.—Here Vincenzo Calmeta said:

"Before you go on, if I heard aright I think you said awhile
ago that the best way to win favours is to deserve them, and that
the Courtier ought to wait for them to be offered him rather than
ask for them presumptuously. I greatly fear this rule is little to
the purpose, and I think experience very clearly teaches us the
contrary. For to-day very few are favoured by their lords, save the
presumptuous; and I know you can give good testimony as to
some, who on finding themselves in small favour with their
princes, have made themselves acceptable solely by their presumption. While as for those who have risen through modesty,
I for my part do not know any, and I even give you time to think
about it and believe you will find few. And if you consider the
court of France, which is to-day one of the noblest in Christendom,
you will find that all men who have universal favour there are
somewhat presumptuous, and not only towards one another but
towards the king himself."

"Now do not say that," replied messer Federico; "for in
France there are very modest and courteous gentlemen. It is true
that they behave with a certain freedom and unceremonious familiarity, which are proper and natural to them; and therefore it
ought not to be called presumption, because in this very manner
of theirs, whilst they deride and make sport of the presumptuous,
yet they rate highly those who seem to them to have worth and
modesty."

Calmeta replied:

"Look at the Spaniards, who it seems are our masters in
Courtiership, and consider how many you will find who are not
very presumptuous with ladies and with gentlemen; and even
more so than the French, because at first sight they show the
greatest modesty. And in this they are truly clever, for as I said,

the princes of our time all favour only those who have such manners."

22.—Then messer Federico replied:

"I will by no means suffer you, messer Vincenzo, to cast this reproach upon the princes of our time. For indeed there are also many who love modesty, which I do not however say alone suffices to make a man acceptable; but I do say that when united to high worth, it greatly honours its possessor. And although it be silent about itself, praiseworthy deeds speak aloud and are far more admirable than if they were accompanied by presumption and rashness. I will not indeed deny that there are many presumptuous Spaniards, but I say that those who are much esteemed are as a rule very modest.

"Again, there are also some men who are so reserved that they shun human company beyond reason, and so far exceed a certain limit of moderation that they come to be regarded as either too timid or too proud. For these I have no praise, nor would I have modesty so dry and arid as to become clownishness; but let the Courtier be fluent on occasion, and prudent and sagacious in discussing statecraft, and let him have the good sense to adapt himself to the customs of the nations where he finds himself; then in lesser matters let him be agreeable and speak well about everything.

"But above all, he should make for right; not envious, not evil-tongued: nor let him ever bring himself to seek grace or favour by foul ways or dishonourable means."

Then Calmeta said:

"I assure you that all other ways are more uncertain and longer than this one which you censure. For to repeat, princes at the present day love only those who tread that path."

"Say not so," then replied messer Federico, "for that would be too clear an argument that the princes of our time are all vicious and wicked,—which is not true, since several good ones are to be found. But if our Courtier should chance to find himself in the service of one who is vicious and malign, let him depart as soon as he discovers it, lest he suffer that keen anguish which all good men feel who serve the wicked."

"We must needs pray God," replied Calmeta, "to send us

good masters, for when we have them, we are forced to endure them such as they are; because an infinity of reasons constrain a gentleman not to leave the patron he has once begun to serve; but the misfortune consists in beginning to serve a bad patron, and Courtiers in this condition are like those unhappy birds that are hatched in a gloomy valley."

"It seems to me," said messer Federico, "that duty ought to outweigh all other reasons. And provided a gentleman does not leave his patron when at war or in adversity,—lest he be thought to have done so to better his fortunes or because he feared that he might lack opportunity for gain,—I think that at any other time he rightly may and ought to leave a service that is like to disgrace him before all good men; for everyone assumes that whoever serves the good is good, and that whoever serves the wicked is wicked."

23.—Then my lord Ludovico Pio said:

"I should like to have you clear a doubt that is in my mind; that is, whether a gentleman in the service of a prince is bound to obey him in all things that he commands, even if they be dishonourable and infamous."

"In dishonourable things we are not bound to obey any man," replied messer Federico.

"And how," returned my lord Ludovico, "if I am in the service of a prince who uses me well and trusts to my doing for him all that can be done, commanding me to go kill a man or do anything else you please,—ought I to refuse to do it?"

"You ought," replied messer Federico, "to obey your lord in all things that are advantageous and honourable to him, not in those that bring him injury and disgrace. Therefore if he were to command you to commit an act of treachery, not only would you not be bound to do it, but you would be bound not to do it,— both for your own sake and for the sake of not being a minister to your lord's disgrace. True it is that many things which are evil seem at first sight good, and many seem evil and yet are good. Hence in our lords' service it is sometimes permitted to kill not one man but ten thousand, and to do many other things that would seem evil to a man who did not rightly consider them, and yet are not evil."

////////////////////////////////////////////////////////////

Then my lord Gaspar Pallavicino replied:

, "On your faith, I pray you discuss this a little, and teach us how the really good can be distinguished from that which only seems so."

"Pardon me," said messer Federico; "I am unwilling to enter upon that, for there would be too much to say; but let the whole matter be left to your own wisdom."

24.—"At least clear another doubt for me," returned my lord Gaspar.

"And what doubt?" said messer Federico.

"It is this," replied my lord Gaspar. "I should like to know, —my lord having charged me exactly what I must do in an enterprise or any other business whatever, if I being engaged upon it think that my doing more or less or otherwise than I was charged, may make the affair turn out better and more advantageously for him who gave me the task,—whether I ought to govern myself by the original plan without exceeding the limits of my command, or on the contrary to do that which seems to me better."

Then messer Federico replied:

"In this I should give you the precept and example of Manlius Torquatus (who in like case slew his son, from too stern a sense of duty), if I thought he deserved much credit, which I do not.[165] And yet I dare not blame him against the verdict of so many centuries. For without doubt it is a very perilous thing to deviate from our superiors' commands, relying more on our own judgment than on theirs whom we ought in reason to obey; because if our expectation fails and the affair turns out ill, we run into the error of disobedience and ruin that which we have to do, without any possibility of excuse or hope of pardon. On the other hand, if the affair turns out according to our wish, we must give the credit to fortune and be content at that. Moreover in this way a fashion is set of rating the commands of our superiors lightly; and following the example of one man who happened to succeed and who perhaps was prudent and had reasoned well and been aided by fortune too,—a thousand other ignorant featherheads will make bold to do as they please in the most important matters, and for the sake of showing that they are sagacious and have authority, to deviate from their masters' commands; which is a very evil thing and often the cause of numberless mistakes.

"But I think that in such a case the man whom it concerns ought to consider carefully, and as it were to place in the balance the profit and advantage that he stands to win by acting contrary to orders, in case his designs turn out according to his hopes; and on the other hand to weigh the evil and disadvantage that will accrue if the affair chances to turn out ill through his disobedience of orders. And if he finds the damage in case of failure to be greater and more serious than the gain in case of success, he ought to restrain himself and carry out his orders to the letter; while on the contrary if the gain in case of success is like to be more serious than the damage in case of failure, I think he may properly venture to do that which his reason and judgment dictate, and somewhat disregard the very letter of his orders,—so as to act like good merchants, who to gain much risk little, but never risk much to gain little.

"I strongly approve of the Courtier's observing above all the character of the prince whom he serves, and of his governing himself accordingly: for if it be severe, as is the case with many, I should never advise anyone who was my friend to change one jot the order given him; lest that might befall him which is recorded as having befallen a master engineer of the Athenians, to whom Publius Crassus Mucianus,[166] when he was in Asia and wished to besiege a fortified place, sent to ask for one of two ship's masts that he had seen at Athens, in order to make a ram wherewith to batter down the wall, and said he wished the larger one. Being very intelligent, the engineer knew that the larger mast was unsuitable for the purpose, and as the smaller one was easier to transport and better adapted for making the machine in question, he sent it to Mucianus. The latter, hearing how things had gone, sent for the poor engineer, asked why he had disobeyed his orders, and refusing to listen to any excuse from him, caused him to be stripped naked and so flogged and scourged with rods that he died, because it seemed to Mucianus that instead of obeying, the man had tried to offer advice. So we had best use great caution with these rigorous men.

25.—"But now let us leave this subject of intercourse with princes, and come to conversation with our equals or with those that are nearly so: for we must pay heed to this also, since it is universally more practised and a man more often finds himself engaged in it than in conversation with princes.

"There are however some simpletons, who, even in the company of the best friend they have in the world, on meeting a man who is better dressed, at once attach themselves to him, and then if they happen on one still better dressed, they do the like to him. And later, when the prince is passing through the squares or churches or other public places, they elbow their way past everyone until they reach his side: and even if they have naught to say to him, they still must talk, and go on babbling, and laugh and clap their hands and head, to show they have business of importance, so that the crowd may see them in favour. But since these fellows deign to speak only with their lords, I would not have us deign to speak of them."

26.—Then the Magnifico Giuliano said:

"As you have mentioned those who are so fond of the company of well dressed men, I should like you to show us, messer Federico, in what manner the Courtier ought to dress, and what costume is suitable to him, and in what way he ought to govern himself in all matters of bodily adornment. For in this we find an infinite variety: some who dress after the French fashion, some after the Spanish, some who wish to appear German; nor is there lack of those who even dress after the style of Turks: some who wear their beards, some not. Hence in this medley it were well to know how to choose the best."

Messer Federico said:

"Indeed I should not know how to give a precise rule about dress, except that a man ought to follow the custom of the majority; and since (as you say) this custom is so various, and the Italians are so fond of arraying themselves after foreign fashions, I think every man may dress as he pleases.

"But I do not know by what fate it happens that Italy has not, as it was wont to have, a costume that should be recognized as Italian: for although the putting of these new fashions into use may have made the former ones seem very rude, yet the old ones were perhaps a badge of freedom, as the new ones have proved an augury of servitude, which I think is now very clearly fulfilled.[167] And as it is recorded that when Darius had the Persian sword which he wore at his side fashioned after the Macedonian style, the year before he fought with Alexander, this was interpreted by the soothsayers to signify that they into whose fashion Darius had transformed his Persian sword, should come to rule over Persia.[168] So our having changed our Italian garb for that of strangers seems to signify that all those for whose garb we have exchanged our own must come to conquer us: which has been but too true, for there is now left no nation that has not made us its prey: so that little more is left to prey upon, and yet they do not cease preying upon us.

27.—"But I do not wish to touch on painful subjects. Therefore it will be well to speak of our Courtier's clothes; which I think, provided they be not out of the common or inappropriate to his profession, may do very well in other respects if only they satisfy him who wears them. True it is that I for my part should not like them to be extreme in any wise, as the French are sometimes wont to be in over amplitude, and the Germans in over scantiness,—but as they both are, only corrected and improved in form by the Italians. Moreover I always like them to tend a little towards the grave and sober rather than the gay. Thus I think black is more suitable for garments than any other colour is; and if it is not black, let it at least be somewhat dark. And this I say of ordinary attire, for there is no doubt that bright and cheerful colours are more suitable over armour, and for gala use also dress may be fringed, showy and magnificent; likewise on public occasions, such as festivals, shows, masquerades, and the like. For such garments carry with them a certain liveliness and gaiety that accord very well with arms and sports. But for the rest I would have our Courtier's dress display that sobriety which the Spanish nation greatly affect, for things external often bear witness to the things within."

Then messer Cesare Gonzaga said:

"This would give me little concern, for if a gentleman is of worth in other things, his attire will never enhance or lessen his reputation."

"You say truly," replied messer Federico. "Yet what one of us is there, who, on seeing a gentleman pass by with a garment on his back quartered in divers colours, or with a mass of strings and knotted ribbons and cross lacings, does not take him for a fool or a buffoon?"

"Neither for a fool," said messer Pietro Bembo, "nor for a buffoon would he be taken by anyone who had lived any time in Lombardy, for all men go about like that."

"Then," said my lady Duchess, laughing, "if all men go about like that, we must not cast it at them as a fault, since this attire is as fitting and proper to them as it is for the Venetians to wear puffed sleeves,[169] or for the Florentines to wear the hood."

"I am not speaking," said messer Federico, "more of Lombardy than of other places, for both the foolish and the wise are to be found in every nation. But to say what I think is important in attire, I wish that our Courtier may be neat and dainty throughout his dress, and have a certain air of modest elegance, yet not of a womanish or vain style. Nor would I have him more careful of one thing than of another, like many we see who take such pains with their hair that they forget the rest; others devote themselves to their teeth, others to their beard, others to their boots, others to their bonnets, others to their coifs;[170] and the result is that these few details of elegance seem borrowed by them, while all the rest, being very tasteless, is recognized as their own. And this kind of dress I would have our Courtier shun, by my advice; adding also that he ought to consider how he wishes to seem and of what sort he wishes to be esteemed, and to dress accordingly and contrive that his attire shall aid him to be so regarded even by those who neither hear him speak nor witness any act of his."

28.—Then my lord Gaspar Pallavicino said:

"Methinks it is not fitting, or even customary among persons of worth, to judge men's quality by their dress rather than by their words and acts; for many would make mistakes, nor is it without reason that we have the proverb, 'dress makes not the monk.' "

"I do not say," replied messer Federico, "that fixed opinions of men's worth are to be formed only in this way, or that they are not better known by their words and acts than by their dress: but I do say that dress is no bad index of the wearer's fancy, although it may be sometimes wrong; and not only this, but all ways and manners, as well as acts and words, are an indication of the qualities of the man in whom they are seen."

"And what things do you find," replied my lord Gaspar, "from which we may form an opinion, that are neither words nor acts?"

Then messer Federico said:

"You are too subtle a logician. But to tell you what I mean, there are some acts that still endure after they are performed, such as building, writing, and the like; others do not endure, such as those I have now in mind. In this sense, therefore, I do not say that walking, laughing, looking, and the like, are acts,— and yet all these outward things often give knowledge of those within. Tell me, did you not judge that friend of ours, of whom we were speaking only this morning, to be a light and frivolous man as soon as you saw him walking with that twist of his head, wriggling about, and with affable demeanour inviting the by-standers to doff their caps to him? So, too, when you see anyone gazing too intently with dull eyes after the manner of an idiot, or laughing as stupidly as those goitrous mutes in the mountains of Bergamo,[171]—do you not set him down a very simpleton, although he neither speak nor do aught else? Thus you see that these ways and manners (which I do not for the present regard as acts) in great measure make men known to us.

29.—"But another thing seems to me to give and to take away from reputation greatly, and this is our choice of the friends with whom we are to live in intimate relations; for doubtless reason requires that they who are joined in close amity and fast companionship, shall have their desires, souls, judgments and minds also in accord. Thus, he who consorts with the ignorant or wicked, is deemed ignorant or wicked; and on the contrary, he who consorts with the good, the wise, and the discreet, is himself deemed to be the like. Because by nature everything seems to join willingly with its like. Therefore I think we ought to use great care in beginning these friendships, for he who knows one of two close friends, at once imagines the other to be of the same quality."

Then messer Pietro Bembo replied:

"I certainly think we ought to take great care to limit ourselves to friends of like mind with us, as you say, not only because of the gain or loss of reputation, but because there are to-day
very few true friends to be found, nor do I believe that the world
any longer contains a Pylades and Orestes, a Theseus and Pirithous, or a Scipio and Lælius.[172] On the contrary, by some fatality
it happens every day that two friends, who have lived in very
cordial love for many years, yet in some way cheat each other
at last, either through malice, or jealousy, or fickleness, or some
other evil cause: and each gives the other the blame which perhaps both deserve.

"Therefore, since it has more than once happened to me to
be deceived by him whom I most loved above every other person,
and by whom I was sure I was loved,—I have sometimes thought
to myself that it would be well for us never to trust anyone in
the world, nor so to give ourselves up to any friend (however
dear and loved he be) as to reveal all our thoughts to him, as we
should to ourselves; for there are so many dark corners and recesses in our minds that it is impossible for human wit to penetrate the deceptions they conceal. Hence I think it were well to
love and serve one more than another according to merit and
worth; yet never to be so sure of friendship's sweet enticement,
that we at last have cause to rue our trust."

30.—Then messer Federico said:

"Verily the loss would be far greater than the gain, if human
intercourse were to be deprived of that highest pitch of friendship which in my opinion gives us all the good our life has in
it; and therefore I will in no wise admit that what you say is
reasonable, nay rather I venture to assert, and for the clearest
reasons, that without this perfect friendship men would be far
unhappier than all other creatures. And if some profanely stain
this sacred name of friendship, we ought not on that account to
uproot it from our hearts, and for the guilt of the wicked deprive
the good of such felicity. And for my part I think there are here
among us more than one pair of friends, whose love is steadfast
and without deceit and lasting unto death with like desires, no
less than if they were those ancients whom you mentioned awhile
ago; and it happens thus when a man chooses a friend, not only

from heaven-born impulse, but like himself in character. And in all this I am speaking of the good and virtuous, for the friendship of the wicked is not friendship.

"I am well pleased that so close a tie as this should not join or bind more than two, for otherwise perhaps it would be dangerous; because, as you know, it is harder to attune three musical instruments together, than two. Therefore, I would that our Courtier might have one special and hearty friend, if possible, of the kind we have described; then that he might love, honour and respect all others according to their worth and merits, and always contrive to consort more with such as are in high esteem and noble and of known virtue, than with the ignoble and those of little worth; in such wise that he may be loved and honoured by them also. And he will accomplish this if he be courteous, kind, generous, affable and mild with others, zealous and active to serve and guard his friends' welfare and honour both absent and present, enduring such of their natural defects as are endurable, without breaking with them for slight cause, and correcting in himself those that are kindly pointed out; never thrusting himself before others to reach the first and most honoured places; nor acting like some, who seem to despise the world and insist with a kind of tiresome preciseness on laying down the law for everyone, and who, besides being unseasonably contentious in every little thing, censure that which they do not do themselves, and are always seeking occasion for complaint against their friends,—which is a very odious thing."

31.—Messer Federico pausing here, my lord Gaspar Pallavicino said:

"I should like to have you speak a little more in detail than you do about this matter of converse with our friends; for in truth you keep much to generalities, and show us things in passing, as it were."

"How 'in passing'?" replied messer Federico. "Perhaps you would have me tell the very words that you must use? Do you not think we have talked enough about this?"

"Enough I think," replied my lord Gaspar. "Yet I should like to hear a few more details about the manner of intercourse with men and women; for the thing seems to me of great importance, seeing that most of our time at courts is given to it; and if it were always the same, it would soon become tedious."

"I think," replied messer Federico, "we have given the Courtier knowledge of so many things, that he can easily vary his conversation and adapt himself to the quality of the persons with whom he has to do, presupposing he has good sense and governs himself by it, and sometimes turns to grave matters and sometimes to festivals and games, according to the occasion."

"And what games?" said my lord Gaspar.

Then messer Federico replied, laughing:

"Let us ask advice of Fra Serafino, who invents new ones every day."

"Jesting apart," answered my lord Gaspar, "do you think it would be a vice in the Courtier to play at cards and dice?"

"Not I," said messer Federico, "unless he did so too constantly and neglected more important matters for them, or indeed unless he played for nothing else but to win money, and cheated the company, and showed such grief and vexation at losing as to argue himself a miser."

"And what," replied my lord Gaspar, "do you say of the game of chess?"

"It is certainly a pleasant and ingenious amusement," said messer Federico. "But I think there is one defect in it. And that is, there is too much to know, so that whoever would excel in the game of chess must spend much time on it, methinks, and give it as much study as if he would learn some noble science or do anything else of importance you please; and yet in the end with all his pains he has learned nothing but a game. Therefore I think a very unusual thing is true of it, namely that mediocrity is more praiseworthy than excellence."

My lord Gaspar replied:

"Many Spaniards excel in this and divers other games, yet without giving them much study or neglecting other things."

"Believe me," replied messer Federico, "they do give much study thereto, although covertly. But those other games you speak of, besides chess, are perhaps like many I have seen played (although of little moment), which serve only to make the vulgar marvel; wherefore methinks they deserve no other praise or reward than that which Alexander the Great gave the fellow who at a good distance impaled chick-peas on the point of a needle.[173]

32.—"But since it appears that fortune exerts immense power over men's opinions as over many other things, we sometimes see that a gentleman, however well conditioned he may be and endowed with many graces, is unacceptable to a prince, and goes against the grain as we say; [174] and this without any apparent reason, so that as soon as he comes into the prince's presence and before he is known by the others, although he be keen and ready with retorts, and display himself to advantage in gestures, manners, words, and all else that is becoming,—the prince will show small esteem for him, nay will soon put some affront upon him. And thus it will come about that the others will follow the prince's lead, and everyone will regard the man as of little worth, nor will there be any to prize or esteem him, or laugh at his amusing talk or hold him in any respect; nay, all will begin to deride and persecute him. Nor will it be enough for the poor man to make good retorts or take things as if said in jest, for the very pages will set upon him, so that even if he were the sturdiest man in the world, he must perforce remain foiled and ridiculed.

"And on the other hand, if the prince shows favour to a very dolt, who knows neither how to speak nor how to act,—his manners and ways (however silly and uncouth they be) will often be praised by everyone with exclamations and astonishment, and the whole court will seem to admire and respect him, and everyone will appear to laugh at his jests and at certain rustic and stupid jokes that ought to excite rather disgust than laughter: to such degree are men firm and fixed in the opinions that are engendered by the favour and disfavour of lords.

"Therefore I would have our Courtier set off his worth as best he can, with cleverness and skill, and whenever he has to go where he is strange and unknown, let him take care that good opinion of him precedes him, and see to it that men there shall know of his being highly rated in other places, among other lords, ladies and gentlemen; for that fame which seems to spring from many judgments, begets a kind of firm belief in a man's worth, which, in minds thus disposed and prepared, is then easily maintained and increased by his conduct: moreover he escapes that annoyance which I feel when asked who I am and what my name is."

33.—"I do not see how this can help," replied messer Bernardo Bibbiena; "for it has several times happened to me, and I think to many others, that having been led by the word of persons of judgment to imagine something to be of great excellence before I saw it,—on seeing it I found it paltry and was much disappointed of what I expected. And the reason was simply that I had put too much trust in report and formed in my mind so high an expectation, that although the real thing was great and excellent, yet when afterwards measured by the fact, it seemed very paltry by comparison with what I had imagined. And I fear it may be so with our Courtier too. Therefore I do not see the advantage of raising such expectations and sending our fame before us; for the mind often imagines things that it is impossible to fulfil, and thus we lose more than we gain."

Here messer Federico said:

"The things that you and many others find inferior to their reputation, are for the most part of such sort that the eye can judge of them at a glance,—as if you had never been at Naples or Rome, and from hearing them so much talked of, you were to imagine something far beyond what they afterwards proved to be when seen; but such is not the case with men's character, because that which is outwardly seen is the least part. Thus, on first hearing a gentleman speak, if you should not find in him that worth which you had previously imagined, you would not at once reverse your good opinion of him, as you would in those matters whereof the eye is instant judge, but you would wait from day to day to discover some other hidden virtue, still holding fast to the good impression you had received from so many lips; and later, if he were thus richly endowed (as I assume our Courtier to be), your confidence in his reputation would be hourly confirmed, because his acts would justify it, and you would be always imagining something more than you saw.

34.—"And surely it cannot be denied that these first impressions have very great weight, and that we ought to be very careful regarding them. And to the end that you may see how important they are, I tell you that in my time I knew a gentleman, who, while he was of very gentle aspect and modest manners and also valiant in arms, yet did not so greatly excel in any of these things but that he had many equals and even superiors. However, fate so willed that a lady chanced to fall most ardently in love with him, and her love increasing daily with the signs that the young man gave of loving her in return, and there being no way for them to speak together, she was moved by excess of passion to reveal her desires to another lady through whom she hoped to secure some assistance. This lady was in no wise inferior to the first in rank or beauty; whence it came to pass, that on hearing the young man (whom she had never seen) spoken of so tenderly, and perceiving that he was extravagantly loved by her friend (whom she knew to be very discreet and of excellent judgment), she straightway imagined him to be the handsomest and wisest and most discreet and in short the most lovable man in the world. And thus, without having seen him, she became so passionately enamoured of him, that she began making every effort to secure him, not for her friend but for herself, and inducing him to return her love: which she succeeded in doing with little effort, for in truth she was a lady rather to be wooed than to woo others.

"Now hear the end of my tale. Not long afterwards it happened that a letter, which this second lady had written to her lover, fell into the hands of still another lady, also very noble and of good character and rarest beauty,—who, being like most ladies curious and eager to learn secrets and especially other ladies', opened this letter, and on reading it saw that it was written with the fervour of ardent love. And the sweet, impassioned words that she read first moved her to compassion for that lady, for she well knew from whom the letter came and to whom it was going; then they gained such power, that as she turned them over in her mind and considered what sort of man he must be who could arouse such love in the lady, she too straightway fell in love with him; and the letter had perhaps a greater effect than if it had been sent by the young man to her. And as it sometimes happens that a poisoned dish, intended for a prince, kills the first comer who tastes it, so in her over greediness this poor lady drank the love poison that had been prepared for another.

*ƒƒƒƒƒƒƒƒƒƒƒƒƒƒƒƒƒƒƒƒƒƒƒƒƒƒƒƒƒƒƒƒƒƒƒƒƒƒƒƒƒƒƒƒƒƒƒƒƒƒƒƒƒ*

"What more shall I say? The affair became well known, and spread abroad so that many other ladies besides these, partly to spite the others and partly to imitate them, used every effort and pains to possess themselves of the man's love, and contended for it with one another as boys contend for cherries. And all this began with the first impression of that lady who saw him so beloved by another."

35.—Here my lord Gaspar Pallavicino replied, laughing:

"To give reasons in support of your opinion, you cite the doings of women, who for the most part are quite unreasonable. And if you cared to tell the whole truth, this favourite of so many women must have been a dunce and at bottom a man of little worth. For their way is always to favour the meanest, and like sheep to do what they see others doing, whether it be good or evil. Moreover they are so jealous among themselves, that even if the man had been a monster, they would have tried to steal him from one another."

Here many began to speak, and nearly everyone wanted to contradict my lord Gaspar; but my lady Duchess imposed silence on all, and then said, laughing:

"If the evil you say of women were not so far from the truth, that the saying of it casts blame and shame on him who says it rather than on them, I should allow you to be answered. But I am not willing that, by being confronted with the arguments which it is possible to cite, you should be cured of this evil habit, in order that you may suffer very grievous punishment for your fault: which shall be the bad opinion wherein you will be held by all who hear you argue in such fashion."

Then messer Federico replied:

"My lord Gaspar, do not say that women are so very unreasonable, even if they are sometimes moved to love by others' judgment rather than by their own; for gentlemen and many wise men do the same. And if I may say the truth, you yourself and all the rest of us here do often and even now trust more to the opinion of others than to our own. And in proof of this, it is not long ago that certain verses, handed about this court under the name of Sannazaro,[115] seemed very excellent to everyone and were praised with wonder and applause; then, it being known for certain that they were by another hand, they promptly sank in reputation and were thought less than mediocre. And a certain motet,[176] which was sung before my lady Duchess, found no favour and was not thought good until it was known to be the work of Josquin de Près.[177]

"What clearer proof of the weight of opinion would you have? Do you not remember that in drinking a certain wine, you at one time pronounced it perfect, and at another most insipid? And this because you believed there were two kinds of wine, one from the Genoese Riviera, and the other from this country; and even when the mistake was discovered, you would not at all believe it,—so firmly fixed in your mind was that wrong opinion, although you had received it from the report of others.

36.—"Hence the Courtier ought to take great care to make a good impression at the start, and to consider how mischievous and fatal a thing it is to do otherwise. And they of all men run this danger, who pride themselves on being very amusing and on having acquired by these pleasantries of theirs a certain freedom that makes it proper and permissible for them to do and say whatever occurs to them, without taking thought about it. Thus they often begin a thing they know not how to finish, and then try to help matters by raising a laugh; and yet they do this so clumsily that it does not succeed, insomuch that they rouse the utmost disgust in him who sees or hears them, and fail most lamentably.

"Sometimes, thinking it to be droll and witty, they say the foulest and most indecent things before and even to honourable ladies; and the more they make these ladies blush, the more they rate themselves good Courtiers, and they laugh and pride themselves on having such a fine accomplishment, as they deem it. Yet they commit all this folly with no other aim than to be esteemed jovial fellows: this is the one name which seems to them worthy of praise and of which they boast more than of any other; and to acquire it, they utter the grossest and most shameful vileness in the world. Often they throw one another down-stairs, clap billets of wood and bricks on one another's backs, cast handfulls of dust in one another's eyes, make one another's horses run into ditches or down some hill; then at table they throw soups, sauces, jellies and every kind of thing in one another's faces: [178] and then they laugh. And he who can excel the others in these things, esteems himself to be the best Courtier and the most gallant, and thinks he has won great glory. And if they sometimes invite a gentleman to these carouses of theirs, and he does not choose to join in their unmannerly jokes, they at once say he stands too much on his dignity, and holds himself aloof, and is not a jovial fellow. But I have worse to tell you. There are some who rival one another and award the palm to him who can eat and drink the vilest and most offensive things; and they devise dishes so abhorrent to human sense that it is impossible to recall them without extreme disgust."

37.—"And what may these be?" said my lord Ludovico Pio.

Messer Federico replied:

"Ask the Marquess Febus, who has often seen them in France, and perhaps has taken part."

The Marquess Febus replied:

"I have seen none of these things done in France that are not done in Italy as well. But what is good among the Italians in dress, sports, banquets, handling arms, and in everything else that befits a Courtier,—all comes from the French."

Messer Federico replied:

"I do not say that very noble and modest cavaliers are not also to be found among the French, and I myself have known many who were truly worthy of every praise. But some are little circumspect, and generally speaking it seems to me that as regards breeding the Spaniards have more in common with the Italians than the French have; because that grave reserve peculiar to the Spaniards befits us far more than the quick vivacity which among the French we see in almost every movement, and which is not unseemly in them, nay is charming, for it is so natural and proper to them as not to seem at all affected. There are very many Italians who earnestly strive to copy this manner; and they can only shake their heads in speaking and make clumsy crosswise bows, and walk so fast that their lackeys cannot keep up with them when they pass through the city. And with these ways they seem to themselves to be good Frenchmen and to have the same freedom of manner, which in truth rarely happens save with those who have been bred in France and have acquired the manner in their youth.

"The same is true of knowing many languages; which I approve highly in the Courtier, especially Spanish and French, because the intercourse of both these nations with Italy is very frequent, and they have more in common with us than any of the others have; and their two princes,[179] being very powerful in war and very glorious in peace, always have their courts full of noble cavaliers, who spread throughout the world; and it is necessary for us also to converse with them.

38.—"I do not care at present to go more into detail in speaking of things that are too well known, such as that our Courtier ought not to avow himself a great eater or drinker, or given to excess in any evil habit, or vile and ungoverned in his life, with certain peasant ways that recall the hoe and plough a thousand miles away; because a man of this kind not only may not hope to become a good Courtier, but can be set to no more fitting business than feeding sheep.

"And finally I say it were well for the Courtier to know perfectly that which we have said befits him, so that every possible thing may be easy to him, and everyone may marvel at him,— he at no one. But be it understood that there ought not to be in him that lofty and ungenial indifference which some men have who show they are not surprised at what others do because they imagine they can do it better, and who disparage it by silence as not worth speaking of; and they almost seem to imply that no one is their equal or even able to fathom the profundity of their knowledge. Wherefore the Courtier ought to shun these odious ways, and to praise the fine achievements of other men with kindness and good will; and although he may feel that he is admirable and far superior to all, yet he ought to appear not to think so.

"But since such complete perfection as this is very rarely and perhaps never found in human nature, a man who is conscious of being lacking in some particular, ought not to despond thereat or lose hope of reaching a high standard, even though he cannot attain that perfect and supreme excellence to which he aspires. For in every art there are many grades that are honourable besides the highest, and whoever aims at the highest will seldom fail to rise more than half-way. Therefore if our Courtier excels in anything besides arms, I would have him get profit and esteem from it in fine fashion; and I would have him so discreet and sensible as to be able with skill and address to attract men to see and hear that wherein he thinks he excels, always appearing not to do it from ostentation, but by chance and at others' request rather than by his own wish. And in everything he has to do or say, let him if possible come ready and prepared, yet appearing to act impromptu throughout. In those things, however, wherein he feels himself to be mediocre, let him touch in passing, without dwelling much upon them, albeit in such fashion that he may be thought to know more about them than he shows himself to know: like certain poets, who sometimes touched lightly upon the profoundest depths of philosophy and other sciences, of which perhaps they understood little. Then, in that of which he knows he is wholly ignorant, I would never have him make any pretence or seek to win any fame; nay if need be, let him frankly confess his ignorance."

39.—"That," said Calmeta, "is not what Nicoletto [180] would have done, who was a very excellent philosopher but knew no more about law than about flying. When a Podestà [181] of Padua had decided to give him a lectureship in law, he was never willing (although urged thereto by many scholars) to undeceive the Podestà and confess his ignorance,—always saying that he did not agree with the opinion of Socrates in this matter, and that it was not seemly for a philosopher ever to say that he was ignorant of anything."

Messer Federico replied:

"I do not say that of his own notion and unasked by others, the Courtier should volunteer to tell his ignorance; for I too dislike this folly of self-accusal and depreciation. And therefore I sometimes inwardly laugh at certain men, who needlessly and of their own accord narrate things that perhaps occurred without their fault but yet imply a shade of disgrace; like a cavalier whom you all know, and who, whenever he heard mention made of the battle that was fought against King Charles in the Parmesan, [182] at once began to tell the manner of his flight, nor seemed to have seen or heard aught else that day; again, speaking of a certain famous joust, he always described how he had fallen, and in his conversation he often seemed to seek an opportunity to tell how he had received a sound cudgelling one night as he was on his way to meet a lady.

"I would not have our Courtier tell such follies. It seems to me, however, that when occasion offers for displaying himself in something of which he is quite ignorant, he ought to avoid it; and if compelled by necessity, he ought to confess his ignorance frankly rather than put himself to that risk. And in this way he will escape the censure that many nowadays deserve, who from some perverse instinct or unreasonable design always set themselves to do that which they do not know, and forsake that which they do know. And as an instance of this, I know a very excellent musician, who, having abandoned music, gave himself up wholly to composing verses, and thinks himself very great therein, and makes all men laugh at him; and now he has lost even his music.

"Another man, one of the first painters of the world, despises the art wherein he is most rare, and has set himself to study philosophy; in which he has such strange conceptions and new chimeras, that he could not with all his painter's art depict them.[183] And of such as these, a countless number could be found.

"Some indeed there are who know they excel in one thing and yet make their chief business of another, of which they are not ignorant either; but every time they have occasion to display themselves in that wherein they feel themselves proficient, they do it gallantly. And it sometimes comes to pass that the company, seeing them do well in that which is not their profession, think they can do far better in that which they make their profession. This art, if it be accompanied by good judgment, is by no means unpleasing to me."

40.—Then my lord Gaspar Pallavicino replied:

"This seems to me not art but mere deceit; nor do I think it fitting for him who would be a man of honour, ever to deceive."

"It is an embellishment, which graces what he does," said messer Federico, "rather than deceit; and even if it be deceit, it is not to be censured. Will you not also say that of two men fencing, the one who touches the other, deceives him? And this is because the one has more art than the other. And if you have a jewel that is beautiful without setting, and it afterwards comes into the hands of a good goldsmith, who by skilful setting makes it look far more beautiful, will you not say that this gold-smith deceives the eyes of anyone who sees it? And yet he deserves praise for his deceit, for with good judgment and art his master hand often adds grace and beauty to ivory or silver, or to a beautiful stone by encircling it with fine gold. Therefore let us not say that art,—or such deceit as this, if you will call it so,—deserves any censure.

"Nor is it unseemly for a man who is conscious of doing something well, dexterously to seek occasion for showing himself therein, and at the same time to conceal what he thinks undeserving of praise,—but always with a touch of wary dissimulation. Do you not remember that without appearing to seek them, King Ferdinand [32] found opportunities now and then to go about in his doublet? and this because he felt himself to be very agile; and that, as his hands were not over good, he rarely or almost never took off his gloves? And there were very few that perceived his cunning. Moreover I think I have read that Julius Cæsar liked to wear the laurel wreath to hide his baldness.[184] But in all these matters it is needful to be very cautious and to use good judgment, in order not to go beyond bounds; for in avoiding one error a man often runs into another, and in his wish to win praise, receives censure.

41.—"Hence in our mode of life and conversation, it is a very safe thing to govern ourselves with a certain decorous discretion, which in truth is a very great and very strong shield against envy, which we ought to avoid as much as possible. Moreover I wish our Courtier to guard against getting the name of a liar or a boaster, which sometimes befalls even those who do not deserve it. Therefore in his talk let him always take care not to go beyond the probable, and also not to tell too often those truths that have the look of falsehood,[185]—like many who never speak save of miracles, and wish to carry such authority that every incredible thing shall be believed from them. Others, at the beginning of a friendship and in order to gain favour with their new friend, swear the first day they speak with him that there is no one in the world whom they love more than him, and that they would gladly die to do him service, and like things be yond reason. And when they part from him, they pretend to weep and to be unable to speak a word from grief. Thus, in their wish to be thought very loving, they come to be esteemed liars and silly flatterers.

"But it would be too long and tedious to recount all the faults that may be committed in our manner of conversation. Hence as regards what I desire in the Courtier, let it suffice to say, besides the things already said, that he should be of such sort as never to be without something to say that is good and well suited to those with whom he is speaking, and that he should know how to refresh the minds of his hearers with a certain sweetness, and by his amusing witticisms and pleasantries to move them cleverly to mirth and laughter, so that without ever becoming tedious or producing satiety, he may give pleasure continually.

42.—"At last I think my lady Emilia will give me leave to be silent. And if she refuse me, I shall by my own talk stand convicted of not being the good Courtier whereof I have spoken; for not only does good talk (which perhaps you have neither now nor ever heard from me), but even such talk as I usually have at command (whatever that may be worth), quite fail me."

Then my lord Prefect said, laughing:

"I am not willing to let this false opinion,—that you are not a most admirable Courtier,—rest in the mind of any of us; for it is certain that your desire to be silent proceeds rather from a wish to escape labour than from lack of something to say. So, to the end that nothing may seem to be neglected in such worthy company as this and such admirable talk, be pleased to teach us how we must employ the pleasantries that you have just mentioned, and to show us the art that pertains to all this kind of amusing talk, so as to excite laughter and mirth in gentle fashion; for indeed methinks it is very important and well befitting the Courtier."

"My Lord," replied messer Federico, "pleasantries and witticisms are the gift and grace of nature rather than of art; but in this matter certain nations are to be found more ready than

others, like the Tuscans, who in truth are very clever. It seems
to me that the use of witticism is very natural to the Spaniards
too. Yet there are many, both of these and of all other nations,
who from over loquacity sometimes go beyond bounds and become silly and pointless, because they do not consider the kind
of person with whom they are speaking, the place where they
are, the occasion, or the soberness and modesty which they ought
above all things to maintain."

43.—Then my lord Prefect replied:

"You deny that there is any art in pleasantries, and yet by
speaking ill of those who use them not with modesty and soberness and who regard not the occasion and the persons with whom
they are speaking, methinks you show that even this can be taught
and has some method in it."

"These rules, my Lord," replied messer Federico, "are so
universal that they fit and apply to everything. But I said there
is no art in pleasantries, because I think there are only two kinds
of them to be found: one of which stretches out in long and
continuous talk, as we see in the case of certain men who narrate
and describe so gracefully and amusingly something that has
happened to them or that they have seen or heard, that they
set it before our eyes with gestures and words and almost make
us touch it with the hand; and for lack of other word, we may
perhaps call this the humorous or urbane manner. The other
kind of witticism is very short, and consists solely in sayings
that are quick and sharp, such as are often heard among us, or
biting; nor are they acceptable unless they sting a little. By the
ancients also they were called apothegms: at present some call
them *arguzie*.[186]

"So I say that in the first kind, which is humorous narrative, there is no need of any art, because nature herself creates
and fashions men fitted to narrate amusingly, and gives them features, gestures, voice and words proper to imitate what they will.
In the other kind, that of *arguzie*, what can art avail? For whatever it be, a pungent saying must dart forth and hit the mark
before he who utters it shall seem to have given it a thought;
otherwise it is flat and has no savour. Therefore I think it is all
the work of intellect and nature."

Then messer Pietro Bembo took up the talk, and said:

"My lord Prefect does not deny what you say, that nature and intellect play the chief part, especially as regards conception. Still it is certain that every man's mind, however fine his intellect may be, conceives both good things and bad, and more or less; yet judgment and art then polish and correct them, and cull out the good and reject the bad. So lay aside what pertains to intellect, and explain to us what consists in art; that is, of the pleasantries and witticisms that excite laughter, tell us what are befitting the Courtier and what are not, and in what time and way they should be used; for this is what my lord Prefect asks of you."

44.—Then messer Federico said laughingly:

"There is no one of us here to whom I do not yield in everything, and especially in being jocular; unless perhaps nonsense, which often makes others laugh more than bright sayings, be also counted as pleasantry." And then turning to Count Ludovico and to messer Bernardo Bibbiena, he said: "Here are the masters of witticism, from whom I must first learn what to say if I am to speak of jocose sayings." [187]

Count Ludovico replied:

"Methinks you are already beginning to practise what you say you know nothing of, I mean in that you try to make these gentlemen laugh by ridiculing messer Bernardo and me; for every one of them knows you far excel us in that for which you praise us. If you are fatigued, then, you had better beg my lady Duchess to postpone the rest of our talk until to-morrow, instead of trying to escape fatigue by subterfuge."

Messer Federico began to make answer, but my lady Emilia quickly interrupted him and said:

"It is not in order for the discussion to spend itself in your praises; it is enough that you are all well known. But as I remember, Sir Count, that you accused me last evening of not distributing the labour equally, it were well to let messer Federico rest awhile, and to give messer Bernardo Bibbiena the task of speaking about pleasantries, because we not only know him to be very amusing in continuous talk, but we remember that he has several times promised us to try to write upon this subject, and hence we may believe that he has already thought much about it, and therefore ought to satisfy us fully. Afterwards, when we have finished discussing pleasantries, messer Federico shall go on with what he has left to say about the Courtier."

Thereupon messer Federico said:

"My Lady, I do not know what I have left to say; but like the wayfarer at noon, weary with the fatigue of his long journey, I will refresh myself with messer Bernardo's talk and the sound of his words, as if under some delightful and shady tree, with the soft murmur of a plashing spring. Then perhaps, being revived a little, I shall be able to say something more."

Messer Bernardo replied, laughing:

"If I show you my head, you shall see what shade is to be expected from the leafage of my tree.[188] As for listening to the murmur of that plashing spring, perhaps you may; for I was once turned into a spring, not by any of the ancient gods but by our friend Fra Mariano,[60] and I have never stood in need of water from then till now."

Then everyone began to laugh, for this pleasantry referred to by messer Bernardo happened at Rome in the presence of Cardinal Galeotto of San Pietro ad Vincula,[189] and was well known to all.

45.—The laughter having ceased, my lady Emilia said:

"Now stop making us laugh by your use of pleasantries, and teach us how we are to use them, and from what they are derived, and all you know about the subject. And to lose no more time, begin at once."

"I fear," said messer Bernardo, "that the hour is late; and to the end that my talk about pleasantries may not itself lack pleasantry and be tedious, perhaps it will be well to postpone it until to-morrow."

Here many replied together that it was still far from the usual hour for ending the discussion. Then, turning to my lady Duchess and to my lady Emilia, messer Bernardo said:

"I do not wish to escape this task; although, just as I am wont to marvel at the presumption of those who venture to sing to the viol before our friend Giacomo Sansecondo,[190] so I ought not to talk about pleasantries before an audience who understand what I should say far better than I.

"However, not to give any of these gentlemen a pretext for refusing the charge that may be laid upon them, I will tell as briefly as I can what occurs to me concerning the causes that excite laughter; which is so peculiar to us that in defining man we are wont to say that he is a laughing animal. For laughter is found only among men, and is nearly always the sign of a certain hilarity felt inwardly in the mind, which is by nature drawn towards amusement and longs for repose and recreation; wherefore we see many things devised by men to this end, such as festivals and different kinds of shows. And since we love those who furnish us this recreation, it was the custom of ancient rulers (Roman, Athenian and many others), in order to gain the people's good will and to feast the eyes and minds of the multitude, to erect great theatres and other public edifices, and therein to exhibit new sports, horse and chariot races, combats, strange beasts, comedies, tragedies and mimes. Nor were such shows eschewed by grave philosophers, who in sports of this kind and banquets often relaxed their minds when fatigued by lofty discourse and spiritual meditation; which thing all kinds of men also like to do: for not only toilers in the field, sailors, and all those who perform hard and rough labour with their hands, but holy priests, and prisoners awaiting death from hour to hour, all seek continually some remedy and solace for their refreshment. Hence everything that moves to laughter, cheers the mind and gives pleasure, and for the moment frees us from the memory of those weary troubles of which our life is full. So laughter, as you see, is very delightful to all, and greatly to be praised is he who excites it reasonably and in a graceful way.

"But what laughter is, and where it abides, and how it sometimes seizes upon our veins, eyes, mouths and sides, and seems as if it would make us burst, so that with all our effort it cannot be restrained,—I will leave Democritus to tell, who could not even if he were to promise.[191]

46.—"Now the occasion and as it were the source from which the laughable springs, lies in a kind of distortion; for we laugh only at those things that have incongruity in them and that seem amiss without being so. I know not how to explain it otherwise; but if you think of it yourselves, you will see that what we laugh at is nearly always something that is incongruous and yet is not amiss.

"Next I will try to tell you, as far as my judgment shall show me, what the means are that the Courtier ought to use for the purpose of exciting laughter, and within what bounds; because it is not seemly for the Courtier to be always making men laugh, nor yet by those means that are made use of by fools or drunken men, by the silly, the nonsensical, and likewise by buffoons. And although these kinds of men seem to be in demand at courts, yet they deserve not to be called Courtiers, but each by his own name, and to be held for what they are.

"Moreover we must diligently consider the bounds and limits of exciting laughter by derision, and who it is we deride; for laughter is not aroused by jeering at a poor unfortunate nor yet at an open rascal and blackguard, because the latter seems to merit greater punishment than that of being ridiculed, and the mind of man is not prone to flout the wretched, unless they boast of their wretchedness and are proud and saucy. We ought also to treat with respect those who are universal favourites and beloved by all and powerful, for by jeering at these persons a man may sometimes bring dangerous enmities upon himself. Yet it is proper to flout and laugh at the vices of those who are neither so wretched as to excite pity, nor so wicked as to seem worthy of capital punishment, nor so great that a touch of their wrath can do much harm.

47.—"Again, you must know that from the same occasion whence we draw our laughable witticisms, we may likewise draw serious phrases of praise or censure, and sometimes by using the same words. Thus in praising a generous man who shares all he has with his friends, we are wont to say that what he has is not his own; the same may be said in censuring a man who has stolen or by other evil means acquired what he possesses. Also we say, 'That lady is of great price,' meaning to praise her for discretion and goodness; the same thing might be said in dispraise of her, implying that anyone may have her.

"But for this purpose we have a chance to use the same

situations oftener than the same words. Thus recently a lady being at mass in church with three cavaliers, one of whom served her in love,[192] a poor beggar came up and taking his stand before the lady began to beg alms of her; and he repeated his petition several times to her with much importunity and pitiful groaning; yet for all that she gave him no alms, nor still did she refuse it to him with a sign to go in peace, but continued to stand abstracted as if she were thinking of something else. Then the cavalier in love said to his two companions:

" 'You see what I have to expect from my lady, who is so hard-hearted that she not only gives no alms to that naked starving wretch who is begging it of her so eagerly and often, but she will not even send him away. So much does she delight to see a man languishing in misery before her and vainly imploring her pity.'

"One of his two friends replied:

" 'This is not hardness of heart, but a silent lesson from the lady to teach you that she is never pleased with an importunate suitor.'

"The other replied:

" 'Nay, it is a warning to him that while she never grants what is asked of her, still she likes to be entreated for it.'

"You see how the lady's failure to send the poor man away, gave rise to one saying of grave censure, one of moderate praise, and another of biting satire.

48.—"Proceeding now to declare the kinds of pleasantries that are pertinent to our subject, I say that in my opinion there are three varieties, although messer Federico mentioned only two: namely, that which consists in rendering the effect of a thing by means of urbane and amusing long narrative, and that which consists in the swift and keen readiness of a single phrase. But we will add a third sort called practical joking, in which long narratives and short sayings have place, and also some action.

"Now the first, which consists in continuous talk, is of such sort as almost to amount to story-telling. And to give you an instance: just at the time when Pope Alexander the Sixth died and Pius the Third was created pope,[193] your fellow Mantuan, my lady Duchess, messer Antonio Agnello,[194] being at Rome and

✓✓✓✓✓✓✓✓✓✓✓✓✓✓✓✓✓✓✓✓✓✓✓✓✓✓✓✓✓✓✓✓✓✓✓✓✓✓✓✓✓✓✓✓✓✓✓✓✓✓✓✓✓

in the palace, happened to speak of the death of the one pope and of the other's creation, and in discussing this with some of his friends, he said:

" 'My Lords, even in the days of Catullus [195] doors began to speak without a tongue and to listen without ears, and thus to reveal adulteries. Now, although men are not of such worth as they were in those times, it may be that the doors (many of which are made of antique marbles, at least here in Rome) have the same powers that they then had; and for my part I believe that these two here could clear away all our doubts if we cared to learn from them.'

"Then the gentlemen present were very curious, and waited to see how the affair was going to end. Whereupon messer Antonio, continuing to walk up and down, raised his eyes as if by chance to one of the two doors of the hall in which they were strolling, stopped a moment, and pointed out to his companions the inscription over it, which was the name of Pope Alexander, followed by a V and an I, signifying Sixth as you know; and he said:

" 'See what the door says: *Alessandro Papa vi,* which means that he became pope by the violence that he used, and that he accomplished more by violence than by reason. Now let us see if from the other we can learn anything about the new pope.' And turning to the other door as if by accident, he showed the inscription, N PP V, which signified *Nicolaus Papa Quintus;* [196] and he at once said: 'Alas, bad news; this one says, *Nihil Papa Valet.*'

49.—"Now you see how elegant and admirable this kind of pleasantry is, and how becoming to a Courtier, whether the thing that is said be true or not; because in such a case it is allowable for a man to fabricate as much as he pleases, without blame; and in speaking the truth, to adorn it with a little falsity, overstating or understating as the occasion requires. But in these matters perfect grace and true cleverness consist in picturing forth what we wish to say, with both word and gesture, so well and with such ease that they who hear may seem to see before their eyes the thing we tell them. And this graphic method is so

↑↑↑↑↑↑↑↑↑↑↑↑↑↑↑↑↑↑↑↑↑↑↑↑↑↑↑↑↑↑↑↑↑↑↑↑↑↑↑↑↑↑↑↑↑↑↑↑↑↑↑↑↑↑↑↑↑↑

effective that it sometimes adorns and makes highly amusing a
thing that in itself is neither very jocular nor clever.

"And although this kind of narrative requires gesture and
the aid of the speaking voice, its quality is sometimes found in
written compositions also. Who does not laugh, when, in the
Eighth Day of his Decameron,[197] Giovanni Boccaccio tells how
the priest of Varlungo tried to chant a *Kyrie* and a *Sanctus* on
discovering that his Belcolore was in the church. There are amusing narratives also in his stories of Calandrino,[198] and in many
others. Of the same sort seems to be the raising of a laugh by
mimicry or imitation, as we say,—wherein I have thus far seen
no one more admirable than our friend messer Roberto da
Bari." [48]

50.—"This would be no small praise," said messer Roberto,
"if it were true; because I should of course try to imitate the
good rather than the bad, and if I could make myself like some
men I know, I should deem myself very fortunate. I fear, however, that I know how to imitate only those things which excite
laughter, and which you just now said consist essentially in the
imperfect."

Messer Bernardo replied:

"Imperfect, yes; but not unpleasantly so. And you must
know that this imitation of which we are speaking, cannot be
without cleverness; for besides the way of governing words and
gestures and setting before our hearers' eyes the face and manners of the man we are speaking of, we must needs be discreet,
and pay great heed to the place and time, and to the persons
with whom we are speaking, and not descend to buffoonery or go
beyond bounds;—which rules you observe admirably and therefore know them all, I think. For in truth it would little befit a
gentleman to make faces, to weep and laugh, and mimic voices,
to wrestle with himself as Berto [65] does, or dress like a clown
before everyone, like Strascino,[199]—and things of that kind,
which are very fitting in those men because it is their profession.

"But for us it is needful to give only a fleeting and covert
imitation, always preserving the dignity of a gentleman, without
uttering foul words or performing acts that are less than seemly,
without contorting the face or person beyond measure; but to

order our movements in such fashion that whoever hears and
sees us may from our words and gestures imagine far more than
what he sees and hears, and so be moved to laughter.

"Moreover in our imitation we ought to avoid too stinging
jibes, especially at deformities of face or person; for while bodily
defects often furnish excellent material for laughter to a man
who uses them with discretion, yet to employ this method too
bitterly is the act not only of a buffoon but of an enemy. So,
although it be difficult, in this regard we must, as I have said,
keep to the manner of our friend messer Roberto, who mimics
all men and not without marking their defects sharply even to
their face, and yet no one is annoyed or seems to take it amiss.
And I will give no instance of this, because in him we see countless examples of it every day.

51.—"Another thing excites much laughter, although it is
included under the head of narration; and that is to describe
gracefully certain defects of others,—unimportant ones however
and undeserving greater punishment, such as follies, sometimes
mere absurdities or sometimes accompanied by a quick and
pungent dash of liveliness; likewise certain extreme affectations;
sometimes a huge and well-constructed lie. As when, a few days
since, our friend Cesare told of a delightful absurdity, which was
that finding himself before the Podestà of this place,[200] he saw a
peasant come in to complain of being robbed of a donkey. The
fellow told of his poverty and of the trick played upon him by
the thief, and then, to make out his loss the heavier, he said:
'Masters, if you had seen my donkey, you would have better
understood how much cause I have to grieve; for when he had
his pack on, he looked like a very Tullius.'[201]

"And one of our friends, meeting a flock of goats with a
great he-goat at their head, stopped and said with a look of admiration: 'See what a he-goat! He looks like a Saint Paul.'[202]

"My lord Gaspar tells of having known an old servant of
Duke Ercole of Ferrara,[203] who offered the duke his two sons
as pages; but before they could begin their service, both the
boys died. When the duke heard this, he condoled with the father
kindly, saying that he was very sorry, for the only time when
he had seen them, they had seemed to him very pretty and gentle

boys.  The father replied: 'My Lord, you saw nothing; for within
the last few days they had grown far handsomer and more virtuous than I could possibly have believed, and already they sang
together like two sparrow-hawks.'

"And not long since one of our doctors stood looking at a
man who had been condemned to be flogged about the piazza,
and taking pity on him, because (although his shoulders were
bleeding freely) the poor wretch walked as slowly as if he had
been out for a stroll to pass the time, the doctor said to him:
'Step out, poor fellow, and make haste to be done with your
pain.' Whereat the good man turned, and gazing at the doctor
as if amazed, he stood awhile without speaking, and then said:
'When you come to be flogged, you will go your own gait; so I
choose to go mine now.'

"You surely must still remember that absurd story which
my lord Duke [2] lately told of a certain abbot, who, being present
one day when Duke Federico [26] was discussing what to do with
the great mass of earth that had been excavated to lay the foundations of this palace, which was then building, said: 'My Lord,
I have thought of an excellent place to put it. Give orders to have
an immense pit made, and it can be put in without further difficulty.' Duke Federico replied, not without laughter: 'And where
shall we put the earth to be dug out of this pit of yours?' The
abbot continued: 'Have it made large enough to hold both.' And
so, for all the duke repeated several times that the larger the pit
was made, the more earth would be dug out of it, the man could
never get it into his brain that it could not be made large enough
to hold both, and kept replying: 'Make it so much the larger.'
Now you see what good judgment this abbot had."

52.—Then messer Pietro Bembo said:

"And why do you not tell the story of your friend the
Florentine commander who was besieged in Castellina [204] by the
Duke of Calabria? Finding one day some poisoned crossbow
missiles that had been shot in from the camp, he wrote to the
duke that if the warfare was to be carried on so barbarously, he
too would have medicine put on his cannon shot, and then woe
to the one who had the worst of it." [205]

Messer Bernardo laughed, and said:

"Messer Pietro, if you do not hold your peace, I will tell all the things I have seen and heard about your dear Venetians (which are not few), and especially when they try to play the horseman."

"Do not so, I beg of you," replied messer Pietro, "and I will keep quiet about two other delightful tales that I know of the Florentines." [206]

Messer Bernardo said:

"They must have rather been Sienese, who often slip in this way; as was recently the case with one, who, on hearing some letters read in council wherein the phrase 'the aforesaid' was used (to avoid such frequent repetition of the name of the man who was spoken of), said to the man who was reading: 'Stop there a moment and tell me, is this Aforesaid a friend to our commune?' "

Messer Pietro laughed, then said:

"I am speaking of Florentines, not of Sienese."

"Speak out freely then," added my lady Emilia, "and do not stand so much on ceremony."

Messer Pietro continued:

"When the Florentine Signory was waging war against the Pisans,[207] they sometimes found their money exhausted by their great expenses; and the method of finding money for daily needs being discussed in council one day, after many ways had been proposed, one of the oldest citizens said: 'I have thought of two methods whereby we could soon get a goodly sum of money without much trouble. And one of these is, that since we have no revenue greater than from the customs levied at the gates of Florence, and since we have eleven gates, let us at once have eleven more made, and thus we shall double our revenue. The other method is to give orders that the mints be forthwith opened in Pistoia and Prato,[208] just the same as in Florence, and that nothing be done there day and night but mint money, and that all the money be ducats of gold; and in my judgment this course is the quicker and the less costly.' "

53.—There was much laughter at this citizen's keen sagacity: and the laughter being quieted, my lady Emilia said:

"Messer Bernardo, will you allow messer Pietro to ridicule

the Florentines in this fashion, without returning blow for blow.'"

"I forgive him this affront," replied messer Bernardo, still laughing, "for if he has displeased me by ridiculing the Florentines, he has pleased me by obeying you, as I also would always do."

Then messer Cesare said:

"I heard a delightful blunder made by a Brescian who had been at Venice this year for the feast of the Ascension, and in my presence was describing to some of his companions the fine things that he had seen there; and how much merchandise there was, and how much silverware, spices, cloth and stuffs; then the Signory went forth with great pomp to wed the sea in the Bucentaur,[209] on board of which there were so many finely dressed gentlemen, so much music and singing, that it seemed a paradise. And on being asked by one of his companions which kind of music he liked best among those that he had heard, he said: 'They all were good; but among the rest I saw a man playing on a certain strange trumpet, which he thrust down his throat more than two palms at every flourish, and then he straightway drew it out and thrust it down again; so that you never saw a greater marvel.' "

Then everyone laughed, perceiving the silly mistake of the man, who had imagined that the player thrust down his throat that part of the trombone which disappears by sliding into itself.

54.—Messer Bernardo then continued:

"Moreover common affectations are tedious, but they excite much laughter when they are beyond measure: like those we sometimes hear from certain mouths regarding greatness or courage or nobility; or sometimes from women, regarding beauty or fastidiousness. As was not long since the case with a lady who remained sad and abstracted at some great festival; and when asked what she was thinking about that should make her so gloomy, she replied: 'I was thinking of a matter that troubles me greatly whenever it occurs to me, nor can I lift it from my heart; and this is, that on the universal Judgment Day, when all men's naked bodies must rise and appear before the tribunal of Christ, I cannot endure the distress I feel at the thought that my body will have to be seen unclothed among the rest.' Being extravagant, such affectations as these cause laughter rather than tedium.

"You all are familiar with those splendid lies so well composed that they move to laughter. A very excellent one was but lately told me by a friend of ours who never suffers us to be without them."

55.—Then the Magnifico Giuliano said:

"Be that as it may, it cannot be more excellent or more ingenious than one which a fellow-Tuscan of ours, a merchant of Lucca, affirmed the other day as a positive fact."

"Tell it to us," added my lady Duchess.

The Magnifico Giuliano replied, laughing:

"This merchant, so he tells the story, once finding himself in Poland, decided to buy a quantity of sables with the intention of carrying them into Italy and making great profit thereby. And after much effort, being unable to enter Muscovy himself (by reason of the war that was then waging between the King of Poland and the Duke of Muscovy), he arranged with the help of some people of the country, that on an appointed day certain Muscovite merchants should come with their sables to the frontier of Poland, and he promised to be there in order to strike the bargain. Accordingly, proceeding with his companions towards Muscovy, the man of Lucca reached the Dnieper, which he found all frozen as hard as marble, and saw that the Muscovites (who on account of the war were themselves suspicious of the Poles) were already on the other bank, but approached no nearer than the width of the river. So, having recognized each other, the Muscovites after some signalling began to speak with a loud voice, and to ask the price that they wished for their sables; but such was the extreme cold that they were not heard, for before reaching the other bank (where the man of Lucca and his interpreters were) the words froze in the air, and remained there frozen and caught in such manner that the Poles, who knew the custom, set about making a great fire in the very middle of the river; because to their thinking that was the limit reached by the warm voice before it was stopped by freezing, and the river was quite solid enough to bear the fire easily. So, when this was done, the words (which had remained frozen for the space of an hour) in due course began to melt and to fall in a murmur, like snow from the mountains in May; and thus they were at once heard very well, although the men had already gone. But as the merchant thought that the words asked too high a price for the sables, he would not accept the offer and so returned without them." [210]

56.—Thereupon everyone laughed, and messer Bernardo said:

"Of a truth the story I wish to tell you is not so ingenious; however it is a fine one, and runs as follows:

"Speaking a few days since of the country or World recently discovered by the Portuguese mariners,[211] and of the various animals and other things which they bring back to Portugal, that friend of whom I told you affirmed that he had seen a monkey of a form very different from those we are accustomed to see, which played chess most admirably. And among other occasions, the gentleman who had brought her, being one day before the King of Portugal [212] and engaged in a game of chess with her, the monkey made several moves so skilfully as to press him hard and at last checkmated him. Being vexed, as all are wont to be who lose at that game, the gentleman took up the king-piece (which was very large, such as the Portuguese use) and gave the monkey a smart blow upon the head; whereupon she leaped aside crying loudly, and seemed to ask justice of the king for the wrong that had been done her. Then the gentleman invited her to play again; and after refusing awhile by means of signs, she finally began to play once more, and, as she had done the first time, she again had the better of him. At last, seeing that she would be able to checkmate the gentleman, the monkey tried a new trick to guard against being struck again; and without showing what she was at, she quietly put her right paw under the gentleman's left elbow, which was luxuriously resting on a taffety [213] cushion, and (quickly snatching the cushion) with her left paw she at the same time checkmated him with a pawn, while with her right she held the cushion over her head as a shield against his blows; she then leaped joyfully to the king as if to

↑↑↑↑↑↑↑↑↑↑↑↑↑↑↑↑↑↑↑↑↑↑↑↑↑↑↑↑↑↑↑↑↑↑↑↑↑↑↑↑↑↑↑↑↑↑↑↑↑↑↑↑↑↑↑↑↑↑↑↑↑

parade her victory. Now you see how wise, wary and discreet the monkey was."

Then messer Cesare Gonzaga said:

"It must be that this was a doctor among monkeys, and of great authority; and I think that the Republic of Indian Monkeys sent her to Portugal to make a name in a foreign land."

Thereupon everyone laughed, both at the story and at the addition given to it by messer Cesare.

57.—So, continuing the discussion, messer Bernardo said:

"You have now heard what occurs to me concerning those pleasantries that render the effect of a thing by continuous talk; therefore it is now well to speak of those that consist in a single saying and have a quick keenness compressed into a phrase or word. And just as in the first kind,—that of humorous talk,— we must in our narrative and mimicry avoid resembling buffoons and parasites and those who make others laugh by their sheer absurdities, so in these short sayings the Courtier must take care not to appear malicious and spiteful, and not to utter witticisms and *arguzie* solely to annoy and cut to the quick; because for the sin of their tongue such men often suffer in all their members.

58.—"Now of the ready pleasantries that are contained in a short saying, those are keenest that arise from ambiguity. Yet they do not always move to laughter, for they are oftener applauded as ingenious than as comic. As was said a few days since by our friend messer Annibal Paleotto [214] to someone who was recommending a tutor to teach his sons grammar, and who, after praising the tutor as very learned, said that by way of stipend the man desired not only money but a room furnished for living and sleeping, because he had no *letto* (bed): whereupon messer Annibal at once replied: 'And how can he be learned if he has not *letto* (read)?' You see how well he played upon the double meaning of the phrase, *non aver letto* [to have no bed, or, not to have read].

"But while this punning witticism has much sharpness, where a man takes words in a sense different from that in which everyone else takes them, it seems (as I have said) to excite wonderment rather than laughter, except when it is combined with some other kind of saying.

"Now that kind of witticism which is most used to excite laughter, is when we are prepared to hear one thing and the speaker says another, and it is called 'the unexpected.' And if punning be combined with this, the witticism becomes most spicy: as the other day, when there was a discussion about making a fine brick floor (*un bel mattonato*) for my lady Duchess's closet, after much talk you, Giancristoforo, said: 'If we could fetch the Bishop of Potenza [215] and flatten him out well, it would be the very thing, for he is the craziest creature born (*il più bel matto nato*).' Everyone laughed heartily, for by dividing the word *matto-nato* you made the pun. Moreover saying that it would be well to flatten out a bishop and lay him in the floor of a room, was unexpected to the listener; and so the sally was very keen and laughable.

59.—"But of punning witticisms there are many kinds; therefore we must be careful and play very lightly with our words, and avoid those that make the sally flat or that seem forced; and also those (as we have said) that are too biting. As where several companions found themselves at the house of one of their friends who was blind of one eye, and the blind man bade the company stay to dinner, all took their leave save one, who said: 'I will stay with you because I see you have a vacant place for one;' and at the same time he pointed with his finger to the empty socket. You see this is too bitter and rude, for it wounded without cause, and the speaker had not first been stung himself. Moreover he said that which might be said of all blind men; and such universal things give no pleasure, because it seems possible that they may have been thought out beforehand. And of this kind was that gibe at a man without nose: 'And where do you hang your spectacles?' [216] or 'With what do you smell the roses in their season?'

60.—"But among other witticisms those have very good grace that are made by taking the very words and sense from another man's taunt and turning them against him and striking him with his own weapons; as where a litigant—whose adversary had said to him in the judge's presence: 'Why do you bark so?'—at once replied: 'Because I see a thief.'

"And another instance of this was when Galeotto da Narni, [217]

*ソソソソソソソソソソソソソソソソソソソソソソソソソソソソソソソソソソソソソソソソソソソソソソソソソ*

on his way through Siena, stopped in the street to ask for the
inn; and a Sienese, seeing how fat he was, said, laughing: 'Other
men carry their wallets behind, but this one carries his in front.'
Galeotto at once replied: 'That is the way we do in a land of
thieves.'

61.—"There is still another kind, which we call playing on
words,[218] and this consists in changing a word by either adding or
omitting a letter or a syllable; as when someone said: 'You are
better versed in the Latrin tongue than in the Greek.' And you,
my Lady, had a letter addressed to you, 'To my lady Emilia
Impia.'[219]

"Moreover it is a pleasant thing to quote a verse or two,
applying it to a purpose different from that which the author
intends, or some other familiar saw; sometimes to the same purpose, but changing some word. As when a gentleman, who had an
ugly and disagreeable wife, was asked how he was, he replied:
'Judge yourself of my state, when *Furiarum maxima juxta me
cubat.*'[220] And messer Geronimo Donato,[221] while going the
rounds of the *Stazioni*[222] at Rome in Lent with several other
gentlemen, met a bevy of beautiful Roman ladies; and one of
the gentlemen saying: '*Quot coelum stellas, tot habet tua Roma
puellas,*'[223] he at once replied: *Pascua quotque haedos, tot habet
tua Roma cinaedos,*'[224] pointing to a company of young men who
were coming from the other direction.

"In like fashion messer Marcantonio della Torre[225] addressed the Bishop of Padua. There being a nunnery at Padua
in charge of a friar reputed to be of very pure life and learned
as well, it came to pass that, as the friar frequented the convent
familiarly and often confessed the nuns, five of them (more
than half of all there were) became pregnant; and the affair
being discovered, the friar wished to flee but knew not how. The
bishop had him taken into custody, and he soon confessed that
he had brought the five nuns to this pass, being tempted of the
devil; wherefore the bishop was firmly resolved to punish him
roundly. But as the man was learned, he had many friends who
all tried to help him, and along with the rest messer Marcantonio
went to the bishop to implore some measure of pardon for him.
The bishop would in no wise listen to them; and after they had

ↆↆↆↆↆↆↆↆↆↆↆↆↆↆↆↆↆↆↆↆↆↆↆↆↆↆↆↆↆↆↆↆↆↆↆↆↆↆↆↆↆↆↆↆↆↆↆↆↆↆↆↆↆↆↆↆↆↆↆↆↆↆ

pleaded hard, and recommended the culprit, and urged in excuse the opportunities of his position, the frailty of human nature, and many other things,—at last the bishop said: 'I will
do nothing for him, because I shall have to render God an
account of the matter.' And when they repeated their arguments,
the bishop said: 'What answer shall I make to God on the Day
of Judgment, when he says to me, *Give an account of thy
stewardship?*' [226] Then messer Marcantonio at once said: 'My
Lord, say that which the Evangelist says: *Lord, thou deliveredst
unto me five talents: behold I have gained besides them five
talents more.*' [227] Whereupon the bishop could not keep from
laughing, and greatly softened his anger and the punishment
intended for the offender.

62.—"It is also amusing to interpret names, and to pretend
some reason why the man who is spoken of bears such a name,
or why something is done. As a few days ago, when Proto da
Lucca [228] (who is very amusing, as you know) asked for the
bishopric of Caglio, the Pope replied: 'Knowest thou not that
in the Spanish tongue *caglio* means *I keep silence?* And thou art
a babbler; wherefore it would be unseemly for a bishop never to
be able to repeat his title without telling an untruth. So be
thou silent (*caglia*) now.' Here Proto made a reply, which, although it was not of this sort, yet was not less to the point; for
having several times repeated his request, and seeing that it was
of no avail, at last he said: 'Holy Father, if your Holiness grant
me this bishopric, it will not be without advantage, for I shall
leave your Holiness two offices (*ufficii*).' 'And what offices have
you to leave?' said the Pope. Proto replied: 'The full office
(*ufficio grande*), and the Madonna's office (*ufficio della Madonna*).' [229] Then the Pope could not keep from laughing, although he was a very grave man.

"Still another man at Padua said that Calfurnio [230] was so
named because he was accustomed to heat (*scaldare*) ovens
(*forni*). And when I one day asked Fedra [231] why it was that on
Good Friday, while the Church offered prayer not only for Christians but even for pagans and Jews, no mention is made of cardinals along with bishops and other prelates,—he answered me that

cardinals were included in that prayer which says: 'Let us pray for heretics and schismatics.'

"And our friend Count Ludovico said that the reason why I censured a lady for using a certain cosmetic that gave a high polish, was because I saw myself in her face, when it was painted, as in a mirror; and being ill favoured I could have no wish to see myself.

"Of this kind was that retort of messer Camillo Paleotto [232] to messer Antonio Porcaro,[233] who, in speaking of a companion who told the priest at confession that he fasted zealously, attended mass and the sacred offices, and did all the good in the world, said: 'The man praises himself instead of owning his sins;' to which messer Camillo replied: 'Nay, he confesses these things because he thinks it a great sin to do them.'

"Do you not remember what a good thing my lord Prefect said the other day? When Giantommaso Galeotto [234] was surprised at a man's asking two hundred ducats for a horse, because, as Giantommaso said, it was not worth a farthing and among other defects was so afraid of weapons that no one could make it come near them,—my lord Prefect (wishing to twit the man with cowardice) said: 'If the horse has this trick of running away from weapons, I wonder that he does not ask a thousand ducats for it.'

63.—"Moreover the very same word is sometimes employed, but in a sense different from the usual one. As when my lord Duke,[2] being about to cross a very rapid river, said to a trumpeter: 'Cross over' (*passa*); and the trumpeter turned cap in hand, and said respectfully: 'After your Lordship' (*passi la Signoria Vostra*).

"Another amusing kind of banter is where a man takes the speaker's words but not his sense. As was the case this year when a German at Rome, meeting one evening with our friend messer Filippo Beroaldo,[235] whose pupil he was, said: *Domine magister, Deus det vobis bonum sero;* [236] and Beroaldo at once replied: *Tibi malum cito.*[237]

"Again, Diego de Chignones [238] being at the Great Captain's [239] table, another Spaniard, who was eating with them, said:

'*Vino*,' meaning to ask for drink; Diego replied: '*Y no lo cono-cistes*,' [240] meaning to taunt the man with being a heretic. [241]

"Another time messer Giacomo Sadoleto [242] asked Bero-aldo, [235] who was saying how much he wished to go to Bologna: 'What is it that so presses you at this time to leave Rome, where there are so many pleasures, to go to Bologna, which is full of turmoil?' Beroaldo replied: 'On three counts I am forced to go to Bologna,' and lifted three fingers of his left hand to enumerate three reasons for his going; when messer Giacomo quickly interrupted him and said: 'These three Counts that make you go to Bologna are: first, Count Ludovico da San Bonifacio; second, Count Ercole Rangone; third, the Count of Pepoli.' Whereupon everyone laughed, because these three Counts had been pupils of Beroaldo, and were fine youths studying at Bologna. [243]

"Now we laugh heartily at this kind of witticism, because it carries with it a response different from the one we are expecting to hear, and in such matters we are naturally amused by our very mistake and laugh to find ourselves cheated of what we expect.

64.—"But the modes of speech and the figures that are graceful in grave and serious talk, are nearly always becoming in pleasantries and games as well. You see that words set in opposition produce much grace, when one contrasting clause is balanced by another. The same method is often very witty. Thus a Genoese, who was very prodigal in spending, was reproached by a very miserly usurer, who said to him: 'When will you ever cease throwing away your riches?' And he replied: 'When you cease stealing other men's.'

"And since, as we have said, the same situations that give opportunity for biting pleasantries may also give opportunity for serious words of praise,—it is a very graceful and becoming method in either case for a man to admit or confirm what another speaker says, but to interpret it in a manner different from what was intended. Thus a village priest was saying mass to his flock not long since, and after he had announced the festivals of the week, he began the general confession in the people's name, saying: 'I have sinned by doing evil, by saying evil, by thinking evil,' and so forth, making mention of all the deadly sins. Whereupon a friend and close familiar of the priest, in order to make sport of him, said to the bystanders: 'Bear witness all of you to what by his own mouth he confesses he has done, for I mean to report him to the bishop.'

"This same method was used by Sallaza dalla Pedrada [244] in complimenting a lady with whom he was speaking. First he praised her for her virtuous qualities and then for still being beautiful; and she replying that she did not deserve such praise because she was already old, he said to her: 'My Lady, your only sign of age is your resemblance to the angels, who were the first and oldest creatures that God ever made.'

65.—"Just as serious sayings are useful for praising, in like fashion we find great utility also in jocose sayings for taunting, and in well arranged metaphors, especially if they take the form of repartee, and if he who replies preserves the same metaphor used by his interlocutor. And of this kind was the answer made to messer Palla degli Strozzi,[245] who being exiled from Florence, sent back a servant on a certain matter of business and said to him rather threateningly: 'Thou wilt tell Cosimo de' Medici from me that the hen is hatching.' [246] The messenger did the errand commanded him, and Cosimo at once replied without hesitation: 'And thou wilt tell messer Palla from me that hens cannot hatch well away from their nests.'

"Again, with a metaphor messer Camillo Porcaro [247] gracefully praised my lord Marcantonio Colonna; [248] who, having heard that messer Camillo had been extolling in an oration certain Italian gentlemen famous as warriors, and had spoken very highly of him among the rest, he expressed his thanks and said: 'Messer Camillo, you have treated your friends as some merchants treat their money when it is found to contain a false ducat; for in order to be rid of it, they put the piece among many good ones, and in this way pass it on. So you, to do me honour (although I am of little worth), have put me in company with such worthy and excellent cavaliers, that by virtue of their merit I shall perhaps pass as good.' Then messer Camillo replied: 'Those who forge ducats are wont to gild them so well that they seem to the eye much finer than the good ones; so, if there were forgers of men as there are of ducats, we should have reason to suspect that you were false, being as you are of far finer and brighter metal than any of the rest.'

"You see that this situation gave opportunity for both kinds of witticism; and so do many others, of which countless instances could be given and especially in serious sayings. Like the one uttered by the Great Captain, who, being seated at table and all the places being already taken, saw that there remained standing two Italian cavaliers who had served very gallantly in the war; and he at once rose himself and caused all the others to rise and make room for these two, saying: 'Allow these cavaliers to sit at their meat, for had it not been for them, the rest of us should now have no meat to eat.' Another time he said to Diego Garzia,[249] who was urging him to retire from a dangerous position where the cannon shot were falling: 'Since God hath put no fear in your heart, do not try to put any in mine.'

"And King Louis,[250] who is to-day king of France, being told soon after his accession that then was the time to punish his enemies who had so grievously wronged him while he was Duke of Orleans, replied that it was not seemly for the King of France to avenge the wrongs of the Duke of Orleans.

66.—"Taunts are also often humorously uttered with a grave air and without exciting laughter. As when Djem Othman,[251] brother to the Grand Turk,[252] being a captive at Rome, said that jousting as we practise it in Italy seemed to him too great a matter for play and too paltry for earnest. And on being told how agile and active King Ferdinand the Younger was in running, leaping, vaulting, and the like,—he said that in his country slaves practised these exercises, while gentlemen studied the liberal arts from boyhood, and prided themselves thereon.

"Almost of the same kind, too, but somewhat more laughable, was what the Archbishop of Florence said to the Alexandrian cardinal:[253] that men have only their goods, their body, and their soul; their goods are put in peril by the lawyers, their body by the physicians, and their soul by the theologians."

Then the Magnifico Giuliano replied:

"To this you might add what Nicoletto [254] said: that we seldom find a lawyer who goes to law, a physician who takes physic, or a theologian who is a good Christian."

ノノノノノノノノノノノノノノノノノノノノノノノノノノノノノノノノノノノノノノノノノノノノノノノ

67.—Messer Bernardo laughed, then went on:

"Of these there are countless instances, uttered by great lords and very weighty men. But we often laugh at similes also, such as the one that our friend Pistoia [255] wrote to Serafino: 'Send back the wallet that looks like you;' because, if you remember rightly, Serafino looked very like a wallet.

"Moreover there are some who delight to liken men and women to horses, dogs, birds, and often to chests, stools, carts, candlesticks; which is sometimes good and sometimes very flat. Therefore in this it is needful to consider time, place, persons, and the other things that we have mentioned so many times."

Then my lord Gaspar Pallavicino said:

"An amusing comparison was the one that our friend my lord Giovanni Gonzaga [256] made between Alexander the Great and his own son Alessandro." [257]

"I do not know it," replied messer Bernardo.

My lord Gaspar said:

"My lord Giovanni was playing with three dice, and as was his wont had lost many ducats and was still losing; and his son my lord Alessandro (who, although only a lad, is as fond of play as the father is) stood looking at him with great attention and seemed very sad. Count Pianella,[258] who was present with many other gentlemen, said: 'You see, my Lord, that my lord Alessandro is little pleased at your losing, and is waiting anxiously for you to win so that he may have some of your winnings. Therefore put him out of his misery, and before you lose everything give him at least a ducat, in order that he too may go and play with his fellows.' Then my lord Giovanni said: 'You are wrong, for Alessandro is not thinking of any such trifle. But as it is written that when he was a boy, Alexander the Great began to weep on hearing that his father Philip [259] had won a great battle and subdued some kingdom, and when he was asked why he wept, he replied that it was because he feared his father would subdue so many lands as to leave nothing for him to subdue; in the same way my son Alessandro is now grieving and about to weep, seeing that I his father am losing, because he fears I am losing so much that I shall leave nothing for him to lose.' "

68.—After some laughter at this, messer Bernardo continued:

"Moreover we must avoid impiety in our witticism, (because from this it is only a step to try to be jocular by blaspheming and to invent new forms of blasphemy); otherwise we seem to seek applause by that for which we deserve not only blame but heavy punishment, which is an abominable thing. And therefore those of us who like to show their pleasantry by little reverence to God, deserve to be chased from the society of every gentleman.

"And they, no less, who are indecent and foul of speech, and show no respect for ladies' presence and seem to have no other pleasure than to make them blush with shame, and who to that end are continually seeking witticisms and *arguzie*. As in Ferrara this year at a banquet attended by many ladies, there were a Florentine and a Sienese, who are usually hostile, as you know. To taunt the Florentine, the Sienese said: 'We have married Siena to the Emperor and have given him Florence for dowry.' He said this because it was reported at the time that the Sienese had given the Emperor a certain sum of money and that he had taken their city under his protection. The Florentine quickly retorted: 'Siena will first be possessed' (he used the Italian word, but with the French meaning); 'then the dowry will be disputed at leisure.' [260] You see that the retort was clever, but, being made in the presence of ladies, it became indecent and unseemly."

69.—Then my lord Gaspar Pallavicino said:

"Women delight to hear nothing else; and you would deprive them of it. Moreover for my part I have found myself blushing with shame at words uttered by women far oftener than by men."

"Of such women I was not speaking," said messer Bernardo; "but of virtuous ladies, who deserve reverence and honour from every gentleman."

My lord Gaspar said:

"We should have to invent a subtle rule by which to distinguish them, for most often those who are seemingly the best, in fact are quite the contrary."

↑↑↑↑↑↑↑↑↑↑↑↑↑↑↑↑↑↑↑↑↑↑↑↑↑↑↑↑↑↑↑↑↑↑↑↑↑↑↑↑↑↑↑↑↑↑↑↑↑↑↑↑↑↑↑↑↑↑↑.

Then messer Bernardo said, laughing:

"If we had not present here my lord Magnifico, who is everywhere accounted the champion of women, I should undertake to answer you; but I am unwilling to do him wrong."

Here my lady Emilia said, also laughing:

"Women have need of no champion against an accuser of so little weight. So leave my lord Gaspar in his perverse opinion, —which arises from his never having found a lady to look at him, rather than from any fault on their part,—and go on with your talk about pleasantries."

70.—Then messer Bernardo said:

"In truth, my Lady, methinks I have told of many situations from which we can derive sharp witticisms, which then have the more grace the more they are accompanied by fine narrative. Still many others might be mentioned. As when, by overstatement or understatement, we say things that outrageously exceed the probable; and of this sort was what Mario da Volterra [261] said of a prelate, that he held himself so great a man that when he entered St. Peter's, he stooped in order not to strike his head against the architrave of the portal. Again, our friend here the Magnifico said that his servant Galpino was so lean and light that in blowing the fire to kindle it one morning, the fellow had been carried by the smoke all the way up the chimney to the very top; but happening to be brought crosswise against one of the openings, he had the good luck not to be blown away with the smoke.

"Another time messer Agostino Bevazzano [262] said that a miser, who had been unwilling to sell his grain while it was dear, afterwards hanged himself in despair from a rafter of his bedroom when he found that the price had greatly fallen; and one of his servants ran in on hearing the noise, saw the miser hanging, and quickly cut the rope and thus rescued him from death. Then, having come to himself, the miser insisted that his servant should pay him for the rope that had been cut.

"Of the same sort also seems to be what Lorenzo de' Medici said to a dull buffoon: 'You would not make me laugh if you tickled me.' And in like fashion he answered another simpleton who had found him abed very late one morning, and who had reproved him for sleeping so late, saying: 'I have already been at the New Market and the Old, then outside the San Gallo gate and around the walls for exercise, and have done a thousand things besides; and you are still asleep?' Then Lorenzo said: 'What I dreamed in one hour is worth more than what you accomplished in four.'

71.—"It is also fine when in a retort we censure something without apparently meaning to censure it. For instance, the Marquess Federico of Mantua,[263] father to our lady Duchess, being at table with many gentlemen, one of them said after eating an entire bowl of stew: 'Pardon me, my lord Marquess;' and so saying he began to gulp down the broth that remained. Then the Marquess said quickly: 'Ask pardon of the swine, for you do me no wrong at all.'

"Again, to censure a tyrant who was falsely reputed to be generous, messer Niccolò Leonico [264] said: 'Think what generosity rules him, for he gives away not his own things only, but other men's as well!'

72.—"Another very pretty form of pleasantry is that which consists in a kind of innuendo, when we say one thing and tacitly imply another. Of course I do not mean another thing of a completely different kind, like calling a dwarf gigantic and a negro white or a very ugly man handsome, for the difference is too obvious,—although even these sometimes cause laughter; but I mean when with stern and serious air we humorously say something in jest which is not our real thought. For instance, when a gentleman told a palpable lie to messer Agostino Foglietta [265] and affirmed it stoutly on seeing that he had much difficulty in believing it, messer Agostino said at last: 'Fair sir, if I may ever hope to receive kindness from you, do me the favour to be content even if I do not believe anything you say.' But as the other repeated, and under oath, that it was the truth, he finally said: 'Since you will have it so, I will believe it for your sake, for indeed I would do even a greater thing than this for you.'

"Don Giovanni di Cardona [266] said something nearly of this sort about a man who wished to leave Rome: 'To my thinking the fellow is ill advised, for he is so great a rascal that by staying on at Rome he might in time become a cardinal.' Of this sort also is what was said by Alfonso Santacroce,[267] who had shortly before suffered some outrage from the Cardinal of Pavia.[268] While strolling with several gentlemen near the place of public execution outside Bologna, he saw a man who had recently been hanged, and turning towards the body with a thoughtful air, he said loud enough for everyone to hear him: 'Happy thou, who hast naught to do with the Cardinal of Pavia.'

73.—"And this sort of pleasantry which is tinged with irony seems very becoming to great men, because it is dignified and sharp, and can be used in jocose as well as in serious matters. Hence many ancients (and those among the most esteemed) have used it, like Cato and Scipio Africanus the Younger; but above all men, the philosopher Socrates is said to have excelled in it. And in our own times King Alfonso I of Aragon,[269] who, being about to eat one morning, took off the many precious rings that he had on his fingers, in order not to wet them in washing his hands, and so gave them to the first person he happened on, almost without looking to see who it was. This servant supposed that the king had taken no notice who received them, and by reason of weightier cares would easily forget them altogether; and in this he was the more confirmed, seeing that the king did not ask for them again; and as he saw days, weeks and months pass without hearing a word about them, he thought he was surely safe. Accordingly, nearly a year after this had happened, he presented himself again one morning as the king was about to eat, and held out his hand to receive the rings; whereupon the king bent close to his ear and said to him: 'Let the first ones suffice thee, because these will do for someone else.' You see how biting, clever and dignified the sally was, and how truly worthy the exalted spirit of an Alexander.

74.—"Similar to this manner (which savours of the ironical) is another method, that of describing an evil thing in polite terms. As the Great Captain said to one of his cavaliers, who, after the battle of Cerignola,[270] when the danger was over, came forward in the richest armour possible to describe, accoutred as if for battle. And then the Great Captain turned to Don Ugo di Cardona [271] and said: 'Have no more fear of storm, for Saint Elmo has appeared;' and with this polite speech he stung the man to the quick, because you know that Saint Elmo [272] always appears to mariners after the tempest and gives token of fair weather; and thus the Great Captain meant that this cavalier's appearance was a token that the danger was quite passed.

"Another time my lord Ottaviano Ubaldini,[273] being at Florence in the company of some citizens of great influence, and the talk being about soldiers, one of them asked him if he knew Antonello da Forli,[274] who had at that time fled from Florentine territory. My lord Ottaviano replied: 'I do not know him, but have always heard him spoken of as a prompt soldier.' Whereupon another Florentine said: 'You see how prompt he is, when he takes his departure without asking leave.'

75.—"Those witticisms also are very clever in which we take from our interlocutor's lips something that he does not mean. And of this kind, methinks, was my lord Duke's reply to the castellan who lost San Leo [275] when this duchy was taken by Pope Alexander and given to Duke Valentino; [276] and it was this: my lord Duke being in Venice at the time I have mentioned, many of his subjects came continually to give him secret news how things were faring in his state; and among the rest came this castellan, who, after having excused himself as best he could, ascribing the blame to mischance, said: 'Have no anxiety, my Lord, because I still have heart to take measures for the recovery of San Leo.' Then my lord Duke replied: 'Trouble yourself no more about the matter, for the mere loss of it was a measure that rendered its recovery possible.'

"There are certain other sayings when a man known to be clever says something that seems to proceed from foolishness. For instance, messer Camillo Paleotto [232] said of someone the other day: 'He was such a fool that he died as soon as he began to grow rich.'

"Of like kind with this is a spicy and keen dissimulation, where a man (discreet, as I have said) pretends not to understand something that he does understand. Like what was said by the Marquess Federico of Mantua, who,—being pestered by a tiresome fellow who complained that some of his neighbours were snaring doves out of his dovecote, and all the while held one of them in his hand, hanging dead just as he had found it

━━━━━━━━━━━━━━━━━━━━━━━━━━━━━━━━━━━━━━━━━━━━━━━━━━

with its foot caught in the snare,—replied that the matter should
be looked to. The fellow repeated the story of his loss not once
only but many times, always displaying the dove that had been
hanged, and saying: 'And what, my Lord, do you think ought
to be done in this case?' At last the Marquess said: 'I think the
dove ought on no account to be buried in church, for having
hanged itself, it must be believed to have committed suicide.' [277]

    "Somewhat of the same fashion was the retort made by
Scipio Nasica [278] to Ennius. Once when Scipio went to Ennius's
house to speak with him and called him down from the street,
one of his maids replied that he was not at home; and Scipio
distinctly heard Ennius himself tell the maid to say he was not
at home, and so went away. Not long afterwards Ennius came
to Scipio's house and likewise called to him from below; whereupon Scipio himself replied in a loud voice that he was not at
home. Then Ennius replied: 'How? Do I not know thy voice?'
Scipio said: 'Thou art too rude. The other day I believed thy
maid when she said thou wert not at home, and now thou wilt
not believe the like from me in person.'

    76.—"It is also a fine thing when a man is struck in the
very same place where he first struck his fellow. As in the case
of messer Alonso Carillo,[279] who, being at the Spanish court and
having committed some youthful peccadilloes of no great importance, was put in prison by the king's order and left there over-
night. The next day he was taken out, and so going to the palace
in the morning, he reached the hall where there were many
cavaliers and ladies. And as they were laughing at his imprisonment, my lady Boadilla [280] said: 'Signor Alonso, your mishap
weighed on me heavily, for all your acquaintance thought the
king would have you hanged.' Then Alonso said quickly: 'My
Lady, I was much afraid of it myself; but then I had hope that
you would ask me to be your husband.' You see how sharp and
clever this was, because in Spain (as in many other countries too)
the custom is that when a man is led to the gallows, his life is
given him if a public courtesan begs him for her husband.

    "In this manner also the painter Raphael replied to two
cardinals with whom he was on familiar terms, and who (to make
him talk) were finding fault in his presence with a picture that

he had painted,—in which St. Peter and St. Paul were represented,—saying that these two figures were too red in the face.
Then Raphael at once said: 'My Lords, be not concerned; because I painted them so with full intention, since we have reason
to believe that St. Peter and St. Paul are as red in Heaven as
you see them here, for shame that their Church should be governed by such men as you.' [281]

77.—"Very keen also are those witticisms that have a certain
latent spice of fun in them. As where a husband was making
great lament and weeping for his wife, who had hanged herself
on a fig-tree, another man approached him and plucking him by
the robe, said: 'Brother, might I as a great favour have a small
branch of that fig-tree to graft upon some tree in my garden?'

"Some other witticisms need an air of patience and are slowly
uttered with a certain gravity. As where a rustic, who was carrying a box on his shoulders, jostled it against Cato, and then said:
'Have a care.' Cato replied: 'Hast thou aught else but that chest
upon thy shoulders?' [282]

"Moreover we laugh when a man has made a blunder, and
to mend it says something of set purpose that seems silly and yet
tends to the object he has in view, and thus keeps himself in
countenance. For instance, in the Florentine Council not long ago
there were (as often happens in these republics) two enemies, and
one of them, who was of the Altoviti family, fell asleep. And
although his adversary, who was of the Alamanni family, was
not speaking and had not spoken, yet to raise a laugh the man
who sat next Altoviti woke him with a touch of the elbow, and
said: 'Do you not hear what So and So says? Make answer, as
the Signors are asking for your opinion.' Thereupon Altoviti rose
to his feet all drowsy as he was, and said without stopping to
think: 'My Lords, I say just the opposite of what Alamanni said.'
Alamanni replied: 'But I said nothing.' 'Then,' said Altoviti at
once, 'the opposite of whatever you may say.'

"Of this kind also was what your Urbino physician, master
Serafino, said to a rustic, who had received a hard blow in the
eye so that it was forced quite out, yet decided to seek aid from
master Serafino. On seeing him, although aware that it was
impossible to cure him, still in order to force money from his

ЈЈЈЈЈЈЈЈЈЈЈЈЈЈЈЈЈЈЈЈЈЈЈЈЈЈЈЈЈЈЈЈЈЈЈЈЈЈЈЈЈЈЈЈЈЈЈЈЈЈЈ

hands (just as the blow had forced the eye from his head), the
doctor readily promised to cure him, and accordingly demanded
money from him every day, affirming that he would begin to
recover his sight within five or six days. The poor rustic gave
what little he had; then, seeing that the affair was progressing
slowly, he began to complain of the physician, and to say that
he felt no benefit at all and saw no more with that eye than as
if he had it not in his head. At last master Serafino, seeing that
he would be able to extort little more from the man, said:
'Brother, you must have patience. You have lost your eye and
there is no longer any help for it; and may God grant that you
do not lose your other eye as well.' On hearing this, the rustic
began to weep and complain loudly, and said: 'Master, you
have ruined me and stolen my money. I will complain to my
lord Duke;' and he made the greatest outcry in the world. Then,
to clear himself, master Serafino said angrily: 'Ah, wretched
traitor! So you would have two eyes, as city-folk and rich men
have? To perdition with you!' and accompanied these words with
such fury that the poor rustic was frightened into silence and
quietly went his way in peace, believing himself to be in the
wrong.

78.—"It is also fine to explain or interpret a thing jocosely.
As when at the court of Spain there appeared one morning in the
palace a cavalier who was very ugly, and his wife who was very
beautiful, both dressed in white damask (*damasco*),—the
queen [283] said to Alonso Carillo: 'What think you of these two,
Alonso?' 'My Lady,' replied Alonso, 'I think she is the *dama*
(lady), and he is the *asco*,' which means monster.

"Another time Rafaello de' Pazzi [284] saw a letter which the
Prior of Messina [285] had written to a lady of his acquaintance, the
superscription of which read, 'This missive is to be delivered to
the author of my woes.' 'Methinks,' said Rafaello, 'this letter
is intended for Paolo Tolosa.' [286] Imagine how the bystanders
laughed, when everyone knew that Paolo Tolosa had lent the
Prior ten thousand ducats, and that he, being a great spendthrift,
found no means to repay them.

"Akin to this is the giving of friendly admonition in the
form of advice, yet covertly. As Cosimo de' Medici did to one of

his friends, who was very rich but of moderate education and who had secured through Cosimo a mission away from Florence. When on setting out the man asked Cosimo what course he thought ought to be taken in order to do well in the mission, Cosimo replied: 'Wear rose-colour,[287] and say little.' Of the same kind was what Count Ludovico said to a man who wished to travel incognito through a certain dangerous place and knew not how to disguise himself; and being asked about it, the count replied: 'Dress like a doctor or some other man of sense.' Again, Gianotto de' Pazzi [288] said to someone who wished to make a jerkin of as varied colours as he could find: 'Imitate the Cardinal of Pavia in word and deed.'

79.—"We laugh also at some things that have no connection. As when someone said the other day to messer Antonio Rizzo [289] about a certain man from Forli: 'You may know he is a fool, for his name is Bartolommeo.' And another: 'You are looking for a Master Stall, and have no horses!' And: 'All the fellow lacks is money and brains.'

"And we laugh at certain other things that seem to have sequence. As recently, when a friend of ours was suspected of having had the renunciation [290] of a benefice forged, upon another priest's falling sick, Antonio Torello [291] said to our friend: 'Why do you delay to send for that notary of yours and see about filching this other benefice?' Likewise at some things that have no sequence. As the other day, when the pope sent for messer Gianluca da Pontremolo and messer Domenico dalla Porta (who are both hunchbacks, as you know),[292] and made them auditors, saying that he wished to set the Wheel right,—messer Latino Giovenale [293] said: 'His Holiness is in error if he thinks to make the Wheel right with two wrongs (*due torti*).'

80.—"We often laugh also when a man admits everything that is said to him and more too, but pretends to take it in a different sense. As when Captain Peralta was brought out to fight a duel with Aldana, and Captain Molart [294] (who was Aldana's second) asked Peralta on his oath if he wore any amulets or charms to keep him from being wounded; Peralta swore that he wore no amulets or charms or relics or objects of devotion in which he had faith. Whereupon, to taunt him with being a heretic,

ィィィィィィィィィィィィィィィィィィィィィィィィィィィィィィィィィィィィィィィィィィィィィィィィィィィィィィィ

Molart said: 'Do not trouble yourself about it, for without your oath I believe you have no faith in Christ himself.' [295]

"Moreover it is a fine thing to use metaphors seasonably in such cases. As when our friend master Marcantonio said to Bottone da Cesena,[296] who was goading him with words: 'Bottone, Bottone, you will one day be the button (*bottone*), and your button-hole will be the halter.' Another time, master Marcantonio having composed a very long comedy in several acts, this same Bottone said to master Marcantonio: 'To play your comedy, all the timber there is in Slavonia will be needed for the setting.' Master Marcantonio replied: 'While for the setting of your tragedy, three sticks will be quite enough.' [297]

81.—"We often use a word in which there is a hidden meaning remote from the one we seem to intend. As was done by my lord Prefect here, on hearing mention of a certain captain who in his time had for the most part been defeated but just then had chanced to win. And the speaker telling that when the captain made his entry into the place in question, he had on a very beautiful crimson velvet doublet, which he always wore after his victories, my lord Prefect said: 'It must be new.'

"Nor is there less laughter when we reply to something that our interlocutor has not said, or pretend to believe he has done something that he has not but ought to have done. As when Andrea Coscia,[298] having gone to visit a gentleman who rudely kept his seat and left his guest to stand, said: 'Since your Lordship commands me, I will sit down to obey you,' and so sat down.[299]

82.—"We laugh also when a man accuses himself of some fault humorously. As when I told my lord Duke's chaplain the other day that my lord Cardinal [300] had a chaplain who said mass faster than he, he answered me: 'It is not possible,' and coming close to my ear, he said: 'You must know, I do not recite a third of the silent prayers.'

"Again, a priest at Milan having died, Biagino Crivello [301] begged his benefice of the Duke,[302] who however was minded to give it to someone else. At last Biagino saw that further argument was of no avail, and said: 'What! After I have had the priest killed, why will you not give me his benefice?'

"It is often amusing also to express desire for those things that cannot be. As the other day, when one of our friends saw all these gentlemen playing at fence while he was lying on his bed, and said: 'Ah, how glad I should be if this too were a fitting exercise for a strong man and a good soldier!'

"Moreover it is an amusing and spicy style of talk, and especially for grave and dignified persons, to reply the opposite of what the person spoken to desires, but slowly and with a little air of doubtful and hesitating deliberation. As was once the case with King Alfonso I of Aragon,[269] who gave a servant weapons, horses and clothes, because the fellow said he had the night before dreamed that his Highness had given him all these things; and again not long afterwards the same servant said he had that night dreamed that the king gave him a goodly sum of gold florins, whereupon the king replied: 'Put no trust in dreams henceforth, because they are not true.' Of like sort also was the pope's reply to the Bishop of Cervia,[303] who said to him in order to sound his purpose: 'Holy Father, it is said all over Rome, and the palace too, that your Holiness is making me governor.' Then the pope replied: 'Let them talk,—thye are only knaves. Have no fear there is any truth in it.'

83.—"Perhaps, my Lords, I might collect still many other occasions that give opportunity for humorous sallies: such as things said with shyness, with admiration, with threats, out of season, with excessive anger; besides these, certain other conditions that provoke laughter when they occur: sometimes a kind of wondering taciturnity, sometimes mere laughter itself when untimely. But methinks I have now said enough, for I believe that pleasantry which takes the form of words does not exceed the limits we have discussed.

"Then, as to that which is shown in action, although it has numberless forms, it still is comprised under a few heads. But in both kinds the main thing is to cheat expectation and reply otherwise than the hearer looks for; and if the pleasantry is to find favour, it must needs be seasoned with deceit or dissimulation or ridicule or censure or simile, or whatever other style a man chooses to employ. And while pleasantries provoke laughter, yet with this laughter they produce divers other effects: for some contain a certain elegance and modest pleasantness, others a hidden or an open sting, others have a taint of grossness, others move to laughter as soon as they are heard, others the more they are thought of, others make us blush as well as laugh, others rouse a little anger. But in all methods we must consider our hearers' state of mind, for to the afflicted jocosity often brings greater affliction, and there are certain maladies that are aggravated the more medicine is employed.

"Hence if the Courtier pays heed to time, persons and his own rank, in his banter and amusing talk, and uses them not too often (for in truth it begets tedium to be harping on this all day, in all kinds of converse, in season and out), he may be called a man of humour; taking care also not to be so sharp and biting as to be thought spiteful, assailing causelessly or with evident rancour: either those who are too powerful, which is imprudent; or those who are too weak, which is cruel; or those who are too wicked, which is useless; or saying things to offend those he would not offend, which is ignorance. Yet there are some who feel bound to speak and assail recklessly whenever they can, let the consequence be what it may. And among these last, some there are who do not scruple to tarnish the honour of a noble lady, for the sake of saying something humorous; which is a very evil thing and worthy the heaviest punishment, for in this regard ladies are to be numbered among the weak, and so ought not to be assailed, since they have no weapons to defend them.

"Besides these things, he who would be agreeable and amusing must have a certain natural aptitude for all kinds of fun, and must adapt his behaviour, gestures and face accordingly; and the graver and more serious and impassive his face is, the more spicy and keen will he make his sallies seem.

84.—"But you, messer Federico, who thought to take your ease under this leafless tree and in my arid talk, I am sure you have repented of it and think you have found your way to the Montefiore Inn.[304] Therefore it will be well for you, like a practised postman, to rise somewhat earlier than usual and take up your journey, in order to escape from a bad inn."

"Nay," replied messer Federico, "I have come to so good an inn that I mean to tarry in it longer than I first intended. So I

ィィィィィィィィィィィィィィィィィィィィィィィィィィィィィィィィィィィィィィィィィィィィィィィィィィ

shall go on taking my ease until you have finished the whole discourse appointed, of which you have left out one part that you
mentioned in the beginning—that is, practical jokes; and it is not
right for you to cheat the company of this. But as you have
taught us many fine things about pleasantries, and have made us
bold to use them by the example of so many singular geniuses,
great men, princes, kings, and popes,—so too in practical jokes I
think you will give us such daring that we shall venture to try
some even upon you."

Then messer Bernardo said, laughing:

"You will not be the first; but perhaps you may not succeed, for I have already endured so many of them that I am on
my guard against everything, like dogs who are afraid of cold
water after once being scalded with hot. However, since you will
have me speak of this also, I think I can despatch it in a few
words.

85.—"It seems to me that practical joking is naught else but
friendly deceit in things that do not offend or that offend only a
little. And just as in pleasantry it arouses laughter to say something contrary to expectation, so in practical joking it arouses
laughter to do something contrary to expectation. And the clev-
erer and more discreet these jokes are, the more they please and
are applauded for he often gives offence who tries to play a practical joke recklessly, and afterwards quarrels and serious enmities arise in consequence.

"But the occasions that give opportunity for practical jokes
are nearly the same as in the case of pleasantries. So not to repeat them, I will merely say that practical jokes are of two kinds,
each of which kinds might be further divided into classes. One
kind is where anyone is cleverly tricked in a fine and amusing
manner; the other is where a net is cast, as it were, and a little
bait is offered, so that the victim himself hastens to be tricked.

"Of the first kind was the joke that two great ladies, whom
I do not wish to name, lately had played upon them by means of
a Spaniard called Castillo." [305]

Then my lady Duchess said:

"And why do you not wish to name them?"

Messer Bernardo replied:

"I would not have them take offence."

My lady Duchess answered, laughing:

"It is not amiss to play jokes now and then even upon great lords. Indeed I have heard of many being played upon Duke Federico, upon King Alfonso of Aragon, upon Queen Isabella of Spain, and upon many other great princes; and they not only did not take offence, but rewarded the perpetrators liberally."

Messer Bernardo replied:

"Not even for the hope of reward will I name those ladies."

"As you please," answered my lady Duchess.

Then messer Bernardo went on to say:

"It is not long since there arrived at the court (of I know whom) a Bergamasque rustic on business for a courtier gentleman; and this rustic was so well attired and elegantly appointed that, although he had been only used to tend cattle and knew no other trade, anyone who did not hear him speak would have taken him for a gallant cavalier. Now, being told that a Spanish follower of Cardinal Borgia [306] had arrived, and that he was called Castillo and was exceedingly clever, a musician, a dancer, a *ballatore*, [307] and the most accomplished Courtier in all Spain,— these two ladies were filled with extreme desire to speak with him, and straightway sent for him. And after receiving him with ceremony, they made him sit down and began to speak to him with the greatest distinction before all the company; and there were few of those present who did not know that the fellow was a Bergamasque cow-herd. So when these ladies were seen entertaining him with so much respect and honouring him so signally, the laughter was very hearty, the more so as the good man spoke his native Bergamasque dialect all the while. [308] But the gentlemen who played the trick had told these ladies in the beginning that he was among other things a great joker, and spoke all languages admirably and especially rustic Lombard. Thus they continually imagined that he was pretending, and they often turned to each other with an air of surprise, and said: 'Listen to this prodigy, how well he counterfeits the language!' In short, the conversation lasted so long that everyone's sides ached from laughing; and he himself could not help giving so many tokens

↑↑↑↑↑↑↑↑↑↑↑↑↑↑↑↑↑↑↑↑↑↑↑↑↑↑↑↑↑↑↑↑↑↑↑↑↑↑↑↑↑↑↑↑↑↑↑↑↑↑↑↑↑↑↑↑↑↑↑↑↑↑↑↑↑

of his gentility that even these ladies were at last convinced, albeit with great difficulty, that he was what he was.

86.—"We meet practical jokes of this kind every day; but among the rest those are amusing which at first excite alarm and turn out well in the end; for even the victim laughs at himself when he sees that his fears were groundless.

"For instance, I was staying at Paglia [309] one night, and in the same inn where I was there happened to be three companions besides myself (two from Pistoia and the other from Prato), who sat down to play after supper, as men often do. They had not been playing long before one of the two Pistoians lost all he had and was left without a farthing, so that he began to lament and to curse and swear roundly; and he retired to sleep blaspheming thus. After gaming awhile, the other two resolved to play a trick upon the one who had gone to bed. So, making sure that he was really asleep, they put out all the lights and covered the fire; then they began to talk loud and to make as much noise as they could, pretending to quarrel over their play, and one of them said: 'You've drawn the under card,' and the other denied it, saying: 'And you have wagered on four of a suit; let us deal again;' [310] and the like, with such an uproar that the sleeper awoke. And perceiving that his friends were playing and talking as if they saw the cards, he rubbed his eyes a little, and seeing no light in the room, he said: 'What the devil do you mean by shouting all night?' Then he lay back again as if to go to sleep.

"His two friends made no reply, but went on as before; whereat the man began to wonder (now that he was more awake) and seeing that there was really no fire or glimmer of any kind, and that still his friends were playing and quarrelling, he said: 'And how can you see the cards without light?' One of the two replied: 'You must have lost your sight along with your money; don't you see with these two candles we have here?' The man who was abed lifted himself upon his arms, and said rather angrily: 'Either I am drunk or blind, or you are lying.' The two got up and groped their way to the bed, laughing and pretending to think that he was making sport of them; and still he answered: 'I say I do not see you.' Finally the two began to feign great surprise, and one said to the other: 'Alas, methinks he speaks the

truth. Hand me that candle, and let us see if perchance there is
something wrong with his sight.' Then the poor fellow took it for
certain that he had become blind, and weeping bitterly he said:
'Oh my brothers, I am blind;' and he at once began to call on
Our Lady of Loreto, and to implore her to pardon the blasphemies and maledictions that he had heaped upon her for the
loss of his money. His two companions kept comforting him, and
said: 'It can't be that you do not see us; 'tis some fancy you've got
into your head.' 'Alas,' replied the other, 'this is no fancy, for I
see no more than as if I had never had any eyes in my head.'
'Yet your sight is clear,' replied the two, and one said to the other:
'See how well he opens his eyes! And how bright they are! Who
could believe that he doesn't see?' The unhappy man wept more
loudly all the while, and begged mercy of God.

"At last they said to him: 'Make a vow to go in penance to
Our Lady of Loreto,[311] barefoot and naked, for this is the best
remedy that can be found; and meanwhile we will go to Acua-
pendente [312] and those other places hard by to see some doctor,
nor will we fail to do everything we can for you.' Then the poor
fellow quickly knelt by his bed, and with endless tears and bitter
penitence for his blasphemy he made a solemn vow to go naked
to Our Lady of Loreto, and to offer her a pair of silver eyes, and
to eat no flesh on Wednesday or eggs on Friday, and to fast on
bread and water every Saturday in honour of Our Lady, if she
would grant him the mercy of restoring his sight. His two companions went into another room, struck a light, and laughing
their very loudest, came back to the unhappy man, who was relieved of his great anguish, as you may imagine, but was so
stunned by the terror that he had passed through, that he could
neither laugh nor even speak; and his two companions did nothing but tease him, saying that he must fulfil all his vows, because
he had obtained the mercy which he sought.

87.—"Of the other kind of practical joke, where a man deceives himself, I shall give no other example than the one that
was played on me not very long ago.

"During the last carnival, my friend Monsignor of San
Pietro ad Vincula [313] (who knows how fond I am of playing tricks
on the friars when I am masked, and who had carefully arranged

ʡʡʡʡʡʡʡʡʡʡʡʡʡʡʡʡʡʡʡʡʡʡʡʡʡʡʡʡʡʡʡʡʡʡʡʡʡʡʡʡʡʡʡʡʡʡʡʡʡʡʡ

beforehand what he meant to do) came one day with Monsignor of Aragon [315] and a few other cardinals, to certain windows in the *Banchi*,[315] ostensibly for the purpose of seeing the maskers pass, as the custom is at Rome. I came along in my mask, and seeing a friar (somewhat apart) who had a little air of hesitation, I thought I had found my chance and rushed upon him like a hungry falcon on its prey. And first having asked him who he was and received his answer, I pretended to know him, and with many words began to make him think that the chief constable was out in search of him (because of certain evil reports that had been received against him), and to urge him to go with me to the Chancery,[316] where I would put him in safety. Frightened and trembling from head to foot, the friar seemed not to know what to do and said he feared being taken if he went far from San Celso.[317] I said so much to encourage him, however, that he mounted my crupper; and then I thought I had fully succeeded in my scheme. So I at once began to make for the *Banchi*, my horse frisking and kicking the while. Now imagine what a fine sight a friar made on a masker's crupper, with cloak flying and head tossed to and fro, and looking all the time as if he were about to fall.

"At this fine spectacle those gentlemen began to throw eggs on us from the windows, as did all the *Banchi* people and everyone who was there,—so that hail never fell from heaven with greater violence than from those windows fell the eggs, most of which came on me. Being masked as I was, I did not care and thought that all the laughter was for the friar and not for me; and so I went up and down the *Banchi* several times with this fury always at my back, although the friar with tears in his eyes begged me to let him dismount and not to shame his cloth in this way. Then the knave had eggs given him on the sly by some lackeys stationed there for the purpose, and pretending to hold me fast to keep from falling, he broke them over my breast, often over my head, and sometimes on my very brow, until I was completely bedaubed. Finally, when everyone was weary both of laughing and of throwing eggs, he jumped off my crupper, and pushing back his cowl showed me his long hair, and said: 'Messer Bernardo, I am one of the grooms at San Pietro ad Vincula, and it is I who take care of your little mule.'

"I know not which was then greatest, my grief, my anger, or my shame. However, as the least of evils, I set out fast for home, and dared not make an appearance the next morning; but the laughter raised by this trick lasted not only the next day, but nearly until now."

88.—And so, after they had again laughed awhile at the story, messer Bernardo continued:

"There is another very amusing kind of practical joke, which gives opportunity for pleasantry as well, when we pretend to think that a man wishes to do something which in fact he does not wish to do. For instance, one evening after supper, when I was on the bridge at Lyons and jesting with Cesare Beccadello[318] as we walked along, we began to seize each other by the arm as if we were bent on wrestling, for by chance no one else appeared on the bridge at the time. While we were standing thus, two Frenchmen came up, and on seeing our dispute they asked what the matter was, and stopped to try to separate us, thinking that we were quarrelling in earnest. Then I said quickly: 'Help me, Sirs, for this poor gentleman loses his reason at certain changes of the moon, and you see he is now trying to throw himself off the bridge into the water.' Thereupon these two men ran, and with my aid seized Cesare and held him very tight; and he, telling me all the while that I was mad, tried harder to free himself from their hands, and they held him all the tighter. Thus the passers-by gathered to look at the disturbance, and everyone ran up. And the more poor Cesare struck out with his hands and feet (for he was now beginning to grow angry), the more people arrived; and from the great effort that he made, they fully believed he was trying to jump into the river, and on that account held him the tighter. So that a great crowd of men carried him bodily to the inn, all dishevelled, capless, pale with anger and shame; for nothing he said availed him, partly because the Frenchmen did not understand him, and also partly because, as I walked along leading them to the inn, I kept lamenting the poor man's misfortune in being thus stricken mad.

89.—"Now, as we have said, it would be possible to talk at length about practical jokes; but suffice it to repeat that the occa-

sions which give opportunity for them are the same as in the case
of pleasantries. Moreover we have an infinity of examples because
we see them every day. Among others there are many amusing ones
in the *Novelle* of Boccaccio, like those which Bruno and Buffal-
macco played upon their friend Calandrino and upon master Si-
mone,[319] and many others played by women, that are truly clever
and fine.

"I remember having known in my time many other amusing
men of this sort, and among others a certain Sicilian student at
Padua, called Ponzio;[320] who once saw a peasant with a pair of fat
capons. And pretending that he wished to buy them, he struck a
bargain, and told the fellow to come home with him and get some
breakfast besides the price agreed on. So he led the peasant to a
place where there was a bell-tower standing apart from its church [321]
so that one could walk around it; and just opposite one of the four
sides of the tower was the end of a little lane. Here Ponzio, who
had already settled what he meant to do, said to the peasant: 'I have
wagered these capons with one of my friends, who says that this
tower measures quite forty feet around, while I say it does not. And
just before I found you, I had bought this twine to measure it.
Now, before we go home I wish to find out which of the two has
won.' And so saying, he drew the twine from his sleeve, gave one
end of it to the peasant, and said: 'Hand them here.' Thereupon he
took the capons, and holding the other end of the twine as if he
were going to measure, he started to walk around the tower, first
making the peasant stay and hold the twine against that side of it
which was farthest from the one that looked up the little lane.
When he reached this other side, he stuck a nail into the wall, tied
the twine to it, and leaving the man there he quietly went off with
the capons up the little lane. The peasant stood still a long time
waiting for Ponzio to finish the measurement; at last,—after he
had several times said: 'What are you doing there so long?'—he
went to look, and found that it was not Ponzio who was holding the
twine, but a nail stuck in the wall, and that this was all the pay left
him for the capons. Ponzio played numberless tricks of this sort.

"There have also been many other men who were amusing in
like manner, such as Gonnella, Meliolo in his day,[322] and at the
present time our friends Fra Mariano [60] and Fra Serafino [61] here,

and many whom you all know. And doubtless this method is well enough for men who have no other business, but I think the Courtier's practical jokes ought to be somewhat farther removed from scurrility. Care must be taken also not to let practical joking degenerate into knavery, as we see in the case of many rogues, who go through the world with sundry wiles to get money, now pretending one thing and now another. Moreover the Courtier's tricks must not be too rude; and above all let him pay respect and reverence to women in this as in all other things, and especially where their honour may be touched."

90.—Then my lord Gaspar said:

"Indeed, messer Bernardo, you are too partial towards women. And why would you have men pay more respect to women than women to men? Should not our honour be as dear to us, forsooth, as theirs to them? Do you think that women ought to taunt men with words and nonsense without the least restraint in anything, and that men should quietly endure it and thank them into the bargain?"

Then messer Bernardo replied:

"I do not say that in their pleasantries and practical jokes women ought not to use towards men the same respect which we have before described; but I do say they may taunt men with unchastity more freely than men may taunt them. And this is because we have made unto ourselves a law, whereby free living is in us neither vice nor fault nor disgrace, while in women it is such utter infamy and shame that she of whom evil is once spoken is disgraced forever, whether the imputation [323] cast upon her be false or true. Wherefore, since speaking of women's honour brings such risk of doing them grievous harm, I say we ought to attack them in some other way, and to abstain from this; because to strike too hard with our pleasantries and practical jokes, is to exceed the bounds that we have before said are befitting a gentleman."

91.—As messer Bernardo paused a little here, my lord Ottaviano Fregoso said, laughing:

"My lord Gaspar might answer you that this law you refer to, which we have made unto ourselves, is perhaps not so unreasonable as it seems to you. For since women were very imperfect creatures and of little or no worth in comparison with men, and since of

ɟɟɟɟɟɟɟɟɟɟɟɟɟɟɟɟɟɟɟɟɟɟɟɟɟɟɟɟɟɟɟɟɟɟɟɟɟɟɟɟɟɟɟɟɟɟɟɟɟɟɟɟɟ

themselves they were not capable of performing any worthy act,—it was necessary by fear of shame and infamy to lay upon them a restraint that might impart some quality of goodness to them almost against their will. And chastity seemed more needful for them than any other quality, in order to have certainty as to our offspring; hence it was necessary to use every possible skill, art and way to make women chaste, and almost to permit them to be of little worth in all things else and to do constantly the reverse of what they ought. Therefore, since they are allowed to commit all other faults without blame, if we taunt them with those defects which (as we have said) are all permitted to them and therefore not incongruous in them, and of which they take no heed,—we shall never arouse laughter; for you said awhile ago that laughter is aroused by certain things that are incongruous."

92.—Then my lady Duchess said:

"You speak thus of women, my lord Ottaviano, and then you complain that they love you not."

"I do not complain of this," replied my lord Ottaviano, "but rather thank them in that they do not, by loving me, force me to love them. Nor am I speaking my own mind, but saying that my lord Gaspar might use these arguments."

Messer Bernardo said:

"Verily it would be a great gain to women if they could conciliate two such great enemies of theirs as you and my lord Gaspar are."

"I am not their enemy," replied my lord Gaspar, "but you are indeed an enemy of men; for if you would not have women taunted as to their honour, you ought also to impose on them a law that they shall not taunt men for that which is as shameful to us as unchastity is to women. And why was not Alonso Carillo's retort to my lady Boadilla (about hoping to escape with his life by being asked to become her husband) as seemly in him, as it was for her to say that all who knew him thought the king was about to have him hanged? And why was it not as allowable for Riciardo Minutoli to deceive Filippello's wife and get her to go to that resort, as for Beatrice to make her husband Egano [324] get out of bed and be cudgelled by Anichino, after she had long been with the latter? And for that other woman to tie a string to her toe and make her husband believe that she was someone else?—since you say that these women's pranks in Giovanni Boccaccio are so clever and fine."

93.—Then messer Bernardo said, laughing:

"My Lords, as my task was simply to discuss pleasantries, I do not mean to go outside my subject. And I think I have already told why it does not seem to me befitting to attack women in their honour either by word or deed, and have imposed on them as well a rule that they shall not touch men in a tender spot.

"As for the pranks and sallies cited by you, my lord Gaspar, I grant that although what Alonso said to my lady Boadilla may touch a little on her chastity, it still does not displease me, because it is very remote, and is so veiled that it may be taken innocently, and the speaker might disguise his meaning and declare he had not meant it. He said another that was to my thinking very unseemly. And it was this: as the queen [325] was passing my lady Boadilla's house, [280] Alonso saw the door all blackened with pictures of those indecencies that are painted about inns in such variety; and turning to the Countess of Castagneta, [326] he said: 'There, my Lady, are the heads of the game that my lady Boadilla slaps in hunting every day.' You see that while the metaphor is clever and aptly borrowed from hunters (who take pride in having many heads of beasts fastened on their doors), yet it is scurrilous and disgraceful. Besides which, it was not an answer to anything; for it is far less rude to say a thing by way of retort, because then it seems to have been provoked and needs must be impromptu.

"Returning, however, to the subject of tricks played by women, I do not say they do well to deceive their husbands, but I say that some of those deceptions (which Giovanni Boccaccio recounts of women) are fine and very clever, and especially those which you yourself told. But in my opinion the trick played by Riciardo Minutoli goes too far, and is much more heartless than the one played by Beatrice; because Riciardo Minutoli did much greater wrong to Filippello's wife than Beatrice did to her husband Egano, for by his deception Riciardo forced the woman's will and made her do with herself something that she did not wish to do, while Beatrice deceived her husband in order that she might do with herself something that pleased her."

94.—Then my lord Gaspar said:

"Beatrice can be excused on no other plea than that of love, which ought to be allowed in the case of men as well as in that of women."

Then messer Bernardo replied:

"No doubt the passion of love affords great excuse for every fault. But for my part I think that a gentleman of worth, who is in love, ought to be sincere and truthful in this as in all things else; and if it be true that to betray even an enemy is such a vile act and abominable crime, consider how much more heinous the offence ought to be deemed when it is committed against one whom we love.

"Moreover, I think that every gentle lover endures so many toils, so many vigils, braves so many perils, sheds so many tears, employs so many means and ways to please the lady of his love,—not chiefly in order to possess her person, but to capture the fortress of her mind, and to shatter those hardest diamonds, to melt that coldest ice, that often are in the tender breast of woman. This, I think, is the true and sound pleasure and the purposed goal of every noble heart. For myself, were I in love, I certainly should prefer to be assured that she whom I served returned my love from her heart and had given me her mind,—without ever having any other satisfaction from her,—than to enjoy her to the full against her will; for in such case I should deem myself the master of a lifeless body. Hence they who pursue their desires by means of such trickery, which might perhaps be called treachery rather than trickery, do injury to others; nor have they yet that bliss which is to be desired in love, if they possess the body without the will.

"The same I say of certain others who use enchantments in their love, charms and sometimes force, sometimes sleeping potions and such like things. Be assured, too, that gifts much lessen the pleasures of love; for a man may suspect that he is not loved and that his lady makes a show of loving him in order to profit by it. Hence you see that great ladies' love is prized because it could hardly spring from other source than real and true affection, nor is it credible that a great lady should ever pretend to love one of her inferiors unless she loves him truly."

95.—Then my lord Gaspar replied:

ııııııııııııııııııııııııııııııııııııııııııııııııııııı

"I do not deny that the purpose, toils and dangers of lovers ought to have their aim directed chiefly towards the conquest of the mind rather than of the body of their beloved. But I say that these deceits, which you call treachery in men and trickery in women, are excellent means of attaining this aim, for whoever possesses a woman's person is master of her mind as well. And if you remember rightly, Filippello's wife, after much lament over the deceit practised on her by Riciardo, discovered how much more delicious than her husband's were the kisses of her lover, and her coldness to Riciardo changed to sweet affection, so that from that day forth she loved him most tenderly. Thus it came about that what his frequent fond visits, his gifts and countless other tokens shown unceasingly, could not effect, a taste of his embraces soon accomplished. You now see that this same trickery, or treachery as you would call it, was a good way to capture the fortress of her mind."

Then messer Bernardo said:

"You advance a very false premise, for if women always surrendered their mind to the man who possessed their person, no wife would be found who did not love her husband more than every other person in the world; the contrary of which we find to be the case. But Giovanni Boccaccio was very unjustly hostile to women, as you are also." [327]

96.—My lord Gaspar replied:

"I am not at all hostile to them; but there are very few men of worth who as a rule make any account of women whatever, although for their own purposes they sometimes pretend the contrary."

Then messer Bernardo replied:

"You wrong not women only, but also all men who hold them in respect. However, as I said, I do not wish for the present to go outside my original subject of practical joking, and enter upon so difficult an enterprise as would be the defence of women against you, who are a most redoubtable warrior. So I will make an end of this talk of mine, which has perhaps been far longer than was necessary, and certainly less amusing than you expected. And since I see the ladies sit so quiet, enduring your insults thus patiently as they do, I shall henceforth regard a part of what my lord Ottaviano said as true, namely, that they care not what other evil is said of them, provided they be not taunted with lack of chastity."

Then at a signal from my lady Duchess, many of the ladies rose to their feet, and all ran laughing towards my lord Gaspar, as if to shower blows upon him and treat him as the bacchants treated Orpheus,[328]—meanwhile saying:

"You shall see now whether we care if evil be said of us."

97.—Thus, partly because of the laughter and partly because everyone rose to his feet, the drowsiness that had seized the eyes and mind of some, seemed to flee away; but my lord Gaspar began to say:

"You see that being in the wrong, they would fain use force and thus end the discussion by giving us a Braccesque leave, as the saying is."[329]

Then my lady Emilia replied:

"Nay, that shall not help you; for when you saw messer Bernardo wearied by his long talk, you began to say all manner of evil about women, thinking to have no antagonist. But we shall put a fresh champion in the field to fight you, to the end that your offence may not go long unpunished."

So, turning to the Magnifico Giuliano, who had thus far spoken little, she said:

"You are accounted the defender of women's honour; wherefore the time has come for you to show that you have not required this title falsely. And if hitherto you have ever found profit in your office, you ought now to consider that by putting down so bitter an enemy of ours, you will render all women still more beholden to you, so much so that although nothing else be ever done but requite you, yet the obligation must always stand and can never fully be requited."

98.—Then the Magnifico Giuliano replied:

"My Lady, methinks you do your enemy much honour, and your defender very little; for so far my lord Gaspar has certainly said nothing against women that messer Bernardo has not most consummately answered. And I believe we all know that it is fitting for the Courtier to show women the greatest reverence, and that he who is discreet and courteous must never taunt them with lack of chastity, either in jest or in earnest. Therefore, to discuss such obvious truth as this, is almost to cast doubt upon that which is undoubted. But indeed I think my lord Ottaviano went rather too far when he said that women are very imperfect creatures, incapable of any worthy action, and possessed of little or no dignity in comparison with men. And as trust is often placed in those who have great authority, even when they say what is not the exact truth and also when they speak in jest,—my lord Gaspar suffered himself to be led by my lord Ottaviano's words to say that wise men make no account of women whatever, which is most false. On the contrary, I have known very few men of merit who did not love and honour women,—whose worth (and so whose dignity) I regard as in no wise inferior to men's.

"Yet if this were to be the subject of dispute, women's cause would be at serious disadvantage; because these gentlemen have described a Courtier so excellent and of such heavenly accomplishments, that whoso undertook to consider him as they have pictured him, would imagine that women's merits could not attain that pitch. But if the contest were to be fair, we should first need to have someone as clever and eloquent as Count Ludovico and messer Federico are, to describe a Court Lady with all the perfections proper to woman, just as they have described the Courtier with the perfections proper to man. And then, if he who defended their cause were of only moderate cleverness and eloquence, I think that with truth for ally, he would clearly prove that women are as full of virtue as men are."

"Nay," replied my lady Emilia, "far more so; and in proof of this, you see that virtue (*la virtù*) is feminine. and vice (*il vizio*) is masculine." [330]

99.—Then my lord Gaspar laughed, and turning to messer Niccolò Frisio, said:

"What think you of this, Frisio?"

Frisio replied:

"I am sorry for my lord Magnifico, who has been beguiled by my lady Emilia's promises and soft words into the error of saying that which I blush for on his behalf."

My lady Emilia replied, still laughing:

"You will be ashamed rather of yourself, when you see my

lord Gaspar confuted, confessing his own and your error, and imploring a pardon that we shall refuse to grant him."

Then my lady Duchess said:

"As the hour is very late, let the whole matter be postponed until to-morrow; especially since it seems to me wise to follow my lord Magnifico's counsel, which is: that before we enter upon this controversy, a Court Lady be described with all her perfections, just as these gentlemen have described the perfect Courtier."

Then my lady Emilia said:

"My Lady, God forbid that we chance to entrust this task to any fellow-conspirator of my lord Gaspar, who will describe us a Court Lady that can do naught but cook and spin."

Frisio said:

"But this is her proper calling."

Then my lady Emilia said:

"I am willing to trust my lord Magnifico, who will (with the cleverness and good sense which I know are his) imagine the highest perfection that can be desired in woman, and will set it forth in beautiful language too; and then we shall have something to offer against my lord Gaspar's false aspersions."

100.—"My Lady," replied the Magnifico, "I am not sure how well advised you are to impose on me an enterprise of such weight that I really do not feel myself sufficient for it. Nor am I like the Count and messer Federico, who have with their eloquence described a Courtier that never was and perhaps never can be. Still, if it pleases you to have me bear this burden, at least let it be upon the same conditions as in the case of these other gentlemen, namely: that everyone may contradict me when he pleases; for I shall take it, not as contradiction, but as aid; and perhaps by the correction of my mistakes we shall discover that perfection of the Court Lady which we seek."

"I hope," replied my lady Duchess, "that your talk will be of such sort that little may be found in it to contradict. So give your whole mind to it, and describe for us such a woman that these adversaries of ours shall be ashamed to say she is not equal in worth to the Courtier; of whom it will be well for messer Federico to say no more, since the Courtier has been only too well adorned by him, especially as there is now need to give him a paragon in woman."

Then messer Federico said:

"My Lady, little or nothing is now left for me to tell about the Courtier; and what I thought of saying has been driven from my mind by messer Bernardo's pleasantries."

"If that be so," said my lady Duchess, "let us come together again early to-morrow, and we shall have time to attend to both matters."

Thereupon all rose to their feet, and having reverently taken leave of my lady Duchess, everyone went to his own room.

## The Third Book

### TO MESSER ALFONSO ARIOSTO

E READ THAT PYTHAGORAS VERY IN-geniously and cleverly discovered the measure of Hercules's body; and the way was this: it being known that the space where the Olympic games were cele-brated every five years, before the temple of Olympian Jove near Elis, in Achaia,[331] had been measured by Hercules, and a stadium made six hundred and twenty-five times the length of his own foot; and that the other stadia which were afterwards established throughout Greece by later generations, were likewise of the length of six hundred and twenty-five feet, and yet were somewhat shorter than the first one: by this proportion Pythagoras easily reckoned how much larger Hercules's foot was than other human feet; and thus, knowing the measure of the foot, from this he argued that the whole body of Hercules was larger than other men's in the same proportion that the first stadium bore to the other stadia.

So you, my dear messer Alfonso, by the same reasoning may clearly see, from this small part of the whole body, how superior the court of Urbino was to all others in Italy, considering how much the games that were devised for the refreshment of minds wearied by the most arduous labours, were superior to those that were practised in the other courts of Italy. And if these were of such sort, think what were the other worthy pursuits to which our minds were bent and wholly given; and of this I confidently make bold to speak with hope of being believed; for I am not praising things so ancient that I might be allowed to invent, but can prove what I affirm by the testimony of many men worthy of faith, who are still living and personally saw and knew the life and behaviour

ʃʃʃʃʃʃʃʃʃʃʃʃʃʃʃʃʃʃʃʃʃʃʃʃʃʃʃʃʃʃʃʃʃʃʃʃʃʃʃʃʃʃʃʃʃʃʃʃʃʃʃʃʃʃʃ

that one time flourished in that court: and I hold myself bound, as far as I can, to strive with every effort to rescue this bright memory from mortal oblivion, and by my writing to make it live in the hearts of posterity.

Wherefore perhaps in the future there will not be lacking some to envy our century for this also; since no one reads the wonderful exploits of the ancients, who in his mind does not conceive a somewhat higher opinion of those that are written of than the books themselves seem able to express, however divinely they be written. Even so we desire that all to whose hands this work of ours shall come (if indeed it shall ever be worthy of such favour as to deserve being seen by noble cavaliers and virtuous ladies) may assume and take for certain that the court of Urbino was far more excellent, and adorned by men of singular worth, that we can express in writing; and if we had as great eloquence as they had merit, we should have no need of other proof to make our words believed by those who saw it not.

2.—Now the company being assembled the next day at the accustomed hour and place, and seated in silence, everyone turned his eyes to messer Federico and to the Magnifico Giuliano, waiting to see which of them would begin the discussion. Wherefore my lady Duchess, having been silent awhile, said:

"My lord Magnifico, everyone desires to see this lady of yours well adorned; and if you do not display her to us in such fashion that all her beauties may be seen, we shall think that you are jealous of her."

The Magnifico replied:

"My Lady, if I deemed her beautiful, I should display her all unadorned and in the same fashion wherein Paris chose to view the three goddesses; [332] but if these ladies here, who well know how, do not aid me to deck her forth, I fear that not only my lord Gaspar and Frisio, but all these other gentlemen, will have just cause to say ill of her. So, while still she stands in some repute for beauty, perhaps it will be better to keep her hidden, and to see what messer Federico has left to say about the Courtier, which without doubt is far more beautiful than my Lady can be."

"What I had in mind," replied messer Federico, "is not so necessary to the Courtier that it may not be omitted without any harm; nay, it is rather different matter from that which has thus far been discussed."

"And what is it, then?" said my lady Duchess.

Messer Federico replied:

"I had thought of explaining, as far as I could, the origin of these companies and orders of knighthood established by great princes under different ensigns: as that of Saint Michael in the House of France; [333] that of the Garter, which bears the name of Saint George, in the House of England; [334] the Golden Fleece in that of Burgundy: [335] and in what manner these dignities are bestowed, and how they who deserve them are deprived thereof; whence they arose, who were the founders of them, and to what end they were established: for even in great courts these knights are always honoured.

"I thought too, if I had time enough, to speak not only of the diversity of customs that are in use at the courts of Christian princes in serving them, in merry-making and in appearing at public shows, but also to say something of the Grand Turk's [252] court, and much more particularly of the court of the Sophi king of Persia. [336] For having heard, from merchants who have been long in that country, that the noblemen there are of great worth and gentle behaviour, and that in their intercourse with one another, in their service to ladies and in all their actions, they practise much courtesy and much discretion, and on occasion much magnificence, much liberality and elegance in their weapons, games and festivals, —I was glad to learn what ways they most prize in these things, and in what their pomp and finery of dress and arms consist; in what they differ from us, and in what they resemble us; what manner of amusement their ladies practise and with what modesty show favour to lovers.

"But indeed it is not fitting to enter upon this discussion now, especially as there is something else to say, and far more to our purpose than this."

3.—"Nay," said my lord Gaspar, "both this and many other things are to the purpose than to describe this Court Lady; seeing that the same rules that are set the Courtier, serve also for the Lady; for she, like the Courtier, ought to have regard to time and place, and (as far as her stupidity permits) to follow all those

*1111111111111111111111111111111111111111111111111111*

other ways that have been so much discussed. And therefore, in place of this, perhaps it would not have been amiss to teach some of the details that pertain to the service of the Prince's person, for it is well befitting the Courtier to know them and to show grace in practising them; or indeed to tell of the method to be pursued in bodily exercises, such as riding, handling weapons and wrestling, and to tell wherein consists the difficulty of these accomplishments."

Then my lady Duchess said, laughing:

"Princes do not employ the personal service of so admirable a Courtier as this: and as for bodily exercises and physical strength and agility, we will leave to our friend messer Pietro Monte the duty of teaching them, when he shall deem the season more convenient; for now the Magnifico must speak of nothing but this Lady, of whom, methinks, you are already beginning to be afraid, and so would make us wander from our subject."

Frisio replied:

"Surely it is irrelevant and little to the purpose to speak of women now, especially when more remains to be said about the Courtier, for we ought not to mix one thing with another."

"You are much in error," replied messer Cesare Gonzaga; "for just as no court, however great it be, can have in it adornment or splendour or gaiety, without ladies, nor can any Courtier be graceful or pleasing or brave, or perform any gallant feat of chivalry, unless moved by the society and by the love and pleasure of ladies: so, too, discussion about the Courtier is always very imperfect, unless by taking part therein the ladies add their touch of that grace wherewith they perfect Courtiership and adorn it."

My lord Ottaviano laughed, and said:

"There you have a taste of that bait which makes men fools."

4.—Then my lord Magnifico, turning to my lady Duchess, said:

"Since so it pleases you, my Lady, I will say what occurs to me, but with very great fear of not satisfying. And in sooth it would be a far lighter task to describe a lady worthy to be queen of the world, than a perfect Court Lady: because of the latter I know not where to take my model; while for the queen I should not need to go far, and it would be enough for me to think of the divine accomplishments of a lady whom I know,[337] and, lost in contemplation, to bend all my thoughts to express clearly in words that which many see with their eyes; and if I could do no more, by merely naming her I should have performed my task."

Then my lady Duchess said:

"Do not wander from your subject, my lord Magnifico, but hold to the order given you and describe the Court Lady, to the end that so noble a Lady as this may have someone competent to serve her worthily."

The Magnifico continued:

"Then, my Lady, to show that your commands have power to induce me to essay even that which I know not how to do, I will speak of this excellent Lady as I would have her; and when I have fashioned her to my liking, not being able then to have another such, like Pygmalion I will take her for my own.[338]

"And although my lord Gaspar has said that the same rules which are set the Courtier, serve also for the Lady, I am of another mind; for while some qualities are common to both and as necessary to man as to woman, there are nevertheless some others that befit woman more than man, and some are befitting man to which she ought to be wholly a stranger. The same I say of bodily exercises; but above all, methinks that in her ways, manners, words, gestures and bearing, a woman ought to be very unlike a man; for just as it befits him to show a certain stout and sturdy manliness, so it is becoming in a woman to have a soft and dainty tenderness with an air of womanly sweetness in her every movement, which, in her going or staying or saying what you will, shall always make her seem the woman, without any likeness of a man.

"Now, if this precept be added to the rules that these gentlemen have taught the Courtier, I certainly think she ought to be able to profit by many of them, and to adorn herself with admirable accomplishments, as my lord Gaspar says. For I believe that many faculties of the mind are as necessary to woman as to man; likewise gentle birth, to avoid affectation, to be naturally graceful in all her doings, to be mannerly, clever, prudent, not arrogant, not envious, not slanderous, not vain, not quarrelsome, not silly, to know how to win and keep the favour of her mistress and of all others, to practise well and gracefully the exercises that befit women. I am quite of the opinion, too, that beauty is more necessary to her than to the Courtier, for in truth that woman lacks much who lacks beauty. Then, too, she ought to be more circumspect and take greater care not to give occasion for evil being said of her, and so to act that she may not only escape a stain of guilt but even of suspicion, for a woman has not so many ways of defending herself against false imputations as has a man.

"But as Count Ludovico has explained very minutely the chief profession of the Courtier, and has insisted it be that of arms, methinks it is also fitting to tell what in my judgment is that of the Court Lady: and when I have done this, I shall think myself quit of the greater part of my duty.

5.—"Laying aside, then, those faculties of the mind that she ought to have in common with the Courtier (such as prudence, magnanimity, continence, and many others), and likewise those qualities that befit all women (such as kindness, discretion, ability to manage her husband's property and her house and children if she be married, and all those capacities that are requisite in a good housewife), I say that in a lady who lives at court methinks above all else a certain pleasant affability is befitting, whereby she may be able to entertain politely every sort of man with agreeable and seemly converse, suited to the time and place, and to the rank of the person with whom she may speak, uniting with calm and modest manners, and with that seemliness which should ever dispose all her actions, a quick vivacity of spirit whereby she may show herself alien to all indelicacy; but with such a kindly manner as shall make us think of her no less chaste, prudent and benign, than agreeable, witty and discreet: and so she must preserve a certain mean (difficult and composed almost of contraries), and must barely touch certain limits but not pass them.

"Thus, in her wish to be thought good and pure, the Lady ought not to be so coy and seem so to abhor company and talk that are a little free, as to take her leave as soon as she finds herself therein; for it might easily be thought that she was pretending to be thus austere in order to hide something about herself which she feared others might come to know; and such prudish manners are always odious. Nor ought she, on the other hand, for the sake of showing herself free and agreeable, to utter unseemly words or practise a certain wild and unbridled familiarity and ways likely to make that believed of her which perhaps is not true; but when she is present at such talk, she ought to listen with a little blush and shame.

"Likewise she ought to avoid an error into which I have seen many women fall, which is that of saying and of willingly listening to evil about other women. For those women who, on hearing the unseemly ways of other women described, grow angry thereat and seem to disbelieve it and to regard it almost monstrous that a woman should be immodest,—they, by accounting the offence so heinous, give reason to think that they do not commit it. But those who go about continually prying into other women's intrigues, and narrate them so minutely and with such zest, seem to be envious of them and to wish that everyone may know it, to the end that like matters may not be reckoned as a fault in their own case; and thus they fall into certain laughs and ways that show they then feel greatest pleasure. And hence it comes that men, while seeming to listen gladly, usually hold such women in small respect and have very little regard for them, and think these ways of theirs are an invitation to advance farther, and thus often go such lengths with them as bring them deserved reproach, and finally esteem them so lightly as to despise their company and even find them tedious.

"And on the other hand, there is no man so shameless and insolent as not to have reverence for those women who are esteemed good and virtuous; because this gravity (tempered with wisdom and goodness) is as it were a shield against the insolence and coarseness of the presumptuous. Thus we see that a word or laugh or act of kindness (however small it be) from a virtuous woman is more prized by everyone, than all the endearments and caresses of those who show their lack of shame so openly; and if they are not immodest, by their unseemly laughter, their loquacity, insolence and like scurrile manners, they give sign of being so.

6.—"And since words that carry no meaning of importance are vain and puerile, the Court Lady must have not only the good sense to discern the quality of him with whom she is speaking, but knowledge of many things, in order to entertain him graciously; and in her talk she should know how to choose those things that are adapted to the quality of him with whom she is speaking, and should be cautious lest occasionally, without intending it, she utter words that may offend him. Let her guard against wearying him by praising herself indiscreetly or by being too prolix. Let her not go about mingling serious matters with her playful or humorous discourse, or jests and jokes with her serious discourse. Let her not stupidly pretend to know that which she does not know, but modestly seek to do herself credit in that which she does know,—in all things avoiding affectation, as has been said. In this way she will be adorned with good manners, and will perform with perfect grace the bodily exercises proper to women; her discourse will be rich and full of prudence, virtue and pleasantness; and thus she will be not only loved but revered by everyone, and perhaps worthy to be placed side by side with this great Courtier as well in qualities of the mind as in those of the body."

7.—Having so far spoken, the Magnifico was silent and sat quiet, as if he had ended his discourse. Then my lord Gaspar said:

"Verily, my lord Magnifico, you have adorned this Lady well and given her excellent qualities. Yet methinks you have kept much to generalities, and mentioned some things in her so great that I think you were ashamed to explain them, and have rather desired than taught them, after the manner of those who sometimes wish for things impossible and beyond nature. Therefore I would have you declare to us a little better what are the bodily exercises proper to a Court Lady, and in what way she ought to converse, and what those many things are whereof you say it befits her to have knowledge; and whether you mean that she should use the prudence, the magnanimity, the continence, and the many other virtues you have named, merely to aid her in the government of her house, children and family (which however you would not have her chief profession), or indeed in her conversation and graceful practice of those bodily exercises; and, by your faith, guard against setting these poor virtues to such menial duty that they must needs be ashamed of it."

The Magnifico laughed, and said:

"My lord Gaspar, you cannot help showing your ill will towards women. But in truth I thought I had said enough, and especially before such hearers; for I am quite sure there is no one here who does not perceive that in the matter of bodily exercises it does not befit women to handle weapons, to ride, to play tennis, to wrestle, and to do many other things that befit men."

Then the Unico Aretino said:

"Among the ancients it was the custom for women to wrestle unclothed with men but we have lost this good custom, along with many others."

Messer Cesare Gonzaga added:

"And in my time I have seen women play tennis, handle weapons, ride, go hunting, and perform nearly all the exercises that a cavalier can."

8.—The Magnifico replied:

"Since I may fashion this Lady as I wish, not only am I unwilling to have her practise such vigorous and rugged manly exercises, but I would have her practise even those that are becoming to women, circumspectly and with that gentle daintiness which we have said befits her; and thus in dancing I would not see her use too active and violent movements, nor in singing or playing those abrupt and oft-repeated diminutions which show more skill than sweetness; likewise the musical instruments that she uses ought, in my opinion, to be appropriate to this intent. Imagine how unlovely it would be to see a woman play drums, fifes or trumpets, or other like instruments; and this because their harshness hides and destroys that mild gentleness which so much adorns every act a woman does. Therefore when she starts to dance or make music of any kind, she ought to bring herself to it by letting herself be urged a little, and with a touch of shyness which shall show that noble shame which is the opposite of effrontery.

"Moreover, she ought to adapt her dress to this intent, and so to clothe herself that she may not seem vain or frivolous. But since women may and ought to take more care for beauty than men,—and there are divers sorts of beauty,—this Lady ought to have the good sense to discern what those garments are that enhance her grace and are most appropriate to the exercises wherein she purposes to engage at the time, and to wear them. And if she is conscious of possessing a bright and cheerful beauty, she ought to set it off with movements, words and dress all tending towards the cheerful; so too, another, who feels that her style is gentle and serious, ought to accompany it with fashions of that sort, in order to enhance that which is the gift of nature. Thus, if she is a little more stout or thin than the medium, or fair or dark, let her seek help from dress, but as covertly as possible; and while keeping herself dainty and neat, let her always seem to give no thought or heed to it.

9.—"And since my lord Gaspar further asks what these many things are whereof she ought to have knowledge, and in what manner she ought to converse, and whether her virtues ought to contribute to her conversation,—I say I would have her acquainted with that which these gentlemen wished the Courtier to know. And of the exercises that we have said do not befit her, I would have her at least possess such understanding as we may have of things that we do not practise; and this in order that she may know how to praise and value cavaliers more or less, according to their deserts.

"And to repeat in a few words part of what has been already said, I wish this Lady to have knowledge of letters, music, painting, and to know how to dance and make merry; accompanying the other precepts that have been taught the Courtier with discreet modesty and with the giving of a good impression of herself. And thus, in her talk, her laughter, her play, her jesting, in short, in everything, she will be very graceful, and will entertain appropriately, and with witticisms and pleasantries befitting her, everyone who shall come before her. And although continence, magnanimity, temperance, strength of mind, prudence, and the other virtues, seem to have little to do with entertainment, I would have her adorned with all of them, not so much for the sake of entertainment (albeit even there they can be of service), as in order that she may be full of virtue, and to the end that these virtues may render her worthy of being honoured, and that her every act may be governed by them."

10.—My lord Gaspar then said, laughing:

"Since you have given women letters and continence and magnanimity and temperance, I only marvel that you would not also have them govern cities, make laws, and lead armies, and let the men stay at home to cook or spin."

The Magnifico replied, also laughing:

"Perhaps even this would not be amiss." Then he added: "Do you not know that Plato, who certainly was no great friend to women, gave them charge over the city, and gave all other martial duties to the men? [339] Do you not believe that there are many to be found who would know how to govern cities and armies as well as men do? But I have not laid these duties on them, because I am fashioning a Court Lady and not a Queen.

"I well know you would like to repeat tacitly that false imputation which my lord Ottaviano cast on women yesterday: namely, that they are very imperfect creatures, incapable of doing any good act, and of very little worth and no dignity by comparison with men: but in truth both he and you would be greatly in the wrong if you were to think this."

11.—Then my lord Gaspar said:

"I do not wish to repeat things already said; but you would fain lead me to say something to offend these ladies' feelings in order to make them my enemies, just as you wish to win their favour by flattering them falsely. But they are so much above other women in discretion that they love truth (even if it be little in their favour) more than false praises; nor do they take it amiss if anyone says that men are of greater dignity, and will admit that you have recounted great miracles and ascribed to the Court Lady certain absurd impossibilities, and so many virtues that Socrates and Cato and all the philosophers in the world are as nothing by comparison. To tell the plain truth, I marvel that you were not ashamed to go so far beyond bounds; for it ought to have been quite enough for you to make this Court Lady beautiful, discreet, chaste, gracious, and able (without incurring infamy) to entertain with dancing, music, games, laughter, witticisms, and the other things which we see used at court every day. But to insist on giving her knowledge of all the things in the world, and to attribute to her those virtues that are so rarely seen in men even in past centuries, is something that cannot be endured or hardly listened to.

"Now, I am far from willing to affirm that women are imperfect creatures, and consequently of less dignity than men, and not capable of those virtues that men are,—because these ladies' worth would suffice to prove me wrong: [340] but I do say that very learned men have left it in writing that since nature always aims and designs to make things most perfect, she would continually bring forth men if she could; and when a woman is born, it is a defect or mistake of nature, and contrary to that which she would wish to do: as is seen also in the case of one who is born blind or halt or with some other defect; and in trees, many fruits that never ripen. Thus woman may be said to be a creature produced by chance and accident; and that this is so, mark a man's acts and a woman's, and judge therefrom the perfection of both. Yet, as these imperfections of women are the fault of nature who has made them so, we ought not on that account to hate them or fail to show them that respect which is their due. But to esteem them above what they are, seems to me plain error."

12.—The Magnifico Giuliano waited for my lord Gaspar to continue further, but seeing that he kept silent, said:

"As to women's imperfection, methinks you have adduced a very weak argument; to which, although perhaps it be not timely to enter upon these subtleties now, I reply (according to the opinion of one who knows and according to truth) that the substance of anything you please cannot receive into itself more or less. For just as no one stone can be more perfectly stone than another as regards the essence of a stone, nor one piece of wood more perfectly wood than another,—so one man cannot be more perfectly man than another; and consequently the male will not be more perfect than the female as regards its essential substance, because both are included in the species man, and that wherein the one differs from the other is an accidental matter and not essential. In case you then tell me that man is more perfect than woman, if not in essence, at least in non-essentials, I reply that these non-essentials must pertain either to the body or to the mind; if to the body (as in that man is more robust, more agile, lighter, or more capable of toil), I say that this is proof of very slight perfection, because even among men, they who have these qualities more than others have, are not more esteemed therefor; and even in wars, where the greater part of the work is laborious and a matter of strength, the strongest are yet not the most prized; if to the mind, I say that all the things that men can understand, the same can women understand too; and where the intellect of the one penetrates, there also can that of the other penetrate."

13.—Having here made a little pause, the Magnifico Giuliano added, laughing:

"Do you not know that in philosophy this proposition is maintained, that those who are tender in flesh are apt in mind? So there is no doubt that women, being tenderer in flesh, are apter in mind, and of capacity better fitted for speculation than men are." Then he continued:

"But leaving this aside, since you have told me to argue concerning the perfection of both from their acts, I say that if you will consider the workings of nature, you will find that she makes women what they are, not by chance, but adapted to the necessary end: for although she makes them not strong in body and of placid spirit, with many other qualities opposed to those of men, yet the characters of both tend to one single end conducive to the same use. For just as by reason of that feebleness of theirs women are less courageous, so for the same reason they are also more cautious: thus the mother nourishes her children, the father instructs them and with his strength earns abroad that which she with anxious care preserves at home, which is not the lesser merit.

"Again, if you examine the ancient histories (albeit men have ever been very chary of writing women's praises) and the modern ones, you will find that worth has continually existed among women as well as among men; and that there have even been those who waged wars and won glorious victories therein, governed kingdoms with the highest prudence and justice, and did everything that men have done. As for the sciences, do you not remember having read of many women who were learned in philosophy? Others who were very excellent in poetry? Others who conducted suits, and accused and defended most eloquently before judges? Of handicrafts it would be too long to tell, nor is there need to bring proof regarding that.

"Therefore, if in essential substance man is not more perfect than woman, nor in non-essentials either (and of this, quite apart

from argument, the effects are seen), I do not know in what
consists this perfection of his.

14.—"And since you said that nature's aim is always to bring
forth the most perfect things, and that she therefore would always bring forth man if she could, and that the bringing forth of
woman is rather an error or defect in nature than of purpose,—
I reply that this is totally denied; nor do I see how you can say
that nature does not aim to bring forth women, without whom
the human species cannot be preserved, whereof this same nature
is more desirous than of everything else. For by means of this
union of male and female she brings forth children, who repay
the benefits received in childhood by maintaining their parents
when old; then in turn they beget other children of their own,
from whom they look to receive in old age that which they in
their youth bestowed upon their parents; thus nature, moving as
it were in a circle, fills out eternity and in this way grants immortality to mortals. Woman being therefore as necessary in this
as man, I do not see how the one was made more by chance than
the other.

"It is very true that nature aims always to bring forth the
most perfect things, and hence means to bring forth man after
his kind, but not male rather than female. Nay, if she were always to bring forth male, she would be working imperfection;
for just as from body and soul there results a compound more
noble than its parts, which is man,—so from the union of male
and female there results a compound which preserves the human
species, and without which its members would perish. And hence
male and female are by nature always together, nor can the one
exist without the other; thus that ought not to be called male
which has no female, according to the definition of each; nor
female, that which has no male. And as one sex alone shows imperfection, the theologians of old attribute both the one and the
other to God: [341] wherefore Orpheus said that Jove was male and
female; and we read in Holy Writ that God formed men male
and female in his own likeness; and often the poets, speaking of
the gods, confuse the sex."

15.—Then my lord Gaspar said:

"I would not have us enter upon such subtleties, because

these ladies will not understand us, and although I answer you with excellent arguments, they will believe (or at least pretend to believe) that I am wrong, and straightway will pronounce judgment to their liking. Yet since we are already begun, I will say merely this, that (as you know is the opinion of very wise men) man resembles form, and woman matter; and therefore, just as form is more perfect than matter,—nay, gives it its being, —so man is far more perfect than woman. And I remember having once heard that a great philosopher says in some of his problems: [342] 'Why is it that a woman always naturally loves the man who first tasted the sweets of love with her? and on the contrary a man holds that woman in hatred who was the first to give herself to him?' And adding the reason, he affirms it to be this: because in this matter the woman receives perfection from the man, and the man imperfection from the woman; and therefore everyone naturally loves that thing which makes him perfect, and hates that which makes him imperfect. And besides this, a great argument for the perfection of man and for the imperfection of woman is that every woman universally desires to be a man, by a certain natural instinct that teaches her to desire her perfection."

16.—The Magnifico Giuliano at once replied:

"The poor creatures do not desire to be men in order to be perfect, but in order to have liberty and to escape that dominion over them which man has arrogated to himself by his own authority. And the analogy that you cite of matter and form does not apply in everything; for woman is not made perfect by man, as matter by form: because matter receives its being from form and cannot exist without it; nay, the more matter forms have, the more they have of imperfection, and are most perfect when separated from it. But woman does not receive her being from man; nay, just as she is made perfect by him, she also makes him perfect. Hence both join in procreation, which neither of them can effect without the other.

"Therefore I will assign the cause of woman's lasting love for the first man to whom she has given herself, and of man's hatred for the first woman, not at all to that which your Philosopher alleges in his problems, but to woman's firmness and constancy, and to man's inconstancy; nor without natural reason: for being warm, the male naturally derives from that quality lightness, movement and inconstancy, while from her frigidity woman on the other hand derives quietness, firm gravity, and more fixed impressions."

17.—Then my lady Emilia turned to my lord Magnifico and said:

"For the love of Heaven, leave these matters and forms of yours awhile, and male and female, and speak in such fashion that you may be understood; for we heard and understood very well the evil that my lord Ottaviano and my lord Gaspar said of us, but now we do not at all understand in what manner you are defending us: so it seems to me that you are straying from the subject and leaving in everyone's mind that bad impression which these enemies of ours have given of us."

"Do not give us that name, my Lady," replied my lord Gaspar, "for it better befits my lord Magnifico, who by bestowing false praises upon women shows that there are none true of them."

The Magnifico Giuliano continued:

"Do not doubt, my Lady, that answer will be made to everything. But I do not wish to utter such inordinate abuse of men as they have uttered of women; and if by chance there were anyone to write down our discussions, I should not like, in a place where these matters and forms are understood, to have the arguments and reasons that my lord Gaspar adduces against you, appear to have been without reply."

"I do not see, my lord Magnifico," my lord Gaspar then said, "how in this matter you will be able to deny that man is by his natural qualities more perfect than woman, who is frigid by temperament, and man warm. And warmth is far nobler and more perfect than cold, because it is active and productive; and, as you know, the heavens send down only warmth upon us here, and not cold, which does not enter into the works of nature. And hence I believe that the frigidity of women's temperament is the cause of their abasement and timidity."

18.—"So you too," replied the Magnifico Giuliano, "wish to enter into subtleties; but you shall see that you will always have the worst of it: and that this is true, listen.

"I grant you that warmth is in itself more perfect than cold;

↗↗↗↗↗↗↗↗↗↗↗↗↗↗↗↗↗↗↗↗↗↗↗↗↗↗↗↗↗↗↗↗↗↗↗↗↗↗↗↗↗↗↗↗↗↗↗↗↗↗↗↗↗↗

but this is not the case with things mixed and composite; for if it were so, that body which is warmer would be more perfect, which is false, because temperate bodies are most perfect. Moreover, I tell you that woman is of frigid temperament by comparison with man, who by excess of warmth is far from temperate; but as for her, she is temperate (or at least more nearly temperate than man is) because she has in her a moisture proportioned to her natural warmth, which in man usually evaporates by reason of excessive dryness and is consumed. Furthermore, her coldness is of the kind that resists and moderates her natural warmth and makes it more nearly temperate; while in man the surplus warmth soon raises his natural heat to the highest pitch, which wastes away for lack of sustenance. And thus, as men lose more in procreation than women do, it often happens that they are less long lived than women; wherefore this perfection also may be ascribed to women, that, living longer than men, they perform better than men that which is the intent of nature.

"Of the warmth that the heavens shed upon us I do not speak now, because it is of a different sort from that which we are discussing; for being preservative of all things under the moon's orb, warm as well as cold, it cannot be hostile to cold. But timidity in women, although it shows some imperfection, yet springs from a praiseworthy source, that is, from the subtlety and readiness of their wits, which picture images to their minds quickly and thus are easily disturbed by things external. You will very often see men who fear neither death nor anything else, and yet cannot be called courageous, because they do not know the danger and go like fools where they see the road open, and think no further; and this proceeds from a certain grossness of dull wits: wherefore we cannot say that a fool is brave. But true loftiness of mind comes from a due deliberation and determined resolve to act thus and so, and from esteeming honour and duty above all the dangers in the world; and from being of such stout heart and courage (although death be manifest), that the senses are not clogged or frightened, but perform their office in speech and thought as if they were most quiet. We have seen and heard that great men are of this sort; likewise many women, who both in ancient and in modern times have displayed greatness of spirit and have wrought upon the world effects worthy of infinite praise, not less than men have done."

19.—Then Frisio said:

"These effects began when the first woman by her transgression led others to transgress against God, and left the human race an heritage of death, sufferings, sorrows, and all the miseries and calamities that are felt in the world to-day."

The Magnifico Giuliano replied:

"Since you too are pleased to enter upon sacred things, do you not know that this transgression was repaired by a Woman, who brought us much greater gain than the other had done us injury, so that the guilt is called most fortunate which was atoned by such merits? But I do not now mean to tell you how inferior in dignity all human creatures are to our Lady the Virgin (in order not to mingle things divine with these light discussions of ours); nor to recount how many women have, with infinite constancy, suffered themselves to be cruelly slain by tyrants for Christ's name, nor those who by learned disputation have confuted so many idolaters. And if you told me that this was a miracle and grace of the Holy Spirit, I say that no virtue merits more praise than that which is approved by the testimony of God. Many other women also, of whom there is less talk, you yourself can see,—especially by reading Saint Jerome, who celebrates certain ones of his time with such admiring praises as might well suffice for the saintliest man on earth.³⁴³

20.—"Then consider how many others there have been, of whom no mention is made at all, because the poor creatures are kept shut up, without the lofty pride to seek the name of saint from the rabble, as many accursed hypocrites do to-day, who,— forgetful or rather regardless of Christ's teaching, which requires that when a man fasts he shall anoint his face in order that he may not seem to fast, and commands that prayers, alms, and other good works shall be done, not in the market-place nor in synagogues, but in secret, so that the left hand shall not know of the right,—affirm that there is no greater good thing in the world than to give a good example: and so, with averted head and downcast eyes, noising it abroad that they will not speak to women or eat anything but raw herbs,—dirty, with cassocks torn, they

ᒣᒣᒣᒣᒣᒣᒣᒣᒣᒣᒣᒣᒣᒣᒣᒣᒣᒣᒣᒣᒣᒣᒣᒣᒣᒣᒣᒣᒣᒣᒣᒣᒣᒣᒣᒣᒣᒣᒣᒣᒣᒣᒣᒣᒣᒣᒣ

beguile the simple. Yet they abstain not from forging wills, setting mortal enmities between man and wife, and sometimes poison, using sorceries, incantations and every sort of villainy. And then they cite a certain authority out of their own head, which says, *si non caste, tamen caute*;[344] and with this they think to cure every great evil, and with good arguments to persuade anyone who is not right wary that all sin, however grave it be, is easily pardoned of God, provided it remain secret and do not give rise to bad example. Thus, under a veil of sanctity and in secret they often turn all their thoughts to corrupt the pure mind of some woman; often to sow hatred between brothers; to govern states; to raise up one and cast another down; to get men beheaded, imprisoned and proscribed; to be ministers of the villainies and as it were receivers of the thefts that many princes commit.

"Others shamelessly delight to appear dainty and fresh, with well-shaven crown and garments fine, and in walking lift the cassock to display their neat hose and their comeliness of person in making salutations. Others use certain glances and gestures even in saying mass, whereby they imagine they are graceful and attract attention. Villainous and wicked men, utter strangers not only to religion but to all good behaviour; and when they are reproved for their loose living, they make a jest of it and laugh at him who speaks to them of it, and almost make a merit of their vices."

Then my lady Emilia said:

"You take such pleasure in speaking ill of friars, that you have entered upon this subject without rhyme or reason. But you are very wrong to murmur against ecclesiastics, and you burden your conscience quite needlessly; since, but for those who pray to God for us, we should have much greater scourges than we have."

Then the Magnifico Giuliano laughed, and said:

"How did you guess so well, my Lady, that I was speaking of friars, when I did not name them? But in truth what I do is not called murmuring, for I speak very openly and plainly; nor am I speaking of the good, but of the bad and guilty, of whom moreover I do not tell the thousandth part of what I know."

"Do not speak of friars now," replied my lady Emilia; "because for my part I esteem it grievous sin to listen to you, and so I shall go away in order not to listen to you."

21.—"I am content," said the Magnifico Giuliano, "to speak no more of this; but returning to the praises of women, I say that my lord Gaspar shall not find me an admirable man, but I will find you a wife or daughter or sister of equal and sometimes greater merit. Moreover, many women have been the cause of countless benefits to their men-folk, and sometimes have corrected many a one of his errors. Wherefore, women being (as we have shown) naturally capable of the same virtues as men, and the effects thereof being often seen, I do not perceive why,— in giving them what it is possible for them to have, what they more than once have had and still have,—I should be regarded as relating miracles, whereof my lord Gaspar has accused me; seeing that there have always been on earth, and now still are, women as like the Court Lady I have fashioned, as men like the man these gentlemen have fashioned."

Then my lord Gaspar said:

"Those arguments that have experience against them do not seem to me good; and certainly if I were to ask you who these great women were that have been as worthy of praise as the great men whose wives or sisters or daughters they were, or that have been the cause of any benefit, and who those were that have corrected the errors of their men-folk,—I think you would be embarrassed."

22.—"Verily," replied the Magnifico Giuliano, "no other thing could make me embarrassed save their multitude; and had I time enough, I should tell you here the story of Octavia,[345] wife of Mark Antony and sister of Augustus; that of Porcia,[346] Cato's daughter and wife of Brutus; that of Caia Cæcilia,[347] wife of Tarquinius Priscus; that of Cornelia,[348] Scipio's daughter; and of countless others who are very celebrated: and not only of our own, but of barbarian nations; as that of Alexandra,[349] wife of Alexander king of the Jews, who,—after her husband's death, when she saw the people kindled with fury and already up in arms to slay the two children that he had left her, in revenge for the cruel and grievous bondage in which the father had always kept them,—so acted that she soon appeased their just wrath, and

by her prudence straightway won over for her children those
minds which the father, by countless injuries during many years,
had made very hostile to his offspring."

"At least tell us," replied my lady Emilia, "how she did it."

"Seeing her children in such peril," said the Magnifico, "she
at once caused Alexander's body to be cast into the middle of the
market-place. Then, having called the citizens to her, she said
that she knew their minds to be kindled with very just wrath
against her husband, because the cruel injuries that he had in-
iquitously done them deserved it; and that, as she had always
wished, while he was alive, that she could make him abstain from
such a wicked life, so now she was ready to give proof of it, and
as far as possible to help them punish him after death; and therefore let them take his body, and give it as food for dogs, and
outrage it in the most cruel ways they could devise: but she prayed
them to have mercy upon her innocent children, who could not
have either guilt or even knowledge of the father's evil deeds.
Of such efficacy were these words, that the fierce wrath before
conceived in the minds of all that people was quickly softened
and turned to a feeling of such pity, that they not only with one
accord chose the children for their rulers, but also gave most
honourable burial to the body of the dead."

Here the Magnifico made a little pause; then he added:

"Do you not know that the wife and daughters of Mithridates showed much less fear of death than Mithridates? [350] And
Hasdrubal's wife than Hasdrubal? [351] Do you not know that Harmonia, daughter of Hiero the Syracusan, chose to perish in the
burning of her native city?" [352]

Then Frisio said:

"Where obstinacy is concerned, it is certain that some women
are occasionally to be found who never change their purpose; like
the one who being no longer able to say 'Scissors' to her husband,
made the sign of them to him with her hands." [353]

23.—The Magnifico Giuliano laughed, and said:

"Obstinacy that tends to a worthy end ought to be called
steadfastness; as was the case of the famous Epicharis, a Roman
freedwoman, who, being privy to a great conspiracy against Nero,
was of such steadfastness that, although racked by all the direst

tortures that can be imagined, she never betrayed one of her accomplices; while in the same peril many noble knights and senators basely accused brothers, friends and the dearest and nearest they had in the world.[354]

"What will you say of that other woman who was called Leæna? In whose honour the Athenians dedicated a tongueless lioness (*leæna*) in bronze before the gate of the citadel, to show in her the steadfast virtue of silence; because being likewise privy to a conspiracy against the tyrants, she was not dismayed by the death of two great men (her friends), and although rent by countless most cruel tortures, she never betrayed one of the conspirators." [355]

Then madonna Margarita Gonzaga said:

"Methinks you narrate too briefly these virtuous deeds done by women; for these enemies of ours, although having heard and read them, yet pretend not to know them and fain would have the memory of them lost: but if you will let us women hear them, we at least shall deem ourselves honoured by them."

24.—Then the Magnifico Giuliano replied:

"So be it. I wish to tell you now of one who did what I think my lord Gaspar himself will admit very few men do," and he began: "In Massilia [356] there was once a custom that is believed to have been brought from Greece, which was that they publicly [357] kept a poison compounded of hemlock, and allowed anyone to take it who proved to the Senate that he ought to lay down his life because of any trouble that he found therein, or for other just cause, to the end that whoever had suffered a too hostile fortune or had enjoyed a too prosperous fortune, should not drag on the one or change the other. Now Sextus Pompey, finding himself—" [358]

Here Frisio, not waiting for the Magnifico Giuliano to go on, said:

"Methinks this is the beginning of a long story."

Then the Magnifico Giuliano turned to madonna Margarita laughing, and said:

"You see that Frisio will not let me speak. I wished to tell you now about a woman who, having shown to the Senate that she had good reason to die, cheerfully and fearlessly took the poison in Sextus Pompey's presence, with such steadfastness of spirit and

with such affectionate and thoughtful remembrances to her family,
that Pompey and all the others who saw such wisdom and confidence on a woman's part in the dread hour of death, were lost in
wonderment and tears."

25.—Then my lord Gaspar said, laughing:

"I too remember having read a speech in which an unhappy
husband asks leave of the Senate to die, and proves that he has just
cause for it in that he cannot endure the continual annoyance of his
wife's chatter, and prefers to drink the poison, which you say was
publicly kept for such purposes, than his wife's words."

The Magnifico Giuliano replied:

"How many poor women would have just cause for asking
leave to die because they cannot endure, I will not say the evil
words, but the very evil deeds of their husbands! I know several
such, who suffer in this world the pains that are said to be in hell."

"Do you not believe," replied my lord Gaspar, "that there are
also many husbands who have such torment of their wives that
they hourly wish for death?"

"And what pain," said the Magnifico, "can wives give their
husbands that is as incurable as are those that husbands give their
wives?—who if not for love, at least for fear, are submissive to
their husbands."

"Certain it is," said my lord Gaspar, "that the little good they
sometimes do proceeds from fear, since there are few in the world
who in their secret hearts do not hate their husbands."

"Nay, quite the contrary," replied the Magnifico; "and if you
recall aright what you have read, we see in all the histories that
wives nearly always love their husbands more than husbands love
their wives. When did you ever see or read of a husband showing
his wife such a token of love as did the famous Camma to her
husband?"

"I do not know," replied my lord Gaspar, "who the woman
was, nor what token she showed."

"Nor I," said Frisio.

"Listen," replied the Magnifico; "and do you, madonna
Margarita, take care to keep it in mind.

26.—"This Camma was a very beautiful young woman,
adorned with such modesty and gentle manners that she was admir-

able no less for this than for her beauty; and above other things with all her heart she loved her husband, who was called Synattus. It happened that another gentleman, who was of much higher station than Synattus and almost tyrant of the city where they lived, became enamoured of this young woman; and after having long tried by every way and means to possess her, and all in vain, he persuaded himself that the love she bore her husband was the sole cause that hindered his desires, and had this Synattus slain.

"So then urging her continually, he was never able to gain other advantage than he had done at first; wherefore, his love increasing daily, he resolved to take her for his wife, although she was far beneath him in station. So, her parents being asked by Sinoris (for thus the lover was called), they began to persuade her to accept him, showing her that her consent would be very advantageous, and her refusal dangerous to her and to them all. After resisting them awhile, she at last replied that she was willing.

"Her parents had the news brought to Sinoris, who was happy beyond measure and arranged that the marriage should be celebrated at once. Both having accordingly come in state for the purpose to the temple of Diana, Camma had a certain sweet drink brought which she had prepared; and so before Diana's image she drank half of it in the presence of Sinoris; then with her own hand (for thus it was the custom to do at marriages) she gave the rest to her spouse, who drank it all.

"When Camma saw that her plan had succeeded, she knelt all joyful at the foot of Diana's image, and said:

" 'O Goddess, thou who knowest the secrets of my heart, be thou sure witness for me how hardly I refrained from putting myself to death after my dear consort died, and with what weariness I bore the sorrow of remaining in this bitter life, wherein I felt no other good or pleasure beyond the hope of that vengeance which now I find I have attained. Joyful and content, then, I go to seek the sweet company of that soul which in life and in death I have loved more than myself. And thou, wretch, who thoughtest to be my husband, instead of the marriage bed give order that thy tomb be made ready for thee, for I offer thee as a sacrifice to the shade of Synattus.'

"Aghast at these words, and already feeling the effect of the poison stir pain within him, Sinoris tried many remedies; but they were of no avail, and Camma had such great good fortune (or whatever else it was), that before dying herself she knew that Sinoris was dead. Learning which thing, she very contentedly laid herself upon her bed with eyes to heaven, continually calling the name of Synattus, and saying:

" 'O sweetest consort, now that I have given both tears and vengeance as last offerings for thy death, nor see that aught else is left me to do for thee, I hasten from the world and this life,—cruel without thee and once dear to me only for thy sake. Come then to meet me, my Lord, and receive this soul as gladly as it gladly comes to thee.'

"And speaking thus, and with arms opened as if she would already embrace him, she died. Now say, Frisio, what do you think of her?" [359]

Frisio replied:

"I think you fain would make these ladies weep. But even supposing this were true, I tell you that such women are no longer to be found in the world."

27.—"Indeed they are to be found," said the Magnifico; "and that this is true, listen:

"In my time there was a gentleman at Pisa, whose name was messer Tommaso; I do not remember of what family, although I often heard it mentioned by my father, who was a great friend of his. Now this messer Tommaso, crossing one day in a small vessel from Pisa to Sicily on business, was surprised by some Moorish galleys which had come up so stealthily that those who commanded the vessel did not suspect it; and although the men who were in her defended themselves stoutly, yet as they were few and the enemy many, the vessel fell into the hands of the Moors, together with all who were in here, both wounded and whole as it chanced, and among them messer Tommaso, who had carried himself bravely and slain with his own hand a brother of one of the captains of the galleys. Wherefore enraged, as you may believe, by the loss of a brother, the captain claimed him as special prisoner, and beating and maltreating him every day, carried him to Barbary, having resolved to keep him there in great misery a captive for life and with grievous pains.

"All the others got free after a time, some in one way and some in another, and returned home and reported to his wife (whose name was madonna Argentina) and to his children, the hard life and sore affliction in which messer Tommaso was living and was like to go on living without hope unless God should aid him miraculously. After she and they were informed of this and had tried several other means to deliver him, and when he himself was quite resigned to die, it came to pass that watchful love so kindled the wit and daring of one of his sons, who was called Paolo, that the youth took no heed of any kind of danger and resolved either to die or to free his father; and this thing was brought about in such sort that the father was conveyed away so privily that he was in Leghorn before it was discovered in Barbary that he had departed thence. From here messer Tommaso wrote in safety to his wife, and informed her of his deliverance and where he was and how he hoped to see her the next day. Overwhelmed with great and unexpected joy at being (through the dutifulness and merit of her son) so soon to see her husband, whom she so dearly loved and firmly believed she would never see again, —the good and gentle lady raised her eyes to heaven when she had read the letter, and calling her husband's name fell dead upon the ground; nor in spite of all the remedies that were employed upon her did the departed spirit return again to her body. Cruel spectacle, and enough to moderate human wishes and restrain their over-longing for too much joy."

28.—Then Frisio said, laughing:

"How do you know that she did not die of grief at hearing that her husband was coming home?"

The Magnifico replied:

"Because the rest of her life did not comport with this; nay, I think that her soul, unable to brook delay in seeing him with the eyes of her body, forsook it, and, drawn by eagerness, quickly flew whither her thought had flown on reading the letter."

My lord Gaspar said:

"It may be that this lady was too loving, for women always run to extremes in everything, which is bad; and you see that by being too loving she wrought evil to herself, and to her husband and children, for whom she turned to bitterness the joy of his perilous and longed-for deliverance. So you ought by no means to cite her as one of those women who have been the cause of such great benefits."

The Magnifico replied:

"I cite her as one of those who bear witness that there are wives who love their hsubands; for of those who have been the cause of great benefits to the world, I could tell you of an endless number, and discourse to you of some so ancient that they almost seem fabulous, and of those who among men have been the inventors of such things, that they deserved to be esteemed as goddesses, like Pallas and Ceres; and of the Sibyls,[360] by whose mouth God has so often spoken and revealed to the world events that were to come; and of those who have instructed very great men, like Aspasia,[361] and like Diotima,[362] who furthermore by her sacrifices delayed for ten years the time of a pestilence that was to come upon Athens. I could tell you of Nicostrate,[363] Evander's mother, who taught the Latins letters; and of still another woman,[364] who was preceptress to the lyric poet Pindar;[365] and of Corinna[366] and of Sappho,[367] who were excellent in poetry; but I do not wish to seek out matters so far afield. I tell you, however (leaving the rest apart), that women were perhaps not less the cause of Rome's greatness than men."

"This," said my lord Gaspar, "would be fine to hear."

29.—The Magnifico replied:

"Then listen to it. After the fall of Troy many Trojans fled who escaped that great disaster, some in one direction and some in another; of whom one part, who were buffeted by many storms, came to Italy at that place where the Tiber flows into the sea. Landing here in search of necessaries, they began to roam about the country: the women, who had remained in the ships, bethought themselves of a good plan that would put an end to their perilous and long wandering by sea and give them a new fatherland in place of that which they had lost; and after consulting together in the absence of the men, they burned the ships; and the first to begin the work bore the name Roma. Yet fearing the wrath of the men, who were returning, they went out to meet these; and embracing and kissing, some their husbands, some their kinsmen, with tokens of affection, they softened the first impulse of anger; then they quietly explained to the men the reason of their wise device. Whereupon the Trojans, either from necessity or from having been kindly received by the natives, were well pleased with what the women had done, and dwelt there with the Latins in the place where afterwards was Rome; and from this arose the ancient custom among the Romans that the women kissed their kinsfolk when they met.[368] Now you see how much these women helped to make a beginning of Rome.

30.—"Nor did the Sabine women contribute less to its increase than the Trojan women did to its beginning. For Romulus, having excited general enmity among all his neighbours by the seizure of their women, was harassed by wars on every side; which (he being a man of ability) were soon brought to a successful issue, except that with the Sabines, which was very great because Titus Tatius, king of the Sabines, was very powerful and wise. Wherefore, a severe conflict having taken place between Romans and Sabines, with very heavy loss on both sides, and a new and cruel battle making ready, the Sabine women,—clad in black, with hair loose and torn, weeping, sorrowful, fearless of the weapons that were already drawn to strike,—rushed in between the fathers and husbands, imploring them to refrain from defiling their hands with the blood of fathers-in-law and sons-in-law. And if the men were still displeased with the alliance, let the weapons be turned against the women, for it were better for them to die than to live widowed or fatherless and brotherless, and to remember that their children were begotten of those who had slain their fathers, or that they themselves were born of those who had slain their husbands. Lamenting thus and weeping, many of them carried their little babes in their arms,[369] some of whom were already beginning to loose the tongue and seemed to try to call and to make merry with their grandsires; to whom the women showed the little ones, and said, weeping: 'Behold your blood, which with such heat and fury you are seeking to shed with your own hands.'

"The women's dutifulness and wisdom wrought such great effect at this pass, that not only were lasting friendship and union established between the two hostile kings, but what was stranger, the Sabines came to live at Rome, and of the two peoples a single one was made. And thus this union greatly increased the power of Rome, thanks to those wise and lofty-minded women, who were rewarded by Romulus in such fashion that in dividing the people into thirty wards he gave thereto the names of the Sabine women."

31.—Here having paused a little, and seeing that my lord Gaspar did not speak, the Magnifico Giuliano said:

"Do you not think that these women were the cause of good to their men-folk and contributed to the greatness of Rome?"

My lord Gaspar replied:

"No doubt they were worthy of much praise; but had you been as willing to tell the sins of women as their good works, you would not have omitted to say that in this war of Titus Tatius a woman betrayed Rome and showed the enemy the way to seize the Capitol, whereby the Romans came near being all destroyed." [370]

The Magnifico Giuliano replied:

"You tell me of a single bad woman, while I tell you of countless good ones; and besides those already mentioned, I could show you a thousand other instances on my side, of benefits done to Rome by women, and could tell you why a temple was dedicated of old to Venus Armata, [371] and another to Venus Calva, [372] and how the Festival of the Handmaidens was instituted in honour of Juno because handmaidens once delivered Rome from the wiles of the enemy. [373] But leaving all these things aside, did not that lofty deed—the discovery of Cataline's conspiracy, whereof Cicero so vaunts himself—spring chiefly from a vile woman? [374]—who for this might be said to have been the cause of all the good that Cicero boasts of having wrought the Roman commonwealth. And had I time enough, I should further show you that women have often corrected many of men's errors; but I fear that this discourse of mine is already too long and wearisome: so, having performed according to my ability the task imposed upon me by these ladies, I think it well to give place to someone who will say things worthier to be listened to than any I can say."

32.—Then my lady Emilia said:

"Do not deprive women of those true praises that are their due; and remember that if my lord Gaspar, and perhaps my lord Ottaviano as well, listen to you with weariness, we and all these other gentlemen listen to you with pleasure."

The Magnifico still wished to stop, but all the ladies began begging him to speak: whereupon he said, laughing:

"In order not to make my lord Gaspar more my enemy than he is, I will tell briefly of a few women who occur to my mind, omitting many that I might mention." Then he continued: "When Philip, son of Demetrius, was laying siege to the city of Chios, he issued an edict promising freedom and their masters' wives to all slaves who should escape from the city and come to him. So great was the women's wrath at this shameful edict that they rushed to the walls in arms, and fought so fiercely that in a short time they drove Philip off with disgrace and loss: which their husbands had not been able to do.[375]

"When these same women came to Leuconia with their husbands, fathers and brothers (who were going into exile), they performed a deed no less glorious than this: the Erythræans,[376] who were there with their allies, waged war upon these Chiotes, who were unable to resist, and so bound themselves to quit the city in tunic and shift only. Hearing of this shameful bargain, the women bewailed and upbraided the men for abandoning their weapons and going forth almost naked among the enemy; and the men answering that they were already bound, the women told them to wear their shields and spears and leave their clothes behind, and to tell the enemy that this was their attire. And thus, acting upon the advice of their women, they in great part atoned for the shame that they could not wholly escape.

"Again, Cyrus having routed an army of Persians in battle, in fleeing to their city they met their women outside the gate, who, stopping in the way, said: 'Whither do ye flee, base men? Would ye perchance hide yourselves in us, from whence ye came?' On hearing these and other like words, and being sensible how inferior they were in courage to their women, the men were ashamed, and returning against the enemy, fought with him anew and routed him." [377]

33.—Having thus far spoken, the Magnifico stopped, and turning to my lady Duchess, said:

"Now, my Lady, you will give me leave to be silent."

My lord Gaspar replied:

"You will forsooth have to be silent, for you do not know what more to say."

The Magnifico said, laughing:

"You provoke me so, that you run risk of having to listen to women's praises all night; and to hear of many Spartan women who rejoiced in the glorious death of their children;[378] and of those who disowned or even slew theirs when seen to behave basely. Then how in the ruin of their country the Saguntine women took up arms against the forces of Hannibal;[379] and how, when Marius overcame the army of the Germans, the women, being unable to get leave to live free at Rome in the service of the Vestal Virgins, all killed themselves and their little children;[380] and of a thousand others whereof all the ancient histories are full."

Then my lord Gaspar said:

"Ah, my lord Magnifico, but God knows how those things happened; for that age is so remote from us that many lies can be told and there is none to refute them."

34.—The Magnifico said:

"If in every age you will compare women's worth with that of men, you will find that they have never been and are not now at all inferior to men in worth; for leaving aside the times that are so ancient, if you come to the time when the Goths ruled in Italy, you will find that there was a queen among them, Amalasontha,[381] who long reigned with admirable wisdom; then Theodolinda,[382] queen of the Lombards, of singular worth; Theodora,[383] the Greek empress; and in Italy among many others the Countess Matilda was a most illustrious lady, of whose praises I will leave Count Ludovico to speak, since she was of his family."[384]

"Nay," said the Count, "that rests with you, for you know it does not become a man to praise what is his own."

The Magnifico continued:

"And how many women in times past do you find belonging

to this most noble house of Montefeltro! [385] How many of the house of Gonzaga, of Este, of Pio! [386] Then, if you wish to speak of the present times, we shall have no need to seek very far for instances, because we have them at home. But I shall not avail myself of those we see before us, lest you pretend to grant me out of courtesy that which you can in no wise deny. And to go outside of Italy, remember that we in our day have seen Queen Anne of France, [387] a very great lady not less in worth than in state; and if you will compare her in justice and clemency, liberality and pureness of life, with Kings Charles [388] and Louis [250] (to both of whom she was consort), you will not find her at all their inferior. You see madonna Margarita [389] (daughter of the Emperor Maximilian) [390] who has until now governed and still governs her state with the utmost wisdom and justice.

35.—"But laying all others aside, tell me, my lord Gaspar, what king or what prince has there been in our days, or even for many years past in Christendom, who deserves to be compared with Queen Isabella of Spain?" [391]

My lord Gaspar replied:

"King Ferdinand, her husband." [392]

The Magnifico continued:

"That I shall not deny; for since the queen judged him worthy to be her husband, and so loved and honoured him, we cannot say that he did not deserve to be compared with her: yet I believe that the fame he had by her was a dowry not inferior to the kingdom of Castile."

"Nay," replied my lord Gaspar, "I think that Queen Isabella had credit for many of King Ferdinand's deeds."

Then the Magnifico said:

"Unless the people of Spain,—lords, commons, men and women, poor and rich,—have all agreed to live in praise of her, there has not been in our time on earth a brighter example of true goodness, of lofty spirit, of wisdom, of piety, of purity, of courtesy, of liberality,—in short, of every virtue,—than Queen Isabella; and although the fame of that illustrious lady is very great in every place and among every nation, those who lived in her company and were witness to her actions, do all affirm that this fame sprang from her virtue and merits. And whoever will

ↆↆↆↆↆↆↆↆↆↆↆↆↆↆↆↆↆↆↆↆↆↆↆↆↆↆↆↆↆↆↆↆↆↆↆↆↆↆↆↆↆↆↆↆↆↆↆↆↆↆↆↆↆↆↆↆↆↆↆↆↆↆↆↆↆ

consider her deeds will easily perceive such to be the truth. For leaving aside countless things that give proof of this and could be told if it were our theme, everyone knows that when she came to reign she found the greater part of Castile usurped by the grandees; yet she recovered the whole so righteously and in such fashion that the very men who were deprived of it, remained very devoted to her and content to give up that which they possessed.

"A very noted thing also is with what courage and wisdom she always defended her realms against very powerful enemies; and likewise to her alone can be given the honour of the glorious conquest of the kingdom of Granada; for in this long and difficult war against obstinate enemies,—who were fighting for property, for life, for religion, and (to their thinking) for God,—she always showed, both in her counsel and in her very person, such virtue that perhaps few princes in our time have had the hardihood, I will not say to imitate, but even to envy her.

"Besides this, all who knew her affirm that she had such a divine manner of ruling that her mere wish seemed enough to make every man do quietly that which he ought to do; so that men hardly dared in their own houses and secretly to do anything they thought would displease her: and in great part the cause of this was the admirable judgment she had in discerning and choosing right agents for the duties she meant to employ them in; and so well did she know how to unite the rigour of justice with the gentleness of mercy and liberality, that in her day there was no good man who complained of being ill rewarded, nor any bad man of being too severely punished. Thus there sprang up among the people an exceeding great reverence for her, composed of love and fear, which still remains so implanted in the minds of all, that they almost seem to think that she looks down upon them from heaven and must bestow praise or blame upon them from above; and thus those realms are still governed by her name and the methods she ordained, so that although her life is at an end, her authority lives,—like a wheel which, long revolved with force, still turns of itself for a good space, although nothing more impels it.

"Consider also, my lord Gaspar, that in our times nearly all the men in Spain who are great or famous for anything whatever, were made so by Queen Isabella; and Consalvo Ferdinando, the

Great Captain, was far prouder of this than of all his famous victories, and of those eminent and worthy deeds which have made him so bright and illustrious in peace and war, that if fame is not very thankless, she will always herald his immortal praises to the world, and give proof that we have in our age had few kings or great princes who have not been surpassed by him in magnanimity, wisdom, and in every virtue.

36.—"Returning now to Italy, I say that here too there is no lack of very admirable ladies; for in Naples we have two remarkable queens; [393] and a short time since there died at Naples also the other queen of Hungary,[394] you know how admirable a lady, and worthy to be the peer of the unconquerable and glorious king, Matthias Corvinus, her husband.[395] Likewise the Duchess Isabella of Aragon, worthy sister to King Ferdinand of Naples; who (like gold in the fire) showed her virtue and worth amid the storms of fortune.[396]

"If you come to Lombardy, you will find my lady Isabella, Marchioness of Mantua; [397] to whose very admirable virtues injustice would be done in speaking as soberly as in this place anyone must needs do who would speak of her at all. I regret, too, that you did not all know her sister the Duchess Beatrice of Milan, in order that you might never more have need to marvel at woman's capacity.[398] And Eleanora of Aragon, Duchess of Ferrara and mother of both these two ladies whom I have mentioned, was of such sort that her very admirable virtues bore good witness to all the world that she not only was a worthy daughter of a king, but deserved to be queen over a much greater realm than all her ancestors had possessed.[399] And to tell you of another, how many men do you know in the world who have borne the cruel blows of fortune as patiently as Queen Isabella of Naples has done? [400]—who, after the loss of her kingdom, the exile and death of her husband King Federico [401] and of two children, and the captivity of her first-born, the Duke of Calabria,[402] still shows herself to be a queen, and so endures the grievous burdens of bitter poverty as to give all men proof that although her fortunes are changed, her rank is not.

"I refrain from mentioning countless other ladies, and also women of low degree; like many Pisan women, who in defence of their city against the Florentines displayed that generous daring, without any fear of death, which might have been displayed by the most unconquerable souls that have ever been on earth; wherefore some of them have been celebrated by many noble poets.[403]

"I could tell you of some who were very excellent in letters, in music, in painting, in sculpture; but I do not wish to go on selecting from among these instances that are perfectly well known to you all. It is enough that if you reflect upon the women whom you yourselves know, it is not difficult for you to perceive that they are for the most part not inferior in worth and merits to their fathers, brothers and husbands; and that not a few have been the source of good to men and often have corrected many a one of his errors; and if there are not now to be found on earth those great queens who march to the conquest of distant lands, and erect great buildings, pyramids and cities,—like that famous Tomyris, Queen of Scythia, Artemisia, Zenobia, Semiramis or Cleopatra,[404]—neither are there men like Cæsar, Alexander, Scipio, Lucullus and those other Roman commanders."

37.—"Say not so," replied Frisio, laughing; "for now more than ever are there women to be found like Cleopatra or Semiramis; and if they have not such great states, power and riches, yet they lack not the good will to imitate those queens in giving themselves pleasure, and in satisfying as far as they can all their appetites."

The Magnifico Giuliano said:

"You always wish to go beyond bounds, Frisio; but if there are some Cleopatras to be found, there is no lack of countless Sardanapaluses, which is far worse." [405]

Then my lord Gaspar said:

"Do not draw these comparisons, or imagine that men are more incontinent than women; and even if they were so, it would not be worse, for from women's incontinence countless evils result that do not from men's. Therefore, as was said yesterday, it is wisely ordained that women are allowed to fail in all other things without blame, to the end that they may be able to devote all their strength to keeping themselves in this one virtue of chastity; without which their children would be uncertain, and that tie would be dissolved which binds the whole world by blood and by the natural love of each man for what he has produced. Hence loose living is more forbidden to women than to men, who do not carry their children for nine months within them."

38.—Then the Magnifico replied:

"Verily these are fine arguments which you cite, and I do not see why you do not commit them to writing.

"But tell me why it is not ordained that loose living is as disgraceful a thing in men as in women, seeing that if men are by nature more virtuous and of greater worth, they could all the more easily practise this virtue of continence also; and their children would be neither more nor less certain, for although women were unchaste, they could of themselves merely and without other aid in no wise bear children, provided men were continent and did not take part in women's unchastity. But if you will say the truth, even you know that we men have of our own authority arrogated to ourselves a licence, whereby we insist that the same sins are in us very trivial and sometimes praiseworthy, and in women cannot be sufficiently punished, unless by shameful death or perpetual infamy at least.

"Wherefore, since this opinion is prevalent, methinks it were a fitting thing to punish severely those also who with lies cast infamy on women; and I think that every noble cavalier is bound always to defend the truth with arms where there is need, and especially when he knows some woman to be falsely accused of little chastity."

39.—"And I," replied my lord Gaspar, laughing, "not only affirm that which you say is the duty of every noble cavalier, but I think that it is an act of great courtesy and gentleness to conceal the fault a woman may have committed through mischance or over-love; and thus you may see that I am more on the side of women, where reason permits it, than you are.

"I do not, indeed, deny that men have taken a little liberty; and this because they know that according to universal opinion loose living does not bring them the infamy that it does to women; who by reason of the frailty of their sex are much more inclined towards their appetites than men are; and if they some-

times refrain from satisfying their desires, they do so from
shame and not because their will is not quite ready. Therefore
men have put the fear of infamy upon them as a bridle to keep
them almost by force to this virtue, without which they were in
truth little to be prized; for the world has no good from women
except the bearing of children.

"But this is not the case with men, who rule cities and
armies, and do so many other things of importance. Since you
will have it so, I do not care to deny that women can do these
things; it is enough that they do not. And when men have seen
fit to set a pattern of continence, they have excelled women in
this virtue as well as in the others also, although you do not
admit it. And as to this I will not rehearse so many histories and
fables as you have done, but merely refer you to the continence
of two very great young lords, and to their victory, which is wont
to make even men of lowest rank insolent. One is that of Alexander the Great towards the very beautiful women of Darius,—an
enemy, and a vanquished one at that;[406] the other, of Scipio,
who having at the age of twenty-four years taken a city in Spain
by force, there was brought before him a very beautiful and noble
young woman, captured along with many others; and hearing
that she was the bride of a gentleman of the country, Scipio not
only abstained from any wanton act towards her, but restored
her unspotted to her husband, bestowing a rich gift upon her
besides.[407]

"I could tell you of Xenocrates,[408] who was so continent that
a very beautiful woman having laid herself down unclothed beside him, and employing all the caresses and using all the arts
that she knew, whereof she was an admirable mistress, she had
not the power to make him show the slightest sign of impudicity,
although she tried one whole night long; and of Pericles, who
on merely hearing someone praise a boy's beauty with over-
warmth, reproved him sharply;[409] and of many others who have
been very continent of their own choice, and not from shame or
fear of punishment, which move most women who practise this
virtue: who for all that deserve to be highly praised, and he who
falsely casts the infamy of unchasteness upon them is worthy of
the heaviest punishment, as you have said."

40.—Then messer Cesare, who had been silent a long while, said:

"Think in what fashion my lord Gaspar is wont to speak in blame of woman, if these are the things that he says in their praise. But if my lord Magnifico will let me say a few things in his stead by way of reply to such matters as my lord Gaspar has, to my thinking, said falsely against women, it were well for both of us; as he will rest awhile and then be better able to go on to declare some other excellence of the Court Lady, and I shall hold myself much favoured at having an opportunity to share with him this duty of a good cavalier—that is, to defend the truth."

"Nay, I pray you do so," replied my lord Magnifico; "for methinks I have already fulfilled my duty to the extent of my powers, and this discussion is now outside my subject."

Messer Cesare continued:

"I am far from wishing to speak of the good that women do in the world besides the bearing of children, for it has been sufficiently shown how necessary they are not only to our being, but to our well-being; but I say, my lord Gaspar, that if they are as you say more inclined to their appetites than men, and if for all that they abstain therefrom more than men, which you admit, —they are as much worthier of praise as their sex is less strong to resist their natural appetites. And if you say they do it from shame, methinks that in place of a single virtue you give them two; for if shame is stronger in them than appetite and they for that reason abstain from evil acts, I think that this shame (which in short is nothing else but fear of infamy) is a very rare virtue and one possessed by very few men. And if I could, without infinite disgrace to men, tell how many of them are plunged in shamelessness (which is the vice opposed to this virtue), I should pollute these chaste ears that hear me. These offenders against God and nature are for the most part men already old, who make a calling, some of the priesthood, some of philosophy, some of sacred law; and govern public affairs with a Catonian severity of countenance that gives promise of all the integrity in the world; and always allege the feminine sex to be very incontinent; nor do they ever lament anything more than their loss of natural

vigour, which renders them unable to satisfy the abominable desires that still linger in their thoughts after being denied by nature to their bodies; and hence they often find ways wherein
strength is not necessary.

41.—"But I do not wish to say more; and it is enough for
me that you grant me that women abstain from unchaste living
more than men; and certain it is that they are restrained by no
other bridle than that which they themselves put on. That this
is true, the greater part of those who are confined with too close
care, or beaten by their husbands or fathers, are less chaste than
those who have some liberty.

"But a great bridle to women generally is their love of true
virtue and their desire for honour, whereof many whom I have
known in my time make more account than of their very life;
and if you will say the truth, every one of us has seen very noble
youths, discreet, wise, valiant and beautiful, spend many years
in love, without omitting aught of care, of gifts, of prayers, of
tears, in short, of anything that can be imagined; and all in vain.
And but that I might be told that my qualities have never made
me worthy of ever being loved, I should call myself as witness,
who have more than once been nigh to death because of a
woman's unchangeable and too stern chastity."

My lord Gaspar replied:

"Marvel not at that: for women who are always wooed refuse to please him who wooes them; and they who are not wooed,
woo others." [410]

42.—Messer Cesare said:

"I have never known these men who are wooed by women;
but very many who, on finding that they have tried in vain and
spent time foolishly, resort to this noble revenge, and say they
have had an abundance of that which they have only imagined,
and think it a kind of courtiership to speak evil and invent tales
to the end that slanderous stories of some noble lady may spring
up among the rabble. But such as these, who make vile boast
(whether true or false) of conquering a gentle lady, deserve punishment or torture most severe; and if they sometimes meet it,
we cannot measure the praise due to those who perform the
office. For if they are telling lies, what villainy can be greater

than to steal from a worthy lady that which she values more than life? And for no other reason than that which ought to win endless praise for her? Again, if they are telling the truth, what punishment could suffice for a man who is so vile as to reward with such ingratitude a woman, who,—vanquished by false flatteries, by feigned tears, by continual wooing, by laments, by arts, tricks and perjuries,—has suffered herself to be led into too great love, and then without reserve has fondly given herself a prey to such a malign spirit?

"But to answer you further touching that unheard-of continence of Alexander and Scipio which you have cited, I say I am unwilling to deny that both performed an act worthy of much praise; yet to the end that you may not be able to say that in rehearsing ancient matters I tell you fables, I wish to cite a woman of low degree in our own times, who showed far more continence than these two great men.

43.—"I say, then, that I once knew a beautiful and gentle girl, whose name I do not tell you lest you give food for slander to many fools, who conceive a bad opinion of a woman as soon as they hear of her being in love. Well, this girl having been long loved by a noble and well-conditioned youth, began to love him with all her mind and heart; and of this not only I (to whom she voluntarily confided everything as if I had been, I will not say her brother, but her dearest sister), but all those who saw her in the presence of the beloved youth, were very certain of her passion. Loving thus as fervently as a very loving soul can love, she maintained such continence for two years that she never gave this youth any token of loving him, except such as she could not hide; neither would she ever speak to him or receive letters from him or gifts, although a day never passed but she was besought to do both. And I well know how she longed for it, because if she was sometimes able to possess anything secretly that had been the youth's, she held it so dear that it seemed to be the source of her life and all her weal; and never in all that time would she grant him other pleasure than to see him and let herself be seen, and to dance with him as with the others when she took part in public festivals.

"And since they were well suited to each other in condition, the girl and the youth desired that their great love might end happily, and that they might be man and wife together. The same was desired by all the other men and women of their city, except her cruel father, who out of perverse and strange caprice wished to marry her to another and richer man; and to this the unhappy girl opposed naught but very bitter tears. And the ill-starred marriage having been concluded, with much pity from the people and to the despair of the poor lovers, even this blow of fortune did not avail to destroy the love so deeply rooted in their hearts; which still endured for the space of three years, although she very prudently concealed it and sought in every way to stifle those desires that now were hopeless. And all this time she kept her stern resolve of continence; and as she could not honourably possess him whom alone in the world she adored, she chose not to wish for him in any wise, and to follow her custom of accepting neither messages nor gifts nor even glances from him; and in this fixed resolve, the poor girl, overcome by sharpest anguish and grown very wasted from long passion, died at the end of three years, preferring to renounce the joys and pleasures so eagerly desired, and at last her very life, rather than her honour. Nor was she without ways and means of satisfying herself quite secretly and without risk of disgrace or any other harm; and yet she abstained from that which she herself so greatly desired and towards which she was so urged continually by the person whom alone in the world she desired to please: nor was she moved therein by fear or any other motive than mere love of true virtue.

"What will you say of another, who for six months spent nearly every night with a dearly cherished lover; yet, in a garden full of sweetest fruits, invited by her own most ardent longing and by the prayers and tears of one dearer to her than life itself, she refrained from tasting them; and although she was caught and held in the fast bonds of those beloved arms, she never yielded herself vanquished, but preserved the flower of her chastity immaculate.

44.—"Do you think, my lord Gaspar, that these acts of continence are equal to Alexander's?—who (being most ardently enamoured, not of Darius's women, but of that fame and greatness which incited him by thirst for glory to endure toils and dangers to make himself immortal) spurned not only other things, but his own life, in order to win renown above all other men. And do we marvel that with such thoughts at heart he abstained from something he did not much desire? For since he had never seen the women before, he could not possibly love them in a moment, but perhaps even loathed them because of his enemy Darius; and in that case every wanton act of his towards them would have been outrage and not love. Hence it is no great thing that Alexander, who conquered the world no less by magnanimity than by arms, abstained from doing outrage to women.

"Scipio's continence also is much to be praised. Yet if you consider rightly, it is not to be compared with these two women's; for he too likewise abstained from something not desired;—being in a hostile country, newly in command, at the beginning of a very important enterprise; having left great expectations of himself at home, and bound to render an account to very strict judges, who often punished very small mistakes as well as great, and among whom he knew he had enemies; conscious also that if he acted otherwise (the lady being very noble and married to a very noble lord), he might arouse so many enemies and in such fashion that they might long hinder and perhaps quite snatch away his success. Hence, for reasons thus many and important, he abstained from a light and harmful wish, displaying continence and generous uprightness; which, as it is written, gave him the entire good will of those nations, and was worth another army to him, wherewith by gentleness to conquer hearts that perhaps would have been unconquerable by force of arms.[411]

.   .   .   .   .   .   .   .

"Forgive me, my lord Gaspar, if I say the truth, for in short these are the miraculous continences that men write about themselves while accusing women of incontinence, in whom we every day see countless tokens of continence; for in truth, if you consider well, there is no fortress so impregnable and well defended that, if it were assailed with a thousandth part of the wiles and tricks that are employed to overcome the steadfast heart of woman, it would not surrender at the first assault.

"How many creatures of great lords,—enriched by them and

placed in very high esteem, entrusted with their castles and
fortresses, whereon depend their whole state, life and weal,—
have basely and sordidly surrendered these to such as had no
right thereto, without shame or fear of being called traitors?
And would to God there were so great a dearth of such men in
our days, that we might have no more trouble to find a man who
had done his duty in this regard, than to name those who have
failed in theirs. Do we not see many others who daily go about
slaying men in the forest and scouring the sea solely to steal
money?

"How many prelates sell the property of God's church!
How many lawyers forge wills! How many perjurers bear false
witness only to get money! How many physicians poison the
sick to the same end! Again, how many do the vilest things from
fear of death! And yet a tender and delicate girl often resists
all these sharp and hard encounters; for many have been found
who preferred death rather than lose their chastity."

47.—Then my lord Gaspar said:

"These, messer Cesare, I believe are not on earth to-day."

Messer Cesare replied:

"I will not cite the ancients now but I tell you this, that
many would be and are to be found, who in such case do not fear
to die. And now I remember that when Capua was sacked by the
French (which was not so long ago that you cannot recall it very
well),[412] a beautiful young Capuan lady being led out of her
house, where she had been captured by a company of Gascons,
when she reached the river that flows through Capua,[413] she pretended that she wished to tie her shoe, so that he who was leading her let her go a little, and she suddenly threw herself into
the river.

"What will you say of a peasant girl, who not many months
ago, at Gazuolo in the Mantuan territory,[414] went with her sister
to reap corn in the fields, and being overcome with thirst, entered
a house for a drink of water; and the master of the house, who
was a young man, seeing that she was very beautiful and alone,
took her in his arms, and first with soft words, and then with
threats, sought to persuade her to his wishes; and she resisting
more and more stubbornly, he at last overcame her with many

blows and with force. So, dishevelled and weeping, she went back to her sister in the field, nor would she for all her sister's urgent questioning tell what outrage she had received in that house; but on the way home, feigning to grow calmer little by little and to speak quite without agitation, she gave her sister some directions. Then when she came to the Oglio, which is the river that flows by Gazuolo,[415] she left her sister a little behind not knowing or imagining what she meant to do, and suddenly threw herself in. Wailing and weeping her sister ran after her as fast as possible along the bank of the river, which was bearing her down-stream very rapidly: and each time the poor creature rose to the surface, her sister threw her a cord which they had to bind the corn, and although the cord reached her hands several times (for she was still near the bank), the steadfast and determined girl always refused it and put it from her; and thus rejecting every aid that might save her life, she soon died: nor was she moved by nobility of birth, nor by fear of most cruel death or of infamy, but solely by grief for her lost virginity.[416]

"Now from this you can understand how many other women, who are not known, perform acts most worthy of praise; for although this one gave such proof of her virtue only three days since, as one may say, there is no talk of her and even her name is unknown. But if the death of our lady Duchess's uncle, the Bishop of Mantua,[417] had not occurred at that time, the bank of the Oglio, at the place where she threw herself in, would have been graced by a very beautiful monument to the memory of that glorious soul, which deserved so much the brighter fame after death, because in life it dwelt in a less noble body."

48.—Here messer Cesare made a little pause; then he continued:

"At Rome, in my day, there happened another like case; and it was that a beautiful and noble Roman girl, being long pursued by one who seemed to love her much, was never willing to favour him at all, even with a single look. So, by means of money he corrupted one of her women; who, desirous of satisfying him in order to get more money from him, persuaded her mistress to visit the church of San Sebastiano on a certain day of small solemnity,[418] and having made everything known to the lover and shown him what he must do, she led the girl to one of those dark caves which nearly all who go to San Sebastiano are wont to visit; and in this the young man was already hidden secretly.

"Finding himself alone with her whom he loved so much, he began in all ways to beg her as gently as he could to have pity on him and change her former hardness to love. But after he saw all his prayers to be in vain, he had resort to threats, which failing too, he began to beat her cruelly; at last, although firmly resolved to attain his end, by force if necessary, and therein employing the help of the infamous woman who had led her thither, he was never able to bring her to consent. Nay, with both word and deed (although she had little strength), the poor girl defended herself to the last: so that partly from anger at seeing that he could not obtain what he desired, partly from fear lest her relatives might make him suffer for it when they learned the thing, this wretch, with the help of the servant (who feared the like), strangled the unhappy girl and left her there; and having fled, he took means not to be discovered. Blinded by her very crime, the servant could not flee, and being taken into custody on suspicion, confessed everything and so was punished as she deserved.

"The body of the steadfast and noble girl was taken from that cave with the greatest honour and brought to Rome for burial, with a laurel crown upon her head, and accompanied by a countless host of men and women; among whom there was no one who went home without tears in his eyes; and thus was this rare soul universally mourned as well as praised by all the people.

49.—"But to speak to you of those whom you yourselves know, do you not remember having heard that when my lady Felice della Rovere was journeying to Savona,[419] and feared that some sails that were sighted were vessels of Pope Alexander in pursuit of her, she made ready with fixed resolve to cast herself into the sea, in case they should come up and there was no remedy by flight: and it is no wise to be believed that she acted in this from lightness, for you know as well as any other with what intelligence and wisdom this lady's singular beauty was accompanied.

"Nor can I refrain from saying a word of our lady Duchess, who having for fifteen years lived like a widow in company with her husband, not only was steadfast in never revealing this to anyone in the world, but when urged by her own people to lay aside her widowhood, she chose rather to endure exile, poverty and every other sort of hardship, than to accept that which seemed to all others great favour and blessing of fortune;" [420] and as messer Cesare was going on to speak of this, my lady Duchess said:

"Speak of something else, and go no further with this subject, for you have many other things to say."

Messer Cesare continued:

"Yet I know you will not deny this, my lord Gaspar, nor you, Frisio."

"Indeed no," replied Frisio; "but one does not make a host."

50.—Then messer Cesare said:

"It is true that such great results as these are met in few women: still, those also who withstand the assaults of love are all admirable; and those who are sometimes overcome deserve much pity: for certainly the urgence of lovers, the arts they use, the snares they spread, are so many and so continual that it is but too great a wonder that a tender girl can escape. What day, what hour, ever passes that the persecuted girl is not besought by the lover with money, gifts and all things that must please her? When can she ever go to her window, but she shall always see her persistent lover pass, silent in word but with eyes that speak, with sad and languid face, with those burning sighs, often with most abundant tears? When does she ever go forth to church or other place, but he is always before her, and meets her at every turn of the street with his melancholy passion depicted in his eyes, as if he were expecting instant death? I leave aside the fripperies, inventions, mottoes, devices, festivals, dances, games, masques, jousts, tourneys!—all which things she knows are made for her.

"Then at night she can never wake but she hears music, or at least his unquiet spirit sighing about the house walls and making lamentable sounds. If by chance she wishes to speak to one of her women, the wench (already corrupted with money) soon has ready a little gift, a letter, a sonnet or some such thing to give her on the lover's behalf, and then coming in opportunely, makes her understand how the poor man is burning with love, and in her service cares naught for his own life; and how he seeks nothing from her that is less than seemly, and only desires to speak with her. Then remedies are found for all difficulties, false keys, rope ladders, sleeping potions; the thing is painted as of little consequence; instances are given of many other women who do far worse. Thus everything is made so easy that she has no further trouble than to say, 'I am willing.' And even if the poor girl holds back for a time, they add so many inducements, find so many ways, that with their continual battering they break down that which stays her.

"And when they see that blandishments do not avail them, there are many who have resort to threats and say they will accuse the woman to her husband of being what she is not. Others bargain boldly with the fathers and often with the husbands, who for money or to get favours give their own daughters and wives as an unwilling prey. Others seek by incantations and sorceries to steal from them that liberty which God has bestowed upon their souls: whereof startling results are seen.

"But I could not in a thousand years rehearse all the wiles that men employ to bring women to their wishes, for the wiles are infinite; and besides those that every man finds for himself, writers have not been lacking who have ingeniously composed books and therein taken every pains to teach how women are to be duped in these matters.[421] Now, among so many snares, think how there can be any safety for these simple doves, lured by such sweet bait. And what wonder is it, then, if a woman (seeing herself thus loved and adored for many years by a beautiful, noble and accomplished youth, who a thousand times a day puts himself in danger of death to serve her, nor ever thinks of aught but to please her) is finally brought to love him by continual wearing (as water wears the hardest marble), and, conquered by this passion, contents him with that which you say she in the weakness of her sex desires more than her lover? Do you think that this error is so grave that the poor creature who has been caught by so many flatteries, does not deserve even that pardon which is often vouchsafed to homicides, thieves, assassins and traitors? Will you insist that this offence is so heinous that because you find some woman commits it, womankind ought to be wholly despised and held universally devoid of continence, without regard to the many who are found unconquerable, and who are proof against love's continual incitements, and firmer in their infinite constancy than rocks against the surges of the ocean?"

51.—Messer Cesare having ceased speaking, my lord Gaspar then began to reply, but my lord Ottaviano said, laughing:

"For the love of Heaven, pray grant him the victory, for I know you will profit little; and methinks I see that you will make not only all these ladies your enemies, but the greater part of the men also."

My lord Gaspar laughed, and said:

"Nay, the ladies have great cause to thank me; for if I had not gainsaid my lord Magnifico and messer Cesare, all these praises which they have bestowed upon women would not have been heard."

Then messer Cesare said:

"The things that my lord Magnifico and I have said in praise of women, and many others too, were very well known and hence superfluous.

"Who does not know that without women we can feel no content or satisfaction throughout this life of ours, which but for them would be rude and devoid of all sweetness and more savage than that of wild beasts? Who does not know that women alone banish from our hearts all vile and base thoughts, vexations, miseries, and those turbid melancholies that so often are their fellows? and if you will consider well the truth, we shall also see that in our understanding of great matters women do not hamper our wits but rather quicken them, and in war make men fearless and brave beyond measure. And certainly it is impossible for vileness ever again to rule in a man's heart where once the flame of love has entered; for whoever loves desires always to make himself as lovable as he can, and always fears lest some disgrace befall him that may make him to be esteemed lightly with her by whom he desires to be esteemed highly. Nor does he stop at risking his life a thousand times a day to show himself worthy of her love: hence whoever could form an army of lovers and have them fight in the presence of the ladies of their love, would conquer all the world, unless there were opposed to it another army similarly in love. And be well assured that Troy's ten years' resistance against all Greece proceeded from naught else but a few lovers, who on sallying forth to battle, armed themselves in the presence of their women; and often these women helped them and spoke some word to them at leaving, which inflamed them and made them more than men. Then in battle they knew that they were watched by their women from the walls and towers; wherefore it seemed to them that every act of hardihood they performed, every proof they gave, won them their women's praise, which was the greatest reward they could have in the world.

"There are many who think that the victory of King Ferdinand of Spain and Queen Isabella against the King of Granada was in great part due to women; for very often when the Spanish army went out to meet the enemy, Queen Isabella went out also with all her maids of honour, and in the army went many noble cavaliers who were in love. These always went conversing with their ladies until they reached the place where the enemy were seen, then taking leave each of his own lady, they went on in this presence to meet the enemy with that fierce spirit which was aroused in them by their love and by the desire to make their ladies sensible of being served by men of valour; thus a very few Spanish cavaliers were often found putting a host of Moors to flight and to death, thanks to gentle and beloved women.

"So I do not see, my lord Gaspar, what perversity of judgment has led you to cast reproach on women.

52.—"Do you not know that the origin of all the graceful exercises that give pleasure in the world is to be ascribed to none other than to women? Who learns to dance and caper gallantly for aught else than to please women? Who studies the sweetness of music for other cause than this? Who tries to compose verses, in the vernacular at least, unless to express those feelings that are inspired by women? Think how many very noble poems we should be deprived of, both in the Greek tongue and in the Latin, if women had been lightly esteemed by the poets. But to pass all the others by, would it not have been a very great loss if messer Francesco Petrarch, who so divinely wrote his loves in this language of ours, had turned his mind solely to things Latin, as he would have done if the love of madonna Laura had not sometimes drawn him from them? [422] I do not name you the bright geniuses now on earth and present here, who every day put forth some noble fruit and yet choose their subject only from the beauties and virtues of women.

"You see that Solomon, wishing to write mystically of things lofty and divine, to cover them with a graceful veil composed a fervent and tender dialogue between a lover and his sweetheart, deeming that he could not here below find any similitude more apt and befitting things divine than love for women; and in this way he tried to give us a little of the savour of that divinity which he both by knowledge and by grace knew better than the rest. [423]

"Hence there was no need, my lord Gaspar, to dispute about this, or at least so wordily: but by gainsaying the truth you have prevented us from hearing a thousand other fine and weighty matters concerning the perfection of the Court Lady."

My lord Gaspar replied:

"I believe nothing more is left to say; yet if you think that my lord Magnifico has not adorned her with enough good qualities, the fault lay not with him, but with the one who arranged that there are not more virtues in the world; for the Magnifico gave her all there are."

My lady Duchess said, laughing:

"You shall now see that my lord Magnifico will find still others."

The Magnifico replied:

"Indeed, my Lady, methinks I have said enough, and for my part I am content with this Lady of mine; and if these gentlemen will not have her as she is, let them leave her to me."

53.—Here everyone remaining silent, messer Federico said:

"My lord Magnifico, to spur you on to say something more, I should like to put you a question concerning what you would have the chief business of the Court Lady, and it is this: that I wish to hear how she ought to conduct herself with respect to one detail which seems to me very important; for although the excellent qualities wherewith you have endowed her include genius, wisdom, good sense, ease of bearing, modesty, and so many other virtues, whereby she ought in reason to be able to converse with everyone and on every theme, still I think that more than anything else she needs to know that which belongs to discussions on love. For as every gentle cavalier uses those noble exercises, elegances and fine manners that we have mentioned, as a means to win the favour of women, to this end likewise he employs words; and not only when he is moved by passion, but often also to do honour to the lady with whom he is speaking, since he thinks that to give signs of love for her is a proof that she is worthy of it, and that her beauty and merits are so great that they compel every man to serve her.

"Hence I fain would know how this lady ought to converse on such a theme discreetly, and how reply to him who loves her truly, and how to him who makes a false pretence thereof; and whether she ought to feign not to understand, whether to return his love or to refuse, and how conduct herself."

54.—Then my lord Magnifico said:

"It would be needful to teach her first to distinguish those who pretend to love and those who love truly; then, as to returning love or not, I think she ought not to be governed by any others' wish but her own."

Messer Federico said:

"Then teach her what are the surest and safest signs to discern false love from true, and with what proof she ought to be content in order to be sure of the love shown her."

The Magnifico replied, laughing:

"I know not, for men to-day are so cunning that they make false pretences without end, and sometimes weep when they have great wish to laugh; hence it were necessary to send them to Isola Ferma under the True Lovers' Arch.[424]

"But to the end that this Lady of mine (of whom it behooves me to take special care, since she is my creation) may not fall into those errors wherein I have seen many others fall, I should tell her not to be quick to believe herself loved, nor act like some who not only do not feign not to understand when court is paid to them even covertly, but at the first word accept all the praise that is given them, or decline it with a certain air that is rather an invitation to love for those with whom they are speaking, than a refusal.

"Therefore the course of conduct that I wish my Court Lady to pursue in love talk, will be to refuse always to believe that whoever pays court to her for that reason loves her: and if the gentleman shall be as pert as many are, and speak to her with small respect, she will give him such answer that he may clearly understand he is causing her annoyance. Again, if he shall be discreet and use modest phrases and words of love covertly, with that gentle manner which I think the Courtier fashioned by these gentlemen will employ, the lady will feign not to understand and will apply his words in another sense, always modestly trying to change the subject with that skill and prudence which have been said befit her. If, again, the talk is such that she cannot feign not to understand, she will take it all as a jest, pretending to be aware that it is said to her more out of compliment to her than because it is true, depreciating her merits and ascribing the praises that he gives her to the gentleman's courtesy; and in this way she will win a name for discretion and be safer against deceit.

"After this fashion methinks the Court Lady ought to conduct herself in love talk."

55.—Then messer Federico said:

"My lord Magnifico, you discourse of this matter as if everyone who pays court to women must needs speak lies and seek to deceive them: if the which were true, I should say that your teachings were sound; but if this cavalier who is speaking loves truly and feels that passion which sometimes so sorely afflicts the human heart, do you not consider in what pain, in what calamity and mortal anguish you put him by insisting that the lady shall never believe anything he says on this subject? Ought his supplications, tears, and many other signs to go for naught? Have a care, my lord Magnifico, lest it be thought that besides the natural cruelty which many of these ladies have in them, you are teaching them still more."

The Magnifico replied:

"I spoke not of him who loves, but of him who entertains with amorous talk, wherein one of the most necessary conditions is that words shall never be lacking. But just as true lovers have glowing hearts, so they have cold tongues, with broken speech and sudden silence; wherefore perhaps it would not be a false assumption to say: 'Who loves much, speaks little.' Yet as to this I believe no certain rule can be given, because of the diversity of men's habits; nor could I say anything more than that the Lady must be very cautious, and always bear in mind that men can declare their love with much less danger than women can."

56.—Then my lord Gaspar said, laughing:

"Would you not, my lord Magnifico, have this admirable Lady of yours love in return even when she knows that she is loved truly? For if the Courtier were not loved in return, it is not conceivable that he should go on loving her; and thus she would lose many advantages, and especially that service and reverence with which lovers honour and almost adore the virtue of their beloved."

"As to that," replied the Magnifico, "I do not wish to give advice; but I do say that I think love, as you understand it, is proper only for unmarried women; for when this love cannot end in marriage, the lady must always find in it that remorse and sting which things illicit give her, and run risk of staining that reputation for chastity which is so important to her."

Then messer Federico replied, laughing:

"This opinion of yours, my lord Magnifico, seems to me very austere, and I think you have learned it from some preacher —one of those who rebuke women for loving laymen, in order to have themselves the better part therein. And methinks you impose too hard a rule on married women, for many of them are to be found whose husbands bear the greatest hatred without cause, and affront them grievously, sometimes by loving other women, sometimes by causing them all the annoyances possible to devise; some against their will are married by their fathers to old men, infirm, loathsome and disgusting, who make them live in continual misery. If such women were allowed to be

ィィィィィィィィィィィィィィィィィィィィィィィィィィィィィィィィィィィィィィィィィィィィィィィィィィィィ
divorced and separated from those with whom they are ill mated,
perhaps it would not be fitting for them to love any but their
husbands; but when, either by enmity of the stars or by unfitness
of temperament or by other accident, it happens that the marriage
bed, which ought to be a nest of concord and of love, is strewn
by the accursed infernal fury with the seed of its venom, which
then brings forth anger, suspicion and the stinging thorns of
hatred to torment those unhappy souls cruelly bound by an un-
breakable chain until death,—why are you unwilling that the
woman should be allowed to seek some refuge from the heavy
lash, and to bestow on others that which is not only spurned but
hated by her husband? I am quite of the opinion that those who
have suitable husbands and are loved by them, ought not to do
them wrong; but the others wrong themselves by not loving
those who love them."

"Nay," replied the Magnifico, "they wrong themselves by
loving others than their husbands. Still, since not to love is often
beyond our power, if this mischance shall happen to the Court
Lady (that her husband's hate or another's love brings her to
love), I would have her yield her lover nothing but her spirit;
nor ever let her show him any clear sign of love (either by words
or by gestures or by any other means) by which he may be sure
of it."

57.—Then messer Roberto da Bari said, laughing:

"I appeal from this judgment of yours, my lord Magnifico,
and think I shall have many with me; but since you will teach
married women this rusticity, so to speak, do you wish also to
have the unmarried equally cruel and discourteous?—and com-
plaisant to their lovers in nothing whatever?"

"If my Court Lady be unmarried," replied my lord Magnifico, "and must love, I wish her to love someone whom she can
marry; nor shall I account it an error if she shows him some
sign of love: as to which matter I wish to teach her one universal
rule in a few words, to the end that she may with little pains be
able to bear it in mind; and this is, let her show him who loves
her every token of love except such as may imbue her lover's
mind with the hope of obtaining something wanton from her.
And it is necessary to give great heed to this, for it is an error

committed by countless women, who commonly desire nothing
more than to be beautiful: and since to have many lovers seems
to them proof of their beauty, they take every pains to get as
many as they can. Thus they are often carried into reckless behaviour, and forsaking that temperate modesty which so becomes
them, they employ certain pert looks with scurrile words and acts
full of immodesty, thinking that they are gladly seen and listened
to for this and that by such ways they make themselves loved:
which is false; for the demonstrations that are made to them
spring from desire excited by a belief in their willingness, not
from love. Wherefore I wish that my Court Lady may not by
wanton behaviour seem to offer herself to anyone who wants her
and to do her best to lure the eyes and appetite of all who look
upon her, but that by her merits and virtuous conduct, by her
loveliness, by her grace, she may imbue the mind of all who see
her with that true love which is due to all things lovable, and with
that respect which always deprives him of hope who thinks of
any wantonness.

"Moreover, he who is loved by such a woman ought to content himself with her every slightest demonstration, and to prize
a single loving look from her more than complete possession of
any other woman; and to such a Lady I should not know how
to add anything, unless to have her loved by so excellent a Courtier as these gentlemen have described, and to have her love him
also, to the end that they may both attain their complete perfection."

58.—Having thus far spoken, my lord Magnifico was silent;
whereupon my lord Gaspar said, laughing:

"Now, in sooth, you will not be able to complain that my
lord Magnifico has not described a most excellent Court Lady;
and henceforth, if such an one is found, I admit that she deserves
to be esteemed the Courtier's equal."

My lady Emilia replied:

"I engage to find her, provided you will find the Courtier."

Messer Roberto added:

"Verily it cannot be denied that the Lady described by my
lord Magnifico is most perfect: nevertheless, as to those last conditions of love, methinks he has made her a little too austere,

especially when he would have her deprive her lover of all hope, by words, gestures and behaviour, and do all she can to plunge the man in despair. For as everyone knows, human desires do not spend themselves upon those things whereof there is not some hope. And although a few women may have indeed been found, haughty perhaps by reason of their beauty and worth, whose first word to anyone who paid them court was that he must never expect to have anything from them that he wished,—yet afterwards they have been a little more gracious to him in look and manner, so that by their kindly acts they have somewhat tempered their haughty words. But if this Lady by acts and words and manner removes all hope, I think our Courtier, if he is wise, will never love her; and thus she will have the imperfection of being without a lover."

59.—Then the Magnifico said:

"I do not wish my Court Lady to remove hope of everything but only of wanton things, which (if the Courtier be as courteous and discreet as these gentlemen have described him) he will not only not hope for, but will not even wish for. Because if the beauty, behaviour, cleverness, goodness, knowledge, modesty, and the many other worthy qualities that we have given the Lady, are the cause of the Courtier's love for her, the end of his love will necessarily be worthy too: and if nobility, excellence in arms and letters and music, if gentleness and the possession of so many graces in speech and conversation, be the means whereby the Courtier is to win the lady's love, the end of that love must needs be of like quality with the means whereby it is attained.

"Moreover, just as there are divers sorts of beauty in the world, so too there are divers tastes in men; and thus it happens that when they see a woman of that serious beauty, which (whether she be going or staying or joking or jesting or doing what you will) always so tempers her whole behaviour as to induce a certain reverence in anyone who looks upon her,—many are abashed and dare not serve her; and lured by hope, they oftener love attractive and enticing women, so soft and tender as to display in words and acts and looks a certain languorous passion that promises easily to pass and be changed into love.

"To be safe against deceits, some men love another sort of

women, who are so free of eye and word and movement as to do
the first thing that comes into their mind with a certain simplicity which does not hide their thoughts. Nor are there lacking
other generous souls, who—(esteeming that worth is shown in
difficulty, and that it would be a victory most sweet to conquer
what to others seems unconquerable), in order to give proof that
their valour is able to force a stubborn mind and persuade to love
even wills that are contrary and recusant thereto,—readily turn
to love the beauties of those women who by eyes and words and
behaviour show more austere severity than the others. Wherefore
these men who are so self-confident, and who account themselves
secure against being deceived, willingly love certain women also
who by cunning and art seem to conceal a thousand wiles with
beauty; or else some others, who along with their beauty have
a coquettishly disdainful manner of few words and few laughs,
with almost an air of prizing little every man who looks upon
them or serves them.

"Then there are certain other men who deign to love only
those women who in face and speech and every movement carry
all elegance, all gentle manners, all knowledge, and all the graces
heaped together,—like a single flower composed of all the excellences in the world. Thus if my Court Lady have a dearth of
those loves that spring from evil hope, she will not on that account be left without a lover; for she will not lack those loves
that spring both from her merits and from her lovers' confidence
in their own worth, whereby they will know themselves to be
worthy of being loved by her."

60.—Messer Roberto still objected, but my lady Duchess
held him in the wrong, supporting my lord Magnifico's argument; then she continued:

"We have no cause to complain of my lord Magnifico, for I
truly think that the Court Lady described by him may stand on
a par with the Courtier, and even with some advantage; for he
has taught her how to love, which these gentlemen did not do for
their Courtier."

Then the Unico Aretino said:

"It is very fitting to teach women how to love, for rarely
have I seen any that knew how: since they nearly all accompany

their beauty with cruelty and ingratitude towards those who serve them most faithfully and deserve the reward of their love by nobility of birth, gentleness and worth; and then they often give themselves a prey to men who are very silly, base, and of small account, and who not only love them not, but hate them.

"So, to avoid such grievous errors as these, perhaps it was well to teach them first how to make choice of a man who shall deserve to be loved, and then how to love him; which is not needful in the case of men, who know it but too well of themselves. And here I can be a good witness; for love was never taught me save by the divine beauty and divinest behaviour of a Lady whom it was beyond my power not to adore, wherein I had no need of art of any master;[425] and I think that the same happens with all who love truly. Hence it were fitting to teach the Courtier how to make himself loved rather than how to love."

61.—Here my lady Emilia said:

"Then discourse of this now, my lord Unico."

The Unico replied:

"Methinks reason would require that ladies' favour should be won by serving and pleasing them; but by what they deem themselves served and pleased, I think must needs be learned from ladies themselves, who often desire things so strange that there is no man who would imagine the same, and sometimes they do not themselves know what they desire. Hence it is right that you, my Lady, who are a woman and so must surely know what pleases women, should undertake this task, to do the world so great a benefit."

Then my lady Emilia said:

"The very great favour that you always find with women is good proof that you know all the ways by which their grace is won; hence it is quite fitting that you should teach them."

"My Lady," replied the Unico, "I could give a lover no more useful warning than to look to it that you have no influence over the lady whose favour he seeks; for such good qualities as the world once thought were in me, together with the sincerest love that ever was, have not had so much power to make me loved as you have to make me hated."

62.—Then my lady Emilia replied:

"My lord Unico, God forbid that I should even think, much less do, anything to make you hated; for besides doing what I ought not, I should be esteemed of little sense for attempting the impossible. But since you urge me thus to speak of that which pleases women, I will speak; and if you shall be displeased, blame yourself for it.

"I think, then, that whoever would be loved must love and be lovable; and that these two things suffice to win women's favour.

"Now to answer that which you accuse me of, I say that everyone knows and sees that you are very lovable; but whether you love as sincerely as you say, I am very much in doubt, and perhaps the others too. For your being too lovable has brought it to pass that you have been loved by many women: and great rivers divided into many parts become little streams; so love, bestowed upon more than one object, has little strength. But these continual laments of yours, and complaints of ingratitude in the women you have served (which is not probable, in view of your great merits), are a certain sort of mystery to hide the favours, contentments and pleasures attained by you in love, and to assure the women who love you and have given themselves to you, that you will not betray them; and hence also they are content that you should thus openly display feigned love for others to hide their real love for you. So, if the women whom you now pretend to love are not so ready to believe it as you would like, the reason is because this artfulness of yours in love is beginning to be understood, not because I make you hated."

63.—Then my lord Unico said:

"I do not wish to try again to confute your words, because I at last perceive that it is as much my fate not to be believed when I say truth, as it is yours to be believed when you say untruth."

"Say rather, my lord Unico," replied my lady Emilia, "that you do not love as you would have us believe; for if you loved, all your desire would be to please your beloved lady and to wish what she wishes, because this is the law of love; but your thus complaining of her denotes some deceit, as I said, or indeed gives proof that you wish what she does not wish."

"Nay," said my lord Unico, "indeed I wish what she wishes,

which is proof that I love her; but I complain that she does not wish what I wish, which is a token that she loves me not, according to that same rule that you have cited."

My lady Emilia replied:

"He who begins to love ought also to begin to please his beloved and bend himself wholly to her wishes, and govern his by hers; and make his own desires her slaves, and his very soul like unto an obedient handmaid, nor ever think of aught but to let it be transformed, if possible, into that of his beloved, and to account this as his highest happiness; for they do thus who love truly."

"Assuredly," said my lord Unico, "my highest happiness would be to have a single wish rule her soul and mine."

"It rests with you to have it so," replied my lady Emilia.

64.—Then messer Bernardo interrupted and said:

"Certain it is that he who loves truly bends all his thoughts to serve and please the lady of his love, without being shown the way by others; but as these loving services are sometimes not clearly perceived, I think that besides loving and serving it is further necessary to make some other demonstration of his love so evident that the lady cannot hide her knowledge that she is loved; yet with such modesty withal that he may not seem to have small respect for her. And since you, my Lady, began to tell how the lover's soul must be the obedient handmaid of his beloved, I pray you explain this secret also, which seems to me very important."

Messer Cesare laughed, and said:

"If the lover is so modest that he is ashamed to tell her of his love, let him write it to her."

My lady Emilia added:

"Nay, if he is as discreet as becomes him, he ought to be sure of not offending her before he declares himself to her."

Then my lord Gaspar said:

"All women like to be sued in love, even though they mean to refuse that which they are sued for."

The Magnifico Giuliano replied:

"You are very wrong; nor should I advise the Courtier ever to employ this method, unless he be certain of not being repulsed."

65.—"Then what is he to do?" said my lord Gaspar.

The Magnifico continued:

"If he must speak or write, let him do it with such modesty and so warily that his first words shall try her mind, and shall touch so ambiguously upon her wish as to leave a way and certain loophole that may enable her to feign not to see that his discourse imports love, to the end that he may retreat in case of difficulty and pretend that he spoke or wrote to some other end, in order to enjoy in safety those intimate caresses and coquetries that a woman often grants to him who she thinks accepts them in friendship, and then withholds them as soon as she finds they are received as demonstrations of love. Hence those men who are too precipitate and venture thus presumptuously with a kind of fury and stubbornness, often lose these favours, and deservedly; for every noble lady regards herself as little esteemed by him who rudely wooes her before having done her service.

66.—"Therefore in my opinion the way that the Courtier ought to take to make his love known to the Lady, seems to me to be by showing it to her in manner rather than in words;—for verily more of love's affection is sometimes revealed in a sigh, in reverence, in timidity, than in a thousand words;—next by making his eyes to be faithful messengers to bear the embassies of his heart, since they often show the passion that is within more clearly than the tongue itself or letters or other couriers: so that they not only disclose thoughts, but often kindle love in the beloved's heart. Because those quick spirits that issue from the eyes, being generated near the heart, enter again by the eyes (whither they are aimed like an arrow at the mark), and naturally reach the heart as if it were their abode, and mingling with those other spirits there and with that subtle quality of blood which they have in them, they infect the blood near the heart to which they have come, and warm it, and make it like themselves and ready to receive the impression of that image which they have brought with them. Travelling thus to and fro over the road from eyes to heart, and bringing back the tinder and steel of beauty and grace, little by little these messengers fan with the breath of desire that fire which glows so ardently and never ceases to burn because they are always bringing it the fuel of hope to feed on.

"Hence it may be well said that eyes are the guide in love, especially if they are kind and soft; black, of a bright and gentle blackness, or blue; merry and laughing, so gracious and keen of glance, like some wherein the channels that give the spirits egress seem so deep that through them we can see the very heart. Then the eyes lie in wait, just as in war soldiers lurk in ambush; and if the form of the whole body is fair and well proportioned, it attracts and allures anyone who looks upon it from afar until he approaches, and, as soon as he is near, the eyes dart forth and bewitch like sorcerers; and especially when they send out their rays straight to the eyes of the beloved at a moment when these are doing the same; because the spirits meet, and in that sweet encounter each receives the other's quality, as we see in the case of an eye diseased, which by looking fixedly into a sound one imparts thereto its own disease. So methinks in this way our Courtier can in great part manifest his love for his Lady.

"True it is that if the eyes are not governed with skill, they often most disclose a man's amourous desires to whom he least would do so; for through them there shines forth almost visibly that ardent passion which (while wishing to reveal it only to his beloved) the lover often reveals also to those from whom he most would hide it. Therefore he who has not lost the bridle of reason, governs himself cautiously and observes time and place, and abstains when needful from such intent gazing, sweetest food though it be; for an open love is too difficult a thing."

67.—Count Ludovico replied:

"Sometimes even openness does no harm, for in this case men often think such a love affair is not tending to the end which every lover desires, seeing that little care is taken to hide it, nor any heed given whether it be known or not; and so, by not denying it, a man wins a certain freedom that enables him to speak openly with his beloved and to be with her without suspicion; which those do not win who try to be secret, because they seem to hope for and to be near some great reward that they would not have others discover.

"Moreover I have often seen very ardent love spring up in a woman's heart towards a man for whom she had at first not had the least affection, simply from hearing that many deemed them to be in love; and I think the reason of this was because such an universal opinion as that seemed to her sufficient proof to make her believe the man worthy of her love, and it seemed as if report brought her messages from the lover much truer and worthier of belief than he himself could have sent by letters and words, or another for him.

"Thus, this public report not only sometime does no harm, but helps."

The Magnifico replied:

"Love affairs that have report for their minister put a man in great danger of being pointed at with the finger; and hence he who would travel this road safely, must feign to have less fire within him than he has, and content himself with that which seems little to him, and conceal his desires, jealousies, griefs and joys, and often laugh with his mouth when his heart is weeping, and feign to be prodigal of that whereof he most is chary; and these things are so difficult to do, that they are almost impossible. Therefore if our Courtier would follow my advice, I should exhort him to keep his love affairs secret."

68.—Then messer Bernardo said:

"There is need, then, for you to teach him how, and methinks it is of no small importance; for, besides the signals which men sometimes make so covertly that almost without a motion the person whom they wish reads in their face and eyes what is in their heart,—I have sometimes heard a long and free love talk between two lovers, of which, however, those present could understand clearly no details at all or even be sure that the talk was about love. And the reason of this lay in the speakers' discretion and precaution; for without showing any sign of annoyance at being listened to, they whispered only those words that signified, and spoke aloud the rest, which could be construed in different senses."

Then messer Federico said:

"To speak thus minutely about these precautions of secrecy would be a journey into the infinite; hence I would rather have some little discussion as to how the lover ought to maintain his lady's favour, which seems to me much more necessary."

69.—The Magnifico replied:

"I think that those means which serve to win it serve also to maintain it; and all this consists in pleasing the lady of our love without ever offending her. Wherefore it would be difficult to give any fixed rule for it; since in countless ways he who is not very discreet sometimes makes mistakes that seem little and yet grievously offend the lady's spirit; and this befalls those, more than others, who are overmastered by passion: like some who, whenever they have means of speaking to the lady whom they love, lament and complain so bitterly and often wish for things that are so impossible, that they become wearisome by their very importunity. Others, when they are stung by any jealousy, allow themselves to be so carried away by their grief that they heedlessly run into speaking evil of him whom they suspect, and sometimes without fault either on his part or on the lady's, and insist that she shall not speak to him or even turn her eyes in the direction where he is. And by this behaviour they often not only offend the lady, but are the cause that leads her to love the man: because the fear that lovers sometimes display lest their lady forsake them for another, shows that they are conscious of being inferior to him in merits and worth, and with this idea the lady is moved to love him, and perceiving that evil is said of him to put him out of favour, she believes it not although it be true, and loves him all the more."

70.—Then messer Cesare said, laughing:

"I own I am not so wise that I could abstain from speaking evil of my rival, except you were to teach me some other better means of ruining him."

My lord Magnifico replied, laughing:

"There is a proverb which says that when our enemy is in the water up to the belt, we must offer him our hand and lift him out of peril; but when he is in up to the chin, we must set our foot on his head and drown him outright. Thus there are some who do this with their rival, and as long as they have no safe way of ruining him, go about dissimulating and pretend to be rather his friend than otherwise; then if an opportunity offers—such that they know they can overwhelm him with certain ruin by saying all manner of evil of him (whether it be true or false),—they do it without mercy, with craft, deception and all the means they know how to invent.

"But since it would never please me to have our Courtier use any deceit, I would have him deprive his rival of the lady's favour by no other craft than by loving and serving her, and by being worthy, valiant, discreet and modest; in short, by deserving her better than his rival, and by being in all things wary and prudent, abstaining from all stupid follies, wherein many dunces fall and in diverse ways. For in the past I have known some who use Poliphilian words in writing and speaking to women,[426] and so insist upon the niceties of rhetoric, that the women are diffident of themselves and account themselves very ignorant, and think each hour of such discourse a thousand years, and rise before the end. Others are immoderately boastful. Others often say things that redound to their own discredit and damage, like some I am wont to laugh at, who profess to be in love and sometimes say in the presence of women: 'I have never found a woman to love me;' and they do not perceive that those who hear them at once conclude that this can arise from no other reason than that they deserve neither love nor the water they drink, and hold them for men of slight account, and would not love them for all the gold in the world, thinking that to love them would be to stand lower than all the other women who loved them not.

"Still others are so silly that for the purpose of bringing odium upon some rival of theirs, they say in the presence of women: 'So and So is the luckiest man on earth; for although he is not at all handsome, discreet or valiant, and cannot do or say more than the rest, yet all the women love him and run after him,' and thus showing themselves to be envious of the man's good luck, they incite belief that (although he shows himself to be lovable in neither looks nor acts) he has in him some hidden quality for which he deserves so many women's love; hence those who hear him thus spoken of are by this belief even much more moved to love him."

71.—Then Count Ludovico laughed, and said:

"I assure you that the discreet Courtier will never use these stupidities to win favour with women."

Messer Cesare Gonzaga replied:

"Nor yet that one which was used in my time by a gentleman of great repute, whose name for the honour of men I will not mention."

My lady Duchess replied:

"At least tell what he did."

Messer Cesare continued:

"Being loved by a great lady, at her request he came secretly to the place where she was; and after he had seen her and conversed with her as long as she and the time allowed, taking his leave with many bitter tears and sighs, in token of the extreme sorrow that he felt at such a parting, he besought her to keep him continually in mind; and then he added that she ought to pay his board and lodging, for as he had been invited by her, it seemed to him reasonable that he should be at no charge for his coming."

Then all the ladies began to laugh and to say that he was quite unworthy to be called a gentleman; and many of the men were ashamed, with that shame which the man himself would have rightly felt if he had at any time found wit enough to be conscious of such a shameful fault.

My lord Gaspar then turned to messer Cesare, and said:

"It was better to refrain from telling this thing for the honour of women, than to refrain for the honour of men from naming him; for you can well imagine what good judgment that great lady had in loving such a senseless animal, and also that of the many who served her perhaps she had chosen this one as the most discreet, forsaking and misliking men whose lackey he was unworthy to be."

Count Ludovico laughed, and said:

"Who knows that he was not discreet in other things, and failed only as to board and lodging? But many times men commit great follies in their excessive love; and if you will say the truth, perhaps it has befallen you to commit more than one."

72.—Messer Cesare replied, laughing:

"By your faith, do not expose our errors."

"Nay, it is necessary to expose them," replied my lord Gaspar, "in order that we may know how to correct them," then he added: "My lord Magnifico, now that the Courtier knows how to win and maintain his lady's favour and to deprive his rival of it, you must teach him how to keep his love affairs secret."

The Magnifico replied:

"Methinks I have said enough; so now choose someone else to speak of this secrecy."

Then messer Bernardo and all the others began to urge him anew; and the Magnifico said, laughing:

"You wish to tempt me. All of you are too well practised in love: yet if you would know more, go read it in Ovid."

"And how," said messer Bernardo, "should I hope that his precepts are of any service in love, when he recommends and says it is a very good thing that a man should pretend to be drunk in the presence of the beloved? [427] See what a fine way of winning favour! And he cites as a fine method of making one's love known to a lady at a banquet, to dip a finger in wine and write it on the table." [428]

The Magnifico replied, laughing:

"In those days it was not amiss."

"And therefore," said messer Bernardo, "since such a filthy trick as this was not offensive to the men of that time, we may believe that they did not have so gentle a manner of serving women in love as we have. But let us not forsake our first subject, of teaching how to keep love secret."

73.—Then the Magnifico said:

"In my opinion, in order to keep love secret it is needful to avoid the causes that make it public, which are many; but there is one chief cause, which is the wish to be too secret and not trust any person whatever. For every lover desires to make his passion known to his beloved, and being alone he is forced to make many more and stronger demonstrations than if he were aided by some loving and faithful friend; because the demonstrations that the lover himself makes arouse much greater suspicion than those he makes through intermediaries. And since the human mind is naturally curious to find things out, as soon as a stranger begins to suspect, he employs such diligence that he learns the truth, and having learned it, makes no scruple to publish it—nay, sometimes delights to do so; which is not the case with a friend, who besides helping with comfort and advice, often repairs those mistakes which the blind lover commits, and always contrives secrecy and provides for many things for which he himself cannot provide. Moreover very great relief is felt in telling our passion and unburdening it to a trusty friend, and likewise it greatly enhances our joys to be able to impart them."

74.—Then my lord Gaspar said:

"Another cause discloses love more than this."

"And what is it?" replied the Magnifico.

My lord Gaspar continued:

"The vain ambition joined with madness and cruelty of women; who, as you yourself have said, try to have as great a number of lovers as they can, and if it were possible would have all of these burn and (once made ashes) after death return alive to die once more. And even although they be in love, still they delight in their lover's torment, because they think that pain and afflictions and continual calling for death give good proof that they are loved, and can, by their beauty, make men wretched and happy, and bestow death and life, as they please. Hence they feed only on this food, and are so eager for it that (in order not to be without it) they do not satisfy or ever quite dishearten their lovers; but to keep these continually in anguish and desire, they use a certain domineering severity of threats mingled with encouragement, and fain would have a word, a look, a nod of theirs esteemed as highest bliss. And to be deemed modest and chaste, not only by their lovers but by all the rest, they take care to make their harsh and discourteous behaviour public, to the end that everyone may think that if they thus maltreat those who are worthy to be loved, they must treat the unworthy much worse.

"And in this belief, thinking they thus have artfully made themselves secure against infamy, they often spend every night with vilest men whom they scarcely know; and so, to enjoy the calamities and continual laments of some noble cavalier whom they love, they deny themselves those pleasures which they might perhaps attain with some excuse; and they are the cause that forces the poor lover in sheer desperation to behaviour which brings to light that which every care ought to be taken to keep most secret.

"Some others there are, who, if by trickery they succeed in

leading many a man to think himself loved by them, nourish the
jealousy of each by bestowing caresses and favour on one in the
presence of another; and when they see that he too whom they
most love is nearly sure of being loved because of the demonstrations shown him, they often put him in suspense by ambiguous
words and pretended anger, and pierce his heart, feigning to care
nothing for him and to wish to give themselves wholly to another;
whence arise hatreds, enmities and countless scandals and manifest ruin, for in such a case a man must show the passion that he
feels, even though it result in blame and infamy to the lady.

"Others, not content with this single torment of jealousy,
after the lover has given all proofs of love and faithful service,
and after they have received the same with some sign of returning it with good will, they begin to draw back without cause and
when it is least expected, and pretend to believe that he has grown
lukewarm, and feigning new suspicions that they are not loved,
they give sign of wishing to break with him absolutely. And so,
because of these obstacles, the poor fellow is by very force compelled to go back to the start and pay court as if his service were
beginning; and daily to walk the earth, and when the lady stirs
abroad to accompany her to church and everywhere she goes,
never to turn his eyes another way: and now he returns to plaints
and sighs and heaviness of heart, and if he can speak with her,
to supplications, blasphemies, despairings, and all those ragings
to which unhappy lovers are put by these fierce monsters, who
have a greater thirst for blood than tigers have.

75.—"Such woeful demonstrations as these are but too much
seen and known, and often more by others than by her who occasions them and thus in a few days they become so public that
not a step can be taken, nor the least signal given, that is not noted
by a thousand eyes. Then it happens that long before there are
any sweets of love between them, they are believed and judged
by all the world; for when women see that the lover, now nigh to
death and overwhelmed by the cruelty and tortures inflicted on
him, is firmly and really resolving to withdraw, they at once
begin to show him that they love him heartily, and to do him all
manner of kindness, and to yield to him, to the end that (his
ardent desire having failed) the fruits of love may be less sweet

to him and he may have less to thank them for, in order to do everything amiss.

"And their love being now very well known, at the same time all the results that proceed from it are also very well known; thus the women are dishonoured, and the lover finds that he has lost time and pains and has shortened his life in sorrows, without the least advantage or pleasure; for he attained his desires, not when they would have made him very happy with their pleasantness, but when he cared little or nothing for them, because his heart was already so deadened by his cruel passion that it had no feeling left wherewith to enjoy the delight or contentment which was offered him."

76.—Then my lord Ottaviano said, laughing:

"You held your peace awhile and refrained from saying evil of women; then you hit them so hard that it seems as if you were gathering strength, like those who draw back in order to strike the harder; and verily you are in the wrong and ought henceforth to be gentler."

My lady Emilia laughed, and turning to my lady Duchess, said:

"You see, my Lady, that our adversaries are beginning to quarrel and differ among themselves."

"Call me not so," replied my lord Ottaviano, "for I am not your adversary. This contest has displeased me much, not because I was sorry to see the victory in favour of women, but because it has led my lord Gaspar to revile them more than he ought, and my lord Magnifico and messer Cesare to praise them perhaps a little more than their due; besides which, owing to the length of the discussion, we have missed hearing many other fine things that remained to say about the Courtier."

"You see," said my lady Emilia, "that you are our adversary after all; and for that reason you are displeased with the late discussion, and fain would not have had so excellent a Court Lady described; not because you had anything more to say about the Courtier (for these gentlemen have·said all they knew, and I think that neither you nor anyone else could add anything whatever), but because of the envy that you have of women's honour."

77.—"Certain it is," replied my lord Ottaviano, "that be-

sides the things that have been said about the Courtier, I should
like to hear many others. Still, since everyone is content to have
him as he is, I also am content; nor should I change him in aught
else, unless in making him a little more friendly to women than
my lord Gaspar is, albeit perhaps not so much so as some of these
other gentlemen."

Then my lady Duchess said:

"By all means we must see whether your talents are so great
that they can give the Courtier greater perfection than these gentlemen have given him. So please to say what you have in mind:
else we shall think that even you cannot add anything to what
has been said, but that you wished to detract from the praises of
the Court Lady because you think her the equal of the Courtier,
who you would therefore have us believe could be much more
perfect than these gentlemen have described him."

My lord Ottaviano laughed, and said:

"The praise and censure that have been bestowed on women
beyond their due have so filled the ears and mind of the company as to leave no room for anything else to lodge; besides this,
in my opinion the hour is very late."

"Then," said my lady Duchess, "we shall have more time by
waiting till to-morrow; and meanwhile this praise and censure,
which you say have been on both sides bestowed excessively on
women, will leave these gentlemen's minds, and thus they will
better appreciate that truth which you will tell them."

So saying, my lady Duchess rose to her feet, and courteously
dismissing the company, retired to her more private room, and
everyone went to rest.

## The Fourth Book

### TO MESSER ALFONSO ARIOSTO

THINKING TO WRITE OUT THE DISCUSSIONS that were held on the fourth evening, after those mentioned in the previous Books, among various reflections I feel one bitter thought that strikes my heart, and makes me mindful of human miseries and our deceptive hopes: and how fortune, often in mid-course and sometimes near the end, shatters our frail and vain designs, and sometimes wrecks them before the haven can be even seen afar.

Thus I recall that not long after these discussions took place, importunate death deprived our court of three very rare gentlemen while they were in the flower of robust health and hope of honour. And of these the first was my lord Gaspar Pallavicino, who being assailed by an acute disease and more than once brought low, although his courage was of such vigour that for a season it held spirit and body together in spite of death, yet ended his natural course far before his time; [429] a very great loss not only to our court and to his friends and family, but to his native land and to all Lombardy.

Not long afterwards died messer Cesare Gonzaga, who to all those who had acquaintance with him left a bitter and painful memory of his death; [430] for since nature produces such men as rarely as she does, it seemed only fitting that she should not so soon deprive us of this one: because it certainly may be said that messer Cesare was carried off just when he was beginning to give something more than promise of himself, and to be esteemed as his admirable qualities deserved; for already, by many meritorious efforts he had given good proof of his worth, which shone

240

forth not only in noble birth, but also in the ornament of letters and of arms, and in every kind of laudable behaviour, so that, by reason of his goodness, capacity, courage and wisdom, there was nothing so great that it might not be expected from him.

No long time passed before the death of messer Roberto da Bari also inflicted deep sorrow upon the whole court; [48] for it seemed reasonable that everyone should lament the death of a youth of good behaviour, agreeable, fair of aspect, and of very rare personal grace, and of as stout and sturdy temper as could be wished.

2.—If, then, these men had lived, I think they would have reached such eminence that they would have been able to give everyone who knew them clear proof how worthy the court of Urbino was of praise, and how adorned with noble cavaliers; which nearly all the others have done who were reared there. For verily the Trojan Horse did not send forth so many lords and captains as this court has sent forth men singular in worth and most highly prized by everyone. Thus, as you know, messer Federico Fregoso was made Archbishop of Salerno; Count Ludovico, Bishop of Bayeux; my lord Ottaviano, Doge of Genoa; messer Bernardo Bibbiena, Cardinal of Santa Maria in Portico; messer Pietro Bembo, secretary to Pope Leo; my lord Magnifico rose to the dukedom of Nemours and to that greatness where he now is. My lord Francesco Maria della Rovere also, Prefect of Rome, was made Duke of Urbino: [431] albeit much higher praise may be accorded to the court where he was nurtured, because he there became a rare and excellent lord in every quality of worth, as we now see, than because he attained the dukedom of Urbino; nor do I believe that a small cause of this was the noble company in whose daily converse he always saw and heard laudable behaviour.

However, it seems to me that the cause, whether chance or favour of the stars, which has so long granted excellent lords to Urbino, still continues and produces the same results; and hence we may hope that fair fortune must further so bless these good works, that the welfare of the house and state shall not only not wane but rather wax from day to day: and of this many bright auguries are already to be seen, among which I esteem the chief to be Heaven's bestowal of such a mistress as is my lady Eleanora Gonzaga, the new Duchess; [432] for if ever in a single body there were joined wisdom, grace, beauty, capacity, tact, humanity, and every other gentle quality,—in her they are so united that they form a chain which completes and adorns her every movement with all these qualities at once.

Let us now continue the discussion about our Courtier, in the hope that after us there ought to be no lack of those who will find bright and honoured examples of worth in the present court of Urbino, just as we now do in that of bygone times.

3.—It seemed, then, as my lord Gaspar Pallavicino used to relate, that the following day after the discussions contained in the preceding Book, little was seen of my lord Ottaviano; hence many thought that he had retired in order that he might without hindrance think carefully of what he had to say. Thus, the company having betaken themselves to my lady Duchess at the accustomed hour, search had to be made far and wide for my lord Ottaviano, who did not appear for a good space; so that many cavaliers and maids of honour of the court began to dance and engage in other pastimes, thinking that for that evening there would be no more talk about the Courtier. And indeed all were busied, some with one thing and some with another, when my lord Ottaviano arrived, after he had almost been given up; and seeing that messer Cesare Gonzaga and my lord Gaspar were dancing, he bowed to my lady Duchess and said, laughing:

"I quite expected to hear my lord Gaspar say some evil about women again this evening; but seeing him dance with one, I think that he has made his peace with all of them; and I am glad that the dispute (or rather the discussion) about the Courtier has ended thus."

"It is by no means ended," replied my lady Duchess; "for I am no such enemy of men as you are of women, and therefore I am unwilling that the Courtier should be deprived of his due honour, and of those ornaments that you promised him last evening;" and so saying, she directed that as soon as the dance was finished, everyone should sit down in the usual order, which was done; and when all were giving close attention, my lord Ottaviano said:

"My Lady, since my wish to have the Courtier possess many other good qualities is taken as a promise to tell what they are, I am content to speak about them, not with any hope of saying all that might be said, but merely enough to clear your mind of the charge that was made against me last evening, to wit: that I spoke as I did rather for the purpose of detracting from the Court Lady's praises (by raising a false belief that other excellences can be ascribed to the Courtier, and by thus artfully making him her superior), than because what I said was true. Wherefore, to adapt myself to the hour, which is later than it is wont to be when we begin our discussions, I shall be brief.

4.—"So, to pursue these gentlemen's discourse, which I wholly approve and confirm, I say that of the things that we call good, there are some which simply and in themselves are always good, like temperance, fortitude, health, and all the virtues that bestow tranquillity upon the mind; others, which are good in various respects and for the object to which they tend, like law, liberality, riches, and other like things. Hence I think that the perfect Courtier, such as Count Ludovico and messer Federico have described, may be a truly good thing and worthy of praise, not however simply and in himself, but in respect to the end to which he may be directed. For indeed if by being nobly born, graceful, agreeable, and expert in so many exercises, the Courtier brought forth no other fruit than merely being what he is, I should not deem it right for a man to devote so much study and pains to acquiring this perfection of Courtiership, as anyone must who wishes to attain it. Nay, I should say that many of those accomplishments that have been ascribed to him (like dancing, merry-making, singing and playing) were follies and vanities, and in a man of rank worthy rather of censure than of praise: for these elegances, devices, mottoes, and other like things that pertain to discourse about women and love, although perhaps many other men think the contrary, often serve only to effeminate the mind, to corrupt youth, and to reduce it to great wantonness of living; whence then it comes to pass that the Italian name is brought into opprobrium, and but few are to be found who dare, I will not say to die, but even to run into danger.

"And surely there are countless other things, which, if industry and study were spent upon them, would be of much greater utility in both peace and war than this kind of Courtiership in itself merely; but if the Courtier's actions are directed to that good end to which they ought, and which I have in mind, methinks they are not only not harmful or vain, but very useful and deserving of infinite praise.

5.—"I think then that the aim of the perfect Courtier, which has not been spoken of till now, is so to win for himself, by means of the accomplishments ascribed to him by these gentlemen, the favour and mind of the prince whom he serves, that he may be able to say, and always shall say, the truth about everything which it is fitting for the prince to know, without fear or risk of giving offence thereby; and that when he sees his prince's mind inclined to do something wrong, he may be quick to oppose, and gently to make use of the favour acquired by his good accomplishments, so as to banish every bad intent and lead his prince into the path of virtue. And thus, possessing the goodness which these gentlemen have described, together with readiness of wit and pleasantness, and shrewdness and knowledge of letters and many other things,—the Courtier will in every case be able deftly to show the prince how much honour and profit accrue to him and his from justice, liberality, magnanimity, gentleness, and the other virtues that become a good prince; and on the other hand how much infamy and loss proceed from the vices opposed to them. Therefore I think that just as music, festivals, games, and the other pleasant accomplishments are as it were the flower, in like manner to lead or help one's prince towards right, and to frighten him from wrong, are the true fruit of Courtiership.

"And since the merit of well-doing lies chiefly in two things, one of which is the choice of an end for our intentions that shall be truly good, and the other ability to find means suitable and fitting to conduce to that good end marked out,—certain it is that that man's mind tends to the best end, who purposes to see to it that his prince shall be deceived by no one, shall hearken not to flatterers or to slanderers and liars, and shall distinguish good and evil, and love the one and hate the other.

6.—"Methinks, too, that the accomplishments ascribed to the Courtier by these gentlemen may be a good means of arriving at that end; and this because among the many faults which to-day we see in many of our princes, the greatest are ignorance and self-esteem. And the root of these two evils is none other than falsehood: which vice is deservedly hateful to God and to men, and more injurious to princes than any other; because they have greatest lack of that whereof they most need to have abundance— I mean of someone to tell them the truth and to put them in mind of what is right: for their enemies are not moved by love to perform these offices, but are well pleased to have them live wickedly and never correct themselves; on the other hand, their enemies dare not accuse them openly, for fear of being punished. Then of their friends there are few who have free access to them, and those few are chary of censuring them for their errors as freely as in the case of private persons, and to win grace and favour often think of nothing but how to suggest things that may delight and please their fancy, although the same be evil and dishonourable; thus from being friends these men become flatterers, and to derive profit from their intimacy, always speak and act complaisantly, and for the most part make their way by means of falsehoods, which beget ignorance in the prince's mind, not only of outward things but of himself; and this may be said to be the greatest and most monstrous falsehood of all, for the ignorant mind deceives itself and lies inwardly to itself.

7.—"From this it follows that, besides never hearing the truth about anything whatever, rulers are intoxicated by that licence which dominion carries with it, and by the abundance of their enjoyments are drowned in pleasures, and so deceive themselves and have their minds so corrupted,—always finding themselves obeyed and almost adored with such reverence and praise, without the least censure or even contradiction,—that from this ignorance they pass to boundless self-esteem, so that they then brook no advice or persuasion from others. And since they think that to know how to rule is a very easy thing, and that to succeed therein they need no other art or training than mere force, they bend their mind and all their thoughts to the maintenance of that power which they have, esteeming that true felicity lies in being able to do what one likes.

"Therefore some princes hate reason and justice, thinking

that it would be a kind of bridle and a means of reducing them to bondage, and of lessening the pleasure and satisfaction which they have in ruling, if they were willing to follow it; and that their dominion would not be perfect or complete if they were constrained to obey duty and honour, because they think that he who obeys is no true ruler. Therefore, following these principles and allowing themselves to be transported by self-esteem, they become arrogant, with haughty looks and stern behaviour, with splendid dress, gold and gems, and by letting themselves be almost never seen in public they think to win authority among men and to be held almost as gods. And to my thinking they are like the colossi that last year were made at Rome the day of the festival in the Piazza d'Agone,[433] which outwardly showed a likeness to great men and horses in a triumph, and within were full of tow and rags. But princes of this sort are much worse, in that the colossi keep upright merely by their great weight; while the princes, since they are ill balanced within and placed haphazard on uneven bases, fall to their ruin by reason of their own weight, and from one error run into many; for their ignorance, together with the false belief that they cannot err and that the power which they have proceeds from their own wisdom, leads them to seize states boldly by fair means or foul, whenever they can.

8.—"But if they were resolved to know and to do that which they ought, they would be as set on not ruling as they are set on ruling; for they would perceive how monstrous and pernicious a thing it is when subjects, who are to be governed, are wiser than the princes who are to govern.

"You see that ignorance of music, of dancing, of horsemanship, is not harmful to any man; nevertheless, he who is no musician is ashamed and dares not sing in the presence of others, or dance if he knows not how, or ride if he has not a good seat. But from not knowing how to govern people there spring so many woes, deaths, destructions, burnings, ruins,—that it may be said to be the deadliest pest that is to be found on earth. And yet some princes who are very ignorant of government are not ashamed to undertake to govern, I will not say in the presence of four or of six men, but before all the world, for their rank is set so high that all eyes gaze on them, and hence not only their great but their least defects are always noted. Thus it is written that Cimon was accused of loving wine, Scipio of loving sleep, Lucullus of loving feasts.[434] But would to God that the princes of our time might couple their sins with as many virtues as did those ancients; who, although they erred in some respects, yet did not avoid the reminders and advice of anyone who seemed to them competent to correct those errors, but rather sought with all solicitude to order their lives after the precepts of excellent men: as Epaminondas after that of Lysis the Pythagorean,[435] Agesilaus after that of Xenophon, Scipio after that of Panætius, and countless others.[436]

"But if some of our princes were to happen upon a stern philosopher or any man who was willing openly and artlessly to show them the frightful face of true virtue, and to teach them what good behaviour is and what a good prince's life ought to be, I am certain that they would loathe him like an asp, or in sooth deride him as a thing most vile.

9.—"I say, then, that since princes are to-day so corrupted by evil customs and by ignorance and mistaken self-esteem, and since it is so difficult to give them knowledge of the truth and lead them on to virtue, and since men seek to enter into their favour by lies and flatteries and such vicious means,—the Courtier, by the aid of those gentle qualities that Count Ludovico and messer Federico have given him, can with ease and should try to gain the good will and so charm the mind of his prince, that he shall win free and safe indulgence to speak of everything without being irksome. And if he be such as has been said, he will accomplish this with little trouble, and thus be able always to disclose the truth about all things with ease; and also to instil goodness into his prince's mind little by little, and to teach continence, fortitude, justice, temperance, by giving a taste of how much sweetness is hidden by the little bitterness that at first sight appears to him who understands vice; which is always hurtful and displeasing, and accompanied by infamy and blame, just as virtue is profitable, blithe and full of praise. And thereto he will be able to incite his prince by the example of the famous captains and other eminent men to whom the ancients were wont to make statues of bronze and of marble and sometimes of gold, and to erect the same in public places, both for the honour of these men and as a stimulus to others, so that they might be led by worthy emulation to strive to reach that glory too.

10.—"In this way the Courtier will be able to lead his prince along the thorny path of virtue, decking it as with shady leafage and strewing it with lovely flowers to relieve the tedium of the weary journey to one whose strength is slight; and now with music, now with arms and horses, now with verses, now with love talk, and with all those means whereof these gentlemen have told, to keep his mind continually busied with worthy pleasures, yet always impressing upon him also, as I have said, some virtuous practice along with these allurements, and playing upon him with salutary craft; like cunning doctors, who often anoint the edge of the cup with a sweet cordial, when they wish to give some bitter-tasting medicine to sick and over-delicate children.

"If, therefore, the Courtier put the veil of pleasure to such a use, he will reach his aim in every time and place and exercise, and will deserve much greater praise and reward than for any other good work that he could do in the world. For there is no good thing that is of such universal advantage as a good prince, nor any evil so universally noxious as a bad prince: hence, too, there is no punishment so harsh and cruel as to be a sufficient penalty for those wicked courtiers who use their gentle and pleasant ways and fine accomplishments to a bad end, and therewith seek their prince's favour, in order to corrupt him and entice him from the path of virtue and lead him into vice; for such as these may be said to taint with deadly poison not a single cup from which one man alone must drink, but the public fountain used by all men."

11.—My lord Ottaviano was silent, as if he did not wish to say more; but my lord Gaspar said:

"It does not seem to me, my lord Ottaviano, that this rightmindedness and continence, and the other virtues which you wish the Courtier to show his lord, can be learned; but I think that the men who have them are given them by nature and by God. And that this is true, you see that there is no man in the world so wicked and ill conditioned, or so intemperate and perverse, as to confess that he is so when he is asked; nay, everyone, however wicked he be, has pleasure in being deemed just, continent and good: which would not be the case if these virtues could be learned; for it is no disgrace not to know that to which one has given no study, but it seems a reproach indeed not to have that wherewith we ought to be adorned by nature. Hence everyone tries to hide his natural defects both of mind and of body too; which is seen in the blind, the halt and the crooked, and in others who are maimed or ugly; for although these imperfections may be ascribed to nature, still everyone dislikes to be sensible of them in himself, because he seems by nature's own testimony to have that defect as it were for a seal and token of his wickedness.

"Moreover my opinion is confirmed by that story which is told of Epimetheus, who knew so ill how to distribute the gifts of nature among men that he left them much poorer in everything than all other creatures: wherefore Prometheus stole from Minerva and from Vulcan that artful cunning whereby men find the means of living; [437] but still they did not have the civic cunning to gather together in cities and live orderly lives, for this was guarded in Jove's castle by very watchful warders, who so frightened Prometheus that he dared not approach them; wherefore Jove had compassion for the misery of men, who were torn by wild beasts because they could not stand together for lack of civic faculty, and sent Mercury to earth to bring them justice and shame, to the end that these two things might adorn their cities and unite the citizens. And he saw fit that they should not be given to men like the other arts, wherein one expert suffices for many ignorant (as in the case of medicine), but that they should be impressed upon each man; and he ordained a law that all who were without justice and shame should be exterminated and put to death like public pests. So you see, my lord Ottaviano, that these virtues are vouchsafed by God to men, and are not acquired, but natural."

12.—Then my lord Ottaviano said, smiling:

"Do you then insist, my lord Gaspar, that men are so unhappy and perverse, that they have by industry discovered an art to tame the natures of wild beasts, bears, wolves, lions, and by it are able to teach a pretty bird to fly whither they like, and to return willingly from its woods and natural freedom to cages and

ᚇᚇᚇᚇᚇᚇᚇᚇᚇᚇᚇᚇᚇᚇᚇᚇᚇᚇᚇᚇᚇᚇᚇᚇᚇᚇᚇᚇᚇᚇᚇᚇᚇᚇᚇᚇᚇᚇᚇᚇᚇᚇᚇᚇᚇᚇᚇᚇᚇᚇᚇ

captivity,—and yet that they cannot or will not by the same industry find arts to help themselves and improve their minds with diligence and study? To my thinking this would be as if physicians were to study with all diligence to acquire the mere art of healing sore nails and scurf in children, and were to leave off curing fevers, pleurisy and other serious maladies; and how out of all reason this would be, everyone can consider.

"Therefore I think that the moral virtues are not in us by nature wholly, for nothing can ever become used to that which is naturally contrary to it; as we see in the case of a stone, which although it were thrown upwards ten thousand times would never become used to move thither of itself; hence if virtue were as natural to us as weight is to the stone, we should never become used to vice. Nor, on the other hand, are the vices natural in this sense, for we should never be able to be virtuous; and it would be too unfair and foolish to chastise men for those defects that proceed from nature without our fault; and this error would be committed by the law, which does not inflict punishment upon malefactors on account of their past error (since what is done can not be undone), but has regard to the future, to the end that he who has erred may err no more nor be the cause of others erring through his bad example. And thus the law presumes that the virtues can be learned, which is very true; for we are born capable of receiving them and the vices also, and hence custom creates in us the habit of both the one and the other, so that we first practise virtue or vice, and then are virtuous or vicious.

"The contrary is observed in things that are bestowed by nature, which we first have the power to practise and then do practise: as is the case with the senses; for first we are able to see, hear and touch, then we see, hear and touch, although also many of these functions are perfected by training. Wherefore good masters teach children not only letters, but also good and seemly manners in eating, drinking, speaking and walking, with certain appropriate gestures.

13.—"Therefore as in the other arts, so too in virtue it is necessary to have a master, who by instruction and good reminders shall arouse and awake in us those moral virtues whereof we have the seed enclosed and buried in our soul, and like a good husbandman shall cultivate them and open the way for them by freeing us from the thorns and tares of appetite, which often so overshadow and choke our minds as not to let them blossom or bring forth those happy fruits which alone we should desire to have spring up in the human heart.

"In this sense, then, justice and shame, which you say Jove sent upon earth to all men, are natural in each one of us. But just as a body without eyes, however strong it be, often fails if it moves towards any object, so the root of these virtues potentially engendered in our minds often comes to naught if it be not helped by cultivation. For if it is to ripen into action and perfect character, nature alone is not enough, as has been said, but there is need of studied practice and of reason, to purify and clear the soul by lifting the dark veil of ignorance, from which nearly all the errors of men proceed,—because if good and evil were well perceived and understood, everyone would always prefer good and shun evil. Thus virtue may almost be said to be a kind of prudence and wit to prefer the good, and vice a kind of imprudence and ignorance which lead us to judge falsely; for men never prefer evil deeming it to be evil, but are deceived by a certain likeness that it bears to good."

14.—Then my lord Gaspar replied:

"There are, however, many who know well that they are doing evil, and yet do it; and this because they have more thought for the present pleasure which they feel, than for the chastisement which they fear must come upon them: like thieves, homicides, and other such men."

My lord Ottaviano said:

"True pleasure is always good, and true suffering always evil; therefore these men deceive themselves in taking false pleasure for true, and true suffering for false; hence by false pleasures they often run into true sufferings. Therefore that art which teaches how to discern the true from the false, may well be learned; and the faculty whereby we choose that which is truly good and not that which falsely seems so, may be called true wisdom and more profitable to human life than any other, because it dispels the ignorance from which, as I have said, all evils spring."

ᔓᔓᔓᔓᔓᔓᔓᔓᔓᔓᔓᔓᔓᔓᔓᔓᔓᔓᔓᔓᔓᔓᔓᔓᔓᔓᔓᔓᔓᔓᔓᔓᔓᔓᔓᔓᔓᔓᔓᔓᔓᔓᔓᔓᔓᔓᔓᔓᔓᔓ

15.—Then messer Pietro Bembo said:

"I do not know, my lord Ottaviano, whether my lord Gaspar ought to grant you that all evils spring from ignorance; and that there are not many who well know that they are sinning when they sin, and do not in the least deceive themselves as to true pleasure, nor yet as to true suffering. For it is certain that those who are incontinent judge reasonably and rightly, and know that to be evil to which they are prompted by their lusts in spite of duty, and therefore resist and set reason against appetite, whence arises a conflict of pleasure and pain against judgment. Conquered at last by too potent appetite, reason yields, like a ship which resists awhile the buffetings of the sea, but finally beaten by the too furious violence of the gale, with anchor and rigging broken, suffers herself to be driven at fortune's will, without use of helm or any guidance of compass to save her.

"Therefore the incontinent commit their errors with a certain doubtful remorse, and as it were in their own despite; which they would not do if they did not know that what they are doing is evil, but would follow appetite without restraint of reason and wholly uncontrolled, and would then be not incontinent but intemperate, which is much worse. Thus incontinence is said to be a diminished vice, because it has a grain of reason in it; and likewise continence is said to be an imperfect virtue, because it has a grain of passion in it. Therefore in this, methinks, we cannot say that the errors of the incontinent proceed from ignorance, or that they deceive themselves and that they do not sin, when they well know that they are sinning."

16.—My lord Ottaviano replied:

"In truth, messer Pietro, your argument is fine; yet to my thinking it is specious rather than sound, for although the incontinent sin hesitatingly, and reason struggles with appetite in their mind, and although that which is evil seems evil to them,—yet they have no perfect perception of it, nor do they know it so thoroughly as they need. Hence they have a vague idea rather than any certain knowledge of it, and thus allow their reason to be overcome by passion; but if they had true knowledge of it, doubtless they would not err: since the thing by which appetite conquers reason is always ignorance, and true knowledge can never be overcome by passion, which is derived from the body and not from the mind, and becomes virtue if rightly ruled and governed by reason; if not, it becomes vice.

"But reason has such power that it always reduces the senses to submission and enters in by wonderful means and ways, provided ignorance does not seize that which it ought to possess. So that although the spirits and nerves and bones have no reason in them, yet when a movement of the mind starts in us, as if thought were spurring and shaking the bridle on our spirits, all our members make ready,—the feet to run, the hands to take or to do that which the mind thinks; and moreover this is clearly seen in many who at times unwittingly eat some loathsome and disgusting food, which to their taste seems very delicious, and then learning what thing it was, not only suffer pain and distress of mind, but the body so follows the mental sense, that they must perforce cast up that food."

17.—My lord Ottaviano was continuing his discourse further, but the Magnifico Giuliano interrupted him and said:

"If I heard aright, my lord Ottaviano, you said that continence is an imperfect virtue because it has a grain of passion in it; and when there is a struggle waging in our minds between reason and appetite, I think that the virtue which battles and gives reason the victory, ought to be esteemed more perfect than that which conquers without opposition of lust or passion; for there the mind seems not to abstain from evil by force of virtue, but to refrain from doing evil because it has no inclination thereto."

Then my lord Ottaviano said:

"Which captain would you deem of greater worth, the one who fighting openly puts himself in danger and yet conquers the enemy, or the one who by his ability and skill deprives them of their strength, reducing them to such straits that they cannot fight, and thus conquers them without any battle or danger whatever?"

"The one," said the Magnifico Giuliano, "who more safely conquers is without doubt more to be praised, provided this safe victory of his do not proceed from the cowardice of the enemy."

My lord Ottaviano replied:

"You have judged rightly; and hence I tell you that continence may be likened to a captain who fights manfully, and although the enemy be strong and powerful, still conquers them, albeit not without great difficulty and danger. While temperance unperturbed is like that captain who conquers and rules without opposition, and having not only abated but quite extinguished the fire of lust in the mind where she abides, like a good prince in time of civil strife, she destroys her seditious enemies within, and gives reason the sceptre and whole dominion.

"Thus this virtue does not compel the mind, but infusing it by very gentle means with a vehement belief that inclines it to righteousness, renders it calm and full of rest, in all things equal and well measured, and disposed on every side by a certain self-accord which adorns it with a tranquillity so serene that it is never ruffled, and becomes in all things very obedient to reason and ready to turn its every act thereto and to follow wherever reason may wish to lead it, without the least unwillingness; like a tender lambkin, which always runs and stops and walks near its dam, and moves only with her.

"This virtue, then, is very perfect and especially befitting to princes, because from it spring many others."

18.—Then messer Cesare Gonzaga said:

"I do not know what virtues befitting to a lord can spring from this temperance, if it is the one which removes the passions from the mind, as you say. Perhaps this would be fitting in a monk or hermit; but I am by no means sure whether it would befit a prince (who was magnanimous, liberal and valiant in arms) never to feel, whatever might be done to him, either wrath or hate or good will or scorn or lust or passion of any kind, and whether he could without this wield authority over citizens or soldiers."

My lord Ottaviano replied:

"I did not say that temperance wholly removes and uproots the passions from the human mind, nor would it be well to do this, for even the passions contain some elements of good; but it reduces to the sway of reason that which is perverse in our passions and recusant to right. Therefore it is not well to extirpate the passions altogether, in order to be rid of disturbance; for this would be like making an edict that no one must drink wine, in order to be rid of drunkenness, or forbidding everyone to run, because in running we sometimes fall. You know that those who tame horses do not keep them from running and leaping, but would have them do so seasonably and in obedience to the rider.

"Thus, when moderated by temperance, the passions are helpful to virtue, like the wrath that aids strength, hatred of evil-doers aids justice, and likewise the other virtues are aided by the passions; which, if they were wholly removed, would leave the reason very weak and languid, so that it could effect little, like the master of a vessel abandoned by the winds in a great calm.

"Now do not marvel, messer Cesare, if I have said that many other virtues are born of temperance, for when a mind is attuned to this harmony, it then through the reason easily receives true strength, which makes it bold, and safe from every peril, and almost superior to human passions. Nor is this less true of justice (unspotted virgin, friend of modesty and good, queen of all the other virtues), because she teaches us to do that which it is right to do, and to shun that which it is right to shun; and therefore she is most perfect, because the other virtues perform their works through her, and because she is helpful to whomsoever possesses her, both to himself and to others: without whom (as it is said) Jove himself could not rule his kingdom rightly. Magnanimity also follows these and enhances them all; but she cannot stand alone, for whoever has no other virtue, cannot be magnanimous. Then the guide of these virtues is foresight, which consists in a certain judgment in choosing well. And in this happy chain are joined liberality, magnificence, thirst for honour, gentleness, pleasantness, affability and many others which there is not now time to name.

"But if our Courtier will do that which we have said, he will find them all in his prince's mind, and will daily see spring therefrom beautiful flowers and fruits, such as all the delightful gardens in the world do not contain; and he will feel within him very great content when he remembers that he gave his prince, not that which fools give (which is gold or silver, vases, raiment, and the like, whereof the giver has very great dearth, and the recipient very great abundance), but that faculty which of all things human is perhaps the greatest and rarest—that is, the man-

ner and mode of ruling and reigning rightly: which would of
itself alone suffice to make men happy and to bring back once more
to earth that age of gold which is said to have been when Saturn
reigned."

19.—My lord Ottaviano having here made a little pause as
if to rest, my lord Gaspar said:

"Which do you think, my lord Ottaviano, the happier rule,
and the more able to bring back to earth that age of gold which
you have mentioned,—the rule of so good a prince, or the government of a good republic?"

My lord Ottaviano replied:

"I should always prefer the rule of a good prince, because
such dominion is more accordant with nature, and (if it is allowed
to compare small things with infinitely great) more like that of
God, who governs the universe singly and alone.

"But leaving this aside, you see that in those things that are
wrought by human skill,—such as armies, great fleets, buildings
and the like,—the whole is referred to one man who governs to
his liking. So too in our body all the members labour and are
employed at the command of the heart. Moreover it seems fitting
that the people should be ruled by one prince, as is the case also
with many animals, to whom nature teaches this obedience as a
very salutary thing. You know that stags, cranes and many other
birds, when on their flight, always set up a leader, whom they
follow and obey; and the bees obey their king as it were by process
of reason, and with as much reverence as the most obedient people
on earth; and hence all this is very strong proof that the dominion
of princes is more accordant with nature than that of republics."

20.—Then messer Pietro Bembo said:

"Yet it seems to me that since liberty has been given us by
God as a supreme gift, it is not reasonable that we should be deprived of it, nor that one man should have a larger share of it
than another: which happens under the dominion of princes, who
for the most part hold their subjects in closest bondage. But in
rightly ordered republics this liberty is fully preserved: besides
which, both in judgments and in councils, it more often happens
that one man's opinion singly is wrong, than that of many; because disturbance arising from anger or scorn or lust more easily

enters the mind of one man than that of the many, who are almost like a great body of water, which is less liable to corruption than a small one.

"I say, too, that the example of the animals does not seem to me apposite; for stags, cranes and the rest do not always set up the same one to follow and obey, but on the contrary change and vary, giving the dominion over them now to one, now to another, and thus come to be a kind of republic rather than a monarchy; and this may be called true and equal liberty, when those who command to-day in turn obey to-morrow. Neither does the example of the bees seem to be pertinent, for that king of theirs is not of their own species; and therefore whoever would give men a truly worthy lord, would need to find one of another species and of more excellent nature than that of men, if men must of reason obey him, like the herds which obey not an animal of their own kind but a herdsman, who is a man and of higher species than theirs.

"For these reasons, my lord Ottaviano, I think the rule of a republic is more desirable than that of a king."

21.—Then my lord Ottaviano said:

"Against your opinion, messer Pietro, I wish to cite only one argument; which is, that of the modes of ruling people well, three kinds only are to be found: one is monarchy; another, the rule of the good, whom the ancients called optimates; the other, popular government. And the excess and opposite extreme, so to speak, wherein each one of the forms of rule falls to ruin and decay, is when monarchy becomes tyranny; and when the rule of the optimates changes to government by a few powerful and bad men; and when popular government is seized by the rabble, which breaks down distinctions and commits the government of the whole to the caprice of the multitude. Of these three kinds of bad government, it is certain that tyranny is the worst of all, as could be proved by many arguments; then it follows that monarchy is the best of the three kinds of good government, because it is the opposite of the worst; for, as you know, the results of opposite causes are themselves opposite.

"Now as to what you said about liberty, I reply that we ought not to say that true liberty is to live as we like, but to live according to good laws. Nor is it less natural and useful and necessary to obey than it is to command; and some things are born and thus appointed and ordained by nature to command, as certain others are to obey. True it is that there are two modes of ruling: the one imperious and violent, like that of masters towards their slaves, and in this way the soul commands the body; the other more mild and gentle, like that of good princes by means of laws over their subjects, and in this way the reason commands the appetite: and both of these modes are useful, for the body is by nature created apt for obedience to the soul, and so is appetite for obedience to reason. Moreover there are many men whose actions have to do only with the use of the body; and such as these are as far from virtuous as the soul from the body, and although they are rational creatures, they have only such share of reason as to recognize it but not to possess or profit by it. These, therefore, are naturally slaves, and it is better and more profitable for them to obey than to command."

22.—Thereupon my lord Gaspar said:

"In what mode then are the discreet and virtuous, and those who are not by nature slaves, to be ruled?"

My lord Ottaviano replied:

"With that gentle rule, kingly and civic. And to such men it is well sometimes to give the charge of those offices for which they are fitted, to the end that they too may be able to command and govern those less wise than themselves, but in such manner that the chief rule shall wholly depend upon the supreme prince. And since you said that it is an easier thing for the mind of one man to be corrupted than for that of many, I say that it is also an easier thing to find one good and wise man than many. And to be good and wise ought to be deemed possible for a king of noble race, inclined to worthiness by his natural instinct and by the illustrious memory of his predecessors, and practised in good behaviour; and if he be not of another species more than human (as you said of the bee-king), being aided by the teachings and by the education and skill of so prudent and excellent a Courtier as these gentlemen have described,—he will be very just, continent, temperate, strong and wise, full of liberality, magnificence, religion and clemency. In short, he will be very glorious, and very dear to men and to God (by whose grace he will attain that heroic worth which will make him exceed the limits of humanity), and may be called a demigod rather than a mortal man.

"For God delights in and protects, not those princes who wish to imitate Him by displaying great power and making themselves adored of men, but those who, besides the power that makes them mighty, strive to make themselves like Him in goodness and wisdom, whereby they wish and are able to do good and to be His ministers, distributing for men's weal the benefits and gifts which they receive from Him. Thus, just as in heaven the sun and moon and other stars show the world as in a mirror some likeness of God, so on earth a much liker image of God is found in those good princes who love and revere Him, and show their people the shining light of His justice and a reflection of His divine reason and mind; and with such as those God shares His righteousness, equity, justice and goodness, and those other happy blessings which I know not how to name, but which display to the world much clearer proof of divinity than the sun's light, or the continual revolving of the heavens and the various coursing of the stars.

23.—"Accordingly men have been placed by God under the ward of princes, who for this reason ought to take diligent care of them, in order to render Him an account of them like good stewards to their lord, and ought to love them, and regard as personal to themselves every good and evil thing that happens to them, and provide for their happiness above every other thing. Therefore the prince ought not only to be good, but also to make others good, like that square used by architects, which not only is straight and true itself, but also makes straight and true all things to which it is applied. And a very great proof that the prince is good is when his people are good, because the prince's life is law and preceptress to his subjects, and upon his behaviour all the others must needs depend; nor is it fitting for an ignorant man to teach, nor for an unordered man to give orders, nor for one who falls to raise up others.

"Hence if the prince would perform these duties rightly, he must devote every study and diligence to wisdom; then he must set before himself and follow steadfastly in everything the law of reason (unwritten on paper or metal, but graven upon his own mind), to the end that it may be not only familiar to him, but ingrained in him, and abide with him as a part of himself; so that day and night, in every place and time, it may admonish him and speak inwardly to his heart, freeing him from those disturbances that are felt by intemperate minds, which—because they are oppressed on the one hand as it were by the very deep sleep of ignorance, and on the other by the travail which they suffer from their perverse and blind desires—are tossed by relentless fury, as a sleeper sometimes is by strange and dreadful visions.

24.—"Moreover, by adding greater power to evil wish, greater harm is added also; and when the prince is able to do that which he wishes, then there is great danger that he will not wish that which he ought. Hence Bias well said that office shows what men are: [438] for just as vases with some crack in them cannot easily be detected so long as they are empty, yet if liquid be poured in they at once show where the flaw is;—so corrupt and vicious minds seldom disclose their defects except when they are filled with authority; because then they do not suffice to bear the heavy weight of power, and hence run all lengths and scatter on every side the greeds, the pride, the bad temper, the insolence, and those tyrannical practices, which they have within them. Thus they recklessly persecute the good and wise and exalt the wicked, and in their cities they permit neither friendships nor unions nor understandings among their subjects, but maintain spies, informers and murderers, in order that they may frighten and make men cowardly, and sow discords to keep men disunited and weak. And from these ways there then ensue countless ruin and losses to the unhappy people, and often cruel death (or at least continual fear) to the tyrants themselves; because good princes are not afraid for themselves, but for those whom they rule, while tyrants fear even those whom they rule; hence the greater the number of people they rule and the more powerful they are, so much the more do they fear and so many more enemies do they have.

"How frightened and of what uneasy mind do you think was Clearchus, tyrant of Pontus, [439] every time he went into the market-place or theatre, or to a banquet or other public place? who, as

it is written, was wont to sleep shut up in a chest. Or that other
tyrant, Aristodemus the Argive? [440] who made a kind of prison of
his bed: for in his palace he had a little room hung in air, and
so high that it could be reached only by a ladder; and here he
slept with one of his women, whose mother took away the ladder
at night and replaced it in the morning.

"A wholly different life from this, then, ought that of the
good prince to be, free and safe and as dear to his subjects as
their very own, and so ordered as to partake both of the active
and of the contemplative, as much as may comport with his people's weal."

25.—Then my lord Gaspar said:

"And which of these two lives, my lord Ottaviano, seems to
you more fitting for the prince?"

My lord Ottaviano replied, laughing:

"Perhaps you think I imagine myself to be that excellent
Courtier who ought to know so many things and apply them to
that good end which I have set forth; but remember that these
gentlemen have described him with many accomplishments that
are not in me. Therefore let us first take care to find him, for I
leave to him both this and all things else that belong to a good
prince."

Then my lord Gaspar said:

"I think that if any of the accomplishments ascribed to the
Courtier are lacking in you, they are music and dancing and others
of small importance, rather than those that belong to the mould-
ing of the prince and to this end of Courtiership."

My lord Ottaviano replied:

"None of those are of small importance that help to win the
prince's favour, which is necessary (as we have said) before the
Courtier risks trying to teach him virtue; which I think I have
proved can be learned, and in which there is as much profit as
there is loss in ignorance, whence spring all sins, and especially
that false esteem which men cherish of themselves. But methinks
I have said enough, and perhaps more than I promised."

Then my lady Duchess said:

"We shall be the more beholden to your courtesy, the more
your performance outstrips your promise; so do not weary of

saying what occurs to you about my lord Gaspar's question; and by your faith, tell us also everything that you would teach your prince if he had need of instruction, and imagine yourself to have won completely his favour, so that you are allowed to tell him freely what comes into your mind."

26.—My lord Ottaviano laughed, and said:

"If I had the favour of a certain prince whom I know, and were to tell him freely what I think, I fear that I should soon lose it; moreover, to teach him, I myself should first need to learn.

"Yet since it pleases you to have me answer my lord Gaspar further concerning this, I say that I think princes ought to lead both the two lives, but more especially the contemplative life, because in their case this is divided into two parts: one of which consists in perceiving rightly and in judging; the other in commanding (justly and in those ways that are fitting) things reasonable and those wherein they have authority, and in requiring the same of such men as have in reason to obey, and at appropriate times and places; and of this Duke Federico spoke when he said that whoever knows how to command is always obeyed. And as command is always the chief office of princes, they ought often to see with their own eyes and be present at the execution of their commands, and ought also sometimes to take part themselves, according to the time and need; and all this partakes of action: but the aim of the active life ought to be the contemplative, as peace is that of war, repose that of toil.

27.—"Therefore it is also the good prince's office so to establish his people, and under such laws and ordinances, that they may live at ease and peace, without danger and with dignity, and may worthily enjoy this end of their actions, which ought to be tranquillity. For many republics and princes are often found that have been very prosperous and great in war, and as soon as they have had peace they have gone to ruin and lost their greatness and splendour, like iron laid aside. And this has come about from nothing else but from their not having been well established for living at peace, and from their not knowing how to enjoy the blessing of ease. And to be always at war, without seeking to arrive at the end of peace, is not permitted: albeit some princes think that their chief aim ought to be to lord it over their neigh-bours, and therefore they train their people to a warlike ferocity for spoil, killing and the like, and give rewards to excite it, and call it virtue.

"Thus it was once a custom among the Scythians that who-ever had not slain an enemy might not drink from the bowl which was handed about to the company at solemn feasts. In other places they used to set up, around a tomb, as many obelisks as he who was buried there had slain enemies; and all these things were done to make men warlike, solely in order to lord it over others: which was almost impossible, because the undertaking was end-less (until the whole world should be subjugated) and far from reasonable according to the law of nature, which will not have us pleased with that in others which is displeasing to us in our-selves.

"Therefore princes ought not to make their people warlike for lust of rule, but for the sake of being able to defend them-selves and their people against him who would reduce them to bondage or do them wrong in any wise; or to drive out tyrants and govern those people well who were ill used, or to reduce to bondage those who are by nature such as to deserve being made slaves, with the object of governing them well and giving them ease and rest and peace. To this end also the laws and all the or-dinances of justice ought to be directed, by punishing the wicked, not from hatred, but in order that they may not be wicked and to the end that they may not disturb the tranquillity of the good. For in truth it is a monstrous thing and worthy of blame for men to show themselves valiant and wise in war (which is bad in it-self) and in peace and quiet (which are good) to show themselves ignorant and of so little worth that they know not how to enjoy their happiness.

"Hence, just as in war men ought to apply themselves to the qualities that are useful and necessary to attain its end, which is peace,—so in peace, to attain its end also, which is tranquillity, they ought to apply themselves to the righteous qualities that are the end of the useful. And thus subjects will be good, and the prince will have much more to praise and reward than to punish; and dominion will be very happy for the subjects and for the

ↆↆↆↆↆↆↆↆↆↆↆↆↆↆↆↆↆↆↆↆↆↆↆↆↆↆↆↆↆↆↆↆↆↆↆↆↆↆↆↆↆↆↆↆↆↆↆↆↆↆↆↆↆↆↆↆↆↆↆↆↆↆↆↆↆↆↆↆↆↆↆↆↆↆↆ

prince—not imperious, like that of master over slave, but sweet and gentle, like that of a good father over a good son."

28.—Then my lord Gaspar said:

"I should much like to know what these virtues are that are useful and necessary in war, and what ones are righteous in peace."

My lord Ottaviano replied:

"All virtues are good and helpful, because they tend to a good end; but of especial utility in war is that true courage which so frees the mind from the passions that it not only fears not dangers, but even pays no heed to them; likewise steadfastness, and that enduring patience, with a mind staunch and undisturbed by all the shocks of fortune. It is also fitting in war, and always, to have all the virtues that make for right,—like justice, continence, temperance; but much more in time of peace and ease, because men placed in prosperity and ease, when good fortune smiles upon them, often become unjust, intemperate, and allow themselves to be corrupted by pleasures: hence those who are in such case have very great need of these virtues, for ease too readily engenders evil behaviour in human minds. Therefore it was anciently said as a proverb, slaves should be given no ease; and it is believed that the pyramids of Egypt were made to keep the people busy, because it is very good for everyone to be accustomed to bear toil.

"There are still many other virtues that are all helpful, but let it suffice for the present that I have spoken until now; for if I knew how to teach my prince and instruct him in this kind of worthy education such as we have planned, merely by so doing I should deem myself to have attained sufficiently well the aim of the good Courtier."

29.—Then my lord Gaspar said:

"My lord Ottaviano, since you have highly praised good education, and seemed almost to think that it is the chief means of making a man virtuous and good, I should like to know whether this instruction, which the Courtier must give his prince, ought to be begun with practice and with daily behaviour as it were, so as to accustom him to right doing without his perceiving it; or whether a beginning ought to be made by demonstrating to his reason the quality of good and evil, and by making him understand, before he sets out, which is the good way and the one to follow, and which is the bad way and the one to avoid: In short whether his mind ought to be first imbued and implanted with the virtues through the reason and intelligence or through practice."

My lord Ottaviano said:

"You start me upon too long a discourse; still, in order that you may not think I abstain from lack of will to answer your questions, I say that just as our mind and body are two things, so too the soul is divided into two parts, of which one has the reason in it, and the other has the appetite. Then, just as in generation the body precedes the soul, so the unreasoning part of the soul precedes the reasoning part: which is clearly perceived in children, in whom anger and lust are seen almost as soon as they are born, but with the lapse of time reason appears. Hence care must be taken of the body earlier than of the soul, and of appetite earlier than of reason; but care of the body with a view to the soul, and of the appetite with a view to reason: for just as intellectual worth is perfected by instruction, so is moral worth perfected by practice. We ought, therefore, first to teach through habit, which is able to govern the as yet unreasoning appetites and to direct them towards the good by means of that fair use; next we ought to establish them through the understanding, which, although it shows its light more tardily, still furnishes a mode of making the virtues more perfectly fruitful to one whose mind is well trained by practice,—wherein, to my thinking, lies the whole matter."

30.—My lord Gaspar said:

"Before you go further, I should like to know what care ought to be taken of the body, since you said that we ought to take care of it earlier than of the soul."

"As to that," replied my lord Ottaviano, laughing, "ask those who nourish their bodies well, and are plump and fresh; for mine, as you see, is not too well conditioned. Yet of this also it would be possible to say much, as of the proper time for marriage, to the end that the children may not be too near or too far from their father's age; of the exercises and education to be fol-

ﬀﬀﬀﬀﬀﬀﬀﬀﬀﬀﬀﬀﬀﬀﬀﬀﬀﬀﬀﬀﬀﬀﬀﬀﬀﬀﬀﬀﬀﬀﬀﬀﬀﬀﬀﬀﬀﬀﬀﬀﬀﬀﬀﬀﬀﬀﬀﬀﬀﬀﬀﬀ

lowed from birth and during the rest of life, in order to make them handsome, strong and sturdy."

My lord Gaspar replied:

"That which would best please women for making their children handsome and beautiful, methinks would be that community wherein Plato in his Republic wishes them to be held, and after that manner." [441]

Then my lady Emilia said, laughing:

"It is not in the compact that you should fall to speaking ill of women again."

"I think," replied my lord Gaspar, "that I give them great praise in saying that they wish to bring in a custom approved by so great a man."

Messer Cesare Gonzaga said, laughing:

"Let us see whether this could have place among my lord Ottaviano's precepts (I do not know if he has rehearsed them all), and whether it were well for the prince to make it law."

"The few that I have rehearsed," replied my lord Ottaviano, "might perhaps suffice to make a prince good, as princes go nowadays; although if one cared to look into the matter more minutely, he would still have much more to say."

My lady Duchess added:

"Since it costs us nothing but words, tell us on your faith everything that it would occur to your mind to teach your prince."

31.—My lord Ottaviano replied:

"Many other things, my Lady, would I teach him, provided I knew them; and among others, that he should choose from his subjects a number of the noblest and wisest gentlemen, with whom he should consult on everything, and that he should give them authority and free leave to speak their mind to him about all things without ceremony; and that he should preserve such demeanour towards them, that they all might perceive that he wished to know the truth about everything and held all manner of falsehood in hatred. Besides this council of nobles, I should advise that there be chosen from the people other men of lower rank, of whom a popular council should be made, to communicate with the council of nobles concerning the affairs of the city, both public and private. And in this way there would be made of the prince (as of the head) and of the nobles and commonalty (as of the members) a single united body, the government of which would spring chiefly from the prince and yet include the others also; and this state would thus have the form of the three good kinds of government, which are Monarchy, Optimates, and People.[442]

32.—"Next I should show him that of the cares which belong to the prince, the most important is that of justice; for the maintenance of which wise and well-tried men ought to be chosen to office, whose foresight is true foresight accompanied by goodness, for else it is not foresight, but cunning; and when this goodness is lacking, the pleaders' skill and subtlety always work nothing but ruin and destruction to law and justice, and the guilt of all their errors must be laid on him who put them in office.

"I should tell how justice also fosters that piety towards God which is the duty of all men, and especially of princes, who ought to love Him above every other thing and direct all their actions to Him as to the true end; and as Xenophon said, to honour and love Him always, but much more when they are in prosperity, so that afterwards they may the more reasonably have confidence to ask Him for mercy when they are in some adversity.[443] For it is impossible to govern rightly either one's self or others without the help of God; who to the good sometimes sends good fortune as His minister to relieve them from grievous perils; sometimes adverse fortune, to prevent their being so lulled by prosperity as to forget Him or human foresight, which often repairs evil fortune, as a good player repairs bad throws of the dice by placing his board well.[444] Moreover I should not cease reminding the prince to be truly religious—not superstitious or given to the vanities of incantation and soothsaying; for by adding divine piety and true religion to human foresight, he would have good fortune too and a protecting God always to increase his prosperity in peace and in war.

33.—"Next I should tell how he ought to love his land and people, not holding them too much in bondage, lest he make himself odious to them, from which thing there arise seditions, conspiracies and a thousand other evils; nor yet in too great freedom, lest he be despised, from which proceed licentious and

dissolute life among his people, rapine, theft, murder, without
any fear of the law; often the ruin and total destruction of city
and realms. Next, how he ought to love those near him according to their degree, maintaining among all men an even equality
in some things, as in justice and liberty; and in certain other
things a judicious inequality, as in being generous, in rewarding,
in distributing honours and dignities according to the inequality
of their merits, which always ought not to exceed but to be exceeded by their rewards; and that in this way he would be not
merely loved but almost adored by his subjects. Nor would there
be need that he should turn to aliens for the safeguard of his
life, because his own people for their very profit would guard it
with their own, and all men would gladly obey the laws, when
they found that he himself obeyed and was as it were the guardian
and incorruptible minister of the same; and thus he would make
so strong an impression in this matter, that even if he sometimes chanced to infringe the laws in some particular, everyone
would feel that it was done for a good end, and the same respect
and reverence would be paid to his wish as to the law itself.

"Thus the minds of his subjects would be so tempered that
the good would not seek for more than they needed, and the bad
could not; for excessive riches are oftentimes the cause of great
ruin, as in poor Italy, which has been and still is exposed as a
prey to foreign nations, both because of bad government and because of the great riches of which it is full. Hence it were well to
have the greater part of the citizens neither very rich nor very
poor, for the over-rich often become insolent and rash; the poor,
base and dishonest; but men of moderate fortune do not lay
snares for others, and live safe from being snared: and being the
greater number, these men of moderate fortune are also more
powerful; and therefore neither the poor nor the rich can con-
spire against the prince or other men, nor can they sow seditions;
wherefore, in order to avoid this evil, it is a very wholesome thing
to preserve a mean in all things.

34.—"I should say then, that the prince ought to employ
these and many other suitable precautions, so that there may not
arise in his subjects' mind a desire for new things and for a change
of government; which they most often bring to pass either for

gain or else for honour which they hope for, or because of loss or else of shame which they fear. And this unrest is engendered in their minds sometimes by hatred and anger driving them to despair, by reason of the wrongs and insults that have been wrought upon them through the avarice, insolence and cruelty or lust of their superiors; sometimes by the contempt that is aroused in them by the neglect and baseness and unworthiness of their princes. These two errors ought to be avoided by winning the people's love and obedience; as is done by benefiting and rewarding the good, and by prudently and sometimes severely precluding the bad and seditious from becoming powerful, which is much easier to prevent before they have become so than to deprive them of power after they have once acquired it. And I should say that to prevent a subject from running into these errors, there is no better way than to keep him from evil practices, and especially from those that spread little by little; for they are secret pests that infect cities before it is possible to cure or even to detect them.

"By such means I should advise that the prince contrive to keep his subjects in a tranquil state, and to give them the blessings of mind and body and fortune; but those of the body and of fortune, in order to be able to exercise those of the mind, which are the more profitable the greater and more superabundant they are; which is not true of those of the body and of fortune. If, then, the subjects be good and worthy and rightly directed towards the goal of happiness, their prince is a very great lord; for that is a true and great dominion, under which the subjects are good and well governed and well commanded."

35.—Then my lord Gaspar said:

"I think that he would be a small lord under whom all the subjects were good, for in every place the good are few."

My lord Ottaviano replied:

"If some Circe were to change all the subjects of the King of France into wild beasts, would he not seem to you a small lord for all he ruled over so many thousand animals? [445] And on the other hand, if only the flocks that roam our mountains here for pasture were to become wise men and worthy cavaliers, would you not think that those herdsmen who governed them and were obeyed by them, had become great lords instead of herdsmen? You see then, that it is not the number but the worth of their subjects that makes princes great."

36.—My lady Duchess and my lady Emilia and all the others had been for a good space very attentive to my lord Ottaviano's discourse; but since he now made a little pause, as if he had finished his discourse, messer Cesare Gonzaga said:

"Verily, my lord Ottaviano, it cannot be said that your precepts are not good and useful; nevertheless I should think that if you fashioned your prince after them, you would rather deserve the name of a good school-master than of a good Courtier, and he rather that of a good governor than of a great prince. I am far from saying that the care of lords should not be to have their people well ruled with justice and good uses; nevertheless methinks it is enough for them to select good ministers to dispose of such matters, and that their true office is much greater.

"Therefore if I felt myself to be that excellent Courtier which these gentlemen have described, and to possess the favour of my prince, I certainly should not lead him into anything vicious; but, to pursue that good end which you tell of, and which I agree ought to be the fruit of the Courtier's toils and actions, I should seek to impress upon his mind a certain greatness, together with that regal splendour and readiness of mind and unconquered valour in war which should make him loved and revered by everyone to such a degree that he should be famous and illustrious in the world chiefly for this. I should tell him also that he ought to accompany his greatness with a familiar gentleness, with that sweet and amiable humanity, and a fine manner of caressing both his subjects and strangers with discrimination, more or less according to their merits,—always preserving, however, the majesty suited to his rank, so as not to allow his authority to abate one jot from over-condescension, nor on the other hand to excite hatred by too stern severity; that he ought to be very generous and splendid, and to give to all men without reserve, because God, as the saying runs, is the treasurer of generous princes; that he ought to give magnificent banquets, festivals, games, public shows; to have a great number of excellent horses (for use in war and for pleasure in time of peace), falcons, hounds, and all things else that pertain to the pleasures of great lords and of the people. as in our days we have seen done by my lord Francesco Gonzaga, Marquess of Mantua, who in these matters seems rather King of Italy than lord of a city.[446]

"I should seek also to induce him to erect great buildings, both to win honour in his lifetime and to give a memorial of himself to posterity: as Duke Federico did in the case of this noble palace,[447] and as Pope Julius is now doing in the case of St. Peter's Church [448] and of that street which leads from the Palace to his pleasure pavilion the Belvedere,[449] and many other buildings: as also the ancient Romans did, whereof we see so many remains at Rome and at Naples, at Pozzuoli, at Baja, at Civita Vecchia, at Porto,[450] and out of Italy too, and many other places,—which are great proof of the worth of those divine minds.[451] So did Alexander the Great also, for not content with the fame that he had justly won by having conquered the world with arms, he built Alexandria in Egypt, Bucephalia in India,[452] and other cities in other countries; and he thought of reducing Mount Athos to the form of a man, and of building a very spacious city in its left hand, and in its right a great basin in which were to be gathered all the rivers that take their rise there, and from it they were to flow over into the sea: [453] a truly great thought and one worthy of Alexander the Great.

"These, my lord Ottaviano, are things which I think befit a noble and true prince, and make him very glorious in peace and war; and not setting his mind to so many trifles, and taking care to fight solely in order to rule or conquer those who deserve to be ruled, or for his subjects' profit, or to deprive those of power who yield it ill. For if the Romans, Alexander, Hannibal and the others had had these aims, they would not have reached that height of glory to which they did attain."

37.—Then my lord Ottaviano replied, laughing:

"Those who had not these aims, would have done better if they had; although if you think, you will find many that did, and particularly those first ancients, like Theseus and Hercules. And do not imagine that Procrustes and Sciron, Cacus, Diomed, Antæus, Geryon, were other than cruel and impious tyrants, against whom these lofty-minded heroes waged perpetual and deadly war.[454] Therefore, for having delivered the world from such intolerable monsters (for only thus ought tyrants to be called), temples were raised and sacrifices offered to Hercules, and divine honours paid to him; since the extirpation of tyrants is a benefit so profitable to the world that he who confers it deserves much greater reward than any befitting to a mortal.[455]

"And of those whom you named, do you not think that by his victories Alexander did good to the peoples whom he conquered, having taught so many good customs to those barbarous tribes which he overcame, that out of wild beasts he made them men? He built so many fine cities in lands that were ill-inhabited, and introduced right living there, and as it were united Asia and Europe by the bond of friendship and holy laws, that those who were conquered by him were happier than the others. For to some he taught marriage, to others agriculture, to others religion, others he taught not to kill but to support their fathers when grown old, others to abstain from union with their mothers, and a thousand other things that could be told in proof of the benefit which his victories conferred upon the world.

38.—"But leaving the ancients aside, what more noble and glorious enterprise and more profitable could there be than for Christians to devote their power to subjugating the infidels?[456] Do you not think that this war, if it succeeded prosperously and were the means of turning so many thousand men from the false sect of Mahomet to the light of Christian truth, would be as profitable to the vanquished as to the victors? And truly, as Themistocles once said to his family, being banished from his native land and received by the King of Persia and caressed and honoured with countless and very rich gifts: 'My friends, we should have been undone for our undoing,'[457] so with reason might the Turks and Moors then say the same, because in their loss would lie their salvation.

"Therefore I hope that we shall yet see this happiness, if God grant life enough for Monseigneur d'Angoulême to attain the crown of France,[458] who gives such promise of himself as my lord Magnifico told of four evenings since; and for my lord Henry, Prince of Wales,[459] to attain that of England, who now is growing up under his great father in every sort of virtue,[460] like a tender shoot under the shade of an excellent and fruit-laden tree, to renew it with much greater beauty and fruitfulness when the time shall be; for as our friend Castiglione writes thence,[461] and promises to tell more fully on his return, it seems that nature wished in this lord to show her power by gathering in a single body enough excellences to adorn a host."

Then messer Bernardo Bibbiena said:

"Very great promise is shown also by Don Carlos, Prince of Spain, who (although not yet arrived at the tenth year of his age) already shows so much capacity and such certain signs of goodness, of foresight, of modesty, of magnanimity and of every virtue, that if the empire of Christendom shall be (as men think) in his hands, we may believe that he must eclipse the name of many ancient emperors, and equal the fame of the most famous that have been on earth."[462]

39.—My lord Ottaviano added:

"I think, then, that such divine princes as these have been sent by God on earth, and by Him made to resemble one another in youth, in martial power, in state, in beauty and bodily shape, to the end that they may be of one accord for this good purpose also. And if there must ever be any envy or emulation among them, it may be solely in wishing to be each the first and most fervent and zealous for so glorious an enterprise.

"But let us leave this discourse and return to our subject. I say, then, messer Cesare, that the things which you wish the prince to do are very great and worthy of much praise; but you ought to understand that if he does not know that which I have said he ought to know, and has not formed his mind after that pattern and directed it to the path of virtue, he will hardly know how to be magnanimous, generous, just, courageous, foreseeing, or to possess any of those other qualities that are looked for in him. Nor yet would I have him such merely for the sake of being able to exercise these qualities: for just as those who build are not all good architects, so those who give are not all generous; because virtue never harms any man, and there are many who rob in order to give away, and thus are generous with the property of others; some give to those they ought not, and leave in misfortune and distress those to whom they are beholden; others

✝✝✝✝✝✝✝✝✝✝✝✝✝✝✝✝✝✝✝✝✝✝✝✝✝✝✝✝✝✝✝✝✝✝✝✝✝✝✝✝✝✝✝✝✝✝✝✝✝✝✝✝✝✝

give with a certain bad grace and almost spite, so that men see they
do so on compulsion; others not only make no secret of it, but
call witnesses and almost proclaim their generosities; others foolishly empty the fountain of their generosity at a draught, so that
it can be no more used again.

40.—"Hence in this, as in other things, it is needful to know
and to govern one's self with that foresight which is the necessary
companion of all the virtues; which being midway are near the
two extremes—that is, the vices; and thus he who does not know,
easily runs into them. For just as it is difficult to find the central
point in a circle, which is the mean, so is it difficult to find the point
of virtue set midway between the two extremes (vicious, the one
because of excess, the other because of deficiency); and to these
we are inclined, sometimes to one and sometimes to the other. We
perceive this in the pleasure or displeasure that we feel within us,
for by reason of the one we do that which we ought not, and by
reason of the other we fail to do that which we ought; but the
pleasure is much the more dangerous, because our judgment allows
itself to be easily corrupted by it.

"But since it is a difficult thing to perceive how far a man is
from the central point of virtue, we ought of our own accord to
withdraw step by step in the direction opposite to the extreme
towards which we perceive ourselves to be inclined, as those do
who straighten crooked timbers; for in such wise we approximate
to virtue, which (as I have said) consists in that central point.
Hence it happens that we err in many ways and perform our office
and duty in only one way, just like archers, who hit the mark by
one way only and miss the target by many. Thus, in his wish to be
humane and affable, one prince often does countless things beneath
his dignity, and so abases himself that he is despised; another, to
preserve his grave majesty with becoming authority, becomes
austere and intolerable; another, to be held eloquent, strays into
a thousand strange fashions and long mazes of affected words,
listening to himself to such a degree that others cannot listen to
him for weariness.

41.—"Therefore do not call anything a trifle, messer Cesare,
that can improve a prince in any particular, however slight it be;

ʼʼʼʼʼʼʼʼʼʼʼʼʼʼʼʼʼʼʼʼʼʼʼʼʼʼʼʼʼʼʼʼʼʼʼʼʼʼʼʼʼʼʼʼʼʼʼʼʼʼʼʼʼʼ

nor must you suppose that I think you disparage my precepts
when you say that by them a good governor would be fashioned
rather than a good prince; for perhaps no greater or more fitting
praise can be given to a prince than to call him a good governor.
Hence if it lay with me to instruct him, I would have him take care
to heed not only the matters already mentioned, but those which
are much smaller, and as far as possible understand all details
affecting his people, nor ever so believe or trust any one of his
ministers as to confide to that one alone the bridle and control of
all his government. For there is no man who is very apt for all
things, and much greater harm arises from the credulity of lords
than from their incredulity, which not only sometimes does no
harm, but often is of the greatest advantage: albeit in this matter
there is need of good judgment in the prince, to perceive who
deserves to be believed and who does not.

"I would have him take care to understand the acts and be
the overseer of his ministers; to settle and shorten disputes among
his subjects; to be the means of making peace among them, and
of allying them in marriage; to have his city all united and agreed
in friendship like a private family, populous, not poor, peaceful,
full of good artificers; to favour merchants and even to aid them
with money; to be generous and splendid in hospitality towards
foreigners and ecclesiastics; to moderate all superfluities, for
through the errors that are committed in these matters, small
though they seem, cities often come to ruin. Wherefore it is reasonable that the prince should set a limit upon the too sumptuous
houses of private folk, upon feasts, upon the excessive doweries of
women, upon their luxury, upon their display in jewels and vesture,
which is naught but a proof of their folly; for besides often wasting
their husbands' goods and substance through the ambition and the
envy which they bear one another, they sometimes sell their honour
to anyone who will buy it, for the sake of a trinket or some other
like trifle."

42.—Then messer Bernardo Bibbiena said, laughing:
"My lord Ottaviano, you are taking sides with my lord Gaspar and Frisio."

My lord Ottaviano replied, also laughing:

⁄⁄⁄⁄⁄⁄⁄⁄⁄⁄⁄⁄⁄⁄⁄⁄⁄⁄⁄⁄⁄⁄⁄⁄⁄⁄⁄⁄⁄⁄⁄⁄⁄⁄⁄⁄⁄⁄⁄⁄⁄⁄⁄⁄⁄⁄⁄⁄⁄⁄⁄⁄⁄⁄⁄⁄⁄⁄⁄⁄⁄⁄⁄⁄

"The dispute is finished, and I am far from wishing to renew it; so I shall say no more of women, but return to my prince."

Frisio replied:

"You can very well leave him now, and rest content that he should be such as you have described him. For without doubt it would be easier to find a lady with the qualities mentioned by my lord Magnifico, than a prince with the qualities mentioned by you; hence I fear that he is like Plato's Republic, and that we are never to see his equal, unless perhaps in Heaven."

My lord Ottaviano replied:

"Although they be difficult, things that are possible may still be hoped to come to pass. Therefore we shall in our times perhaps yet see him on earth; for although the heavens are so chary of producing excellent princes that hardly one is seen in many centuries, this good fortune may fall to us."

Then Count Ludovico said:

"I certainly trust that it may be so; for, besides those three great princes whom we have named, to whom we may look for that which has been said to befit the highest type of a perfect prince,—there are also to be found in Italy to-day several princes' sons, who, although they are not likely to have such great power, will perhaps fill its place with worth. And the one among them all who shows the best natural bent, and gives greater promise than any of the others, seems to me to be my lord Federico Gonzaga, eldest son of the Marquess of Mantua and nephew to our lady Duchess here.[463] For besides the gentleness of behaviour and the discretion which he shows at such a tender age, those who have charge of him tell wonderful things of his capacity, eagerness for honour, magnanimity, courtesy, generosity, love of justice; so that from so good a beginning we cannot but hope for the best of ends."

Then Frisio said:

"No more of this at present; we will pray God that we may see this hope of yours fulfilled."

43.—Here my lord Ottaviano, turning to my lady Duchess with an air of having finished his discourse, said:

"There, my Lady, is what occurs to me to say about the aim of the Courtier; wherein, if I shall not have wholly given satisfaction, it will at least be enough for me to have shown that some further perfection could be given him in addition to the things mentioned by these gentlemen; who, methinks, omitted both this and all that I might say, not because they did not know it better than I, but in order to save themselves trouble; therefore I will leave them to continue, if they have anything left to say."

Then my lady Duchess said:

"Not only is the hour so late that it will soon be time to stop for the evening, but it seems to me that we ought not to mingle any other discourse with this; wherein you have gathered so many different and beautiful things, that we may say (touching the aim of Courtiership) not only that you are the perfect Courtier whom we seek, and competent to instruct your prince rightly, but if fortune shall be favourable to you, that you ought also to be an admirable prince, which would be of great advantage to your country." [464]

My lord Ottaviano laughed, and said:

"If I held such rank, my Lady, perhaps it would be with me as it is wont to be with many others, who know better how to speak than to act."

44.—Here the matter having been debated back and forth awhile among the whole company, with some little contradiction albeit in praise of what had been said, and it being suggested that it was not yet time to go to rest, the Magnifico Giuliano said, laughing:

"My Lady, I am so great an enemy to guile, that I am forced to contradict my lord Ottaviano, who, from having (as I fear) conspired secretly with my lord Gaspar against women, has fallen into two errors to my thinking very grave: one of which is, that in order to set this Courtier above the Court Lady and make him transcend the bounds that she can reach, my lord Ottaviano has set the Courtier also above the prince, which is most unseemly; the other is in setting him such a goal that it is always difficult, and sometimes impossible for him to reach it, and that even when he does reach it, he ought not to be called a Courtier."

"I do not understand," said my lady Emilia, "how it should be so difficult or impossible for the Courtier to reach this goal of his, nor yet how my lord Ottaviano has set him above the prince." [465]

"Do not grant him these things," replied my lord Ottaviano, "for I have not set the Courtier above the prince, nor do I think I have fallen into any error touching the aim of Courtiership."

Then the Magnifico Giuliano replied:

"You cannot say, my lord Ottaviano, that the cause which gives a certain quality to a result, does not always have more of that quality than its result has. Thus the Courtier, through whose instruction the prince is to become so excellent, must needs be more excellent than his prince; and in this way he will also be of greater dignity than the prince himself, which is most unseemly.

"Then, as for the aim of Courtiership, what you said may be true when the prince's age is little different from the Courtier's, but still not without difficulty, for where there is small difference in age, it is natural that there should be small difference in knowledge also; while if the prince is old and the Courtier young, it is fitting that the old prince should know more than the young Courtier; and if this does not always happen, it happens sometimes, and then the goal which you set the Courtier is impossible. Again, if the prince is young and the Courtier old, the Courtier can hardly win the prince's mind by means of those accomplishments that you have ascribed to him. For to say the truth, jousting and other exercises of the person belong to young men and do not befit old men, and music and dancing and festivals and games and love-making are ridiculous in old age; and methinks they would be very ill-befitting a director of the prince's life and behaviour, who ought to be a very sober person of authority, mature in years and experience, and (if possible) a good philosopher, a good commander, and ought to know almost everything.

"Therefore I think that whoever instructs the prince ought not to be called a Courtier, but deserves a far higher and more honoured name. So pardon me, my lord Ottaviano, if I have exposed your fallacy; for methinks I am bound to do so for the honour of my Lady, whom you, forsooth, would have of less dignity than this Courtier of yours, and I will not allow it."

45.—My lord Ottaviano laughed, and said:

"My lord Magnifico, it would be more praise to the Court

ꬸꬸꬸꬸꬸꬸꬸꬸꬸꬸꬸꬸꬸꬸꬸꬸꬸꬸꬸꬸꬸꬸꬸꬸꬸꬸꬸꬸꬸꬸꬸꬸꬸꬸꬸꬸꬸꬸꬸꬸꬸꬸꬸꬸꬸꬸꬸꬸꬸꬸꬸ

Lady to exalt her until she equalled the Courtier, than to abase the
Courtier until he equalled the Court Lady, for it would be by no
means forbidden the Lady to teach the mistress also, and with her
to tend towards that aim of Courtiership which I said befits the
Courtier with the prince. But you seek more to censure the Courtier
than to praise the Court Lady; hence I too shall be allowed to
take the Courtier's part.

"To reply, then, to your objections, I declare I did not say
that the Courtier's instruction ought to be the sole cause of making the prince such as we would have him. For if he were not by
nature inclined and fitted to be so, all the Courtier's care and reminders would be in vain: just as any good husbandman also
would labour in vain if he were to set about cultivating barren
sea-sand and sowing it with excellent seed, because such barren-
ness is natural in that place; but when to good seed in fertile
soil, and to mildness of climate and rains suited to the season,
there is added also the diligence of human culture, very abundant
crops are always found to spring up plenteously. Nor is it on
that account true that the husbandman alone is the cause of this,
although without him all the other things would avail little or
nothing. Thus there are many princes who would be good if their
minds were rightly cultivated; and it is of these that I am
speaking, not of those who are like barren ground, and by nature
so alien to good behaviour that no training avails to lead their
minds in the straight path.

46.—"And since, as we have already said, our habits are
what our actions make them, and virtue consists in action, it is
not impossible or marvellous that the Courtier should turn the
prince to many virtues, like justice, generosity, magnanimity, the
practice whereof the prince by his greatness can easily put in use
and convert into habit; which the Courtier cannot do, because he
has not the means to practise them; and thus the prince, allured
to virtue by the Courtier, may become more virtuous than the
Courtier. Moreover you must know that the whetstone, although
it cuts nothing, yet makes iron sharp. Hence it seems to me that
although the Courtier instructs the prince, he need not on that
account be said to be of more dignity than the prince.

"That the aim of this Courtiership is difficult and sometimes impossible, and that even when the Courtier attains it, he ought not to be called a Courtier, but deserves a greater name,—I say that I do not deny this difficulty, since it is not less difficult to find so excellent a Courtier than to attain such an end. Yet methinks there is no impossibility, even in the case that you cited: for if the Courtier is too young to know that which we have said he ought to know, we need not speak of him, since he is not the Courtier we are presupposing, nor is it possible that one who has to know so many things should be very young.

"And if, indeed, the prince shall chance to be so wise and good by nature that he has no need of precepts and counsel from others (although everyone knows how difficult this is), it will be enough for the Courtier to be such a man as could make the prince virtuous if he had need of it. And then the Courtier will be at least able to perform the other part of his duty,—not to allow his prince to be deceived, always to make known the truth about everything, and to set himself against flatterers and slanderers and all those who plot to debase his prince's mind with unworthy pleasures. And in this way he will also attain his end in great part, although he cannot put everything in practice: which will not be a reason for finding fault with him, since he refrains therefrom for so good a cause. For if an excellent physician were to find himself in a place where everyone was in health, it would not for that reason be right to say that this physician failed in his aim, although he healed no sick. Thus, just as the physician's aim ought to be men's health, so the Courtier's ought to be his prince's virtue; and it is enough for them both to have their aim latent within their power, if their failure to attain it openly in acts arises from the subject to which the aim is directed.

"But if the Courtier were so old that it would not become him to practise music, festivals, games, arms, and the other personal accomplishments, still we cannot say that it is impossible for him to win his prince's favour by that road. For if his age prevents his practising those things, it does not prevent his understanding them, and if he has practised them in his youth, it does not prevent his having the more perfect judgment regarding them, and his knowing the more perfectly how to teach them to his prince, in proportion as years and experience bring more knowledge of everything. Thus, although the old Courtier does not practise the accomplishments ascribed to him, he will yet attain his aim of instructing his prince rightly.

47.—"And if you are unwilling to call him Courtier, it does not trouble me; for nature has not set such limit upon human dignities that a man may not mount from one to another. Thus, common soldiers often become captains; private persons, kings; and priests, popes; and pupils, masters; and thus, together with the dignity, they acquire the name also. Hence perhaps we might say that to become his prince's instructor was the Courtier's aim. However, I do not know who would refuse this name of perfect Courtier, which in my opinion is worthy of very great praise. And it seems to me that just as Homer described two most excellent men as patterns of human life,—the one in deeds (which was Achilles), the other in sufferings and endurance (which was Ulysses),—so also he described a perfect Courtier (which was Phœnix), who, after narrating his loves and many other youthful affairs, says that he was sent to Achilles by the latter's father, Peleus, as a companion and to teach the youth how to speak and act: which is naught else but the aim which we have marked out for our Courtier.[466]

"Nor do I think that Aristotle and Plato would have scorned the name of perfect Courtier, for we clearly see that they performed the works of Courtiership and wrought to this end,—the one with Alexander the Great, the other with the kings of Sicily. And since the office of a good Courtier is to know the prince's character and inclinations, and thus to enter tactfully into his favour according to need and opportunity, as we have said, by those ways that afford safe access, and then to lead him towards virtue,—Aristotle so well knew the character of Alexander, and tactfully fostered it so well, that he was loved and honoured more than a father by Alexander.[467] Thus, among many other tokens that Alexander gave him of good will, the king ordered the rebuilding of his native city, Stagira, which had been destroyed;[468] and besides directing Alexander to that most glorious aim,—which was the desire to make the world as one single universal country, and all men as a single people to live in amity and mutual concord under a single government and a single law, which should shine equally on all like the light of the sun,[469]— Aristotle so instructed him in the natural sciences and in the virtues of the mind as to make him most wise, brave, continent, and a true moral philosopher, not only in words but in deeds; for a nobler philosophy cannot be imagined than to bring into civilized living such savage people as those who inhabited Bactria and Caucasia, India, Scythia; [470] and to teach them marriage, agriculture, honour to their fathers, abstention from rapine, murder and other evil ways; to build so many very noble cities in distant lands;—so that countless men were by his laws reduced from savage life to civilization. And of these achievements of Alexander the author was Aristotle, using the means of a good Courtier: which Callisthenes knew not how to do, although Aristotle showed him; [471] for in his wish to be a pure philosopher and austere minister of naked truth, without mingling Courtiership therewith, he lost his life and brought not help but rather infamy to Alexander.

"By these same means of Courtiership, Plato schooled Dio of Syracuse; [472] and having afterwards found the tyrant Dionysius like a book all full of faults and errors and in need of complete erasure rather than of any change or correction (since it was not possible to remove from him that tinge of tyranny wherewith he had so long been stained), Plato was unwilling to practise the ways of Courtiership upon him, thinking that they all would surely be in vain. Which our Courtier also ought to do, if by chance he finds himself in the service of a prince of so evil a disposition as to be inveterate in vice, like consumptives in their malady; for in such case he ought to escape that bondage, in order not to receive blame for his lord's evil deeds, and in order not to feel that distress which all good men feel who serve the wicked."

48.—Here my lord Ottaviano having ceased speaking, my lord Gaspar said:

"I did not in the least suspect that our Courtier was so honoured; but since Aristotle and Plato are his fellows, I think that no one ought henceforth to scorn this name. Still I am far from sure whether I believe that Aristotle and Plato ever danced or made music in their lives, or performed any other acts of chivalry."

My lord Ottaviano replied:

"It is hardly permitted to think that these two divine spirits did not know everything, and hence we may believe that they practised what pertains to Courtiership, for on occasion they write of it in such fashion that the very masters of the subjects written of by them perceive that they understood the same to the marrow and deepest roots. Wherefore there is no ground for saying that all the accomplishments ascribed to him by these gentlemen do not befit a Courtier (or instructor of the prince, as you like to call him) who contributes to that good end which we have mentioned, even though he were a very stern philosopher and most saintly in his behaviour, because they are not at variance with goodness, discretion, wisdom, worth, at every age and in every time and place."

49.—Then my lord Gaspar said:

"I remember that in discussing the accomplishments of the Courtier last evening, these gentlemen desired that he should be in love; and since, by reviewing what has thus far been said, we might conclude that a Courtier who has to allure his prince to virtue by his worth and authority, must almost of necessity be old (because knowledge very rarely comes before years, and especially in those things that are learned by experience),—I do not know how becoming it is for him (being advanced in age) to be in love. For as has been said this evening, love does not sit well upon old men, and those things which in young men are delights, courtesies and elegances very pleasing to women, in old men are extravagances and ridiculous incongruities, and for him who practises them win hatred from women and derision from others.

"So if your friend Aristotle, the old Courtier, were in love, and did those things which young lovers do, like some whom we have seen in our days,—I fear he would forget to instruct his prince, and perhaps children would mock at him behind his back, and women would get little pleasure from him except to deride him."

Then my lord Ottaviano said:

"As all the other accomplishments ascribed to the Courtier befit him although he be old, methinks we ought by no means to deprive him of this enjoyment of loving."

"Nay," said my lord Gaspar, "to deprive him of love is to give him an added perfection, and to make him live at ease remote from misery and calamity."

50.—Messer Pietro Bembo said:

"Do you not remember, my lord Gaspar, that although he is little skilled in love, yet in his game the other evening my lord Ottaviano seemed to know that there are some lovers who call sweet the scorns and ires and warrings and torments which they have from their ladies; whence he asked to be taught the cause of this sweetness? Therefore if our Courtier, although old, were inflamed with those loves that are sweet without bitterness, he would feel no calamity or misery in them; and if he were wise, as we suppose him to be, he would not deceive himself by thinking that all was befitting to him which befits young men; but if he loved, perhaps he would love in a way that would bring him not only no blame, but much praise and highest happiness unaccompanied by any pain, which rarely and almost never happens with young men; and thus he would not fail to instruct his prince, nor would he do aught to deserve the mockery of children."

Then my lady Duchess said:

"I am glad, messer Pietro, that you have had little fatigue in our discussion this evening, for now we shall with more assurance impose on you the burden of speaking, and of teaching the Courtier this love which is so happy that it brings with it neither blame nor discomfort; for perhaps it will be one of the most important and useful attributes that have thus far been ascribed to him: therefore tell us, on your faith, all you know about it."

Messer Pietro laughed, and said:

"I should be sorry, my Lady, that my saying it is permissible for old men to love should be a reason for these ladies to regard me as old; therefore please to give this task to someone else." [473]

My lady Duchess replied:

"You ought not to shun being reputed old in wisdom, even if you are young in years; so speak on, and make no more excuse."

✓✓✓✓✓✓✓✓✓✓✓✓✓✓✓✓✓✓✓✓✓✓✓✓✓✓✓✓✓✓✓✓✓✓✓✓✓✓✓✓✓✓✓✓✓✓✓✓✓✓✓✓

Messer Pietro said:

"Indeed, my Lady, if I must talk about this matter, I should need to go take counsel with my Lavinello's Hermit." [474]

Then my lady Emilia said, half vexed:

"Messer Pietro, there is no one in the company who is more disobedient than you; therefore it will be well for my lady Duchess to inflict some chastisement upon you."

Messer Pietro said, again smiling:

"Be not angry with me, my Lady, for love of God; for I will tell what you wish."

"Then tell it at once," replied my lady Emilia.

51.—Whereupon messer Pietro, having first remained silent awhile, then settled himself a little as if about to speak of something important, and spoke thus: [475]

"My Lords, in order to prove that old men can love not only without blame but sometimes more happily than young men, it will be needful for me to make a little discourse to explain what love is, and in what consists the happiness that lovers may enjoy. So I pray you hear me with attention, for I hope to make you see that there is no man here whom it does not become to be in love, even though he were fifteen or twenty years older than my lord Morello."

And then after some laughter, messer Pietro continued:

"I say, then, that according to the definition of the ancient sages love is naught but a certain desire to enjoy beauty; and as desire longs only for things that are perceived, perception must needs always precede desire, which by its nature wishes good things, but in itself is blind and does not perceive them. Therefore nature has so ordained that to every faculty of perception there is joined a certain faculty of appetite; and since in our soul there are three modes of perceiving, that is, by sense, by reason, and by intellect: from sense springs appetite, which we have in common with the brutes; from reason springs choice, which is peculiar to man; from the intellect, by which man is able to commune with the angels, springs will. Thus, just as sense perceives only things that are perceptible by the senses, appetite desires the same only; and just as intellect is directed solely to the contemplation of things intellectual, the will feeds only upon spiritual benefits. Being by nature rational and placed as a mean between these two extremes, man can at pleasure (by descending to sense or mounting to intellect) turn his desires now in the one direction and now in the other. In these two ways, therefore, it is possible to desire beauty, which universal name applies to all things (whether natural or artificial) that are framed in good proportion and due measure according to their nature.

52.—"But speaking of the beauty we have in mind, which is only that which is seen in the bodies and especially in the faces of men, and which excites this ardent desire that we call love,—we will say that it is an effluence of divine goodness, and that although it is diffused like the sun's light upon all created things, yet when it finds a face well proportioned and framed with a certain pleasant harmony of various colours embellished by lights and shadows and by an orderly distance and limit of outlines, it infuses itself therein and appears most beautiful, and adorns and illumines that object whereon it shines with grace and wonderful splendour, like a sunbeam falling upon a beautiful vase of polished gold set with precious gems. Thus it agreeably attracts the eyes of men, and entering thereby, it impresses itself upon the soul, and stirs and delights her with a new sweetness throughout, and by kindling her it excites in her a desire for its own self.

"Then, being seized with desire to enjoy this beauty as something good, if the soul allows herself to be guided by the judgment of sense, she runs into very grievous errors, and judges that the body wherein the beauty is seen is the chief cause thereof; and hence, in order to enjoy that beauty, she deems it necessary to join herself as closely to that body as she can; which is false: and accordingly, whoever thinks to enjoy the beauty by possessing the body deceives himself, and is moved, not by true perception through reasonable choice, but by false opinion through sensual appetite: wherefore the pleasure also that results therefrom is necessarily false and vicious.

"Hence all those lovers who satisfy their unchaste desires with the women whom they love, run into one of two errors: for as soon as they have attained the end desired, they either not only feel satiety and tedium, but hate the beloved object as if

ィィィィィィィィィィィィィィィィィィィィィィィィィィィィィィィィィィィィィィィィィィィィィィィィィィィ

appetite repented its error and perceived the deceit practised upon it by the false judgment of sense, which made it believe evil to be good; or else they remain in the same desire and longing, like those who have not truly attained the end they sought. And although, by reason of the blind opinion wherewith they are intoxicated, they think they feel pleasure at the moment, as the sick sometimes dream of drinking at some clear spring, nevertheless they are not contented or appeased. And since the possession of a wished-for joy always brings quiet and satisfaction to the mind of the possessor, if that joy were the true and worthy object of their desire, they would remain quiet and satisfied in possessing it; which they do not. Nay, deceived by that likeness, they soon return to unbridled desire, and with the same distress they felt at first, they find themselves furiously and very ardently athirst for that which they vainly hope to possess perfectly.

"Such lovers as these, therefore, love most unhappily; for either they never attain their desires (which is great unhappiness), or if they do attain thereto, they find they have attained their woe, and finish their miseries with other miseries still greater; because even in the beginning and midst of their love naught else is ever felt but anguish, torments, sorrows, sufferings, toils. So that to be pale, melancholy, in continual tears and sighs, to be sad, to be ever silent or lamenting, to long for death, in short, to be most unhappy, are the conditions that are said to befit lovers.

53.—"The cause, then, of this havoc in the minds of men is chiefly sense, which is very potent in youth, because the vigour of flesh and blood at that period gives to it as much strength as it takes away from reason, and hence easily leads the soul to follow appetite. For, finding herself plunged into an earthly prison and deprived of spiritual contemplation by being set the task of governing the body, the soul cannot of herself clearly comprehend the truth; wherefore, in order to have perception of things, she must needs go begging first notions from the senses, and so she believes them and bows before them and allows herself to be guided by them, especially when they have so much vigour that they almost force her; and as they are fallacious, they fill her with errors and false opinions.

"Hence it nearly always happens that young men are

wrapped in this love which is sensual and wholly rebellious to reason, and thus they become unworthy to enjoy the graces and benefits which love bestows upon its true subjects; nor do they feel any pleasures in love beyond those which the unreasoning animals feel, but anguish far more grievous.

"This premise being admitted then,—and it is most true,— I say that the contrary happens to those who are of maturer age. For if such as these (when the soul is already less weighed down by bodily heaviness and when the natural heat begins to become tepid) are inflamed by beauty and turn thereto a desire guided by rational choice,—they are not deceived, and possess beauty perfectly. Therefore their possession of it always brings them good; because beauty is good, and hence true love of beauty is most good and holy, and always works for good in the mind of those who restrain the perversity of sense with the bridle of reason; which the old can do much more easily than the young.

54.—"Hence it is not beyond reason to say further that the old can love without blame and more happily than the young; taking this word old, however, not in the sense of decrepit, nor when the bodily organs have already become so weak that the soul cannot perform its functions through them, but when our knowledge is at its true prime.

"I will not refrain from saying also this: which is, that I think that although sensual love is evil at every age, yet in the young it deserves excuse, and is perhaps in a measure permitted. For although it gives them anguish, dangers, toils, and those woes that have been told, still there are many who, to win the favour of the ladies of their love, do worthy acts, which (although not directed to a good end) are intrinsically good; and thus from that mass of bitterness they extract a little sweet, and through the adversities which they endure they at last perceive their error. Hence, just as I deem those youths divine who control their appetites and love in reason, so I excuse those who allow themselves to be overcome by sensual love, to which they are so strongly inclined by human frailty: provided they show therein gentleness, courtesy and worth, and the other noble qualities of which these gentlemen have told; and provided that when they are no longer of youthful age, they abandon it altogether, shunning this sensual desire as it were the lowest round of the ladder by which true love can be attained. But if, even after they are old, they preserve the fire of appetite in their chill heart and subject stout reason to frail sense, it is not possible to say how much they are to be blamed. For like fools they deserve to be numbered with perpetual infamy among the unreasoning animals, since the thoughts and ways of sensual love are too unbecoming to mature age."

55.—Here Bembo paused a little, as if to rest; and as everyone remained silent, my lord Morello da Ortona said:

"And if an old man were found more vigorous and sturdy and of better looks than many youths, why would you not have him allowed to love with that love wherewith young men love?"

My lady Duchess laughed, and said:

"If young men's love is so unhappy, my lord Morello, why do you wish to have old men love thus unhappily also? But if you were old, as these gentlemen say, you would not thus contrive evil for old men."

My lord Morello replied:

"Methinks it is messer Pietro Bembo who is contriving evil for old men, in that he wishes to have them love in a certain way which I for my part do not understand; and methinks that to possess this beauty which he so highly praises, without the body, is a dream."

Then Count Ludovico said:

"Do you believe, my lord Morello, that beauty is always as good as messer Pietro Bembo says?"

"Not I indeed," replied my lord Morello; "nay, I remember having seen many beautiful women who were very bad, cruel and spiteful; and this seems to be almost always so, for beauty makes them proud, and pride makes them cruel."

Count Ludovico said, laughing:

"To you, perhaps, they seem cruel because they do not grant you what you would have; but have yourself taught by messer Pietro Bembo in what way old men ought to desire beauty, and what they ought to seek from women, and with what they ought to be content; and if you do not exceed these limits, you shall ʃʃʃʃʃʃʃʃʃʃʃʃʃʃʃʃʃʃʃʃʃʃʃʃʃʃʃʃʃʃʃʃʃʃʃʃʃʃʃʃʃʃʃʃʃʃʃʃʃʃʃʃ

see that they will not be either proud or cruel, and will grant
you what you wish."

Then my lord Morello seemed a little vexed, and said:

"I have no wish to know what does not concern me; but do
you have yourself taught how this beauty ought to be desired by
young men who are less vigorous and sturdy than their elders."

56.—Here messer Federico, to quiet my lord Morello and
turn the conversation, did not allow Count Ludovico to reply, but
interrupted him and said:

"Perhaps my lord Morello is not altogether wrong in saying
that beauty is not always good; for women's beauty is often the
cause that brings upon the world countless evils, hatreds, wars,
deaths and destructions; of which good proof can be found in
the fall of Troy. And beautiful women are for the most part
either proud or cruel, or (as has been said) immodest; but this
would not seem to my lord Morello a fault. There are also many
wicked men who have the gift of fair looks, and it seems that
nature made them thus to the end that they should be better
fitted to deceive, and that this gracious seeming is like the bait
upon the hook."

Then messer Pietro Bembo said:

"Do not believe that beauty is not always good."

Here Count Ludovico, in order to return to the original subject, interrupted and said:

"Since my lord Morello does not care to know what so deeply
concerns him, teach it to me, and show me how old men attain
this happiness in love, for I shall not mind having myself thought
old, provided it help me."

57.—Messer Pietro laughed, and said:

"I wish first to free these gentlemen's minds from their
error; then I will satisfy you too." Resuming thus, he said:

"My lords, I would not have any of us, like profane and
sacrilegious men, incur God's wrath by speaking ill of beauty,
which is a sacred thing. Therefore, to the end that my lord
Morello and messer Federico may be warned, and not lose their
sight, like Stesichorus (which is a very fitting punishment for one
who scorns beauty),[476] I say that beauty springs from God, and
is like a circle of which goodness is the centre. And hence, as there

can be no circle without a centre, there can be no beauty without
goodness. Thus a wicked soul rarely inhabits a beautiful body,
and for that reason outward beauty is a true sign of inward goodness. And this grace is impressed upon bodies, more or less, as an
index of the soul, whereby she is known outwardly, as in the case
of trees, in which the beauty of the blossom gives token of the
excellence of the fruit. The same is true in the case of human
bodies, as we see that the Physiognomists often recognize in the
face the character and sometimes the thoughts of men; and what
is more, in beasts also we discern from the aspect the quality of
the mind, which is expressed as much as possible in the body.
Think how clearly we read anger, ferocity and pride in the face
of the lion, the horse, the eagle; a pure and simple innocence in
lambs and doves; cunning malice in foxes and wolves, and so of
nearly all other animals.

58.—"The ugly are therefore for the most part wicked too,
and the beautiful are good: and we may say that beauty is the
pleasant, gay, acceptable and desirable face of good, and that
ugliness is the dark, disagreeable, unpleasant and sad face of evil.
And if you will consider all things, you will find that those which
are good and useful always have a charm of beauty also.

"Look at the state of this great fabric of the world, which
was made by God for the health and preservation of every
created thing. The round firmament, adorned with so many heavenly lights, and the earth in the centre, surrounded by the elements and sustained by its own weight; the sun, which in its
revolving illumines the whole, and in winter approaches the lowest sign, then little by little mounts to the other side; the moon,
which derives her light from it, according as it approaches her or
withdraws from her; and the five other stars, which separately
travel the same course.[477] These things have such influence upon
one another through the linking of an order thus precisely framed,
that if they were changed for an instant, they could not hold
together, and would wreck the world; they have also such beauty
and grace that human wit cannot imagine anything more beautiful.

"Think now of the shape of man, which may be called a
little world; wherein we see every part of the body precisely composed with skill, and not by chance; and then the whole form

together so beautiful that we could hardly decide whether more utility or more grace is given to the human features and the rest of the body by all the members, such as the eyes, nose, mouth, ears, arms, breast, and other parts withal. The same can be said of all the animals. Look at the feathers of birds, the leaves and branches of trees, which are given them by nature to preserve their being, and yet have also very great loveliness.

"Leave nature, and come to art. What thing is so necessary in ships as the prow, the sides, the yards, the masts, the sails, the helm, the oars, the anchors and the cordage? Yet all these things have so much comeliness, that it seems to him who looks upon them that they are thus devised as much for beauty as for use. Columns and architraves support lofty galleries and palaces, yet they are not on that account less pleasing to the eyes of him who looks upon them, than useful to the buildings. When men first began to build, they set that middle ridge in their temples and houses, not in order that the buildings might have more grace, but to the end that the water might flow off conveniently on either side; yet to utility soon was added comeliness, so that if a temple were built under a sky where no hail or rain falls, it would not seem able to have any dignity or beauty without the ridge.

59.—"Much praise is therefore bestowed, not only upon other things, but upon the world, by saying that it is beautiful. We praise when we say: 'Beautiful sky, beautiful earth, beautiful sea, beautiful rivers, beautiful lands, beautiful woods, trees, gardens; beautiful cities, beautiful churches, houses, armies.' In short, this gracious and sacred beauty gives highest ornament to everything; and we may say that the good and the beautiful are in a way one and the same thing, and especially in the human body; of whose beauty I think the most immediate cause is beauty of the soul, which (as partaker of true divine beauty) brightens and beautifies whatever it touches, and especially if the body wherein it dwells is not of such base material that it cannot impress thereon its quality. Therefore beauty is the true trophy of the soul's victory, when with power divine she holds sway over material nature, and by her light overcomes the darkness of the body.

"Hence we must not say that beauty makes women proud

or cruel, although it may seem so to my lord Morello; nor yet ought we to ascribe to beautiful women those enmities, deaths and destructions of which the immoderate appetites of men are the cause. I do not by any means deny that it is possible to find beautiful women in the world who are also immodest, but it is not at all because their beauty inclines them to immodesty; nay, it turns them therefrom and leads them to the path of virtuous behaviour, by the connection that beauty has with goodness. But sometimes evil training, the continual urgence of their lovers, gifts, poverty, hope, deceits, fear and a thousand other causes, overcome the steadfastness even of beautiful and good women; and through these or similar causes beautiful men also may become wicked."

60.—Then messer Cesare said:

"If that is true which my lord Gaspar alleged yesterday, there is no doubt that beautiful women are more chaste than ugly women."

"And what did I allege?" said my lord Gaspar.

Messer Cesare replied:

"If I remember rightly, you said that women who are wooed always refuse to satisfy him who wooes them, and that those who are not wooed woo others. Certain it is that the beautiful are always more wooed and besought in love than are the ugly; therefore the beautiful always refuse, and hence are more chaste than the ugly, who, not being wooed, woo others."

Bembo laughed, and said:

"To this argument no answer can be made." Then he added: "It often happens also that our sight deceives us like our other senses, and accounts a face beautiful which in truth is not beautiful; and since in some women's eyes and whole aspect a certain wantonness is seen depicted, together with unseemly blandishments,—many (who like such manner because it promises them ease in attaining what they desire) call it beauty: but in truth it is disguised immodesty, unworthy a name so honoured and so sacred."

Messer Pietro Bembo was silent, and those gentlemen still urged him to speak further of this love and of the mode of enjoying beauty truly; and he at last said:

"Methinks I have shown clearly enough that old men can love more happily than young, which was my thesis; therefore it does not become me to go further."

Count Ludovico replied:

"You have better shown the unhappiness of youths than the happiness of old men, whom as yet you have not taught what road to follow in this love of theirs, but have only told them to be guided by reason; and by many it is thought impossible for love to abide with reason."

61.—Bembo still sought to put an end to his discourse, but my lady Duchess begged him to speak; and he began anew thus:

"Too unhappy would human nature be, if our soul (wherein such ardent desire can spring up easily) were forced to feed it solely upon that which is common to her with the beasts, and could not direct it to that other nobler part which is peculiar to herself. Therefore, since so indeed it pleases you, I have no wish to avoid discoursing upon this noble subject. And as I feel myself unworthy to speak of Love's most sacred mysteries, I pray him so to inspire my thought and tongue that I may be able to show this excellent Courtier how to love beyond the manner of the vulgar crowd; and since from boyhood up I have dedicated my whole life to him, so now also may my words comport with this intent and with his praise.

"I say, then, that as in youth human nature is so greatly prone to sense, the Courtier may be allowed to love sensually while he is young. But if afterwards in maturer years he chances still to be kindled with this amorous desire, he must be very wary and take care not to deceive himself by allowing himself to be led into those calamities which in the young merit more compassion than blame, and, on the contrary, in the old more blame than compassion.

62.—"Therefore when the gracious aspect of some fair woman meets his view, accompanied with such sweet behaviour and gentle manners that he, as an adept in love, feels that his spirit accords with hers: as soon as he finds that his eyes lay hold upon her image and carry it to his heart; and that his soul begins to contemplate her with pleasure and to feel that influence within which stirs and warms it little by little; and that those

ƔƔƔƔƔƔƔƔƔƔƔƔƔƔƔƔƔƔƔƔƔƔƔƔƔƔƔƔƔƔƔƔƔƔƔƔƔƔƔƔƔƔƔƔƔƔƔƔƔƔƔƔƔƔ

quick spirits which shine out through the eyes continually add
frooh tindor to tho firo, ho ought at thio firot otago to provido n
speedy cure, and arouse his reason, and therewith arm the fortress of his heart, and so shut the way to sense and appetite that
they cannot enter there by force or trickery. Thus, if the flame
is extinguished, the danger is extinguished also; but if it survives or grows, then the Courtier, feeling himself caught, must
resolve on shunning wholly every stain of vulgar love, and thus
enter on the path of divine love, with reason for guide. And first
he must consider that the body wherein this beauty shines is not
the fountain whence it springs, but rather that beauty (being an
incorporeal thing and, as we have said, a heavenly beam) loses
much of its dignity when it finds itself joined to vile and corruptible matter; for the more perfect it is the less it partakes
thereof, and is most perfect when wholly separate therefrom.
And he must consider that just as one cannot hear with the palate
or smell with the ears, so too can beauty in no wise be enjoyed,
nor can the desire which it excites in our minds be satisfied, by
means of touch, but by that sense of which this beauty is the very
object, namely, the power of vision.

"Therefore let him shun the blind judgment of sense, and
with his eyes enjoy the splendour of his lady, her grace, her
amorous sparkle, the laughs, the ways and all the other pleasant
ornaments of her beauty. Likewise with his hearing let him enjoy the sweetness of her voice, the concord of her words, the harmony of her music (if this beloved be a musician). Thus will he
feed his soul on sweetest food by means of these two senses—
which have little of the corporeal and are ministers of reason—
without passing in his desire for the body to any appetite less than
seemly.

"Next let him obey, please and honour his lady with all reverence, and hold her dearer than himself, and prefer her con-
venience and pleasures to his own, and love in her not less the
beauty of mind than that of body. Therefore let him take care
not to leave her to fall into any kind of error, but by admonition
and good advice let him always seek to lead her on to modesty,
to temperance, to true chastity, and see to it that no thoughts
find place in her except those that are pure and free from every

stain of vice; and by thus sowing virtue in the garden of her fair
mind, he will gather fruits of fairest behaviour too, and will taste
them with wonderful delight. And this will be the true engen-
dering and manifesting of beauty in beauty, which by some is
said to be the end of love.

"In such fashion will our Courtier be most acceptable to his
lady, and she will always show herself obedient, sweet and affable
to him, and as desirous of pleasing him as of being loved by him;
and the wishes of both will be most virtuous and harmonious, and
they themselves will thus be very happy."

63.—Here my lord Morello said:

"To engender beauty in beauty, forsooth, would be to beget
a beautiful child in a beautiful woman; and pleasing him in this
would seem to me a much clearer token that she loved her lover
than treating him with the affability of which you speak."

Bembo laughed, and said:

"You must not go beyond bounds, my lord Morello; nor
does a woman give small token of her love when she gives her
lover her beauty, which is so precious a thing, and by the ways
that are the avenues to her soul (that is, sight and hearing) sends
the glances of her eyes, the image of her face, her voice, her
words, which strike home to the lover's heart and give him proof
of her love."

My lord Morello said:

"Glances and words may be, and often are, false proofs;
therefore he who has no better pledge of love is, in my judgment,
far from sure; and truly I quite expected you to make this lady of
yours a little more courteous and generous to the Courtier than
my lord Magnifico made his; but methinks that both of you are
in like case with those judges who pronounce sentence against
their friends for the sake of appearing wise."

64.—Bembo said:

"I am very willing that this lady should be much more
courteous to my unyouthful Courtier, than my lord Magnifico's
is to the youthful Courtier; and with reason, for my Courtier will
desire only seemly things, and therefore the lady can grant him
all of them without blame; while my lord Magnifico's lady, who
is not so sure of the youthful Courtier's modesty, ought to grant

him only seemly things, and to refuse him the unseemly. Hence my Courtier, to whom is granted what he asks, is more happy than the other, to whom part is granted and part refused.

"And to the end that you may still better understand that rational love is happier than sensual, I say that the same things ought sometimes to be refused in sensual love and granted in rational love, because they are unseemly in the one and seemly in the other. Thus, to please her worthy lover, besides granting him pleasant smiles, familiar and secret discourse, and leave to joke and jest with her and to touch her hand, the lady may in reason even go so far as kissing without blame, which is not permitted in sensual love according to my lord Magnifico's rules. For since the kiss is the union of body and soul, there is danger lest the sensual lover incline more in the direction of the body than in that of the soul; while the rational lover perceives that although the mouth is part of the body, yet it gives issue to words, which are interpreters of the soul, and to that inward breath which is itself even called soul. Hence a man delights to join his mouth to that of his beloved in a kiss, not in order to arouse any unseemly desire in him, but because he feels that bond to be the opening of a passage between their souls, which, being each drawn by desire for the other, pour themselves each into the other's body by turn, and so commingle that each has two souls, and a single soul (thus composed of these two) rules as it were over two bodies. Hence the kiss may be oftener said to be a joining of soul than of body, because it has such power over the soul that it draws her to itself and separates her from the body. On this account all chaste lovers desire to kiss as a joining of the soul; and thus the divinely enamoured Plato says that in kissing the soul came to his lips to escape his body. And since the separation of the soul from things material, and its complete union with things spiritual, may be denoted by the kiss, Solomon, in his divine book of the Song, says: 'Let him kiss me with the kiss of his mouth,' to express desire that his soul might be so transported with divine love to the contemplation of celestial beauty, that by joining closely therewith she might forsake the body."

65.—Everyone gave closest heed to Bembo's discourse; and

ﾉﾉﾉﾉﾉﾉﾉﾉﾉﾉﾉﾉﾉﾉﾉﾉﾉﾉﾉﾉﾉﾉﾉﾉﾉﾉﾉﾉﾉﾉﾉﾉﾉﾉﾉﾉﾉﾉﾉﾉﾉﾉﾉﾉﾉﾉﾉﾉﾉﾉﾉﾉﾉﾉﾉﾉﾉ

he, having made a little pause and seeing that no one else spoke, said:

"As you have made me begin to teach our unyouthful Courtier happy love, I fain would lead him a little farther; for it is very dangerous to stop at this stage, seeing that the soul is very prone to the senses, as has many times been said; and although reason and argument choose well and perceive that beauty does not spring from the body, and although they therefore put a bridle upon unseemly desires, still, always contemplating beauty in the body often perverts sound judgment. And even if no other evil flowed therefrom, absence from the beloved object brings much suffering with it, because the influence of her beauty gives the lover wonderful delight when she is present, and by warming his heart weakens and melts certain dormant and frozen forces in his soul, which (being nourished by the warmth of love) spread and blossom about his heart, and send forth through the eyes those spirits that are very subtle vapours made of the purest and brightest part of the blood, which receive the image of her beauty and fashion it with a thousand various ornaments. Hence the soul delights, and trembles with awe and yet rejoices, and as in a stupor feels not only pleasure, but that fear and reverence which we are wont to have for sacred things, and speaks of being in paradise.

66.—"Therefore the lover who considers beauty in the body only, loses this blessing and felicity as soon as his beloved lady by her absence leaves his eyes without their splendour, and his soul consequently widowed of its blessing. Because, her beauty being far away, that amorous influence does not warm his heart as it did in her presence; wherefore his pores become arid and dry, and still the memory of her beauty stirs a little those forces of his soul, so that they seek to scatter abroad the spirits; and these, finding the ways shut, have no exit, and yet seek to issue forth; and thus hemmed in by those goads, they sting the soul and give it keenest suffering, as in the case of children when the teeth begin to come through the tender gums. And from this proceed the tears, the sighs, the anguish and the torments of lovers, because the soul is ever in affliction and travail, and becomes almost raging until her dear beauty appears to it again; and then it suddenly is calmed and breathes, and all intent upon that beauty it feeds on sweetest food, nor would ever part from so delightful a spectacle.

"Hence, to escape the torment of this absence and to enjoy beauty without suffering, there is need that the Courtier should, with the aid of reason, wholly turn his desire from the body to the beauty alone, and contemplate it in itself simple and pure, as far as he can, and fashion it in his imagination apart from all matter; and thus make it lovely and dear to his soul, and enjoy it there, and have it with him day and night, in every time and place, without fear of ever losing it; bearing always in mind that the body is something very different from beauty, and not only does not enhance it, but diminishes its perfection.

"In this wise will our unyouthful Courtier be beyond all the bitterness and calamities that the young nearly always feel: such as jealousies, suspicions, disdainings, angers, despairings, and certain furies full of madness whereby they are often led into such error that some of them not only beat the women whom they love, but deprive themselves of life. He will do no injury to the husband, father, brothers or kinsfolk of his beloved lady; he will put no infamy upon her; he will never be forced to bridle his eyes and tongue with such difficulty in order not to disclose his desires to others, or to endure suffering at partings or absences;—because he will always carry his precious treasure with him shut up in his heart, and also by force of his imagination he will inwardly fashion her beauty much more beautiful than in fact it is.

67.—"But besides these blessings the lover will find another much greater still, if he will employ this love as a step to mount to one much higher; which he will succeed in doing if he continually considers within himself how narrow a restraint it is to be always occupied in contemplating the beauty of one body only; and therefore, in order to escape such close bounds as these, in his thought he will little by little add so many ornaments, that by heaping all beauties together he will form an universal concept, and will reduce the multitude of these beauties to the unity of that single beauty which is spread over human nature at large. In this way he will no longer contemplate the particular beauty of one woman, but that universal beauty which adorns all bodies; and thus, bewildered by this greater light, he will not heed the lesser, and glowing with a purer flame, he will esteem lightly that which at first he so greatly prized.

"This stage of love, although it be very noble and such as few attain, still cannot be called perfect; for since the imagination is merely a corporeal faculty and has no perception except through those means that are furnished it by the senses, it is not wholly purged of material darkness; and hence, although it considers this universal beauty in the abstract and intrinsically, yet it does not discern that beauty very clearly or without some ambiguity, because of the likeness which phantoms bear to substance. Thus those who attain this love are like tender birds beginning to put on feathers, which, although with their frail wings they lift themselves a little in flight, yet dare not go far from their nest or trust themselves to the winds and open sky.

68.—"Therefore when our Courtier shall have reached this goal, although he may be called a very happy lover by comparison with those who are plunged in the misery of sensual love, still I would have him not rest content, but press boldly on following along the lofty path after the guide who leads him to the goal of true felicity. And thus, instead of going outside himself in thought (as all must needs do who choose to contemplate bodily beauty only), let him have recourse to himself, in order to contemplate that beauty which is seen by the eyes of the mind, which begin to be sharp and clear when those of the body lose the flower of their loveliness. Then the soul,—freed from vice, purged by studies of true philosophy, versed in spiritual life, and practised in matters of the intellect, devoted to the contemplation of her own substance,—as if awakened from deepest sleep, opens those eyes which all possess but few use, and sees in herself a ray of that light which is the true image of the angelic beauty communicated to her, and of which she then communicates a faint shadow to the body. Grown blind to things earthly, the soul thus becomes very keen-sighted to things heavenly; and sometimes, when the motive forces of the body are absorbed by earnest contemplation or fettered by sleep, being unhampered by them, she is conscious of a certain far-off perfume of true angelic beauty, and ravished by the splendour of that light, she begins to kindle and pursues it so eagerly that she almost becomes phrensied with desire to unite herself to that beauty, think-

ing that she has found God's footstep, in the contemplation of
which she seeks to rest as in her beatific end. And thus glowing in
this most happy flame, she rises to her noblest part, which is the
intellect; and here, no longer darkened by the gloomy night of
things earthly, she sees the divine beauty; but still she does not yet
quite enjoy it perfectly, because she contemplates it in her own
particular intellect only, which cannot be capable of the vast universal beauty.

"Wherefore, not well content with this boon, love gives the
soul a greater felicity; for just as from the particular beauty of one
body it guides her to the universal beauty of all bodies, so in the
highest stage of perfection it guides her from the particular to the
universal intellect. Hence the soul, kindled by the most sacred fire
of true divine love, flies to unite herself with the angelic nature, and
not only quite forsakes sense, but has no longer need of reason's discourse; for, changed into an angel, she understands all things intelligible, and without veil or cloud views the wide sea of pure divine
beauty, and receives it into herself, and enjoys that supreme felicity of which the senses are incapable.

69.—"If, then, the beauties which with these dim eyes of ours
we daily see in corruptible bodies (but which are naught but dreams
and faintest shadows of beauty) seem to us so fair and gracious that
they often kindle most ardent fire in us, and of such delight that we
deem no felicity able to equal that which we sometimes feel at a
single glance coming to us from a woman's beloved eyes,—what
happy wonder, what blessed awe, shall we think is that which fills
the souls that attain to the vision of divine beauty! What sweet
flame, what delightful burning, must that be thought which springs
from the fountain of supreme and true beauty!—which is the
source of every other beauty, which never waxes nor wanes: ever
fair, and of its own self most simple in every part alike; like only
to itself, and partaking of none other; but fair in such wise that all
other fair things are fair because they derive their beauty from it.

"This is that beauty identical with highest good, which by its
light calls and attracts all things to itself, and not only gives intellect to the intellectual, reason to the rational, sense and desire for
life to the sensual, but to plants also and to stones communicates

motion and that natural instinct of their quality, as an imprint of itself.

"Therefore this love is as much greater and happier than the others, as the cause that moves it is more excellent; and hence, just as material fire refines gold, so does this most sacred fire in our souls destroy and consume that which is mortal there, and quickens and beautifies that celestial part which at first, by reason of the senses, was dead and buried in them. This is the Pyre whereon the poets write that Hercules was burned on the crest of Mount Œta, and by such burning became divine and immortal after death.[478] This is the Burning Bush of Moses, the Cloven Tongues of fire, the Fiery Chariot of Elias,[479] which doubles grace and felicity in the souls of those who are worthy to behold it, when they leave this earthly baseness and take flight towards heaven.

"Let us, then, direct all the thoughts and forces of our soul to this most sacred light, which shows us the way that leads to heaven; and following after it, let us lay aside the passions wherewith we were clothed at our fall, and by the stairway that bears the shadow of sensual beauty on its lowest step, let us mount to the lofty mansion where dwells the heavenly, lovely and true beauty, which lies hidden in the inmost secret recesses of God, so that profane eyes cannot behold it. Here we shall find a most happy end to our desires, true rest from our toil, certain cure for our miseries, most wholesome medicine for our diseases, safest refuge from the boisterous storms of this life's tempestuous sea.

70.—"What mortal tongue, then, O most holy Love, can praise thee worthily? Most fair, most good, most wise, thou springest from the union of beauty and goodness and divine wisdom, and abidest in that union, and by that union returnest to that union as in a circle. Sweetest bond of the universe, joining things celestial to things terrestrial, thou with benignant sway inclinest the supernal powers to rule the lower powers, and turning the minds of mortals to their origin, joinest them thereto. Thou unitest the elements in concord, movest nature to produce—and that which is born, to the perpetuation of life. Thou unitest things that are separate, givest perfection to the imperfect, likeness to the unlike, friendship to the unfriendly, fruit to the earth, tranquillity to the sea, vital light to the heavens.

"Thou art father of true pleasure, of grace, of peace, of gentleness and good will, enemy to rustic savagery and sloth—in short, the beginning and the end of every good. And since thou delightest to inhabit the flower of beautiful bodies and beautiful souls, and thence sometimes to display thyself a little to the eyes and minds of those who are worthy to behold thee, methinks that now thy abode is here among us.

"Deign, then, O Lord, to hear our prayers, pour thyself upon our hearts, and with the splendour of thy most holy fire illumine our darkness and, like a trusted guide, in this blind labyrinth show us the true path. Correct the falseness of our senses, and after our long pursuit of vanities give us true and solid good; make us to inhale those spiritual odours that quicken the powers of the intellect, and to hear the celestial harmony with such accord that there may no longer be room in us for any discord of passion; fill us at that inexhaustible fountain of content which ever delights and never satiates, and gives a taste of true beatitude to all who drink of its living and limpid waters; with the beams of thy light purge our eyes of misty ignorance, to the end that they may no longer prize mortal beauty, and may know that the things which first they seemed to see, are not, and that those which they saw not, really are.

"Accept our souls, which are offered thee in sacrifice; burn them in that living flame which consumes all mortal dross, to the end that, being wholly separated from the body, they may unite with divine beauty by a perpetual and very sweet bond, and that we, being severed from ourselves, may, like true lovers, be able to transform ourselves into the beloved, and rising above the earth may be admitted to the angels' feast, where, fed on ambrosia and immortal nectar, we may at last die a most happy and living death, as died of old those ancient fathers whose souls thou, by the most glowing power of contemplation, didst ravish from the body and unite with God."

71.—Having thus far spoken, with such vehemence that he almost seemed transported and beside himself, Bembo remained silent and motionless, keeping his eyes towards heaven, as if wrapped in ecstasy; when my lady Emilia, who with the others had been listening most attentively to his discourse, took him by the border of his robe, and shaking him a little, said: [480]

"Have a care, messer Pietro, that with these thoughts your soul, also, does not forsake your body."

"My Lady," replied messer Pietro, "that would not be the first miracle that love has wrought upon me."

Then my lady Duchess and all the others again began urging Bembo to continue his discourse: and everyone seemed almost to feel in his mind a spark of that divine love which inspired the speaker, and all desired to hear more; but Bembo added:

"My Lords, I have said that which love's sacred phrensy dictated to me at the moment; now that it seems to inspire me no further, I should not know what to say: and I think love is not willing that its secrets should be further disclosed, or that the Courtier should pass beyond that stage which it has been pleased to have me show him; and therefore perhaps it is not permitted to speak more of this matter."

72.—"Verily," said my lady Duchess, "if the unyouthful Courtier should prove able to follow the path that you have shown him, he ought in all reason to content himself with such great felicity, and to have no envy of the youthful Courtier."

Then messer Cesare Gonzaga said:

"The road which leads to this felicity seems to me so steep that I believe it is very hard to travel."

My lord Gaspar added:

"I believe it is hard for men to travel, but impossible for women."

My lady Emilia laughed, and said:

"My lord Gaspar, if you return to wronging us so often, I promise you that you will not be pardoned again."

My lord Gaspar replied:

"No wrong is done you by saying that women's souls are not so purged of passion as those of men, nor given to contemplation, as messer Pietro said those must be who would taste divine love. Thus we do not read that any woman has had this grace, but that many men have had it, like Plato, Socrates and Plotinus,⁴⁸¹ and many others; and so many of our holy Fathers, like St. Francis, upon whom an ardent spirit of love impressed the most holy seal of the five wounds: ⁴⁸² nor could aught but the power of love lift

St. Paul to the vision of those mysteries whereof man is not allowed to speak; [483] nor show St. Stephen the opened heavens." [484]

Here the Magnifico Giuliano replied:

"In this, women will by no means be outdone by men; for Socrates himself confesses that all the mysteries of love which he knew were revealed to him by a woman, who was the famous Diotima; [362] and the angel who wounded St. Francis with the fire of love, has also made several women of our age worthy of the same seal. You must remember, too, that St. Mary Magdalen had many sins forgiven her because she loved much, [485] and perhaps with no less grace than St. Paul was she many times lifted to the third heaven by angelic love; and so many others, who (as I narrated yesterday more at large) for the love of Christ's name took no heed of life, nor were afraid of torments or any manner of death however horrible and cruel it might be; and they were not old, as messer Pietro would have our Courtier, but tender and delicate girls, and of that age wherein he says that sensual love ought to be allowed in men."

73.—My lord Gaspar began making ready to reply, but my lady Duchess said:

"Of this let messer Pietro Bembo be the judge, and let us abide by his decision whether or not women are as capable of divine love as men are. But as the controversy between you might be too long, it will be well to postpone it until to-morrow."

"Nay, until this evening," said messer Cesare Gonzaga.

"How until this evening?" said my lady Duchess.

Messer Cesare replied:

"Because it is already day;" and he showed her the light that was beginning to come in through the cracks at the windows.

Then everyone rose to his feet in great surprise, for the discussion did not seem to have lasted longer than usual; but by reason of having been begun much later, and by its pleasantness, it had so beguiled the company that they had not perceived the flight of hours; nor was there anyone who felt the heaviness of sleep upon his eyes, which nearly always happens when the accustomed hour of sleep is passed in watching. The windows having then been opened on that side of the palace which looks towards the lofty crest of Mount Catria, [486] they saw that a beautiful dawn of rosy hue was

already born in the east, and that all the stars had vanished save
Venus, sweet mistress of the sky, who holds the bonds of night and
day; from which there seemed to breathe a gentle wind that filled
the air with crisp coolness and began to waken sweet choruses of
joyous birds in the murmuring forests of the hills hard by.

So, having reverently taken leave of my lady Duchess, they
all started towards their chambers without light of torches, that of
day being enough for them; and as they were about to quit the
room, my lord Prefect turned to my lady Duchess, and said:

"My Lady, to finish the controversy between my lord Gaspar
and my lord Magnifico, we will come with our judge this evening
earlier than we did yesterday."

My lady Emilia replied:

"On condition that if my lord Gaspar wishes to accuse women
and put some fresh imputation upon them, as is his wont, he shall
also give bond to sustain his charge, for I account him a shifty
disputant."

# NOTES

# PRELIMINARY NOTES

BALDESAR CASTIGLIONE was born on his father's estate of Casatico in the Mantuan territory, 6 December 1478. Michelangelo was his senior by four years; Leo X by three years; Titian by one year; Giorgione and Cesare Borgia were born in the year of his birth, while his friend Raphael and also Luther were his juniors by five years.

His surname is said to be derived from the little town at which Bonaparte defeated the Austrians near Mantua in 1796, and which is by some supposed to have taken its name from *Castrum Stiliconis*, Camp of Stilico, a Roman general of the 4th century. One Tealdo Castiglione was Archbishop of Milan as early as 1074, from which time the family is often and honourably mentioned in the annals of northern Italy.

Baldesar's parents were Count Cristoforo Castiglione, a soldier-courtier, and Luigia Gonzaga, a near kinswoman of the Marquess of Mantua. The boy studied at Milan,—learning Latin from Giorgio Merula and Greek from Demetrios Chalcondylas, an erudite Athenian who had fled from Byzantium about 1447, and of whom another pupil wrote: "It seems to me that in him are figured all the wisdom, the civility and the elegance of those ancients who are so famous and so illustrious. Merely seeing him, you fancy you are looking on Plato; far more when you hear him speak."

Having spent some time at the splendid court of Ludovico Sforza at Milan, Castiglione lost his father in 1499, and (the Sforzas being expelled the same year) he returned to Mantua and entered the service of his natural lord, the Marquess Gianfrancesco Gonzaga; he accompanied this prince to Milan to witness the entry of Louis XII of France, and afterwards on an expedition to aid the French in their vain effort to hold the kingdom of Naples against the Aragonese. When Gonzaga abandoned the French cause (after being defeated by Ferdinand the Catholic's "Great Captain," Consalvo de Cordova, near the Garigliano in 1503), Castiglione obtained leave to go to Rome, and there met Duke Guidobaldo di Montefeltro, who had come to pay homage to the newly elected Pope Julius II. He entered the duke's service, and soon became one of the brightest ornaments of that brilliant company of statesmen, prelates, scholars, poets, wits and ladies, known as the Court of Urbino.

In 1504 he took part, under Duke Guidobaldo, in the papal siege of

Cesena against the Venetians. The next year he attended the duke on a diplomatic visit to Rome. In 1506 he was sent to the court of Henry VII of England to receive the insignia of the Order of the Garter on the duke's behalf. As appears from a letter to his mother, he returned to Urbino as early as 5 March 1507, notwithstanding his mention of himself in THE COURTIER as still absent in England at the date (8-11 March) of the dialogues he professes to report at second hand. In the same year he was sent on a mission to Louis XII at Milan.

On Guidobaldo's death in 1508, Castiglione continued in the service of the new duke, Francesco Maria della Rovere ("my lord Prefect" of THE COURTIER), who appointed him governor of Gubbio. In the following year he served in his master's campaign against the Venetians, and contracted a dangerous illness, during which he was tenderly nursed by the dowager duchess, Elisabetta Gonzaga. In 1511 he accompanied the duke to Rome on the occasion of the latter's trial for the murder of Cardinal Alidosi, and was active in Francesco Maria's successful defence. In 1513 the duke created him Count of Novillara and gave him an estate of that name, which however he soon lost through the Medici usurpation of the duchy, and never regained. At the death of Julius II, Castiglione was ambassador to the sacred college, and continued in that office during nearly the whole of Leo X's pontificate. His numerous letters show the variety and importance of the diplomatic business in which he was engaged.

Several plans for his marriage came to nothing, and on one occasion, when the lady's father hesitated, the suitor broke off negotiations, saying: "The wife that I am to take, be she who she may, I desire that she should be given to me with as good will as I take her withal,—yea, if she were the daughter of a king."

Pope Leo having in 1516 basely deprived Francesco Maria of the Duchy of Urbino, Castiglione accepted an invitation to Mantua and there married Ippolita, daughter of Count Guido Torello di Montechiarugolo and Francesca Bentivoglio, a daughter of the former ruler of Bologna. This union proved exceptionally happy and was blessed by three children: a son Camillo, a daughter Anna, and a second daughter Ippolita, whose birth cost the young mother her life in 1520. His son attained the age of eighty years, and is said to have been the true embodiment of the qualities described in THE COURTIER.

Castiglione resided alternately at Mantua and at Rome, where he served as Mantuan ambassador, and where his learning, wit, taste, gentle disposition and integrity earned for him an almost unique eminence at the papal court.

In 1524 he was sent by Pope Clement VII as ambassador to the Emperor Charles V (who was waging war against the French in Italy), but while his counsel and high qualities were appreciated, he was too honest a man to cope with the tortuous politics of the time, and proved unable to avert the capture and sack of Rome (1527) or the imprisonment of the pope. These catastrophes, together with a malicious and easily disproved charge of treason brought against him, preyed upon his health, and despite the many honours conferred upon him by Charles, he failed to rally, and finally died at Toledo, 7 February 1529, without again seeing his native land. His body was afterwards brought to Italy and buried in the church of the Madonna delle Grazie near Mantua, where his tomb was erected from designs by his young friend Giulio Romano.

Besides THE COURTIER, his writings comprise: *Tirsi*, an eclogue of fifty-five stanzas in *ottava rima*, written and recited at the Court of Urbino for the carnival of 1506; a prologue and epilogue for his friend Bibbiena's *Calandra;* a few Italian lyrics of moderate merit; and some better Latin elegies and epigrams; nearly all composed during his embassy at Rome. A large number of his letters also have been preserved.

His fine character is reflected in that of his Courtier, who (as Symonds says) "is, with one or two points of immaterial difference, a modern gentleman, such as all men of education at the present day would wish to be." It may perhaps aid the reader to realize the time in which the author lived, to recall that when Castiglione was born, printing had been practised in Italy for thirteen years, that the earliest Greek grammar had been printed two years, that America was discovered when he was a boy, that the Reformation began when he was in the prime of life, and that the Lutherans were first called Protestants in the year of his death.

The first (Aldine) edition of THE COURTIER was issued thirteen years after the death of *Teobaldo* Manucci, the illustrious founder of the press that continued to bear his name, and consisted of one thousand and thirty-one copies, of which thirty were on large paper and one on vellum. It is a small folio of one hundred and twenty-two leaves, the type-page measuring almost precisely nine and one-quarter inches by five and one-eighth inches. In its ordinary form the book can hardly be called rare, as in 1895 the present translator secured a good copy from Leipsic for forty-five francs.

The earliest Spanish translator, BOSCAN (born at Barcelona about 1493; died in France about 1542), was of gentle birth. Early becoming a soldier, he served with credit in Charles V's Italian campaigns, and thus acquired familiarity with the language and literature of Italy. He is said to have known Castiglione personally. Having been for some time tutor to the young prince who was later known as the Duke of Alva, he married and devoted the rest of his short life to letters. As a writer he is best known as the founder of the Italian poetical school in Spain. Ticknor says that Boscan's version of THE COURTIER hardly professes to be literal, but that perhaps nothing in Castilian prose of an earlier date is written in so classical and finished a style. It has been often reprinted (as recently as 1873), and was found useful by the present translator in doubtful passages.

The earliest French translator, COLIN (died 1547), was a native of Auxerre and enjoyed the favour of Francis I, whom he served as reader and almoner, and who bestowed upon him the abbotship of St. Ambrose at Tours, as well as other ecclesiastical offices. In his prosperity he showed much kindness to his less fortunate brother authors, but he was too free of speech to be permanently successful as a courtier, and lost his preferments. His translation of THE COURTIER, which some writers erroneously ascribe to Jean Chaperon, is little esteemed, was soon issued with corrections by another hand, and then followed by another French version. He translated also parts of Homer and Ovid, and composed original verse in Latin and French. For an account of Castiglione's influence upon French literature and of his many French imitators, consult Pietro Toldo's "Le Courtisan dans la littérature française et ses rapports avec l'œuvre du Castiglione" (Archiv für das Studium der Neueren Sprachen und Litteraturen, C. iv, pp. 75 and 313, and C. v, p. 60).

The earliest English translator, HOBY (born 1530; died 1566), was the son of William and Katherine (Forden) Hoby of Herefordshire. Having studied at Cambridge, he visited France, Italy and other foreign countries. In 1565-6 he was knighted by Queen Elizabeth and sent as ambassador to France, where he soon died, leaving several children and a widow. This lady was the third of Sir Anthony Cooke's five learned daughters, of whom the eldest married Sir William Cecil (afterwards Lord Burleigh), while the second became the mother of Francis Bacon, Lord Verulam. Interesting details of Hoby's life and of the manners of the time are given in his unpublished diary, preserved in the British Museum. His version of THE COURTIER was carefully made, and although rough to our ears and occasionally obscure, it became very popular and was several times republished. A beautiful reprint of the original edition has recently been issued (1900), in a scholarly introduction to which Professor Walter Raleigh traces the influence of the book upon Elizabethan writers. THE COURTIER, and especially Hoby's translation of it, are the subject of a very interesting study by Mary Augusta Scott, Ph.D., printed in the Publications of the Modern Language Association of America, vol.

xvi (1901), no. 4. In 1570 Roger Ascham wrote in his "Schoolmaster": "To join learning with comely exercises, Count Baldesar Castiglione in his book CORTEGIANO doth trimly teach: which book, advisedly read and diligently followed but one year at home in England, would do a young gentleman more good, I wis, than three years' travel abroad in Italy. And I marvel this book is not more read in the Court than it is, seeing it is so well translated into English by a worthy gentleman, Sir Thomas Hobbie, who was many ways well furnished with learning, and very expert in knowledge of divers tongues."

Of the first German translator, LORENZ KRATZER, little more is known than that he was an officer of customs at Burckhausen, in Bavaria, from 1565 to 1588, and that he speaks of having devoted to letters the ample leisure which his duties permitted. Although said to be meritorious, his work can hardly have gained wide currency, as both Noyse (whose German translation of THE COURTIER was published at Dilingen in 1593) and a third German translator (whose version was issued at Frankfort in 1684 under the initials "J. C. L. L. J.") seem to have regarded themselves each as the earliest in the field.

The first Latin translator, TURLER (born 1550; died 1602), was a *Doctor Juris,* and became burgomaster of his native town of Lössnitz, near Leipsic. Besides THE COURTIER, he translated several of Machiavelli's works into Latin.

# NOTES TO THE DEDICATORY LETTER

Note 1, page 1. Dom MIGUEL DE SILVA (born about 1480; died 1556), was the second son of Diogo da Silva and Maria de Ayala, Count and Countess of Portalegre, a province of central Portugal. Having studied at the universities of Paris, Siena and Bologna, he was soon called to the court of Emanuel of Portugal, held various ecclesiastical posts, and was made Bishop of Viseu in the Province of Beira. As ambassador to Popes Leo X, Adrian VI and Clement VII, he paid long visits to Rome, where his friendship with Castiglione probably began. During the twenty years that followed 1521 he served John III of Portugal as *Escribano de la Puridad*; then, having been made a cardinal by Paul III, he spent the remainder of his life in the papal service, died in Rome, and was buried in the church of Santa Maria in Trastevere. Eminent as a prelate and a diplomatist, he also enjoyed no small repute as an author and an elegant Latinist.

Note 2, page 1. GUIDOBALDO DI MONTEFELTRO, Duke of Urbino (born 1472; died 1508), was the only son of Duke Federico di Montefeltro and Battista Sforza, an accomplished niece of the first Sforza duke of Milan. Precocious as a child, he was elaborately yet judiciously educated, and much of the praise bestowed upon him in THE COURTIER is shown by contemporary evidence to have been just. On his father's death in 1482, both he and his State were confided to his cousin Ubaldini (see note 273), who seems to have been loyal to the trust, although next heir to the duchy. From records that have survived, Denistoun extracts some details of the young duke's court: "To all persons composing the ducal household, unexceptionable manners were indispensable. In those of higher rank there were further required competent talents and learning, a grave deportment, and fluency of speech. The servants must be of steady habits and respectable character; regular in all private transactions; of good address, modest and graceful; willing and neat handed in their service. There is likewise inculcated the most scrupulous personal cleanliness, especially of the hands, with particular injunctions as to frequent ablutions, and extraordinary precautions against the unpleasant effects of hot weather on their persons and clothing; in case of need, medical treatment is enjoined to correct the breath. Those who wore livery had two suits a year, generally of fustian, though to some silk doubtlets were given for summer use."

In 1489 Guidobaldo married Elisabetta Gonzaga, a sister of the

Marquess of Mantua. All hopes, however, of an heir were soon abandoned, apparently owing to the young duke's physical infirmities, which were increased by over-exercise and in time unfitted him for all active occupations. Nevertheless he was able to take part in the vain resistance to Charles VIII's invasion of Italy, and later in the expulsion of the French from the kingdom of Naples. While fighting in the service of Pope Alexander VI in 1497, he was taken prisoner and forced to pay a ransom of 30,000 ducats, a sum then equivalent to about twice that number of modern pounds sterling, and raised only at the sacrifice of his duchess's jewels. In 1501 he aided rather than opposed Louis XII's invasion of Naples.

In 1502 the pope's son Cesare Borgia treacherously seized the Duchy of Urbino. To spare his people bloodshed and ruin, Guidobaldo fled in disguise to his brother-in-law at Mantua, and after a vain appeal to Louis XII, found an honourable asylum at Venice. In the same year he regained his dominions for a short time, but was again forced to take flight. On the death of Alexander VI (August 1503), Cesare's power crumbled, Guidobaldo easily recovered his duchy, and his position was soon assured by the election of Julius II, who was not only his personal friend, but also the brother of his sister Giovanna's husband. In 1504 he formally adopted as his heir this sister's son, Francesco Maria della Rovere, and (as we have seen) took into his service the future author of THE COURTIER. His learning, amiability and munificence attracted choice spirits to his court, which came to be regarded as the first in Italy. Pope Julius was splendidly entertained there on his way both to and from his Bologna campaign, and the Courtier dialogues are represented as taking place immediately after his departure for Rome in March 1507.

Long an invalid, Guidobaldo became more and more a martyr to his gout, which was aggravated by a season of exceptional drought and cold and brought him final relief from suffering in April 1508. His fame rests, not upon his military and political achievements, but upon the beauty of his character, the variety of his intellectual accomplishments, the patience with which he endured reverses, illness and forced inaction, and upon the culture and refinement that characterized his court.

Note 3, page 1. FRANCESCO MARIA DELLA ROVERE, Duke of Urbino (born 1490; died 1538), was the son of Giovanni della Rovere and Duke Guidobaldo's sister Giovanna di Montefeltro. Giovanni was a nephew of Pope Sixtus IV (who had made him Prefect of Rome), and a younger brother of Cardinal Giuliano della Rovere, afterwards Pope Julius II.

On his father's death in 1501, Francesco was brought to the court of his uncle Guidobaldo, who secured for him a renewal of the Prefecture and superintended his education. In THE COURTIER he appears as "my lord

Prefect." During the Borgian usurpation of the duchy, he found refuge at the court of Louis XII; and soon ofter the fall of the Borgias and his uncle Julius II's accession, he was adopted as Guidobaldo's heir, while through the mediation of Castiglione a marriage was arranged for him with Eleanora, daughter to the Marquess of Mantua and niece to the Duchess of Urbino. He now resided chiefly with his uncle, acquainting himself with his future subjects and duties. Although he possessed many of the good qualities ascribed to him in THE COURTIER, his temper was ungovernable, and before reaching the age of eighteen he slew one of the members of the court, who was accused of seducing his sister.

Having become duke in 1508, he was married on Christmas Eve of that year. In the following spring he commanded the papal forces in the League of Cambray, and despite the obstacles put in his way by his colleague Cardinal Alidosi (see note 268), he soon reduced the Romagna towns, the recovery of which from Venice was Julius II's chief object in forming the league. In a later campaign against the French, Bologna was lost to the Church (1511) through the treachery of Alidosi, who craftily contrived to have the blame fall upon Francesco, and was murdered by the latter at Ravenna. After a long trial before six cardinals, in which ample proof of the dead man's treason was presented, and an eloquent appeal made by Beroaldo (see note 235),—the young duke was acquitted and restored to the pope's favour.

Although both Francesco and his predecessor had generously befriended the Medici during their exile from Florence (1494-1512), Leo X (Giovanni de' Medici) seized his duchy in 1516, to bestow it on a nephew, Lorenzo de' Medici. It is needless to speak here of Francesco's restoration in 1521, of his failure to relieve Pope Clement VII when Rome was sacked in 1527, or of his later life.

While small in person, Francesco was active and well formed. His manners were gentle and his character forgiving, in spite of his fiery temper. Strict in religious observances and an enemy to blasphemous language, he was also creditably intolerant of those outrages upon womanly honour with which war was then fraught. He was famous chiefly as a soldier, and by so competent a judge as the Emperor Charles V was regarded as master of the military science of his day.

Note 4, page 1. This disclaimer of careful authorship is not to be taken too literally. At least a draft of Books I-III seems to have been made at Urbino between April 1508 and May 1509, while Book IV was probably written at Rome in the earlier part of the interval between September 1513 and March 1516. Castiglione apparently continued to revise his work until

1518, when he sent his MS. to Bembo. See Silvestro Marcello's pamphlet, "La Cronologia del Cortegiano di Baldesar Castiglione." Pisa, 1895.

Note 5, page 1. As has been seen, Castiglione resided at the Spanish court from 1524 until his death in 1529.

Note 6, page 1. VITTORIA COLONNA (born 1490; died 1547), was the daughter of Fabrizio Colonna (grand-nephew of Pope Martin V) and Agnese di Montefeltro, a sister of Duke Guidobaldo. At the age of four she was betrothed to the Marquess of Pescara, whom she married in her nineteenth year at Ischia (the fief and residence of his family), and who afterwards became a famous soldier. During his long absences in the field, she consoled herself with books, and after his death in 1525, her widowhood was spent in retiremen* and finally in semi-monastic seclusion at Rome. The time spared from pious exercises she devoted to study, the composition of poetry, correspondence with illustrious men of letters, and the society of learned persons. Although she never became a convert to Protestantism, the liberality of some of her friends' belief exposed her to ecclesiastical censure in her old age. Her celebrated friendship with Michelangelo began when he was past sixty and she had nearly reached fifty years. They frequently exchanged verses, and he is said to have visited her on her death-bed. Her poems are chiefly sonnets to the memory of her husband or verses on sacred and moral subjects.

Note 7, page 1. The following passage is from a letter written by Castiglione to the Marchioness: "I am the more deeply obliged to your Ladyship, because the necessity you have put me under, of sending the book at once to the printer, relieves me from the trouble of adding many things that I had already prepared in my mind,—things (I need hardly say) of little import, like the rest of the book; so that your Ladyship has saved the reader from tedium, and the author from blame."

Despite the many decrees of popes, emperors and other potentates, literary piracy seems to have been quite as common in Castiglione's time as in ours. He was obviously none too prompt in his precautions, as an apparently unauthorized edition of THE COURTIER was issued at Florence by the heirs of Filippo di Giunta in the October following its first publication at Venice in April 1528.

Note 8, page 2. ALFONSO ARIOSTO (died 1526), was a cousin of the poet Ludovico. Little more seems to be known of him than that his father's name was Bonifazio, that he was a gentle cavalier and brave soldier in the service of the Este family and that he was a friend of Castiglione and of

////////////////////////////////////////////////////////////////

Bembo. His name appears at the head of each of the four dialogues composing THE COURTIER, and they purport to have been written at his suggestion. Señor A. M. Fabié, in his notes to the 1873 reprint of Boscan's translation, affirms that Alfonso Ariosto had nothing to do with the poet Ludovico, belonged to a noble Bolognese family, and enjoyed much favour at the court of Francis I of France.

Note 9, page 2. GIULIANO DE' MEDICI (born 1478; died 1516), was the third son of Lorenzo the Magnificent and Clarice Orsini. His education seems to have been for a time entrusted to the famous scholar-poet Poliziano (see note 105). During his family's exile from Florence (1494-1512), he resided much at the court of Urbino, where he was known as "the Magnifico Giuliano," and where one wing of the great palace was reserved to his use and is still called by his name. He became the father of a boy afterwards known as Cardinal Ippolito de' Medici,—the original of Titian's fine portrait in the Pitti Gallery. On the restoration of the Medici, Giuliano was placed at the head of affairs in his native city and succeeded in winning the good will of the Florentines, but his gentle disposition and love of ease thwarted other ambitious projects formed for his advancement by his brother Leo X, and he was too grateful to the dukes of Urbino for their hospitality to accept the pope's intended appropriation of their duchy for his benefit. In 1515 he married Filiberta of Savoy and was created Duke of Nemours by her nephew Francis I of France. In the same year he was appointed Captain General of the Church, but failing health prevented his actual service, and he soon died of fever at Florence, not without suspicion of poison at the hands of his nephew Lorenzo.

Several of his sonnets have survived, and are said to show no mean poetic faculty. Apart, however, from his appearance as an interlocutor in THE COURTIER and in Bembo's *Prose*, his memory is best preserved by Michelangelo's famous tomb at Florence.

Note 10, page 2. "MESSER BERNARDO" (DOVIZI), better known by the name of his birthplace BIBBIENA (born 1470; died 1520), was of humble parentage. His elder brother Pietro was secretary to Lorenzo de' Medici, and secured his admission to the Magnifico's household, where he shared the education of the young Giovanni and became a devoted friend of that future pope. Following the Medici into exile, he travelled about Europe with Giovanni and attended Giuliano to Urbino, where he received the warm welcome always accorded there to such as combined learning with courtly manners. By the Duke of Urbino he seems to have been so commended to the favour of Julius II, that he was able to aid Michelangelo in securing part payment for the Sistine Chapel frescoes, of which payment,

ๆๆๆๆๆๆๆๆๆๆๆๆๆๆๆๆๆๆๆๆๆๆๆๆๆๆๆๆๆๆๆๆๆๆๆๆๆๆๆๆๆๆๆๆๆๆๆๆ

however, he accepted five per cent. as a gift from the painter. At the death of Julius, he was secretary to his friend Cardinal Giovanni de' Medici, and in that capacity had access to the conclave, where his adroitness was largely helpful in effecting his patron's election as pope. Leo at once made him Cardinal of Santa Maria in Portico and loaded him with lucrative offices. During the Medicean usurpation of the Duchy of Urbino, he showed no gratitude for the kindness enjoyed by him at that court. He became very rich, and was a liberal patron of authors and artists. Raphael devised to him the house of the architect Bramante, which the painter had bought for a sum equivalent to about £6,000, and which was afterwards demolished in extending the piazza in front of St. Peter's.

Besides a large number of his letters, for the most part unpublished, we have his play, *Calandra*, founded upon the *Menœchmi* of Plautus and once esteemed as the earliest Italian prose comedy.

Although he was bald, and although his friend Raphael's portrait hardly justifies the epithet, he was known as the *"Bel Bernardo."* A contemporary MS. in the Vatican describes him as a "a facetious character, with no mean powers of ridicule, and much tact in promoting jocular conversation by his wit and well-timed jests. He was a great favourite with certain cardinals, whose chief pursuit was pleasure and the chase, for he thoroughly knew all their habits and fancies, and was even aware of whatever vicious propensities they had. He likewise possessed a singular pliancy for flattery, and for obsequiously accommodating himself to their whims, stooping patiently to be the butt of insulting and abusive jokes, and shrinking from nothing that could render him acceptable to them. He also had much readiness in council, and was perfectly able seasonably to qualify his wit with wisdom, or to dissemble with singular cunning." On the other hand, Bembo wrote of him to their friend Federico Fregoso: "The days seem years until I see him, and enjoy the pleasing society, the charming conversation, the wit, the jests, the features and the affection of that man."

It was to Bibbiena, a few weeks before his death in 1520, that Isabella d'Este, dowager Marchioness of Mantua (see note 397), entrusted the duty of breaking as gently as possible to Castiglione (then Mantuan ambassador at Rome) the news of the sudden death of the latter's young wife. "We told him the sad news," wrote Bibbiena, "as best we could, . . . none of us could keep back our tears, and we all wept together for some time."

Note 11, page 2. OTTAVIANO FREGOSO (died 1524), belonged to a noble Genoese family that had long distinguished itself in public service and had furnished several doges to the Republic. His parents were Agostino Fregoso and Gentile di Montefeltro, a half-sister of Duke Guidobaldo. Driven from Genoa as early as 1497, he entered his uncle's court at Urbino and rendered important military services, especially during the struggle with Cesare Borgia, in which he gallantly defended the fortress of San Leo (see note 275), and was rewarded with the lordship of Santa Agata in the Apennines. In 1506 he commanded the papal forces for the recovery of Bologna, and later in the League of Cambray against Venice. In 1513 he succeeded in putting an end to French domination in Genoa, was elected doge, and ruled so beneficently for two years that when Francis I regained the city, Fregoso was continued as governor. In 1522 Genoa was captured and sacked by Spanish and German troops, and Fregoso given over to the Marquess of Pescara, treated harshly (despite Castiglione's intercession on his behalf), and carried to Ischia, where he died.

Note 12, page 2. "MY LADY DUCHESS," ELISABETTA GONZAGA (born 1471; died 1526), was the second daughter of the Marquess Federico Gonzaga of Mantua and Margarita of Bavaria. She married Duke Guidobaldo in 1489. In 1502 she reluctantly attended the festivities for the marriage, at Ferrara, of Lucrezia Borgia to Alfonso d'Este, and some of her costumes are thus described by an eye-witness: On entering Ferrara, she rode a black mule caparisoned in black velvet embroidered with woven gold, and wore a mantle of black velvet strewn with triangles of beaten gold, a string of pearls about her neck, and a cap of gold; another day indoors she wore a mantle of brown velvet slashed, and caught up with chains of massive gold; another day a gown of black velvet striped with gold, with a jewelled necklace and diadem; and still another day, a black velvet robe embroidered with gold ciphers.

During the Borgian usurpation of their duchy in the same year, she shared her husband's exile at Venice, and on returning to Urbino earlier than Guidobaldo, she amused herself with a scenic representation of the chief events that had occurred during their absence. She cared for her husband tenderly in his illnesses, administered his government wisely when he was called away, and on his death acted as regent and guardian for his nephew and successor, with whom she maintained affectionate relations as long as she lived, and from appropriating whose dominions she strove to the utmost to dissuade Leo X.

Next to her husband's niece by marriage, Emilia Pia (see note 37), her closest friend seems to have been her brother's wife, the famous Isabella d'Este (see note 397), with whom she often travelled and continually corresponded by letter. Although still young and accounted beautiful at her husband's death, she remained faithful to his memory, and the years of her widowhood were cheered by the companionship of her niece, the young duchess Eleanora of Urbino (see note 432). If we may trust universal contemporary opinion of her virtues and beauty, the author of THE COURTIER

ィィィィィィィィィィィィィィィィィィィィィィィィィィィィィィィィィィィィィィィィィィィィィィィィィィィィ
flattered her as little as did the painter of her portrait in the Uffizi Gallery.

Note 13, page 3. Vittoria Colonna seems to have had this passage in mind when she wrote, 20 September 1524, to Castiglione in praise of his book: "It would not be fitting for me to tell you what I think of it, for the same reason which you say prevents you from speaking of the beauty of my lady Duchess."

Note 14, page 3. GIOVANNI BOCCACCIO (born 1313; died 1375), was the natural son of a Florentine tradesman and a Frenchwoman with whom his father had made acquaintance during a business residence at Paris. In early manhood he engaged in commerce at Naples, and had but little learning in his youth, although he studied law for a time. Erudition and authorship became the serious enthusiasm of his life, owing (it is said) to a chance visit to the supposed tomb of Virgil at Naples. In middle life he began the study of Greek at his friend Petrarch's suggestion; and although he never acquired more than what would now be deemed a superficial knowledge of that language, as a Hellenist he had no precursor in Italy. An ardent if somewhat unappreciative admirer of Dante (whose *Divina Commedia* he transcribed with his own hands), he was the first Italian author to write for the common people, instead of composing books suited only to the learned and patrician classes. His style was formed by tireless study of classic models, and became a standard for imitation by his successors.

Note 15, page 3. It is now known that the considerations that led Boccaccio to underrate his poems and tales, were ethical rather than literary.

Note 16, page 5. THEOPHRASTUS (born 374; died 287 B.C.) was a native of Lesbos, but resided at Athens. The chief disciple and successor of Aristotle, he wrote also upon a great variety of subjects other than philosophy. His best known work, the "Characters," is a collection of sprightly sketches of human types. La Bruyère's famous book of the same name was originally a mere translation from Theophrastus. The incident mentioned in the text is thus described in Cicero's *Brutus:* "When he asked a certain old woman for how much she would sell something, and she answered him and added, 'Stranger, it can't be had for less,'—he was vexed at being taken for a stranger although he had grown old at Athens and spoke to perfection."

Note 17, page 5. I. e., pages 39-54.

Note 18, page 6. The reference here is to Plato's "Republic," Xenophon's *Cyropœdia*, and Cicero's *De Oratore*.

Note 19, page 6. In the letter quoted in note 13, Vittoria Colonna wrote: "I do not marvel at your portraying a perfect courtier well, for by merely holding a mirror before you and considering your inward and outward parts, you could describe him as you have; but our greatest difficulty being to know ourselves, I say that it was more difficult for you to portray yourself than another man."

Note 20, page 6. More than 140 editions of THE COURTIER have been published. Most of these are mentioned in the list printed before the Index of this volume. A few of the editions there set down differ from one another only in title-page; a few others, perhaps, exist only in some bibliographer's erroneous mention. Deductions to be made for such reasons, however, are probably offset by other editions that the present translator has failed to bring to light.

In the bibliographical notes appended by the brothers Volpi to their (1733) edition, THE COURTIER is said to have been translated into Flemish; while in his preface to the Sonzogno (1890) edition, Corio speaks of the introduction of the book into Japan in the 17th century, and also of a Russian translation by Archiuzow.

# NOTES TO THE FIRST BOOK OF THE COURTIER

Note 21, page 7. "Courtiership" is a sadly awkward rendering of the Italian *cortegiania*, which implies not only courtesy and courtliness, but all the many other qualities and accomplishments essential to the perfect Courtier or (what in Castiglione's time was the same) the perfect Gentleman.

Note 22, page 8. The extreme dimensions of the Duchy of Urbino were 64 miles from east to west, and 60 miles from north to south. Its population did not much exceed 150,000.

Note 23, page 8. The first of the four dialogues is represented as having been held on the evening of the day after the close of a certain visit paid by Pope Julius II to Urbino on his return from a successful campaign against Bologna. This visit is known to have lasted from 3 March to 7 March 1507. Castiglione returned from England as early as 5 March, on which date he wrote to his mother from Urbino: "We have had his Holiness here for two days." It seems probable that this fictitious prolongation of his absence in England was simply a graceful excuse for not himself appearing in the dialogues.

Note 24, page 9. There were a fief and Count of Montefeltro as early as 1154, and his son was made Count of Urbino in 1216, from which time their male descendants ruled over a gradually increased territory until 1508, when the duchy passed to the female line. The name Montefeltro is said to have originated in that of a temple to Jupiter Feretrius, which in Roman times occupied the summit of the crag afterwards known as San Leo, in the Duchy of Urbino.

Note 25, page 9. Such a rule as that of the usurping Cesare Borgia (1502-3) can hardly have been welcome to a population accustomed to the mild sway of the Montefeltro family.

Note 26, page 9. "DUKE FEDERICO" DI MONTEFELTRO (born 1422; died 1482), was a natural son of Count Guidantonio di Montefeltro, as appears from the act of legitimation issued by Pope Martin V

*ィィィィィィィィィィィィィィィィィィィィィィィィィィィィィィィィィィィィィィィィィィィィィィィィィィィィィィィ*

and also from his father's testament, by virtue whereof (as well as by the choice of the people) he succeeded his half-brother Count Oddantonio in 1444. In his boyhood he resided fifteen months as a hostage at Venice. Later he studied the theory and practice of war at the Mantuan court, and was trained in the humanities by the famous Vittorino da Feltre. In 1437 he married Gentile Brancaleone, who died childless in 1457. Nearly the whole of his life was spent in military service, as paid ally, now of one prince, now of another. In this capacity he became not only the most noted commander of his time, but always displayed perfect and exceptional fidelity to the causes that he undertook. In 1450 he lost an eye and suffered a fracture of the nose in a tournament; contemporary portraits represent his features in profile. In 1454 he began the construction of the great palace at Urbino. In 1460, at the suggestion of Francesco Sforza (whom he had aided to become Duke of Milan), he married the latter's accomplished niece Battista Sforza, who bore him seven daughters and one son, Guidobaldo. In 1474 he was made Duke of Urbino and appointed Captain General of the Church by Pope Sixtus IV, and was unanimously elected a Knight of the Garter. He died of fever contracted during military operations in the malarial country near Ferrara. The vast sums spent by him on public buildings, art objects and books, and upon the maintenance of his splendid household, were not extorted from his subjects, but were received from foreign states in return for war service. Thus at the close of his life he drew a yearly stipend equivalent to about £330,000.

It is not easy to draw a picture of his character that shall seem unflattered. Vespasiano, who by years of labour collected his famous library for him, says that his "establishment was conducted with the regularity of a religious fraternity, rather than like a military household. Gambling and profanity were unknown, and singular decorum of language was observed, whilst many noble youths, sent there to learn good manners and military discipline, were reared under the most exemplary tuition. He regarded his subjects as his children, and was at all times accessible to hear them personally state their petitions, being careful to give answers without unnecessary delay. He walked freely about the streets, entering their shops and workrooms, and enquiring into their circumstances with paternal interest. . . . In summer he was in the saddle at dawn, and rode three or four miles into the country with half-a-dozen of his court . . . reaching home again when others were just up. After mass, he went into an open garden and gave audience to all comers until breakfast-time. When at table, he listened to the Latin historians, chiefly Livy, except in Lent, when some religious book was read, anyone being free to enter the hall and speak with him then. His fare was plain and substantial, denying ʒʒʒʒʒʒʒʒʒʒʒʒʒʒʒʒʒʒʒʒʒʒʒʒʒʒʒʒʒʒʒʒʒʒʒʒʒʒʒʒʒʒʒʒʒʒʒʒʒʒʒʒʒ

himself sweet dishes and wine, except drinks of pomegranates, cherries, apples, or other fruits. After dinner and supper, an able judge of appeal stated in Latin the causes brought before him, on which the duke gave judgment in that language; . . . When his mid-day meal was finished, if no one appeared to ask audience, he retired to his closet and transacted private business, or listened to reading until evening approached, when he generally walked out, giving patient ear to all who accosted him in the streets. He then occasionally visited . . . a meadow belonging to the Franciscans, where thirty or forty of the youths brought up in his court stripped their doublets, and played at throwing the bar, or at wrestling, or ball. This was a fine sight, which the duke much enjoyed, encouraging the lads, and listening freely to all until supper-time. When that and the audiences were over, he repaired to a private apartment with his principal courtiers, whom, after some familiar talk, he would dismiss to bed, taxing them with their sluggish indulgence of a morning."

Note 27, page 9. In a Greek epigram written in a book borrowed from Duke Guidobaldo, Poliziano (see note 105) praises the lender as the worthy son of a father who never suffered defeat, ἀνικήτοιο πατρὸς γονόν. History shows that this phrase was a rhetorical exaggeration, but it became almost proverbial.

Note 28, page 9. Although long since despoiled of its treasures, the palace is still one of the architectural monuments of Italy. Many writers have described its magnificence,—some of the fullest accounts being those by Bernardino Baldi (1553-1617); Fr. Arnold (*Der Herzogliche Palast von Urbino*; Leipsic: 1857); J. A. Symonds ("Italian Byways;" London: 1883; pp. 129-155); Charles Blanc (*Histoire de la Renaissance Artistique en Italie*; Paris: 1894; ii, 87-90); and Egidio Calzini (*Urbino e i Suoi Monumenti*; Florence: 1899; pp. 9-46). Baldi's description will be found reprinted as an appendix to Rigutini's (1889 and 1892) editions of THE COURTIER.

For more than fourteen years Duke Federico employed from thirty to forty copyists in transcribing Greek and Latin MSS. Not only the classics, but ecclesiastical and mediæval authors, as well as the Italian poets and humanists were represented in his library, which contained 792 MSS. Ultimately the collection was sent to Rome, where it forms part of the Vatican Library.

Note 29, page 9. Born in 1422, Duke Federico was in fact sixty years old when he died.

⅄⅄⅄⅄⅄⅄⅄⅄⅄⅄⅄⅄⅄⅄⅄⅄⅄⅄⅄⅄⅄⅄⅄⅄⅄⅄⅄⅄⅄⅄⅄⅄⅄⅄⅄⅄⅄⅄⅄⅄⅄⅄⅄⅄⅄⅄⅄⅄⅄⅄⅄⅄⅄⅄⅄⅄⅄

Note 30, page 9. In his Latin epistle to Henry VII of England, Castiglione says that Duke Guidobaldo began to be afflicted with gout at the age of twenty-one years.

Note 31, page 10. ALFONSO II of Naples (born 1448; died 1495), was the eldest son of Ferdinand I and Isabelle de Clermont. As Duke of Calabria, commanding the papal forces, he defeated the Florentine league in 1479, and in 1481 drove the Turks out of southern Italy. On his father's death in 1494, he succeeded to the crown of Naples; but having rendered himself obnoxious to his subjects, he abdicated in favour of his son Ferdinand just before the arrival of Charles VIII of France, and took refuge in a Sicilian convent, where he soon died, tortured by remorse for the hideous cruelties that he had perpetrated. His wife was Ippolita Maria, daughter of the first Sforza duke of Milan; while his daughter Isabella's marriage to Giangaleazzo Sforza, the rightful duke, and the usurpation of the latter's uncle Ludovico "il Moro" (see note 302), became the immediate cause of the first French invasion of Italy by Charles VIII.

Note 32, page 10. FERDINAND II of Naples (born 1469; died childless 1496) made a gallant but vain stand against the French, and retired to Ischia with his youthful wife-aunt Joanna. When Charles VIII evacuated Naples after a stay of only fifty days, Ferdinand was soon able, with the help of his cousin Ferdinand the Catholic's famous general Consalvo de Cordova, to regain his dominions, but died a few weeks later. He seems to have had no lack of courage; by his mere presence he once overawed a mob at Naples, and he was beloved by the nation in spite of the odious tyranny of his father and grandfather.

Note 33, page 10. Pope ALEXANDER VI (born 1431; died 1503), was Roderigo, the son of Giuffredo (or Alfonso) Lenzuoli and Juana (or Isabella) Borgia, a sister of Pope Calixtus III, by whom the youth was adopted and whose surname he assumed. He was elected pope in 1492 through bribery, and while striving to increase the temporal power of the Church, directed his chief efforts towards the establishment of a great hereditary dominion for his family. Of his five children, two (Cesare and Lucrezia) played important parts in his plan. In 1495 he joined the league which forced Charles VIII to retire from Italy, although it had been partly at his instigation that the French invaded the peninsula. In 1498 Savonarola was burned at Florence by his orders. In 1501 he instituted the ecclesiastical censorship of books. He is believed to have died from accidentally taking a poison designed by him for a rich cardinal whose possessions he wished to seize. His private life was disgraced by orgies, of which the details are unfit for repetition. His contemporary Machiavelli says: "His entire occupation, his only thought, was deception, and he always found victims. Never was there a man with more effrontery in assertion, more ready to add oaths to his promises, or to break them." While Sismondi terms him "the most odious, the most publicly scandalous, and the most wicked of all the miscreants who ever misused sacred authority to outrage and degrade mankind."

Note 34, page 10. Pope JULIUS II (born 1443; died 1513), was Giuliano, the second son of Raffaele della Rovere (only brother of Pope Sixtus IV) and Teodora Menerola. Made a cardinal soon after his uncle's election, he was loaded with sees and offices, including the legateship of Picene and Avignon, which latter occasioned his prolonged absence from Italy and afforded him an escape from the wiles of his inveterate enemy Alexander VI. The outrages with which Alexander sought to punish his sturdy opposition to the scandals of the Borgian court, aroused in him a fierceness of spirit that was alien to the seeming mildness of his early character and became the bane of his own pontificate. His younger brother Giovanni married a sister of Duke Guidobaldo, a union that cemented the friendship between the two families and furnished the Duchy of Urbino an heir in the person of Francesco Maria della Rovere. When Julius engaged Michelangelo to design his tomb, the old basilica of St. Peter's was found too small to contain it, whereupon the pontiff is said to have decreed that a new church be built to receive it, and blessed the laying of the first stone shortly before setting out on his campaign against Bologna in 1506. In 1508 he formed the League of Cambray for the recovery of certain papal fiefs appropriated by Venice at the time of Cesare Borgia's downfall, and in 1511 the so-called Holy League for the expulsion of the French from Italy. Italian unity was the unavowed but real goal at which his policy aimed.

Although a munificent patron of art and letters, Julius was frugal and severe,—a man of action rather than a scholar or theologian. In giving Michelangelo directions for the huge bronze statue at Bologna, he said: "Put a sword in my hand; of letters I know nothing." Another of his reported sayings is: "If we are not ourselves pious, why should we prevent others from being so?"

Note 35, page 10. Although unexpressed in the original, the word 'learned' seems necessary to complete the obvious meaning of the passage.

From his tutor Odasio of Padua, we learn that in his boyhood Guidobaldo was even for the time exceptionally fond of study. He could repeat whole treatises by heart ten years after reading them, and never forgot what he resolved to retain. Besides his classical attainments, he appreciated the Italian poets, and showed peculiar aptitude for philosophy and history.

Note 36, page 10. The Italian *piacevolezza* conveys somewhat the same suggestion of humour which the word 'pleasantness' carried with it to the English of Elizabeth's time, and which still survives in our 'pleasantry.'

Note 37, page 11. EMILIA PIA (died 1528), was the youngest daughter of Marco Pio, one of the lords of Carpi. Her brother Giberto married a natural daughter of Cardinal Ippolito d'Este (see note 64), while her cousin Alberto Pio (1475-1530) was the pupil and became the patron and financial supporter of the scholar-printer Aldus Manutius. In 1487 she was married very young to the studious Count Antonio di Montefeltro (a natural half-brother of Duke Guidobaldo), who left her a widow in 1500. She resided at Urbino and became the trusted and inseparable companion of the Duchess Elisabetta, whom she accompanied on journeys and in exile, ever faithful in misfortune and sorrow. In the duchess's testament she was named as legatee and executrix. She seems to have died without the sacraments of the Church, while discussing passages of the newly published COURTIER with Count Ludovico Canossa. The part taken by her in these dialogues evinces the charm of her winning manners as well as her possession of a variety of knowledge and graceful accomplishment rare even in that age of womanly genius. Always ready to lead or second the learned and sportive pastimes by which the court circle of Urbino gave zest to their intercourse and polish to their wit, she was of infinite service to the duchess, whose own acquirements were of a less brilliant kind.

Note 38, page 11. It may be doubted whether the duchess's influence always availed to secure what we should now regard as decorous behaviour at her court, and in an earlier draft of THE COURTIER Castiglione allowed himself a freedom, not to say licence, of expression singularly in contrast with the general tone of the version published.

Note 39, page 12. The duchess and her husband were expelled from their dominions by Cesare Borgia in 1502, and again in 1516 she was compelled to leave Urbino for a longer time, when Leo X seized the duchy for his nephew Lorenzo de' Medici. Her conduct on these occasions showed rare fortitude and dignity.

Note 40, page 12. These devices, so much in vogue during the 16th century in Italy, were the "inventions" which Giovio (a contemporary writer upon the subject) says "the great lords and noble cavaliers of our time like to wear on their armour, caparisons and banners, to signify a part of their generous thoughts." They consisted of a figure or picture, and a motto nearly always in Latin. The fashion is said to have been copied from the French at the time of the invasions of Charles VIII and Louis XII.

Note 41, page 12. FEDERICO FREGOSO (born 1480; died 1541), was a younger brother of Ottaviano (see note 11), and was educated for holy orders under the direction of his uncle Duke Guidobaldo, at whose court he also perfected himself in worldly accomplishments. In 1507 Julius II made him Archbishop of Salerno, in the kingdom of Naples, but, owing to his supposed French sympathies, he was not allowed to enjoy this benefice, and the next year was put in charge of the bishopric of Gubbio. In the same year he was sent by Julius with the latter's physician to attend Duke Guidobaldo's death-bed, but arrived too late. During the nine years that followed his brother's election as Doge of Genoa (1513), he by turns commanded the army of the Republic, led her fleet against the Barbary pirates (whom he routed in their own harbours), and represented her at the papal court. During the Spanish siege of Genoa in 1522, he escaped to France, was warmly received by Francis I, and made Abbot of St. Bénigne at Dijon, where he devoted himself to theological study. In 1528 he returned to Italy and was appointed to the see of Gubbio. His piety and zeal for the welfare of his flock won for him the title of "father to the poor and refuge of the distressed." In 1539 he was made a cardinal, and two years later died at Gubbio, being succeeded in that see by his friend Bembo. After his death, a discourse of his on prayer happening to be reprinted together with a work by Luther, he was for a time erroneously supposed to have been heretical. He was a profound student of Hebrew, and an appreciative collector of Provençal poetry. His own writings are chiefly doctrinal, and his reputation rests rather upon his friends' praise of his wit, gentleness, personal accomplishments and learning, than upon the present value of his extant works.

Note 42, page 12. PIETRO BEMBO (born at Venice 1470; died at Rome 1547), was the son of a noble Venetian, Bernardo Bembo (a man of much cultivation, who paid for the restoration of Dante's tomb at Ravenna), and Elena Marcella. Having received his early education at Florence, where his father was Venetian ambassador, he studied Greek at Messina under Lascaris (a native of Hellas, whose grammar of that tongue was the first Greek book ever printed, 1476), and philosophy at Padua and Ferrara, where his father was Venetian envoy and introduced him to the Este court. Here he became acquainted with Lucrezia Borgia, who had recently wedded Duke Ercole's son Alfonso, and to whom he dedicated his dialogues on love, *Gli Asolani*. By some writers indeed he is said to have been her lover, but the report is hardly confirmed by the character of the letters exchanged between the two, 1503-1516. Having been entertained at Urbino in 1505, he spent the larger part of the next six years at that court, where he profited by the fine library, delighted in many congenial spirits, and became the close friend of Giuliano de' Medici, who took him to Rome in 1512 and recommended him to the future pope, Leo X. On attaining the tiara, Leo at once appointed him and his friend Sadoleto (see note 242) papal secretaries, an office for which his learning and courtly accomplishments well fitted him. His laxity of morals and his paganism were no disqualification in the eyes of the pope, whom he served also in several diplomatic missions, and from whom he received benefices and pensions sufficient to enrich him for life. In 1518 his friend Castiglione sent him the MS. of THE COURTIER, requesting him to "take the trouble . . . to read it either wholly or in part," and to give his opinion of it. Ten years later, when the book was printed, it was Bembo to whom the proofs were sent for correction, the author being absent in Spain. Even before the death of Leo X in 1521, Bembo had entered upon a life of literary retirement at Padua, where his library and art collection, as well as the learned society that he drew about him, rendered his house famous. Nor was it less esteemed by reason of the presence, at its head, of an avowed mistress (Morosina), who bore him several children. After her death, he devoted himself to theology, entered holy orders, reluctantly accepted a cardinal's hat in 1539, and in 1541 succeeded his friend Fregoso in the bishopric of Gubbio, to which was added that of Bergamo. His death was occasioned by a fall from his horse, and he was buried at Rome in the Minerva church, between his patrons Leo X and Clement VII. His works are noteworthy less for their substance than for the refining influence exerted by their form. He is said to have subjected all his writings to sixteen (some say forty) separate revisions, and a legend survives to the effect that he advised a young cleric (Sadoleto) to avoid reading the Epistles of St. Paul, lest they might mar the youth's style. His numerous private and official letters have preserved many valuable facts and furnish interesting illustration of contemporary manners and character. Humboldt praises him as the first Italian author to write attractive descriptions of natural scenery, and cites especially his dialogue on Mt. Ætna.

Note 43, page 12. CESARE GONZAGA (born about 1475; died 1512), was a native of Mantua, being descended from a younger branch of the ruling family of that city, and a cousin of Castiglione, with whom he maintained a close friendship. His father's name was Giampietro, and he had a brother Luigi. Having received a courtly and martial education at Milan, and after spending some time with his relatives at Mantua, he entered the service of Duke Guidobaldo of Urbino. In 1504 he shared Castiglione's lodgings after their return from a campaign against Cesare Borgia's strongholds in Romagna, and in the carnival of 1506 they together recited Castiglione's eclogue *Tirsi*, in the authorship of which he is by some credited with a part. A graceful canzonet, preserved in Atanagi's *Rime Scelte*, attests his skill in versification. On Guidobaldo's death in 1508, the two friends remained in the service of the new duke, Francesco Maria. In 1511 Cesare fought bravely against the French at Mirandola, and the next year took part in the reduction of Bologna, where he soon died of an acute fever. Little more is known of him, beyond the fact that he was a knight of St. John of Jerusalem, that Leo X sent him on a mission to Charles V of Spain, and that he was among the many friends of the famous Isabella d'Este (see note 397).

Note 44, page 12. Count LUDOVICO DA CANOSSA (born 1476; died 1532), belonged to a noble Veronese family (still honourably extant), and was a close friend of Castiglione and a cousin of the latter's mother. His boyhood was passed at Mantua, and his happiest years at Urbino, where he was received in 1496. In the pontificate of Julius II he went to Rome, and was made Bishop of Tricario, in southern Italy, 1511. Under Leo X he was entrusted with several embassies, one of which (1514) was to England to reconcile Henry VIII with Louis XII, and another (1515) was to the new French king, Francis I, at whose court he continued to reside, and through whose influence he was made Bishop of Bayeux in 1516. In 1526 and 1527 he served as French ambassador to Venice. His ability and zeal as a diplomatist are shown not only by the importance of the posts that he held, but by his numerous letters that have been preserved. At the time of his friend Bibbiena's death in 1520, Canossa remarked that it was a fixed belief among the French that every man of rank who died in Italy was poisoned.

Note 45, page 12. GASPAR PALLAVICINO (born 1486; died 1511), was a descendant of the marquesses of Cortemaggiore, near Piacenza. He appears in THE COURTIER as the youthful woman-hater of the company, and was a friend of Castiglione and Bembo. For an interesting dis-

↑↑↑↑↑↑↑↑↑↑↑↑↑↑↑↑↑↑↑↑↑↑↑↑↑↑↑↑↑↑↑↑↑↑↑↑↑↑↑↑↑↑↑↑↑↑↑↑↑↑↑↑↑↑↑↑↑

cussion of his rôle in the dialogues, see Miss Scott's paper, cited before (page 312).

Note 46, page 12. LUDOVICO PIO belonged to the famous family of the lords of Carpi (a few miles north of Modena), and was a brave captain in the service of the Aragonese princes, of Duke Ludovico Sforza of Milan, and of Pope Julius II. His father Leonello and more celebrated uncle Alberto had been pupils of Aldus, and were second cousins of Emilia Pia. His wife was the beautiful Graziosa Maggi of Milan, who is immortalized in the paintings of Francia and the writings of Bembo.

Note 47, page 12. SIGISMONDO MORELLO DA ORTONA is presented in THE COURTIER as the only elderly member of the company, and the object of many youthful jests. He is known to have taken part in the ceremony of the formal adoption of Francesco Maria della Rovere as heir to the duchy in 1504, is referred to in Castiglione's *Tirsi*, and seems to have been something of a musician.

Note 48, page 12. Of ROBERTO DA BARI little more is known than that his surname was MASSIMO, and that he was taken ill in the campaign of 1510 against the Venetians and retired to Mantua. Thither Castiglione sent a letter to his mother, warmly recommending Roberto to her hospitality, and saying that he loved the man like a brother.

Note 49, page 12. BERNARDO ACCOLTI (born about 1465; died 1535), was generally known as the UNICO ARETINO, from the name of his birthplace (Arezzo) and in compliment to his 'unique' faculty for extemporising verse. His father Benedetto was a jurist, and the author of a dull Latin history of the First Crusade, from which Tasso is believed to have drawn material for the *Gerusalemme Liberata*. His poetical celebrity commended him to the court of Urbino, where (as at Rome and in other places) he was in the habit of reciting his verses to vast audiences of rich and poor alike. When an exhibition by him was announced, guards had to be set to restrain the crowds that rushed to secure places, the shops were closed, and the streets emptied. His life was a kind of lucrative poetic vagabondage: thus we find him flourishing, caressed and applauded, at the courts of Urbino, Mantua, Naples, and especially at that of Leo X, who bestowed many offices upon him, of which, however, his wealth (acquired by his recitations) rendered him independent, enabling him to indulge in a life of literary ease. His elder brother Pietro became a cardinal, bought Raphael's house, and is said to have had a hand in drafting the papal bull against Luther in 1520. He was an early patron of his notorious fellow-townsman Pietro Aretino. Such of his verse as has survived is so bald and stilted as to excite no little wonderment at the esteem which he enjoyed among his contemporaries. In THE COURTIER he poses as the sentimental and afflicted lover, the "slayer" of duchesses and other noble ladies, who (according to his own account) kept flocking in his train, but who more probably were often making sport of him.

Note 50, page 12. GIANCRISTOFORO ROMANO (born about 1465; died 1512), was the son of Isaia di Pippo of Pisa and the pupil of Paolo Romano. Perhaps best known as a sculptor, he possessed skill also as a goldsmith, medallist, architect and crystal carver, cultivated music and wrote verse. During the last years of the Sforza power at Milan, he accompanied the duke's wife, Beatrice d'Este, from place to place, and is now identified as the author of her portrait bust in the Louvre. He executed also at least two portrait medals of her sister Isabella d'Este, acted as adviser and agent of the Gonzagas in the purchase of art objects, worked at Venice, Cremona, Rome and Naples, and is known to have been at Urbino about the time of the Courtier dialogues. In a long letter written by him to Bembo in 1510, he describes the court of Urbino as "a true temple of chastity, decorum and pudicity." In 1512 he was directing architect at Loreto (see note 311), where he died in May, bequeathing his collection of medals and antiques to a hospital, for the purpose of having three masses said weekly for the repose of his soul.

Note 51, page 12. Of PIETRO MONTE little more is known than that he was a master of military exercises at the Urbino court, and perhaps a captain in the duke's army. He may have been identical with one Pietro dal Monte, who is mentioned as a soldier in the pay of Venice (1509), and described as "blind in one eye, but of great valour, gentle speech, and not unlearned in letters," and as "commanding 1500 infantry, and a man of great experience not only in war but in affairs of the world."

Note 52, page 12. ANTONIO MARIA TERPANDRO, one of the most jovial and welcome visitors at Urbino, is said by Dennistoun to have been a musical ornament of the court. He enjoyed the heartiest friendship of Bembo and Bibbiena.

Note 53, page 12. NICCOLÒ FRISIO or FRIGIO is mentioned in a letter by Bembo as a German, but seems more probably to have been an Italian. Dennistoun speaks of him as a musician. In a letter from Castiglione to his mother (1506), the writer warmly commends to her "one messer Niccolò Frisio, who I hear is there [i.e., in Mantua], and I earnestly hope that you will treat him kindly, for I am under the greatest obligation to him with respect to my Roman illness. . . . I am sure he loves me well." In another letter by a friend of Bembo, Frisio is described (1509) as an Italian long resident in courts, sure of heart, gentle, a good linguist, faithful to his employers, and as having been used by Julius II in negotiating the League of Cambray against Venice. He had relations also with the marchioness Isabella of Mantua (see note 397), whom he aided in the collection of antiquities. Growing weary of worldly life, he became a monk in 1510, and retired to the Certosa of Naples.

Note 54, page 12. According to Cian, *omini piacevoli* (rendered 'agreeable men') here means 'buffoons.'

Note 55, page 13. This passage establishes the date of the first dialogue as 8 March 1507.

Note 56, page 13. My lady Emilia contends that she has already told her choice of a game, in proposing that the rest of the company should tell theirs.

Note 57, page 14. COSTANZA FREGOSA was a sister of the two Fregoso brothers already mentioned, and a faithful companion of the Duchess of Urbino. She married Count Marcantonio Landi of Piacenza, and bore him two worthy children, Agostino and Caterina, to the former of whom Bembo stood sponsor and became a kind of second father. Three letters by the lady have been preserved.

Note 58, page 15. Belief in the efficacy of music as a cure for the bite of the tarantula still survives in Andalusia, Sardinia and parts of southern Italy. In a note on the tarantella dance, Goethe wrote: "It has been remarked that in the case of mental ailments, and of a tarantula bite, which is probably cured by perspiration, the movements of this dance have a very salutary effect on the softer sex." "Travels in Italy" (Ed. Bohn, 1883), page 564.

Note 59, page 15. The *moresca* (mime or morris-dance) seems to have been a kind of ballet or story in dance, often very intricate and fanciful. At the courts of this period, it was generally introduced as an interlude between the acts of a comedy. In a letter quoted by Dennistoun ("Memoirs of the Dukes of Urbino," ii, 141), Castiglione describes a *moresca* on the story of Jason, which was thus performed at the first presentation of Bibbiena's *Calandra* before the court of Urbino, 6 February 1513

Note 60, page 15. FRA MARIANO FETTI (born 1460; died 1531), was a native of Florence, and beginning life as a barber to Lorenzo de' Medici, always remained faithful to that family. At Rome, during the pontificate of Julius II, he won the reputation and enjoyed the privileges of "the prince of jesters," and became even more famous under Leo X, upon whom as a child he had bestowed affectionate care, and who as pope did not forget his kindness. Thus in 1514 he was made *Frate piombatore*, or affixer of lead seals to papal bulls, in which office he followed the architect Bramante, was succeeded by the painter Sebastiano Luciani (better known as "del Piombo"), and admitted earning yearly what would now be the equivalent of about £1600, by turning lead into gold. While it remains uncertain whether he was more buffoon or friar, he had a great love for artists, and even composed verse. He seems to have continued in the enjoyment of fame and favour during the reign of the second Medicean pope, Clement VII.

Note 61, page 16. FRA SERAFINO was probably a Mantuan, and had a brother Sebastiano. He lived long at the Gonzaga court, where he was employed in organizing festivals, and at Urbino, where the few of his letters that have survived show him in familiar relations with other interlocutors in THE COURTIER. While at Rome in 1507, with the suite of the Duchess of Urbino, he was seriously wounded in the head by an unknown assailant, probably in return for some lampoon or scandal of his against the papal court.

Note 62, page 17. This letter S was evidently one of the golden ciphers that ladies of the period were fond of wearing on a circlet about their heads. In her portrait the duchess is represented as wearing a narrow band, from which the image of a scorpion hangs upon her forehead. The S may have been used on this occasion as the initial letter of the word scorpion, and seems in any case to have been an instance of the 'devices' mentioned in note 40.

A sonnet, purporting to be the work of the Unico Aretino, was inserted in the edition of THE COURTIER published by Rovillio at Lyons in 1562 and in several later editions, as being the sonnet here mentioned. In its place, however, Cian prints another sonnet, preserved in the Marciana Library at Venice and possessing higher claims to authenticity. Some idea of the baldness of both may be gained from the following crude but tolerably literal translation of the second sonnet:

Consent, O Sea of beauty and virtue,
That I, thy slave, may of great doubt be freed,
Whether the S thou wearest on thy candid brow
Signifies my Suffering or my Salvation,
   Whether it means Succour or Servitude,
Suspicion or Security, Secret or Silliness,
Whether 'Spectation or Shriek, whether Safe or Sepultured!
Whether my bonds be Strait or Severed:
   For much I fear lest it give Sign
Of Stateliness, Sighing, Severity,
Scorn, Slash, Sweat, Stress and Spite.
   But if for naked truth a place there be,
This S shows with no little art
A Sun single in beauty and in cruelty.

Note 63, page 18. The pains of love were a frequent theme with Bembo, and are elaborately set forth in his *Gli Asolani*. Quite untranslatable into English, his play upon the words *amore* (love) and *amaro* (bitter) is at least as old as Plautus's *Trinummus*.

Note 64, page 22. IPPOLITO D'ESTE (born 1479; died 1520), was the third son of Duke Ercole I of Ferrara (see note 203) and Eleanora of Aragon (see note 399). At the instance of his maternal aunt Beatrice's husband, King Matthias Corvinus of Hungary (see note 395), he was given the rich archbishopric of Strigonio, to which was attached the primacy of that country, and made the journey thither as a mere boy. In 1493 Alexander VI made him a cardinal. Soon after the death of his sister Beatrice, her husband Duke Ludovico Sforza of Milan gave him the vacant archbishopric of that city, and the same year (1497) he exchanged the Hungarian primacy, with its burdensome requirement of foreign residence, for the bishopric of Agria in Crete. In 1502 he was made Archbishop of Capua in the kingdom of Naples, but bestowed the revenues of the see upon his widowed and impoverished aunt, the ex-Queen of Hungary, and a little later was made Bishop of Ferrara,—all before reaching the age of twenty-four years. He was also Bishop of Modena and Abbot of Pomposa. During his brother's reign at Ferrara, the young cardinal took an active part in public affairs, several times governing in the duke's absence, and showing brilliant capacities for military command. After the accession of Leo X, he resided chiefly at Rome, where he was always a conspicuous figure and carefully guarded his brother's interests. He was a friend and protector of Leonardo da Vinci, and maintained Ariosto in his service from 1503 to 1517. A prelate only in name, regarding his many ecclesiastical offices merely as a source of wealth, he united the faults and vices to the grace and culture of his time.

Note 65, page 26. BERTO was probably one of the many buffoons about the papal court in the time of Julius II and Leo X. He is again mentioned in the text (page 126) for his powers of mimicry, etc.

Note 66, page 26. This "brave lady" is by some identified as the famous Caterina Sforza, a natural daughter of Duke Galeazzo Maria Sforza of Milan, who by the last of her three husbands became the mother of the even more famous *condottiere* Giovanni de' Medici delle Bande Nere. She was born in 1462, and died in 1509 after a life of singular vicissitudes. For an extraordinary story of her courage, see Dennistoun's "Memoirs of the Dukes of Urbino," i, 292.

The "one whom I will not name at present" is supposed to have been a certain brave soldier of fortune, Gaspar Sanseverino, who is often mentioned as "Captain Fracassa," and was a brother of the Galeazzo Sanseverino who appears a little later in THE COURTIER (see page 34 and note 72).

Note 67, page 27. The philosopher in question has been variously identified as Democritus and Empedocles.

Note 68, page 29. In Charles V's romantic plan for deciding by single combat his rivalry with Francis I, Castiglione was selected as his second, but declined to violate diplomatic proprieties by accepting the offer,—being at the time papal envoy at Charles's court.

Note 69, page 30. Strictly speaking, the joust was a single contest between man and man, while the tourney was a sham battle between two squadrons. Stick-throwing seems to have been an equestrian game introduced by the Moors into Spain, and by the Spaniards into Italy. In the carnival of 1519 it was played by two companies in the Piazza of St. Peter's before Leo X.

Note 70, page 31. Vaulting on horses seems to have included some of the feats of agility with which modern circus riders have familiarized us.

Note 71, page 33. "Finds grace," i.e. favour: literally "is grateful" (*grato*) in the sense of acceptable or pleasing. Compare the familiar phrase *persona grata*.

Note 72, page 34. GALEAZZO SANSEVERINO was one of the twelve stalwart sons of Roberto Sanseverino, a brave *condottiere* who aided to place Ludovico Sforza in power at Milan, rebelled against that prince, and was slain while fighting for the Venetians in 1486. Galeazzo entered the service of Ludovico, whose favour had been attracted by his personal charm, literary accomplishments and rare skill in knightly exercises. When he married his patron's natural daughter Bianca, in 1489, Leonardo da Vinci arranged the jousts held in honour of the wedding. Thenceforth he adopted the names Visconti and Sforza, and was treated as a member of the ducal family. In 1496, at the head of the Milanese forces, he besieged the Duke of Orleans (afterwards Louis XII) at Novara, but in 1500 he was captured by the French, and after the final downfall of Ludovico (to whom he seems to have remained creditably loyal) he entered the service of Louis XII, who made him Grand Equerry in 1506. The duties of his office included the superintendence of all the royal stables and of an academy for the martial education of young men of noble family. For a further account of his interesting life, and especially of his friendship with Isabella d'Este, see Mrs. Henry Ady's recent volume, "Beatrice d'Este, Duchess of Milan."

Note 73, page 35. The word *sprezzatura* (rendered "nonchalance") could hardly have been new to Castiglione's contemporaries, at least in its primary meaning of disprizement or contempt. He may, however, have been among the first to use it (as here and elsewhere in THE COURTIER) in its modified sense of unconcern or nonchalance. Compare Herrick's 'wild civility' in "Art above Nature" and "Delight in Disorder."

Note 74, page 36. Naturally Venice could hardly be a place well suited for horsemanship; its citizens' awkward riding was a favourite subject of ridicule in the 16th century.

Note 75, page 37. The incident is supposed to have occurred on the occasion of a visit paid by Apelles to Rhodes not long after the death (323 B.C.) of Alexander the Great, whom he had accompanied into Asia Minor. Apelles was eager to meet Protogenes, and on landing in Rhodes went at once to the painter's house. Protogenes was absent, but a large panel stood ready for painting. Apelles took a pencil and drew an exceedingly fine coloured line, by which Protogenes on his return immediately recognized who his visitor had been, and in turn drew a finer line of another colour upon or within the first line. When Apelles saw this line, he added a third line still further subdividing the one drawn by Protogenes. Later the panel was carried to Rome, where it long excited wondering admiration in the Palace of the Cæsars, with which it was finally destroyed by fire. Apelles was the first to stimulate appreciation of the merits of Protogenes by buying several of the latter's works at enormous prices: he maintained however that he excelled Protogenes in knowing when to cease elaborating his paintings.

Note 76, page 37. The play upon words here is untranslatable into English. The Italian *tavola* stands equally well for a dining-table and for the tablet or panel upon which pictures were painted.

Note 77, page 39. 'As those who speak [are present] before those who speak' is a literal translation of the accepted reading of this passage. It is perhaps worth noting, however, that the earliest translator (Boscan) ventures to deviate from the letter of the Italian text for the sake of rendering what surely must have been the author's meaning: *como los que hablan á aquellos con quien hablan,* i.e. "as those who speak [are present] before those *with whom* they speak."

Note 78, page 41. Although the dialect of Bergamo was (and still is) ridiculed as rude and harsh, it possessed a copious popular literature.

Note 79, page 41. FRANCESCO PETRARCA or PETRARCH (born 1304; died 1374), belonged to a family that was banished from Florence at the same time with Dante, whom he remembered seeing in his childhood. He was the first Italian of his time to appreciate the value of public libraries, to collect coins and inscriptions as sources of accurate historical information, and to urge the preservation of ancient monuments. Had he never written a line of verse, he would still be venerated as the apostle of scholarship, as the chief originator of humanistic impulses based upon what Symonds describes as "a new and vital perception of the dignity of man considered as a rational being apart from theological determinations, and . . . the further perception that classic literature alone displayed human nature in the plenitude of intellectual and moral freedom."

Note 80, page 41. In an age when grammatical and rhetorical treatises, in the modern sense of the word, hardly existed, it was natural that the study of classic models should take the form of imitation.

Note 81, page 42. It will be remembered that Giuliano de' Medici was a native Tuscan.

Note 82, page 43. This Tuscan triumvirate was called "the three Florentine crowns:" Dante, Petrarch and Boccaccio.

ァァァァァァァァァァァァァァァァァァァァァァァァァァァァァァァァァァァァァァァァァァァァァァ

Note 83, page 44. Evander was a mythical son of Hermes, supposed to have founded a colony on the Tiber before the Trojan War. Turnus was a legendary king of an Italian tribe, who was slain by Æneas.

Note 84, page 43. The Salian priests were attached to the worship of Mars Gradivus. On the occasion of their annual festival, they went in procession through Rome, carrying the sacred shields of which they were custodians and which they beat in accompaniment to dance and song. The words of their chaunts are said to have become unintelligible even to themselves, and appear to have set forth a kind of theogony in praise of all the celestial deities (excepting Venus), and especially of one Mamurius Veturius, who is by some regarded as identical with Mars.

Note 85, page 43. Marcus Antonius (143-87 B.C.) and Licinius Crassus (140-91 B.C.), the two most famous orators of early Rome, were regarded by Cicero as having been the first to rival their Greek precedessors. Quintus Hortensius Hortalus (114-50 B.C.), the great advocate of the aristocratic party at Rome, yielded the palm of oratory only to Cicero (106-43 B.C.). Marcus Porcius Cato (234-149 B.C.), a Roman soldier, author and reforming statesman, sought to restore the ancient purity and simplicity of the earlier republic. Quintus Ennius (239-169 B.C.), a Roman epic poet and annalist, imparted to the language and literature of his nation much of the impulse that affected their growth for centuries. Virgil was born 70 B.C., and died 19 B.C.

Note 86, page 44. Horace was born 65 B.C., and died 8 B.C. Plautus died 184 B.C.

Note 87, page 44. Sergius Sulpicius Galba was Roman Consul 144 B.C.; Cicero praised his oratory, but found it more old-fashioned than that of Lælius (*flor*. 200 B.C.) and Scipio Africanus the Younger (died 129 B.C.).

Note 88, page 46. In his *Prose*, Bembo says that courtly Italian, especially during the pontificate of the Spaniard, Alexander VI (1492-1503), was full of Spanish expressions,—an assertion amply confirmed by contemporary letters, which are rich also in Gallicisms.

Note 89, page 46. The Spanish *primor* has failed to win Italian citizenship. *Aventurare* has become naturalized in Italy; as also have

↑↑↑↑↑↑↑↑↑↑↑↑↑↑↑↑↑↑↑↑↑↑↑↑↑↑↑↑↑↑↑↑↑↑↑↑↑↑↑↑↑↑↑↑↑↑↑↑↑↑↑↑↑↑↑↑↑↑↑↑↑↑↑↑

*acertare* (in the sense, however, of to assure, to make certain, to verify), *ripassare* (to repass, to repeat, to rebutt), *rimproccio* or *rimprovero,* and *attilato* or *attillato,* which is recognizable in the Spanish *atildado. Creato* (Spanish *criado*) is now replaced by *creatura* in the sense mentioned in the text; in Sicily *creato* is used to mean servant.

Note 90, page 46. The reference here is of course to the Attic, Doric, Ionic and Æolic dialects.

Note 91, page 47. TITUS LIVIUS was born at Padua 59 B.C., and died there 17 A.D. Of the one hundred and forty-two books of his History (which covered the period from the founding of Rome in 750 B.C. down to 9 B.C., and upon which he spent forty years of his life), only thirty-five have survived, together with an anonymous summary of the whole.

Note 92, page 47. Of the four forms here condemned by Castiglione as corrupt, three (*Campidoglio, Girolamo,* and *padrone*) have become firmly established in Italian. *Campidoglio* had been used by Petrarch (*Trionfo d'Amore,* i, 14),—an "old" but certainly not an "ignorant" Tuscan.

Note 93, page 48. Oscan was a pre-Roman language spoken by the Opici, an Italian tribe inhabiting the Campanian coast. Much of the mist that shrouded it for centuries has now been dispelled by the epigraphists. Both Dante and Petrarch were great lovers of Provençal, with which in Castiglione's time his friend Federico Fregoso was familiar.

Note 94, page 49. BIDON was a native of Asti, and one of the most famous choristers in the service of Leo X.

Note 95, page 50. MARCHETTO CARA, a native of Verona, entered the service of the Gonzagas in 1495 and lived nearly thirty years at Mantua, where he was made a citizen by the Marquess Federico. He frequented also the court of Urbino, and is known to have been sent by the Marchioness Isabella to relieve the tedium of her friend and sister-in-law the Duchess Elisabetta's exile at Venice in 1503. In his time he was among the most prolific and successful composers of profane music, especially of ballads and madrigals, and a number of his popular pieces have been preserved.

Note 96, page 50. LEONARDO DA VINCI (born 1452; died 1519), was the natural son of a notary, Pietro Antonio, of the village of Vinci, situated about fourteen miles east of Florence. He studied some three

years with Donatello's pupil Verocchio at Florence. Meeting small pe-
cuniary success there, he removed to Milan about 1483 and entered the
service of Duke Ludovico Sforza, who is said to have paid him the equivalent of £4000 a year while painting the "Last Supper," and for whom
he completed in 1493 the model of a colossal equestrian statue of Duke
Francesco Sforza, never executed in permanent form. He was employed
by Cesare Borgia as military engineer, and in that capacity visited Urbino
in July 1502. His famous portrait known as the "Mona Lisa" or "La
Gioconda," upon which he worked at times for four years, was finished
about 1504 and afterwards sold by him to Francis I. In 1507, he had
been appointed painter to Louis XII, but did not visit France until 1516.
On the election of Leo X in 1513, he journeyed to Rome in the company and service of Giuliano de' Medici, who paid him a monthly stipend
of £66. Although he was received with favour by the new pope and
lodged in the Vatican, his stay in Rome was artistically unprolific, his
interest at the time being chiefly confined to chemistry and physics, and
nature attracting him more than antiquities, of which he spoke as "this
old rubbish" (queste anticaglie). Three years before his death he was
visited at Amboise in France by Cardinal Ludovico of Aragon, who is
mentioned later in THE COURTIER (p. 157), and whose secretary left
an interesting account of an interview with him, describing the painter
as then disabled by paralysis of the hand.

Note 97, page 50. ANDREA MANTEGNA (born 1431; died 1506),
was a native of Vicenza and probably of humble origin. When a mere
child he became the pupil and adopted son of the noted painter and instructor, Francesco Squarcione of Padua, and was soon enrolled in the
painters' guild of that city. In 1449 he began painting for the d'Este at
Ferrara, and between 1453 and 1459 he married Niccolosa, a daughter
of Squarcione's rival Giacopo Bellini, and sister of the more famous
brothers Gentile and Giovanni Bellini. He painted also at Verona, and
about 1460 entered the service of the Gonzagas at Mantua, where the
remainder of his life was chiefly spent, although he worked for Pope
Innocent VIII at Rome about the year 1488, before which date he was
knighted by the Marquess of Mantua. By one writer he is affirmed to
have cast the fine bust which ornaments his tomb at Mantua, and which
is said once to have had diamond eyes. He is known to have understood
bronze casting, and besides the brush and the engraver's burin, he handled
modelling tools, while a sonnet of his has been preserved. Although praised
by Vasari as kindly and in every way estimable, he is shown by contemporary letters to have been rather irritable and litigious in private life.
Albert Dürer tells us that one of the keenest disappointments of his life

was occasioned by the great painter's death before he was able to make an intended journey to Mantua for the purpose of visiting Mantegna.

Note 98, page 50. RAFFAELLO SANTI or SANZI,—euphonized by Bembo as SANZIO,—(born 1483; died 1520), was a native of Urbino and the son of Giovanni Santi and Magia Ciarla. The father was himself a painter of no mean skill, and wrote a quaint rhymed chronicle of the Duchy of Urbino, which is preserved in the Vatican and contains much interesting information. Having lost both parents when he had reached the age of eleven years, and probably having first studied at Urbino under Timoteo della Vite, Raphael was sent by a maternal uncle to the studio of Perugino at Perugia. The rest of his short life was an unbroken course of happy labour and brilliant success. In 1499 he seems to have been at Urbino for the purpose of arranging for the welfare of a sister, and again in 1504, when, after executing several works (including, it is believed, portraits of the duke and duchess) for the ducal family, he went to Florence with a letter of commendation from Guidobaldo's sister. From 1504 to 1508 he resided chiefly at Florence, although he again visited Urbino twice, just before and probably soon after the date of the Courtier dialogues. His friendship with so many members of the Urbino court (Giuliano de' Medici, Bibbiena, Bembo, Canossa, and Castiglione), and even his acquaintance with Julius II, probably began during these later visits to his native city. In 1508 he was called to Rome by Julius, and resided there until his death. On succeeding Bramante as architect of St. Peter's in 1514, he wrote to Castiglione: "Sir Count: I have made drawings in several manners according to your suggestion, and if everyone does not flatter me, I am satisfying everyone; but I do not satisfy my own judgment, because I dread not satisfying yours. I am sending them to you. Pray choose any of them, if you deem any worthy. Our Lord [i.e. Leo X] in honouring me has put a great burden on my shoulders,—that is, the charge of the fabric of St. Peter's. I hope, however, not to fall under it; and the more so, because the model I have made for it pleases his Holiness and is praised by many choice spirits; but in thought I soar still higher. I fain would renew the beautiful forms of ancient buildings, but know not whether my flight will be that of Icarus. Vitruvius affords me much light on the subject, but less than I need. As to Galatea, I should hold myself a great master if she possessed half the fine things you write me; but in your words I recognize the love you bear me: and I tell you that to paint one beautiful woman, I should need to see several beautiful women and to have you with me to choose the best. But as there is dearth of good judgments and of beautiful women, I am using a certain idea that has occurred to my mind. Whether this has any artistic ⅎ ⅎ ⅎ ⅎ ⅎ ⅎ ⅎ ⅎ ⅎ ⅎ ⅎ ⅎ ⅎ ⅎ ⅎ ⅎ ⅎ ⅎ ⅎ ⅎ ⅎ ⅎ ⅎ ⅎ ⅎ ⅎ ⅎ ⅎ ⅎ ⅎ ⅎ ⅎ ⅎ ⅎ ⅎ ⅎ ⅎ ⅎ ⅎ ⅎ ⅎ ⅎ ⅎ ⅎ ⅎ ⅎ ⅎ ⅎ ⅎ ⅎ ⅎ

excellence in it, I know not,—but I am striving for it. Command me."
Passavant affirms that the 'drawings' mentioned at the beginning of this
letter were designs for a medal that Castiglione meant to wear. Raphael
is said to have painted two portraits of Castiglione, one of which (1516)
is in the Louvre and appears as the frontispiece to this volume. His
epitaph was written by Bembo, while Castiglione composed a Latin elegy
in his honour.

Note 99, page 50. MICHELANGELO BUONARROTI (born 1475; died
1564), was a native of Caprese, a village about forty-seven miles south-
east of Florence, and the son of Ludovico Buonarroti Simoni and Francesca, daughter of Neri del Sera. His first schoolmaster seems to have
come from Urbino. Apprenticed at the age of thirteen to Ghirlandajo,
he soon came under the protection of Lorenzo de' Medici. In 1496 he
removed to Rome, and remained there five years. From 1501 to 1504 he
was working upon the great statue of David at Florence, and prepared
his cartoon for a vast fresco on the Battle of Cascina, which, although
never executed, was often copied, and is said to have exerted a greater
influence on the art of the Renaissance than any other single work. In
1505 he was called to Rome to design a colossal mausoleum for Julius II.
The anxieties and disappointments connected with this project became
the continual tragedy of his long life. "Every day," he wrote, "I am
stoned as if I had crucified Christ. My youth has been lost, bound hand
and foot to this tomb." The matter was finally ended by the placing of
his statue of Moses in the church of San Pietro in Vincoli at Rome.
In the spring of 1506 he was present at the unearthing of the Laocoön,
and at the date of the Courtier dialogues he was engaged in casting a
great bronze statue of Julius II at Bologna. Duke Guidobaldo's collection
at Urbino seems to have included a Cupid made by Buonarroti in imitation of the antique, originally owned by Cesare Borgia, regained by him
when he captured Urbino in 1502, and soon presented by him to Guidobaldo's sister-in-law, the Marchioness Isabella d'Este of Mantua. The
famous tomb statue of Giuliano de' Medici at Florence is hardly to be
regarded as a portrait, and was of course executed long after the period
of THE COURTIER. In 1519 the Marquess of Mantua wrote to Castiglione, who was his ambassador at Rome, regarding a monument to his
father that he hoped to have the master design. In 1523 Castiglione
brought to Mantua a sketch made by Buonarroti for a villa which the
marquess intended to build at Marmirolo.

Note 100, page 50. GIORGIO BARBARELLI, known as GIORGIONE
or "Big George" (born about 1478; died 1510), was a native of Castel-

franco, a town about forty miles north-west of Venice, and was reputed to be a natural son of one Giacopo Barbarelli, a Venetian, and a peasant girl. Lack of data renders a consecutive account of his life and work impossible. He was brought up in Venice, and bred as a painter in the school of the Bellini. Vasari says that he played upon the lute and sang well, and was of a gentle disposition. Although he seems to have been exceptionally independent of great people, he enjoyed the especial favour of the Marchioness Isabella d'Este of Mantua. In a letter written from Venice in the year before that of the Courtier dialogues, Albert Dürer declared Giorgione to be the greatest painter in the city, which could then boast of the Bellini, Palma Vecchio, Carpaccio and Titian. One of the most acute of recent critics, Mr. Bernhard Berenson, ascribes to him only seventeen existing pictures, of which the best known is the *Fête Champêtre* in the Louvre, while the only one whose authenticity is entirely free from doubt is the "Madonna and Saints" in the Duomo at Castelfranco. The Urbino collection comprised two portraits by Giorgione, one of which is supposed to have represented Duke Guidobaldo, but unfortunately is lost.

Note 101, page 50. Isocrates (born 436; died 338 B.C.), an Athenian orator, was a pupil of Socrates, and became the instructor of many famous orators. His diction was of the purest Attic, and his writings were highly prized by the Alexandrian grammarians. The first printed edition of his works (1493) was edited by Castiglione's Greek master, Chalcondylas. Lysias, (died about 380 B.C.), an Athenian orator, abandoned the stilted monotony of the older speakers, and employed the simple language of every-day life, but with purity and grace. Æschines, (born 389; died 314 B.C.), was the rival and finally unsuccessful antagonist of Demosthenes.

Note 102, page 50. Caius Papirius Carbo (Consul in 120 B.C.), was an adherent of the Gracchi, but became a renegade and finally committed suicide. He was generally suspected of murdering Scipio Africanus the Younger. While abominating the man's character, Cicero praises his oratory. Caius Lælius Sapiens was Consul in 140 B.C. His friendship with Scipio is commemorated in Cicero's *De Amicitia*. While he was in his own time regarded as the model orator, later grammarians resorted to his works for archaisms. Scipio Africanus the Younger, (died 129 B.C.), captured Carthage in the Third Punic War, and was leader of the aristocratic party at Rome against the popular reforms of the Gracchi. His works, of which only a few fragments survive, are praised by Cicero and were long held in esteem. Galba, see note 87. Publius Sulpicius Rufus, (born 124; died 88 B.C.), was a tribune of the plebs.

*✷✷✷✷✷✷✷✷✷✷✷✷✷✷✷✷✷✷✷✷✷✷✷✷✷✷✷✷✷✷✷✷✷✷✷✷✷✷✷✷✷✷✷✷✷✷✷✷✷*

Cicero says: "Of all the orators I ever heard, Sulpicius was the most dignified, and, so to speak, the most tragic." CAIUS AURELIUS COTTA, (Consul 75 B.C.), is characterized by Cicero, who had argued a cause against him, as a most acute and subtle orator, but his style seems to have been dry and unimpassioned. CAIUS SEMPRONIUS GRACCHUS, (died 121 B.C.), a son of the famous Cornelia, and brother-in-law of Scipio Africanus the Younger, is noted chiefly for his vain struggle in behalf of popular rights. Only fragments of his oratory have survived. MARCUS ANTONIUS and CRASSUS, see note 85.

Note 103, page 50. "In a certain place," i.e. De Oratore, II, xxiii, 97.

Note 104, page 50. The Italian *virtù* has here its Latin meaning of natural vigour. See also note 330.

Note 105, page 51. ANGELO POLIZIANO (born 1454; died 1494), was a native of Montepulciano (about twenty-seven miles south-east of Siena), of which his name is a Latinized form. To English students he is better known as POLITIAN, and as the author of the oft-cited line, "Tempora mutantur, nos et mutamur in illis." His father Benedetto Ambrogini died poor, leaving a widow and five young children almost destitute. At the age of ten, Angelo studied at Florence, and composed Latin poems and Greek epigrams while yet a boy. At thirteen, he published Latin epistles; at sixteen, he began his Latin translation of the Iliad; at seventeen, he distributed Greek poems among the learned men of Florence; and at eighteen, he edited Catullus. He was received into Lorenzo de' Medici's household, and before he was thirty years old, he was professor of Latin and Greek at the University of Florence and was entrusted with the care of Lorenzo's children. His pupils included the chief students of Europe. A born poet, entitled to the middle place of honour between Petrarch and Ariosto, he was the first Italian to combine perfect mastery of Latin and a correct sense of Greek with genius for his own native literature. Towards the close of his life, he entered holy orders and became a canon of the Cathedral at Florence. He was ill formed, and had squinting eyes and an enormous nose. His morals were lax. He was succeeded by Bembo as dictator of Italian letters.

Note 106, page 51. LORENZO DE' MEDICI (born 1448; died 1492), was the grandson of Cosimo, *Pater Patriæ*, and father of Giuliano of THE COURTIER. On the death of his father Pietro in 1469, he succeeded jointly with his brother Giuliano to the family wealth and political

ヿヿヿヿヿヿヿヿヿヿヿヿヿヿヿヿヿヿヿヿヿヿヿヿヿヿヿヿヿヿヿヿヿヿヿヿヿヿヿヿヿヿヿヿヿヿヿ

predominance. Giuliano's assassination in the Pazzi conspiracy of 1478 (which Poliziano witnessed and narrated in Latin) left Lorenzo sole ruler, but like his predecessors, he governed the republic without any title, by free use of money and great adroitness in securing the elevation of his adherents to the chief offices of state. He was a man of marvellous range of mental power,—an epitome of Renaissance versatility. Never relaxing his hold on public affairs, among philosophers he passed for a sage; among men of letters, for an original and graceful poet; among scholars, for a Hellenist sensitive to every nicety of Attic idiom; among artists, for a connoisseur of consummate taste; among libertines, for a merry and untiring roysterer; among the pious, for an accomplished theologian. "He was no less famous for his jokes and repartees than for his pithy apothegms and maxims, as good a judge of cattle as of statues, as much at home in the bosom of his family as in the riot of an orgy, as ready to discourse on Plato as to plan a campaign or to plot the death of a dangerous citizen." (Symonds.)

Note 107, page 51. FRANCESCO CATTANI DA DIACCETO (born 1466; died 1522), was a native of Florence, studied at Pisa, and returning to his native city became intimate with Ficino, of whose philosophy he may be said to have been the heir. For many years he lectured at Florence with such success that the Venetians tried to entice him to the University of Padua, in vain. A partisan of the Medici, he enjoyed the favour of Leo X and of Cardinal Giulio, afterwards Clement VII. All his works (written in Latin) are of a philosophical character. His style is said to be sprightly and correct, and despite the ridicule then cast upon the vulgar tongue, he himself translated several of his books into Italian, notably the *Tre Libri d'Amore*, with which Castiglione shows familiarity in the Fourth Book of THE COURTIER.

Note 108, page 52. CAIUS SILIUS ITALICUS (died 100 A.D.), was Consul under Nero and a follower of Cicero in the art of oratory. After a prosperous public career, he retired to a life of literary ease. His most important work was a long epic poem on the Second Punic War, and soon sank into oblivion. CORNELIUS TACITUS, (died probably after 117 A.D.), was Consul and orator as well as historian.

Note 109, page 53. MARCUS TERENTIUS VARRO (born 116; died about 27 B.C.), was somewhat older than Cæsar, Cicero and Sallust, but outlived them all. He was regarded as the most learned of the Romans, and was made director of the public library by Cæsar, although he had been a partisan of Pompey. Of his seventy-four works, which embraced

ノノノノノノノノノノノノノノノノノノノノノノノノノノノノノノノノノノノノノノノノノノノノノノノノノノ

nearly all branches of knowledge, only two survive. They were much esteemed by the Christian Fathers.

Note 110, page 55. CATULLUS was born about 87 B.C. His 39th ode begins: "Because Egnatius has white teeth, he smiles wherever he goes" (*Egnatius, quod candidos habet dentes, renidet usque quaque*). Later in the same ode, he says: "Nothing is more pointless than a pointless laugh" (*Nam risu inepto res ineptior nulla est*).

Note 111, page 56. MONSEIGNEUR D'ANGOULEME, afterwards FRANCIS I (born 1494; died 1547), was the son of Count Charles d'Angoulême and Louise of Savoy. His governor, Sieur de Boisy, strove to inspire him with a taste for arms and a love of letters and art, and it was from romances of chivalry that he derived much of his education and many of his ideas of government. He succeeded his cousin Louis XII in January 1515, and one of the earliest functions at his court was the marriage of his aunt Filiberta of Savoy to Giuliano de' Medici, who is here represented by Castiglione (with what truth remains uncertain) as having visited the French court shortly before the date of the Courtier dialogues. Writing in 1515, the Venetian ambassador describes the young king as being really handsome (the evidence of our nearly contemporaneous medal illustration to the contrary), courageous, an excellent musician, and very learned for one of his age and rank. Under his rule, relations between France and Italy became closer and more active, and there began to penetrate beyond the Alps that Italian influence which he later greatly increased by marrying his son to Giuliano de' Medici's great-niece Caterina. His education had included a study of Italian literature and customs, and besides Federico Fregoso and Ludovico da Canossa he received and honoured many other illustrious Italians, among whom were Leonardo da Vinci and Benvenuto Cellini. He caused search to be made in Italy for rare MSS. and had them copied for his library. His reign, although clouded by defeats and humiliations, began a true literary and artistic Renaissance in France.

Note 112, page 56. The reference here is to the famous Sorbonne (founded by Robert Sorbon in 1253) towards which Francis was for religious reasons hostile during the early years of his reign, and to which he raised up a rival by founding the Collège de France in 1530.

Note 113, page 57. LUCIUS LICINIUS LUCULLUS, a Roman general and Consul (74 B.C.), noted chiefly for his wealth, luxury, and patronage of art and letters. LUCIUS CORNELIUS SULLA, a Roman general,

Consul (88 B.C.) and dictator, was the first Roman to lead an army against the city, and the first to publish lists of his enemies, proscribing them and offering a reward for their death. CNEIUS POMPEIUS, or POMPEY, (born 106; died 48 B.C.), a member of the Triumvirate with Cæsar and Crassus, and the finally unsuccessful champion of the conservative party against the power of Cæsar. MARCUS JUNIUS BRUTUS, (born 85; died 42 B.C.), a statesman and scholar, who adhered to Pompey, joined Cassius in the assassination of Cæsar, and was finally defeated by Mark Antony. HANNIBAL, (born 247 B.C.), the famous Carthaginian general who conquered Spain, crossed the Alps, overran Italy, was defeated by Scipio the Elder, became chief magistrate of Carthage, and committed suicide in exile about 183 B.C.

Note 114, page 58. In the last chapter of his "Prince," Machiavelli (who was Castiglione's contemporary) says: "Although military excellence seems to be extinct in Italy, this arises from the fact that the old methods were not good and there has been no one who knew how to devise new ones. We have great excellence in the members, if only it were not lacking in the heads. In duels and engagements between small numbers, see how superior the Italians are in strength, in dexterity, in resource. But when it comes to armies, they make no showing; and it all proceeds from the weakness of the heads. Whence it arises that in so much time, in so many battles fought in the last twenty years, when an army has been purely Italian, it has always succeeded ill." Compare this opinion with Montaigne's remark (*Essais*, II, c. 24) that the officers of Charles VIII ascribed their easy Italian conquests to the fact that "the princes and nobility of Italy took more pleasure in becoming ingenious and learned than in becoming vigorous and warlike."

Note 115, page 58. In 1524 Castiglione wrote to his mother at Mantua regarding the education of his son, who had just begun to study the Greek alphabet, as follows: "As to Camillo's learning Greek, I have had a letter also from Michael, who says so many things that he seems to me a flatterer. It is enough that the boy shows good capacity and inclination, and good pronunciation. As for Latin, I should be glad to have him attend more to Greek at present, for those who know are of opinion that one ought to begin with Greek; because Latin is natural to us, and we almost acquire it even though we spend little labour upon it; but Greek is not so."

Note 116, page 58. The reader will hardly need to be reminded that the habit of versification was very prevalent in all ranks of Italian society in Castiglione's day. Varchi (1502-1565) informs us that the vernacular was generally despised in the Florence of that time, and adds: "And I remember, when I was a lad, that the first and most important command which fathers usually gave to their children, and masters to their pupils, was that they must on no account whatever read anything in the vulgar tongue."

Note 117, page 58. In the *Vita Nuova* (c. 25), Dante says: "And the first who began to speak like a native poet was moved thereto because he would have his words understood of woman."

Note 118, page 59. ARISTIPPUS (*flor*. 400 B.C.), was a Greek philosopher, whose school took its name from his birthplace, Cyrene in Africa. He was for some time a follower of Socrates, and afterwards lived at the court of Dionysius, tyrant of Syracuse. Diogenes Laertius relates that when Aristippus was asked what was the greatest thing he had gained from philosophy, he replied: "The power to meet all men with confidence."

Note 119, page 59. Among Plutarch's works is a tract entitled "How to Tell Friend from Flatterer." In 1532 Erasmus published a Latin version of it dedicated to Henry VIII of England.

Note 120, page 60. The first quatrain of a well-known sonnet by Petrarch:

> *Giunto Alessandro alla famosa tomba*
> *Del fero Achille, sospirando disse:*
> *O fortunato, che sì chiara tromba*
> *Trovasti, e chi di te sì alto scrisse!*

of which Mr. John Jay Chapman has kindly furnished the following translation:

> When Alexander reached the sacred mound
> Where dread Achilles sleeps, "O child of Fame,"
> He sighed. "Thy deeds are happy that they found
> Old Homer's tongue to clarion thy name."

In his oration *Pro Archia*, Cicero describes Alexander as exclaiming: "O fortunate youth, who found Homer as herald of thy valour!" (*O fortunate, inquit, adulescens qui tuæ virtutis Homerum præconem inveneris!*)

Note 121, page 62. In an earlier version, this passage reads: "Grasso de' Medici will in this matter have the same advantage over Messer Pietro Bembo that a hogshead has over a barrel." Bembo was slender, while

*Grasso* (fat man) was probably the nickname of a corpulent soldier in the service of the Medici, possibly identical with a certain Grosso to whom Bembo desired to be commended in a letter to Bibbiena, 5 February 1506.

Note 122, page 63. The instrument used in Socrates's time (κιθάρα) was certainly not the modern cithern, but more probably a kind of large lyre, supported by a ribbon and played with a plectrum of metal, wood or ivory.

Note 123, page 63. In a note to this passage, Cian says: "*Abito* [rendered 'habit of mind'] is a special condition or habitual quality of the mind, which manifests itself outwardly in a special *costume* [rendered 'habitual tendency'], or equally habitual behaviour, which in turn reacts upon the disposition and moral attitude of the individual."

Note 124, page 63. LYCURGUS probably lived in the 9th century B.C., and was the reputed author of the Spartan laws and institutions.

Note 125, page 63. EPAMINONDAS, a Theban general, defeated the Spartans of Leuctra in 371 B.C. and at Mantinea in 362 B.C., and lost his life in the latter battle.

Note 126, page 63. THEMISTOCLES, the Athenian statesman and general, persuaded the Greeks to resist the second Persian invasion by naval force at Salamis in 480 B.C.

Note 127, page 63. One of the finest of the Pompeian frescoes represents the centaur Chiron teaching Achilles to play upon the lyre.

Note 128, page 63. The reference here is of course to the familiar story of Orpheus and the beasts.

Note 129, page 63. Castiglione doubtless had in mind the legend of Arion, a Greek poet of Lesbos, who probably flourished about 700 B.C. We have a fragment of his verse addressed to Poseidon and telling of the dolphins, who had wafted the poet safely to land when he had lost his course.

Note 130, page 64. As we shall see, the Magnifico's request was not complied with until the second evening (page 79).

Note 131, page 65. QUINTUS FABIUS PICTOR was a Roman general who served in the Second Punic War, and wrote a Greek history of Rome, much esteemed by the ancients, but now lost. Pliny affirms that Fabius painted the temple in the 450th year after the founding of Rome (i.e. 300 B.C.), and that the painting was still extant about the beginning of our era.

Note 132, page 65. The Apollo Belvedere was discovered in 1503, the Laocoön group in 1506, and other famous antique statues only a few years earlier.

Note 133, page 65. The comparative merits of painting and sculpture were a frequent subject of discussion during this period. The Renaissance writers had inherited from antiquity a fondness for seeking superiority or inferiority in matters between which there exists such a diversity of character as to render comparison unprofitable. According to Vasari, Giorgione maintained "that in one picture the painter could display various aspects without the necessity of walking round his work and could even display, at one glance, all the different aspects that could be presented by the figure of a man, even though the latter should assume several attitudes,—a thing which could not be accomplished by sculpture without compelling the observer to change his place, so that the work is not presented at one view, but at different views. He declared, further, that he could execute a single figure in painting, in such a manner as to show the front, back, and profiles of both sides at one and the same time. . . . He painted a nude figure, with its back turned to the spectator, and at the feet of the figure was a limpid stream, wherein the reflection of the front was painted with the utmost exactitude: on one side was a highly burnished corselet, of which the figure had divested itself, and wherein the left side was reflected perfectly, every part of the figure being clearly apparent: and on the other side was a mirror, in which the right profile of the nude form was also exhibited. By this beautiful and admirable fancy, Giorgione desired to prove that painting is, in effect, the superior art, requiring more talent and demanding higher effort."

In one of his letters, Michelangelo wrote: "My opinion is that all painting is the better the nearer it approaches to relief, and relief is worse in proportion as it inclines to painting. And so I have been wont to think that sculpture is the lamp of painting, and that the difference between them might be likened to the difference between the sun and moon. . . . By sculpture I understand an art which operates by taking away superfluous material; by painting, one that attains its result by laying material on. It is enough that both emanate from the same human intelligence, and consequently sculpture and painting ought to live in amity together, without these lengthy disputations. More time is wasted in talk-

ing about the problem than would go to the making of figures in both
species."

Note 134, page 67. In his "Treatise on Painting," Leonardo da
Vinci says: "The first marvel we find in painting is the apparent detach-
ment from the wall or other plane, and the cheating of keen perceptions
by something that is not separate from the surface."

Note 135, page 67. "Grottoes," i.e. the Catacombs. Speaking in his
autobiography of the remains of ancient art found in the Catacombs,
Benvenuto Cellini says: "These grotesques have received this name from
the moderns because they were found by scholars at Rome in certain
subterranean caverns, which had anciently been rooms, chambers, studios,
halls and the like. Since these scholars found them in these cavernous
places (which had been built by the ancients on the surface and had
become low), and since such low places are known at Rome by the
name Grottoes, for that reason they received the name grotesques." Cellini here tries to explain the origin of the name applied to ornaments
(such as the arabesques of the Renaissance) in which figures, human to
the waist, terminate in scrolls, leafage, etc., and are combined with animal
forms and impossible flowers. In this sense the word was used as early
as 1502 in a contract between the Cardinal of Siena and the painter
Pinturicchio. It had of course not yet reached its modern signification, so
fully discussed in the appendix to Volume IV of Ruskin's "Modern
Painters." In Castiglione's time it was not known that the catacomb
decorations were Christian, and in any case they were founded on pagan
models.

Note 136, page 68. DEMETRIUS I of Macedon (died 283 B.C.),
was the son of Antigonus, who was one of Alexander's most illustrious
generals and succeeded to the Macedonian throne.

Note 137, page 68. Of METRODORUS, nothing more is known than
Pliny's account of the incident recorded in our text.

Note 138, page 68. LUCIUS ÆMILIUS PAULUS (died 160 B.C.),
was a Roman general, Consul, and statesman of the aristocratic party.
The incident mentioned in the text occurred after his victory over King
Perseus of Macedon in 168 B.C.

Note 139, page 69. CAMPASPE, according to Pliny, was the name of
the beautiful slave given by Alexander to Apelles, as narrated at page 67.

ℐℐℐℐℐℐℐℐℐℐℐℐℐℐℐℐℐℐℐℐℐℐℐℐℐℐℐℐℐℐℐℐℐℐℐℐℐℐℐℐℐℐℐℐℐℐℐℐℐℐℐℐℐℐ

Note 140, page 70. ZEUXIS (*flor.* 400 B.C.), belonged to the Ionian school of Greek painting, which was characterized by sensuous beauty and accurate imitation of nature. He lived at Athens, and his idealism is said to have been rather of form than of character. The picture referred to in the text represented Helen of Troy, was regarded as his masterpiece, and was probably identical with a picture mentioned as being at Rome. The story of the five maidens is said to have been cited by Tintoretto in support of his maxim, "Art must perfect Nature."

Note 141, page 70. The Marquesses FEBUS and GERARDINO DI CEVA were sons of the Marquess Giovanni (who was living as late as 1491), and belonged to one of the most illustrious families of Piedmont and indeed of all Italy. They were born towards the close of the 15th century and died about the third decade of the 16th, having obtained the investiture of their fief in 1521. They sided sometimes with the Emperor and sometimes with France, as best suited them, and left rather a bad name. To escape punishment for killing a cousin, Gerardino stabbed himself, and Febus also died "*disperato*," leaving two daughters in grief and shame.

Note 142, page 70. ETTORE ROMANO GIOVENALE was a cavalier of whom little more is known than that he was in Francesco Maria's service, fought successfully as one of the thirteen Italian champions at Barletta, was afterwards in the service of the Duke of Ferrara, who dismissed him for an act of treachery.

Note 143, page 70. COLLO VINCENZO CALMETA of Castelnuovo (died 1508), was a courtly poet and prose writer, who had been secretary to the Duchess Beatrice d'Este of Milan. Later he enjoyed the especial favour of this lady's sister, the Marchioness Isabella d'Este of Mantua, and also of the Duchess of Urbino, who protected him from the displeasure of her brother the Marquess of Mantua, and at whose court he improvised verse somewhat after the manner of the Unico Aretino. In a letter (1504) from Urbino to Isabella d'Este, Emilia Pia wrote: "Of news here there is none that is not known to you, except that Calmeta is continually composing songs and divers other things, and this carnival has written a new comedy, which he would have sent you if he had thought it would give you pleasure." Among Calmeta's works were a verse compendium of Ovid's *Ars Amandi*, and a biography of his friend and fellow improvisatore, Serafino Ciminelli d'Aquila (see note 255). As known to us, his poetical writings do not rise above mediocrity, and wholly fail to explain the esteem in which they were held.

Note 144, page 70. ORAZIO FLORIDO was a native of Fano, one of the Adriatic coast towns nearest to Urbino. Having been chancellor to Duke Guidobaldo, he became secretary to Duke Francesco Maria. When Francesco was combating the usurper Lorenzo de' Medici in 1517, he sent one of his officers with Florido under protection of a safe-conduct to challenge Lorenzo to personal combat. In spite of the safe-conduct, Florido was detained and sent to Leo X at Rome, where he was basely tortured in the hope of extorting political secrets from him. He remained steadfastly faithful to his master, and afterwards made a tour of the courts of Europe seeking aid for his lord.

Note 145, page 72. MARGARITA GONZAGA was a niece of the Duchess of Urbino, being a natural daughter of the Marquess Gianfrancesco of Mantua. She was for many years one of the ornaments of the Urbino court. Various mentions of her in contemporary letters show her as a woman of unusual beauty, sprightly wit and gay disposition. She had several suitors, apparently including Filippo Beroaldo, who is mentioned later in THE COURTIER (page 136).

Note 146, page 72. Of BARLETTA nothing more is known than what is contained in this and another shorter mention of him in THE COURTIER (page 85).

Note 147, page 72. The original reads: *havendo prima danzato una bassa, ballarono una Roegarze*. The *danza bassa* was of Spanish origin and is believed to have consisted of sliding steps and of posturing, in which the feet were not lifted. The verb *ballare* seems to be derived from the low Latin *balla*, a ball. In the Middle Ages the game of ball was accompanied with dance and song, and we may well believe that a class of dances, thus originating and denominated generally *balli*, were more animated than the *danza bassa*. Although a Greek derivation has been ascribed to the word *roegarze*, Cian affirms that the dance thus named was of French origin. The earliest French translator of THE COURTIER renders the word by *rouergoise*, which is apparently derived from *Rouergue*, the name of an ancient French province to the south-west of Lyons.

# NOTES TO THE SECOND BOOK OF THE COURTIER

Note 148, page 73. This passage reflects the medico-philosophical theories which the Renaissance inherited from antiquity, and which regarded "the vital spirits" as something far more tangible and material than what we call the principle of life or vital spark. Compare the early conception of electricity as a fluid substance. "Complexion" is of course here used to mean temperament or constitution, and not the mere colour and texture of the skin.

Note 149, page 75. Duke FILIPPO MARIA VISCONTI (born 1391; died 1447), was the son of Giangaleotto and Caterina Visconti, and brother of Giovanni Maria Visconti, whom he succeeded as Duke of Milan in 1412. He married Beatrice di Tenda (widow of Facino Cane), who brought him nearly a half million of florins dowry, besides her husband's soldiers and cities, and thus enabled him gradually to win back the Lombard part of his father's duchy, which his brother had lost. He was very ugly in person, and so sensitive that he rarely appeared in public. Wily but unstable, he was continually plotting schemes that seemed to have no object, and he mistrusted his own generals, even Francesco Sforza, who turned against him, forced him to a ruinous peace, and after his death was soon able to seize his duchy. In him the cruel selfishness of the Renaissance tyrant did not degenerate into mad thirst for blood, as in the case of his terrible brother. He read Dante, Petrarch and French romances of chivalry, and even dallied with the Latin classics, but genuine learning was neglected and despised at his court.

Duke BORSO D'ESTE (born 1413; died 1471), like his brother and predecessor, was a natural son of Duke Niccolò III. Kindly and just, he was idolized by the Ferrarese and especially by the women. He patronized letters and art and was fond of splendid living, yet in spite of the luxury of his court, he left a treasure of about a million pounds sterling. The art of printing was established at Ferrara shortly before his death. He appears to have been himself ignorant of Latin, and encouraged the literary use of Italian and the study of French romance. Histories of Ferrara, as well as the writings of contemporary humanists, are full of his generous deeds. His mild sway passed into a proverb, and the time of "the good Duke Borso" was long remembered as a kind of golden age.

Note 150, page 75. NICCOLÒ PICCININO (born 1380; died 1444), was so humbly born as to possess no other surname than that conferred on him in ridicule of his small stature. Having served under the famous Braccio da Montone, he married the latter's niece, and achieved such distinction as a soldier as to share with Francesco Sforza the fame of being the first *condottiere* of his day. He became the friend and general of Duke Federico of Urbino. His rough wit was highly esteemed.

Note 151, page 76. This consciousness of the corruption then prevailing in Italy is even more frankly expressed by Machiavelli: "It is but too true that we Italians are in a special degree irreligious and corrupt." (*Discorsi*, I, 12.)

Note 152, page 76. The reference here is to Plato's *Phœdo*, c. 3. Socrates is said to have turned Æsop's fables into verse.

Note 153, page 81. The Italian noun *fierezza* (rendered "boldness") and the adjective *fiero* (more anciently *fero*, the epithet applied by Petrarch to Achilles, see note 120) are derived from the Latin *ferus* (wild, untamed, impetuous), the root of which we see in our English word *fer*ocious. While retaining its etymological signification, *fiero* was used to mean also: haughty, intrepid, strong, sturdy.

Note 154, page 85. "Brawls" (Italian, *brandi*; French, *branles*) were a kind of animated figured dance, said to be of Spanish origin and to have resembled the modern *cotillon*. A letter by Castiglione mentions this dance as having been performed by figures dressed as birds in one of the interludes when Bibbiena's *Calandra* was first presented at Urbino. This and other passages suggest that the use of masks was even more common in Italian society of the author's time, than at the present day.

Note 155, page 86. Castiglione's letters show that he possessed and played upon a variety of musical instruments, and it is known that in Duke Federico's time, the palace of Urbino was well supplied with instruments and musicians.

Note 156, page 86. Viol is the generic name for the family of bowed instruments that succeeded the mediæval fiddle and preceded the violin. Invented in the 15th century, it differed from a violin in having deeper ribs, a flat back, and a broad centre-piece on which the sound post rested. Its neck was broad and thin; it had from five to seven strings, and was made in four sizes, of which the lowest pitched (the *violone* or double bass) is still in use. The tone of the instrument is said to have been penetrating rather than powerful.

Note 157, page 87. Wind instruments, and especially the flute, are here referred to. According to Plutarch, Alcibiades maintained that they were regarded with disfavour by Pallas and Apollo because the face is distorted in playing upon them.

Note 158, page 88. The Pythagoreans supposed the intervals between the heavenly bodies to be determined by the laws of musical harmony. Hence arose the celebrated doctrine of "the music of the spheres" (already referred to by Castiglione in the text, page 62); for in their motion the heavenly bodies must each occasion a certain sound or note depending on their distances and velocities, which notes together formed a musical harmony, inaudible to man because he has been accustomed to it from the first and has never had an opportunity to contrast it with silence, or because it exceeds his powers of hearing. Pythagoras himself (died about 500 B.C.) taught his disciples to sing to the accompaniment of the lyre, and to chaunt hymns to the gods and to virtuous men.

Note 159, page 88. As the Italian commentator, Count Vesme, suggests, the author may have meant to say, "shave twice a day." A weekly visit to the barber may, however, have been usually regarded as sufficient at this time.

Note 160, page 91. In the beginning of his Encomium on Folly (which was well known in Italy when Castiglione wrote THE COURTIER), Erasmus pretends that, "although there has been no lack of those who, at great cost of oil and sleep, have exalted . . . the fourth-day ague, the fly, and baldness, with most tedious praise," Folly is languishing without a eulogist. Among the works of Lucian (*flor.* 160 A.D.) there is a brief humorous book in praise of the fly; the philosopher Favorinus (*flor.* 120 A.D.) is said to have written a eulogy on the fourth-day ague; and there is another on baldness by the early Christian writer, Synesius (*flor.* 400 A.D.). The men of the Renaissance delighted in similar displays of wit.

Note 161, page 92. The Italian *procella* (rendered 'fury') primarily means a tempest, and is so translated in the earliest French and English versions of THE COURTIER (*estourbillon,* storm). The still earlier Spanish version has *pestilencia.*

Note 162, page 93. The Italian *impedito* (rendered 'palsied') literally means entangled as to the feet.

Note 163, page 94. St. Luke, iv, 8 and 10.

Note 164, page 95. In Æsop's fable, *Asinus Domino Blandiens*, an ass receives a sound cudgelling for his efforts to win his master's favour by caresses that he was ill fitted to bestow.

Note 165, page 98. TITUS MANLIUS,—called TORQUATUS from the chain (*torques*) that he took from the body of a gigantic Gaul whom he had slain in single combat,—was a favourite hero of Roman history. The incident referred to here occurred shortly before a Roman victory over the Latins at the foot of Vesuvius. Manlius and his colleague in command had proclaimed that no Roman might engage a Latin singly on pain of death, but a son of Manlius accepted a challenge from one of the enemy, slew his adversary, and bore the bloody spoils in triumph to his father, who thereupon caused the young man to be put to death before the assembled army. Manlius was Consul in 340 B.C.

Note 166, page 99. PUBLIUS LICINIUS CRASSUS MUCIANUS was Roman Consul in 131 B.C. According to Livy, the incident narrated in the text occurred during an unsuccessful campaign against Pergamus, which ended in Crassus's voluntary death.

Note 167, page 101. Rome was sacked only the year before THE COURTIER was first published. Italy had become the plaything of foreign conquest.

Note 168, page 101. DARIUS III was King of Persia 336-330 B.C. This story about his sword seems to be founded on the following passage in Quintus Curtius Rufus's History of Alexander the Great: "At the beginning of his reign, Darius ordered his Persian scabbard to be altered to the form which the Greeks used; whereupon the Chaldeans prophesied that the empire of the Persians would pass to those whose arms he had imitated."

Note 169, page 102. It will be remembered that Bembo was a Venetian.

Note 170, page 102. The coif (*cuffia*) here mentioned seems to have been a kind of turban made of cloth wound about the head, with the two ends hanging at the ears.

Note 171, page 103. These unfortunate creatures still abound near Bergamo.

Note 172, page 104. Pylades and Orestes, like Pirithous and Theseus, are the famous friends of Greek legend. The historical and no less tender love between Scipio and Lælius forms the subject of Cicero's *De Amicitia*. See note 102.

Note 173, page 107. The fellow's reward is said to have been a measure of peas.

Note 174, page 107. The Italian phrase here rendered 'goes against the grain' is *non gli avrà sangue* (more usually *non ci avrà il suo sangue*), and might be more precisely translated 'will not suit his humour.' The 'as we say' suggests that the idiom was of recent origin in Castiglione's time.

Note 175, page 110. GIACOPO SANNAZARO (born 1458; died 1530), was a native of Naples, and the son of Giacopo Niccolò and Masella di San Magno. His boyhood was spent with his mother at San Cipriano, near her birthplace Salerno. He soon made such progress in Latin and Greek that he was admitted to the academy of the famous Pontormo, of whom he became the close friend. Their effigies may be seen together in the Neapolitan church of Monte Oliveto. He received a villa and a pension from the scholarly Aragonese dynasty, to which he remained faithful with pen and sword, following Federico III into exile (see note 401) in 1501, and returning to Naples only after his king's death in 1504. He seems to have had a peaceful and honourable old age, active in works of piety and charity, and employing his leisure in study and in the society of a certain noble lady for whom he had formed a lasting Platonic friendship. His writings include marine eclogues, elegies, etc., in Latin, but his best known work is *L'Arcadia*, an Italian prose romance interspersed with verse, of which sixty editions are said to have appeared before 1600. It is regarded by Mahaffy as having originated the idea that the Greek Arcadia was the especial home of pastoral poetry, and probably served Sidney as a model for his poem of the same name. Hardly less famous were Sannazaro's anti-Borgian epigrams, to which Symonds ascribes no small part of the gruesome legend of Lucrezia's crimes. He was buried in a church built by him near the so-called tomb of Virgil, and his monument behind the high altar bears the Latin inscription by Bembo, in which he is described as "near alike to Virgil's muse and sepulchre."

Note 176, page 111. Motet is "a term which for the last three hundred years has been almost exclusively applied to certain pieces of church music, of moderate length, adapted to Latin words (selected, for the most part, either from Holy Scripture, or the Roman office-books), and intended to be sung at high mass, either in place of, or immediately after, the Plain Chaunt *Offertorium* of the Day." (Grove.) The motet was sometimes founded on the air of some non-sacred song, as in the case of Josquin's *Stabat Mater*, which was based upon the ballad *Comme Femme*. (Ambros.)

Note 177, page 111. JOSQUIN (more properly JOSSE) DE PRÈS (born about 1450; died 1521), seems to have been a native of St. Quentin, Hainault, Belgium, and was one of the celebrated musicians of the Renaissance. Having been the pupil of Ockenheim, the greatest composer of the day, he was at the papal court of Sixtus IV, and successively in the service of Lorenzo de' Medici, Louis XII of France, and the Emperor Maximilian I. He returned to Italy about 1503 and lived at the court of Ferrara. He is the earliest composer whose works are preserved in such quantity as adequately to present his power and was called "the father of harmony" by Dr. Burney. Music began to be printed (1498) when Josquin was in his prime.

Note 178, page 112. Other contemporary evidence amply confirms this account of the occasional grossness that marked the table manners of the period.

Note 179, page 113. The two princes here referred to are Ferdinand the Catholic of Spain (see note 392) and Louis XII of France (see note 250).

Note 180, page 114. PAOLO NICCOLÒ VERNIA, called NICOLETTO (little Nick) from his shortness of stature (died 1499), was a native of Chieti, near the Adriatic. He probably studied at Padua, and remained there teaching physics, although in 1444 he took his degree in philosophy, and fourteen years later in medicine. He wrote chiefly on philosophy, but was noted also as a wit.

Note 181, page 114. "When Frederick Barbarossa attempted to govern the rebellious Lombard cities in the common interest of the Empire, he established in their midst a foreign judge, called 'Podestà,' *quasi habens potestatem Imperatoris in hac parte. . . .* The title of 'Podestà' was subsequently conferred upon the official summoned to

maintain an equal balance between the burghers and the nobles."
Symonds's "Renaissance in Italy," ed. 1883, i, 61.

Note 182, page 114. This was the battle of Fornovo (6 July 1495),
in which the Italian forces under the Marquess Gianfrancesco Gonzaga
of Mantua failed to prevent the retreat of Charles VIII towards France.
Both sides claimed a victory, and the marquess even went so far as to
have it commemorated by Mantegna in a picture, "The Madonna of
Victory" (Louvre), which contains his portrait. Castiglione's father died
from the effect of wounds received in this battle.

Note 183, page 115. The reference here is plainly to Leonardo da
Vinci (see note 96). His contemporaries would naturally regard as
chimerical such devices as steam cannon, paddle wheels for boats, and
flying machines, or such hints as that contained in his *Codex Atlanticus,*
where he suggests the possibility of steam navigation. "He was the first
to explain correctly the dim illumination seen over the rest of the surface
of the moon when the bright part is only a thin crescent. He pointed out
that when the moon was nearly new, the half of the earth which was
then illuminated by the sun was turned nearly directly towards the moon,
and that the moon was in consequence illuminated slightly by this 'earth-
shine,' just as we are by moonshine. This explanation . . . tended to
break down the supposed barrier between terrestrial and celestial bodies."
Arthur Berry's "Short History of Astronomy" (London, 1898), p. 91.

Note 184, page 116. Suetonius mentions this characteristic of Cæsar.

Note 185, page 116. This is one of the few passages in THE
COURTIER that are plainly reminiscent of Dante, who says: "To that
truth which hath the face of falsehood, man must ever close his lips"
(*Sempre a quel ver che ha faccia di menzogna, De' l'uom chiuder le
labbra*). *Inferno,* xvi, 124–5.

Note 186, page 118. The translator admits being at a loss to find
an adequate equivalent for the Italian *arguzie.* Our unfamiliar English
adjective 'argute' suggests that kind of pungent and witty conceits which
Castiglione is describing.

Note 187, page 119. Bibbiena's reputation as a wit was well established, while Canossa seems also to have deserved the same epithet, if
we may judge from a story that has been preserved of him. The count
had at Rome a fine collection of silver plate, including a flagon with

a lid in the form of a tiger. A friend having borrowed this flagon and kept it for two months, returned it only on demand and with the request that the count lend him a certain salt-cellar, which had a crab for a cover. Ludovico sent word that if the tiger, which is the swiftest of beasts, had been two months coming home, the crab, being slower than all others, would by the same rule be absent for years, and that on this account he was unwilling to let it go.

Note 188, page 120. The allusion is of course to Bibbiena's early baldness.

Note 189, page 120. Cardinal GALEOTTO DELLA ROVERE (born about 1477; died 1508), was the favourite nephew of Julius II, being a son of the pope's sister Luchina by her first husband Gianfrancesco Franciotti, a patrician of Lucca. Like all his mother's other children, he was adopted as of the della Rovere name. Having been made Bishop of Lucca, he was created a cardinal on his uncle's election as pope, appointed pontifical vice-chancellor, and soon given a great number of benefices. Generous and amiable, and a patron of artists and authors, he was much beloved at the court of Urbino, as is shown by several documents, among which is a letter by Emilia Pia mentioning two sonnets of his, in one of which (written the day before his last illness) he foretold his early death.

Note 190, page 120. GIACOMO SANSECONDO, a noted musician who flourished between the years 1493 and 1522 at the courts of Milan, Mantua, Ferrara, Urbino and Rome, where he attained a wide celebrity in the pontificate of Leo X. He seems to have ended his days in adversity, in some degree relieved by his friend Castiglione, whose letters contain several affectionate mentions of him.

Note 191, page 121. DEMOCRITUS (*flor.* 400 B.C.), was the atomistic philosopher of Abdera in Thrace. He possessed an ample fortune, and his cheerful disposition led him to look on the bright and humorous side of things, a fact taken by later writers to mean that he laughed at the follies of mankind.

Note 192, page 123. The phrase 'served her in love' and the conventional relation that it denoted, were drawn from mediæval life and literature north of the Alps, and with some changes survived in Italy during the Renaissance, until the *cavalier servente* became in the 18th century a recognized institution. Attendance upon the lady at church was a characteristic feature of the cavalier's service.

Note 193, page 123. Pius III, Francesco Todeschini (born 1439; died 1503), was a native of Siena and a nephew of the illustrious Æneas Silvius Piccolomini (Pius II). The suddenness of his predecessor Alexander VI's death took the sacred college by surprise, and they unanimously elected their weakest member as pope. His short pontificate of twenty-six days was filled with disturbances, and he was believed to have died from poison.

Note 194, page 123. Antonio Agnello (died after 1527), belonged to one of the most noted families of Mantua, and seems to have been the son of Giulio Agnello and Margarita Crema. Besides being an able man of affairs (employed by the Palæologus rulers of Montferrat), he was a graceful poet, and became the friend of Bembo and Castiglione.

Note 195, page 124. The poet Caius Valerius Catullus (born about 87 B.C.), was a native of Verona and a friend of Cæsar and Cicero. His extant works include one hundred and sixteen poems, lyric, epigrammatic, elegiac, etc. His 69th Ode is a dialogue between the author and a door.

Note 196, page 124. Pope Nicholas V, Tommaso Parentucelli (born 1398; died 1455), was a native of Pisa, whence his family were exiled in his infancy. Although his father died when he was nine years old, and in spite of great poverty, he contrived to study at the University of Bologna. Later he served as tutor in the Albizzi and Strozzi families at Florence, thus earning enough money to return and take his theological degree at Bologna. He then entered the service of the archbishop of the latter city, whom he accompanied to Florence, and there became a friend of Cosimo de' Medici and a member of the literary society of the place. In 1443 he was made Bishop of Bologna, and four years later was elected pope, an elevation that he owed solely to his reputation for learning and to the comparatively small esteem in which the office was then held. The humanists were delighted at the election of one of their own number. As pope, he devoted his revenues to maintaining a splendid court, to the rebuilding of the fortifications and palaces of Rome, and to the enrichment of scholars. During his pontificate the city became a workshop of erudition. He founded the Vatican Library, for which he collected five thousand volumes, and the list prepared by him for Cosimo de' Medici to use in beginning the Library of San Marco, was followed also by Duke Federico of Urbino. He was a small, ugly man.

*Nihil Papa Valet,* 'the Pope is good for nothing.'

Note 197, page 125. I.e. in the second tale of the Eighth Day.

Note 198, page 125. Calandrino is an unfortunate and very amusing character appearing in the third and sixth tales of the Eighth Day and in the fifth tale of the Ninth Day.

Note 199, page 125. Niccolò Campani, called STRASCINO (born 1478; died between 1522 and 1533), was an excellent actor of Sienese rustic comedies and farces, and the author of verses and of a Lament that was very popular in the 16th century. He frequented the court of Leo X, and several of Castiglione's letters (1521) tell of efforts to secure the actor's services for the Marquess of Mantua, and of furnishing him with twenty-five ducats, a horse, and a papal pass, for the purpose.

Note 200, page 126. 'This place,' i.e. Urbino.

Note 201, page 126. The reader will hardly need to be reminded that the great Roman orator was often spoken of as Tullius or Tully rather than as Cicero.

Note 202, page 129. When THE COURTIER was expurgated by Antonio Ciccarelli in 1584, Dante's name was here substituted for that of St. Paul. The word *becco* (rendered 'he-goat') has long been used by the Italians as a term of jocose reproach applied to a man whose wife is unfaithful.

Note 203, page 126. Duke ERCOLE D'ESTE (born 1431; died 1505), was the legitimate son of Duke Niccolò III and Rizzarda di Saluzzo. Bred at the Neapolitan court, he became Duke of Ferrara on the death of his half-brother Borso (see note 149) in 1471. In 1473 he married Eleanora of Aragon, daughter of Ferdinand I of Naples. Among the six children of this union were: Isabella, who became Marchioness of Mantua (see note 397); Beatrice, who became Duchess of Milan (see note 398); Alfonso, who married Lucrezia Borgia and succeeded his father as duke; and the Cardinal Ippolito already mentioned (see note 64). Although his reign was far from peaceful, his court was noted for its luxury and for the brilliancy of art and letters with which it was adorned. He was an especial patron of the theatre, no less than five comedies of Plautus being performed during the wedding festivities of his son Alfonso in 1502. On the other hand, he maintained relations with Savonarola, who was a native of Ferrara.

Note 204, page 127. Castellina was a small walled town in the Chianti hills, which was held as a Florentine outpost against Siena. The siege referred to in the text took place in 1478, when the place capitulated to the Neapolitan and papal troops after holding out for forty days. Duke of Calabria was the title regularly borne by the heir of each Aragonese king of Naples. The personage here meant must have been Alfonso the Younger (see note 31).

Note 205, page 127. While the meaning is not free from doubt, the point of the story seems to lie in the absurdity of the Florentine's supposing that after being discharged from a cannon, a projectile would retain any poison previously applied to it.

Note 206, page 128. It will be remembered that Bembo was a Venetian, while Bibbiena's birthplace was a Florentine town.

Note 207, page 128. This war lasted from 1494 to 1509, and proved ruinous to both sides. Castiglione's use of the past tense in speaking of it here doubtless arose from the fact that he was writing several years after the date that he assigns to the dialogues.

Note 208, page 129. Pistoia and Prato were two small cities which lay to the north-west of Florence and were subject to its rule. Modern issues of "fiat" money are but a slight modification of the method proposed by the worthy Florentine.

Note 209, page 131. Bucentaur was the name of the state galley of the Venetian Republic, used (among other occasions) in the symbolic ceremony of wedding the Adriatic, which was enjoined upon the Venetians by Alexander III (pope 1159-1181) to commemorate their victory over the fleet of Frederick Barbarossa. On each Ascension Day a ring was dropped from the Bucentaur into the Adriatic, with the words, "we espouse thee, sea, in token of true and lasting dominion." The vessel bore the image of a centaur as figure-head. Of the last of several successive Bucentaurs (demolished in 1824), a few fragments are preserved in the Arsenal at Venice. In the 15th and 16th centuries the name was applied to state vessels of ceremony elsewhere. By some the word is supposed to be derived from the Greek $\beta o\tilde{v}\varsigma$ (ox) and $\kappa\acute{\epsilon}\nu\iota\alpha\nu\varrho o\varsigma$ (centaur); by others it is regarded as a corruption of the Latin *ducentorum* (of two hundred oars), or of the Italian *buzino d'oro* (golden bark).

Note 210, page 131. This tale, not unworthy of Munchausen, may have been suggested to Castiglione by a passage in one of the minor works of Plutarch, who relates that Antiphanes (a friend of Plato) said that "he visited a certain city where words froze as soon as spoken, by reason of the great cold; and later, sounds uttered in winter melted in the spring and were heard by the inhabitants." Although Plutarch represents the story as told in illustration of the way in which "those who came as young men to listen to Plato's talk, understood it only long afterwards, when they had grown old," it is worth noting that an Antiphanes, of Berga in Thrace, is known as a writer on the marvellous and incredible.

Note 211, page 131. Vasco da Gama rounded the southern extremity of Africa and reached India nine years before the date of the Courtier dialogues.

Note 212, page 131. This must have been Emanuel I, who was King of Portugal from 1495 until his death in 1521, and who promoted the expeditions of da Gama and other Portuguese navigators.

Note 213, page 131. Taffety was a very light soft silk fabric. There is extant a letter of Bembo's (1541), in which the aged cardinal orders two cushions filled with swan's down and covered with crimson taffety. The word is said to be derived from the Persian *taftah* (twisted, woven). Taft is the name of a town in central Persia.

Note 214, page 132. ANNIBAL PALEOTTO (died 1516), belonged to an ancient and honourable Bolognese family (with which Castiglione is known to have been on friendly terms), and was the son of an eminent jurist, Vincenzo Paleotto, who died in 1498. Leo X made Annibal a senator of Bologna in 1514, the brief being written by Bembo.

Note 215, page 133. Giacopo di Nino was BISHOP OF POTENZA from 1506 until 1521, and seems to have been a butt for the ridicule of Leo X's court.

Note 216, page 133. An earlier version of this passage reads: "And of this kind was what Rinaldo in the *Morgante* said to the Giant: 'Where do you hang your spectacles?'" The *Morgante Maggiore* is a serio-burlesque romantic poem by Luigi Pulci (1431-1487), introducing, among other characters of mediæval romance, Rinaldo, his cousin Orlando, and the giant Morgante.

Note 217, page 133. GALEOTTO MARZI DA NARNI (born about 1427; died about 1490), a singular example of the adventurer-humanist, studied at the universities of Padua and Bologna, and taught at the latter place. He twice visited the court of Matthias Corvinus of Hungary, for whom he wrote a book on jests. He was something of an astrologer and also the author of a work on chiromancy. Being accused of heresy, he was imprisoned at Venice in 1477, and condemned to make public recantation in the Piazzetta with a crown of devils on his head. He is said to have been learned and witty. The story given in the text became almost proverbial.

Note 218, page 134. The present form (*bisticcio*) of *bischizzo* (rendered 'playing on words') has a meaning somewhat different from that indicated in the text,—being the term applied to a succession of words the similarity of whose sound renders them difficult to pronounce, e.g. "Peter Piper picked a peck of pickled peppers."

Note 219, page 134. At this time the general use of family names was comparatively recent, and their form was somewhat variable. Thus, such surnames as Pio and Fregoso were treated as still being, what they doubtless originally were, merely personal epithets, and so were given the feminine form (Pia, Fregosa) when applied to women. The adjective *pia* means dutiful, pious, kind, while *impia* or *empia* of course means the reverse.

Note 220, page 134. "The greatest of the Furies is my bedfellow." With a change of one syllable in the Latin, this becomes *Furiarum maxima juxta accubat* ("The greatest of the Furies lies hard by"), Æneid, V, 605-6.

Note 221, page 134. Geronimo Donato (born 1457; died 1511), was a native of Venice, where he held many public offices, besides being sent abroad as ambassador of the Republic, especially to the courts of Alexander VI and Julius II. He also enjoyed no small fame as a cultivator of science, art and letters (particularly Greek and theology). The incident narrated in the text occurred during his embassy to Alexander, to whom on another occasion he made a far wittier retort. Being jestingly asked by the pope where Venice got its right of lordship over the Adriatic, he answered: "Let your Holiness show me the title deed to the Patrimony of St. Peter, and on the back of it will be found inscribed the grant to the Venetians of their dominion over the Adriatic."

Note 222, page 134. In the Roman Church a "station" (*stazione*) is a church where indulgences are granted at certain seasons. In earlier times such churches were visited in solemn procession, which afterwards came to be regarded as an opportunity for social recreation. The word is used also to designate the indulgences earned by visiting, on appointed days, many churches founded by popes.

Note 223, page 134. "As many stars as heaven, so many girls hath thy Rome," Ovid's *Ars Amandi*, I, 59.

Note 224, page 134. "As many kids as the pasture, so many satyrs hath thy Rome," is as close an English rendering as Donato's Latin will bear.

Note 225, page 134. MARCANTONIO DELLA TORRE belonged to an ancient noble family of Verona, was a famous anatomist, and is said to have included Leonardo da Vinci among his pupils. He died at the age of thirty, and was highly praised for his learning. His father Geronimo lectured on medicine at Padua.

Pietro Barozzi became ARCHBISHOP OF PADUA in 1487, and died in 1507. Bandello (who had read THE COURTIER in MS.) relates the same story in somewhat wittier form, but gives the name of the prelate as Gerardo Landriano, Bishop of Como.

Note 226, page 135. St. Luke, xvi, 2.

Note 227, page 135. St. Matthew, xxv, 20.

Note 228, page 135. PROTO DA LUCCA was one of the most famous buffoons who enlivened the pontifical court at the beginning of the 16th century. If, as seems probable, the incident in question occurred in January 1506 (when Bernardino Lei died and was succeeded by Antonio da Castriani as Bishop of Cagli, a town near Urbino), the pope in question must have been Julius II, to whom the epithet 'very grave' would be entirely appropriate.

Note 229, page 135. The play is upon the word 'office' in its two meanings of post or employment, and breviary or prayer-book. In the latter sense, the 'full office' contained the psalms, lessons, etc.,—while the 'Madonna's office' was much abbreviated.

Note 230, page 135. GIOVANNI CALFURNIO (born 1443; died 1503), was a gentle and laborious humanist, born at or near Bergamo, but long resident at Padua, where he held the chair of rhetoric. His chief work consisted in correcting and commenting upon the texts of Latin poets. The 'another man at Padua' was probably Raffaele Regio (a fellow professor with Calfurnio), who publicly ridiculed his colleague as the son of a charcoal-burner. Calfurnio seems to have published very little; on his death he bequeathed his library to the church of San Giovanni in Verdara, from which his tomb and portrait relief have recently been removed to a cloister of the monastery of St. Antony at Padua.

Note 231, page 135. Tommaso Inghirami, "FEDRA" (born 1470; died 1516), was a native patrician of Volterra (a town about midway between Pisa and Siena), being the son of Paolo Inghirami and Lucrezia Barlettani. Having passed his early boyhood at Florence, he removed to Rome in 1483, where he played the part of *Phædra* in Seneca's tragedy *Hippolytus* (upon which Racine founded his *Phèdre*) with such success that the name clung to him for life. The play being interrupted by an accident to the scenery, he filled the interval by improvising Latin verses for the entertainment of the audience. The performance took place in the mausoleum of the Emperor Hadrian, which was afterwards converted into the fortress known as the Castle of St. Angelo. Tommaso was employed by Alexander VI in diplomatic affairs, crowned poet by the Emperor Maximilian I, and made a canon of the Lateran and of the Vatican. He seems to have been connected with the Vatican Library as early as 1505, and became its prefect. Although Erasmus called him the Cicero of his time, his fame now rests rather on his portrait in the Pitti Gallery at Florence, than on his works.

Note 232, page 136. CAMILLO PALEOTTO was a brother of the Annibal Paleotto already mentioned (see note 214). On his father's death in 1498, he went to Rome, where he became the friend of Federico Fregoso, Bembo and Castiglione. He taught rhetoric at Bologna and was Chancellor of the Senate there. There also he is said to have died in 1530, although a letter of Bembo's speaks of him in 1518 as then already dead.

Note 233, page 136. ANTONIO PORCARO, or PORZIO, belonged to a noble Roman family, and was a brother of the Camillo Porcaro mentioned in THE COURTIER (at page 138). He had also a twin brother Valerio, whom he so closely resembled that the two were often mistaken, one for the other, as Bibbiena says in the preface to his *Calandra*,—the plot of which is founded upon a similar resemblance. Little more is known of Antonio than that he suffered some grievous wrong from Alexander VI.

Note 234, page 136. Regarding GIANTOMMASO GALEOTTO, Cian furnishes no information. The Spanish annotator, Fabié, adds Marcio (Marzio) to his name—thus apparently treating him as identical with the

↑↑↑↑↑↑↑↑↑↑↑↑↑↑↑↑↑↑↑↑↑↑↑↑↑↑↑↑↑↑↑↑↑↑↑↑↑↑↑↑↑↑↑↑↑↑↑↑↑↑↑↑↑↑↑↑

Galeotto da Narni mentioned above at page 133,—and says that he "died, by reason of his great corpulence, from a fall from his horse, being in the train of Charles VIII of France, when the latter entered Milan." As "My lord Prefect" was only four years old when Charles entered Milan in 1494, this identification seems clearly erroneous.

Note 235, page 136. FILIPPO BEROALDO (born 1472; died 1518), belonged to a noble Bolognese family. Having been one of his famous uncle Filippo the elder's most brilliant pupils in the classics, he was at the age of twenty-six made professor of literature at Bologna, and afterwards at Rome. In 1511 he successfully defended Duke Francesco Maria of Urbino against the charge of murdering Cardinal Alidosi. Instead of seeking to extenuate the deed, as done in heat and under strong provocation, he boldly justified it on the ground that his client was the instrument chosen by the Almighty to rid the world of a monster of wickedness, and eloquently appealed to the tribunal to spare a hero whose promise of future usefulness was precious to Italy. Beroaldo was secretary to Cardinal Giovanni de' Medici, and on the latter's election as pope, he was made Provost of the Roman Academy, while at Inghirami's death he was made Librarian of the Vatican, as a reward for editing the recently discovered first five books of Tacitus's Annals. He died at Rome, partly (it is said) from vexation at not being paid the stipend of his office. Bembo wrote his epitaph. Although he was celebrated for erudition and eloquence rather than for authorship, he left three books of odes, and one of epigrams,—in Latin.

Note 236, page 136. The pupil obviously used the phrase in its low Latin meaning, "Master, God give you good evening." Beroaldo jocosely accepted it in its classical meaning, "Master, God give you good, late."

Note 237, page 136. "Evil to thee, soon."

Note 238, page 136. DIEGO DE CHIGNONES (died 1512), was a Spanish cavalier, of whom Branthôme writes as follows: "This Great Captain had for lieutenant, with a company of one hundred men-at-arms, Don Diego de Quignones, who supported him in his combats and victories, and was truly a good and brave lieutenant to him. After the Great Captain's death, he had sole command of his company of an hundred men-at-arms, as he well deserved to have. He commanded it at the battle of Ravenna, where he died like a brave and valiant captain. And if all had behaved as he did (say the old Spaniards), the victory that the French

ʔʔʔʔʔʔʔʔʔʔʔʔʔʔʔʔʔʔʔʔʔʔʔʔʔʔʔʔʔʔʔʔʔʔʔʔʔʔʔʔʔʔʔʔʔʔʔʔʔʔ
won there would have cost them dearer than it did, although it cost them
dear."

Note 239, page 136. Don Gonzalvo Hernand y Aguilar, better
known as Consalvo de Cordoba, or THE GREAT CAPTAIN (born 1443;
died 1515), was a native of Montilla, near Cordova, and belonged to an
ancient family of Spanish grandees. His father's name was Pietro, and
his mother's was Elvira Errea. Bred to war in early youth and knighted
on the field of battle at the age of sixteen, he followed the fortunes of
Ferdinand the Catholic, and took an active part in the conquest of
Granada. In 1494 he was sent to Italy to aid Ferdinand II of Naples
against Charles VIII, won a long succession of victories over the French,
and was finally made Constable and Viceroy of Naples. Later, Ferdinand
the Catholic, listening to slanderous reports regarding him, deprived him
of office, and in 1507 recalled him to Spain, where he died in disgrace.
His good qualities were much admired by Castiglione, who had fought
against him, but his fame was not unstained by acts of cruelty and bad
faith, which (it is fair to say) were common at the time and seem to
have been committed only against his master's foes. Giorgione is said to
have painted his portrait at Venice, and a life of him by Paolo Giovio
was published at Florence in 1552.

Note 240, page 137. The Spanish word *vino* means not only "wine"
but also "he came." In pronunciation it would be easily mistaken for
*Y-no.* *Y no lo conocistes* is the Spanish for "And thou knewest Him
not." Compare St. John, i, 11.

Note 241, page 137. The word *marano* (here rendered "heretic")
meant a renegade Moor, and is said by Symonds to have been generally
used in Italy at this time as a term of reproach against Spaniards.

Note 242, page 137. GIACOMO SADOLETO (born 1477; died 1547),
was a native of Modena and the son of a noted jurist, Giovanni Sadoleto.
He studied Latin at Ferrara and Greek at Rome, where he settled in
the pontificate of Alexander VI and acquired a great reputation for
learning. Leo X appointed him a secretary at the same time with Bembo
(who shared with him the name of being the best Latinist of the day),
and soon made him Bishop of Carpentras, a town fifteen miles north-
east of Avignon. He was secretary also to Clement VII, to whom he
boldly declared that the sack of Rome (1527) was inflicted by God as
a punishment for human wickedness. Paul III created him a cardinal
in 1536. A sincerely pious man, he was conscious of the evils of the

Church and did not escape suspicion of heresy. He was a close friend of Vittoria Colonna, and the Roman Academy often met at his house on the Quirinal. Besides Latin poems (one of which, on the newly discovered Laocoön group, made him famous), his works include commentaries on the Psalms and the Epistle to the Romans, and a Latin exhortation to the princes and people of Germany against Lutheran heresies. Although far from rich, he was very charitable, especially in providing young men of his flock with the means of education.

Note 243, page 137. LUDOVICO DA SAN BONIFACIO is identified by Cian as a Paduan, who held the offices of prothonotary and private chamberlain under Leo X, successfully disputed with Bembo the possession of a canonry at Padua in 1514, was sent to different courts by Leo, and died at Padua in 1545.

ERCOLE RANGONE (died 1572), belonged to an illustrious family of Modena, and achieved some note as a soldier and diplomatist, having commanded the Florentine forces in 1529, and served as Ferrarese ambassador to France, Spain and Germany. He was esteemed by Castiglione, of whose wife Ippolita Torello he seems to have been a kinsman.

The COUNT OF PEPOLI probably belonged to a noble Bolognese family of that name, but has not been identified with certainty.

Note 244, page 138. Of SALLAZA DALLA PEDRADA nothing seems to be known beyond the mention of him in the text.

Note 245, page 138. PALLA DEGLI STROZZI (born 1372; died 1462), was a wealthy and cultivated Florentine patrician. Having honourably filled high offices of state, he was banished by Cosimo de' Medici in 1434 for ten years to Padua. Himself an enthusiastic scholar and patron of classical studies, he caused many Greek MSS. to be brought into Italy (including works of Plato, Aristotle and Plutarch), and was the first Italian to collect books for the express purpose of founding a public library, in the execution of which design he was prevented by his exile from anticipating Cosimo. He employed learned Greeks to read to him, and was instrumental in inducing Chrysoloras to teach at Florence,—an engagement regarded by Symonds as having secured the future of Hellenic study in Europe. The story narrated of him in the text is elsewhere told of an exile belonging to the Albizzi family.

Note 246, page 138. COSIMO DE' MEDICI, *Pater Patriæ* (born 1389; died 1464), was a Florentine banker, statesman and patron of literature and art. In his father Giovanni's house of business he cultivated the rare faculty for finance that he afterwards employed in public administration and private commerce. He inherited his father's vast fortune in 1429, and made it a practice to lend money to needy citizens and at the same time to involve the affairs of Florence with his own,—thus not only attaching individuals to his interests, but rendering it difficult to control state expenditures apart from his own bank. He understood also how to use his money without exciting jealousy, and while he spent large sums on public works, he declined the architect Brunelleschi's plans for a residence more befitting a prince than a citizen. He was an early riser, and temperate and simple in his life. While ruling Florence with despotic power, he seemed intent on the routine of his counting-house, and put forward other men to execute his political schemes. Despite occasional checks, he so firmly established the influence of his family as the real rulers of Florence that they were not permanently expelled until the nineteenth century. Much of his power was due to sympathy with the intellectual movement of the age, and although he was not a Greek scholar, he had a solid education, and collected MSS., gems, coins and inscriptions, employing his commercial agents in the work. During a year of exile, he built a library at Venice, and later he built one at Florence and another at Fiesole. His house was the centre of a literary and philosophical society, which included all the wits of Florence and the strangers who flocked to that capital of culture.

Note 247, page 138. CAMILLO PORCARO, or PORZIO (died 1517), was a brother of the Antonio Porcaro already mentioned in THE COURTIER (at page 136; see note 233). He was a professor of rhetoric at Rome, and a canon of St. Peter's. Leo X made him Bishop of Teramo, a town near the Adriatic north-east of Rome. He was a member of the Roman Academy, and some of his Latin verse has survived.

Note 248, page 138. MARCANTONIO COLONNA (died 1522), the son of Pierantonio Colonna and Bernardina Conti, was a second cousin of Vittoria Colonna. His wife Lucrezia Gara della Rovere was a niece of Julius II and sister of the Cardinal Galeotto della Rovere already mentioned (at page 120; see note 189). In 1502 he fled from Rome to escape the persecution of the Borgias, repaired to the kingdom of Naples, and took service under the "Great Captain." He served also in the armies of Julius II, Maximilian I, and Francis I, and took part in nearly all the wars of his time. He was cited as a model of physical beauty and martial prowess.

Note 249, page 139. DIEGO GARZIA is regarded by the Spanish annotator, Fabié, as identical with the famous warrior Diego Garcia de Paredes (born 1466; died 1530), who began the life of a soldier at the age of twelve, and had a brilliant share, with the "Great Captain," in the expulsion of the Moors from Spain and later in the Italian campaigns. He was a man of great height and strength, and is said on one occasion to have stopped the wheel of a rapidly moving wind-mill with his single hand. Charles V made him a Knight of the Golden Spur, and he is often called the Chevalier Bayard of Spain.

Note 250, page 139. LOUIS XII (born 1462; died 1515), was the son of Duke Charles d'Orléans and Anne of Cleves. He accompanied Charles VIII into Italy in 1494, became king on his cousin's death in 1498, and the following year married Charles's widow Anne of Brittany. In 1500 he expelled Duke Ludovico Sforza of Milan, to whose duchy he laid claim as the grandson of Valentina Visconti. The following year he conquered Naples in alliance with Ferdinand the Catholic, but quarrelled with his ally over the division of the country, with the result that his force was defeated by the "Great Captain" at Garigliano in 1503, and withdrew from Naples in 1504. He joined the League of Cambray against Venice in 1508, but in 1511 the Holy League was formed against him, and in 1513 the French were again compelled to leave Italy. On the death of Anne of Brittany in 1514, he married Mary, the youthful sister of Henry VIII of England, to whom in dying (1 January 1515) he is reported to have said: "Dear, I leave thee my death as a New Year's gift." He was sincerely regretted by his subjects, and was known as "The Father of His People." Michelet says of him: "He was a good man, honest by nature, sometimes absurd, indiscreet, talkative, testy; but he had a heart, and the only way for men to flatter him was to persuade him that they desired the good of his subjects." Among his sayings was "Good king, stingy king; I prefer to be ridiculous to my courtiers, than deaf to my people."

Note 251, page 139. DJEM or ZIZIM (born 1459; died 1495), was a son of Mahomet II, the conqueror of Constantinople. On the death of his father in 1481, he tried to dispossess his brother as sultan, but being defeated, he sought refuge at Rhodes, where the Knights of the Order of St. John received him for a while, and then sent him to France. In 1489 he was surrendered to the custody of Innocent VIII, from whom he passed into the hands of Alexander VI. Both these pontiffs received a subsidy for his maintenance from his brother the sultan. In 1495 Charles VIII took him to Naples, where he was imprisoned and soon died from the effect (it is supposed) of poison administered at Rome by order of Alexander VI. Of his life at the papal court, we get the following glimpse in a letter from Mantegna to the Marquess of Mantua: "The Turk's brother is here, strictly guarded in the palace of his Holiness, who allows him all sorts of diversion, such as hunting, music, and the like. He often comes to eat in this new palace where I paint [i.e., the Belvedere], and, for a barbarian, his manners are not amiss. There is a sort of majestic bearing about him, and he never doffs his cap to the Pope, having in fact none; . . . He eats five times a day, and sleeps as often; before meals he drinks sugared water like a monkey. He has the gait of an elephant, but his people praise him much, especially for his horsemanship: it may be so, but I have never seen him take his feet out of the stirrups, or give any other proof of skill. He is a most savage man, and has stabbed at least four persons, who are said not to have survived four hours. A few days ago, he gave such a cuffing to one of his interpreters that they had to carry him to the river, in order to bring him round. It is believed that Bacchus pays him many a visit. On the whole he is dreaded by those about him. He takes little heed of anything, like one who does not understand or has no reason. His way of life is quite peculiar; he sleeps without undressing, and gives audience sitting cross-legged, in the Parthian fashion. He carries on his head sixty thousand yards of linen, and wears so long a pair of trousers that he is lost in them, and astonishes all beholders."

Note 252, page 139. The GRAND TURK in question was Bajazet II (born 1447; died 1512), who succeeded his father (Mahomet II, the conqueror of Constantinople) in 1481, was almost uninterruptedly engaged in war with Hungary, Venice, Egypt and Persia, was deposed by his son Selim, and died soon afterwards. He was repeatedly invited by Alexander VI to invade Europe and fight the pope's Christian enemies. The friendly relations between the two were closely connected with the captivity of Bajazet's brother, just mentioned. As a token of his gratitude, the Turk sent Innocent VIII the "Lance of Longinus," the centurion who was supposed to have pierced the Saviour's side on Calvary and afterwards to have been converted to Christianity. As a reward for the death of his brother, he sent Alexander VI a sum of money equivalent to over £500,000 sterling, and a tunic alleged to have been worn by the Saviour. These, however, were intercepted by the pope's enemy, Giuliano della Rovere, afterwards Julius II.

Note 253, page 139. The Archbishopric of Florence was occupied by Roberto Folco from 1481 until his death in 1530.

'The Alexandrian cardinal' is the name by which Giannantonio di Sangiorgio (born 1439; died 1509), was commonly known. At the age of twenty-seven he became professor of canon law at Pavia. In 1479 he was made Bishop of Alexandria, and soon afterwards called to Rome and made an Auditor of the *Ruota* (see note 292), which office he continued to hold until he was created a cardinal in 1493. He was regarded as the most eminent jurist of his day.

Note 254, page 139. Besides the mention of this NICOLETTO in the text, nothing more seems to be known of him beyond the following anecdote: "Of messer Nicoletto da Orvieto it is narrated that, being in the service of that very courteous pontiff Pope Leo, he once won the lasting favour of his Holiness with only four words; for one day, the talk turning upon a certain vacant benefice which was sought after by a member of the Vitelli family to whom it could be given, he said humorously: 'Holy Father, fitness requires that it be by all means conferred on Vitello (calf), the more because it has no nearer or closer kinsman than he is,'—playing on the word 'vacant,' which he seemed to derive from *vacca* (cow), the mother of the calf." Garzoni's *L'Hospidale de' Pazzi Incurabili* (Piacenza: 1586), page 142.

Note 255, page 140. Antonio Cammelli (born 1440; died 1502), called PISTOIA from the name of his birthplace, was a prolific writer of verse, chiefly sonnets of a humorous and satirical character, which have no small historical value. He spent the larger part of his life in the service of the d'Este at Ferarra, and in that of Duke Ludovico Sforza, of Milan, to whom he remained faithful in adversity. An edition of his verse was published at Turin by Renier in 1888.

This SERAFINO was not our merry interlocutor, but the now almost forgotten lyric poet, Serafino Ciminelli (born 1466; died 1500), who was a native of Aquila (fifty-five miles north-east of Rome), and a welcome guest at the courts of Naples, Rome, Urbino, Mantua and Milan. His verse was by some preferred to that of Petrarch, and the unbounded popularity which he enjoyed was doubtless due to the skill with which he improvised to his own accompaniment on the lute. He was a short ugly man of elfish appearance.

Note 256, page 140. GIOVANNI GONZAGA (born 1474; died 1523), was the third son of the Marquess Federico of Mantua and Margarita of Bavaria. He married Laura Bentivoglio, fought in his youth against Charles VIII, and in 1512 was in the service of the Sforza family. He was employed also by his brother Gianfrancesco, Marquess of Mantua, in

*****************************************************************

political negotiations. In 1519, on the death of Lucrezia Borgia, he wrote
to his nephew, the new Marquess Federico of Mantua: "Lucrezia's death
occasioned much grief throughout the city, and his Ducal Highness in
particular displayed extreme distress. Men here tell wonderful things of
her life: for the last ten years she wore a hair shirt; and for two years
she has been in the habit of confessing every day, and of attending Com-
munion three or four times a month."

Note 257, page 140. Giovanni's son ALESSANDRO GONZAGA was
born in 1497, and died in 1527.

Note 258, page 140. GIACOMO D'ATRI (or d'Adria Picena) was
made Count of PIANELLA by Ferdinand II of Naples in 1496, as a
reward for faithful service. He acted as confidential secretary to the
Marquess Gianfrancesco of Mantua in various wars, and especially in
the campaigns against Charles VIII.

Note 259, page 140. PHILIP II of Macedon, the conqueror of
Greece, was born 382 and died 336 B.C.

Note 260, page 141. This retort has by others been ascribed to a
Florentine ambassador at Siena, and his name given as Guido del Pelagio.

Note 261, page 142. MARIO DE' MAFFEI DA VOLTERRA (born
1464; died 1537), occupied successively the offices of Archpriest at Volterra, Sacristan of the Vatican, Bishop of Aquino, and Bishop of Cavaillon
in France.

Note 262, page 142. AGOSTINO BEVAZZANO or Beazzano (*flor.*
1500-1550), was born at Treviso, near Venice, of which republic his
ancestor Francesco had been chancellor in the 15th century. His own
portrait hung in the Grand Council Chamber at Venice. He lived some time
in Venice, but in 1514 he was employed as secretary by Bembo and sent
to Leo X at Rome, where he resided chiefly until 1526. Besides being a
noted writer of Italian and Latin verse, he acquired great skill in public
affairs and came to be regarded as an oracle at the papal court. Late in
life he was painfully afflicted with gout, and passed the last years of his
life at Verona and at Treviso, where he died and was buried in the
cathedral.

Note 263, page 143. The MARQUESS FEDERICO GONZAGA of Mantua (born 1440; died 1484), was the son of the Marquess Ludovico and

Barbara of Brandenburg, and married Margarita, daughter of Duke Albert III of Bavaria. His family attained sovereign power at Mantua in 1354 and continued to exercise it for nearly four centuries. Having succeeded to the marquisate on the death of his father in 1478, he expelled from Italy the Swiss who were besieging Lugano, joined the Milanese in a league against the pope in 1479, and in 1482 joined another league against Venice. He is said to have committed suicide.

Note 264, page 143. NICCOLÒ LEONICO TOMEO (born 1456; died 1531), was a native of Venice, and belonged to an Albanian family. He studied Greek under Chalcondylas at Florence, and for many years taught philosophy at Padua, being the first Italian to expound Aristotle from the original text. He wrote philosophical and moral dialogues and also some Italian verse. His friend Bembo wrote of him: "An illustrious philosopher both in life and learning, equally versed in Latin and Greek, wherein he lived and dwelt, leaving ambition and thirst for riches to others." He was also a wit.

Note 265, page 143. AGOSTINO FOGLIETTA (died 1527), was a Genoese nobleman, who exercised great authority at Rome under Leo X and Clement VII. He was a warm friend of Castiglione, who received cordial aid from him in the efforts that were made on behalf of Francesco Maria della Rovere. He was slain in the sack of Rome by a shot from an arquebuse. In other MS. versions of THE COURTIER the names of Fedra (Tommaso Inghirami) and Antonio di Tommaso appear in place of Foglietta's.

Note 266, page 143. GIOVANNI DI CARDONA was a Spanish soldier in the service of the "Great Captain" and of Cesare Borgia. He had a brother Ugo (mentioned at page 144, see note 271) and another brother Pedro, who was Count of Gosilano. Giovanni seems to have fallen at the battle of Ravenna in 1512.

Note 267, page 144. Of ALFONSO SANTACROCE nothing more is known than is contained in this mention of him in the text.

Note 268, page 144. Francesco Alidosi, CARDINAL OF PAVIA (died 1511), was descended from the Lords of Imola, being the second son of the Lord of Castel del Rio. Having been educated for the Church, he attached himself to Cardinal Giuliano della Rovere, whose lasting gratitude he won by steadfastly refusing to poison the cardinal at the desire of Alexander VI. On the accession of Julius II, he was rapidly promoted in spite of the objections raised in the consistory on the score of his questionable character. He was made Bishop of Miletus, Bishop of Pavia, a cardinal (1505), Legate of the Patrimony, Legate of Romagna, and Archbishop of Bologna. In these offices he proved violently tyrannical and a ruthless and bloody persecutor, especially of the Bolognese partisans of the Bentivogli; so that the city rose against him in 1511 and drove him out. His assassination by young Francesco Maria della Rovere has been already mentioned (see note 3). The odium connected with his name finds an echo also in another passage in the text, page 151.

Note 269, page 144. ALFONSO I of Naples (born 1385; died 1458), succeeded his father Ferdinand the Just as King of Aragon and Sicily in 1416, and in 1435 managed to enforce against René of Provence his double claim to Naples, based upon his descent from the former Hohenstauffen rulers of that kingdom, and also upon his adoption as heir by the last Angevin queen of Naples. Scholarly, enlightened, generous and benevolent, he was the ideal type of royal Mæcenas and the hero of his century. He often went afoot and alone about his capital, saying that "a father, walking amid his children, has naught to fear." On one occasion when a galley full of soldiers and sailors was about to sink, and the men he had ordered to their rescue were hesitating, he leaped into a skiff, crying, "I prefer to be the companion rather than a spectator of their death." When Constantinople fell into the hands of the Turks in 1453, he welcomed learned refugees to his capital; his court was a meeting-place for the savants of his time; and even when engaged in war, his captains might be seen gathered near their king, listening to his exposition of Livy instead of wasting their leisure at games of chance. He was noted also for his gentle disposition and merry humour and seems to have deserved his title of "the Magnanimous."

Note 270, page 144. The battle of Cerignola (a town in Apulia near Cannæ, the scene of one of Hannibal's victories) was fought 28 April 1503, between the Spanish army under the "Great Captain" and the French forces of Louis XII, and resulted in the defeat of the latter with the loss of more than half their men.

Note 271, page 144. UGO DI CARDONA, a brother of the Giovanni already mentioned, was a Spanish soldier who fought under Cesare Borgia and the "Great Captain," and was killed by the hand of Francis I at the battle of Pavia in 1525.

Note 272, page 145. This is a corruption of the name of St. Erasmus, a Syrian bishop who suffered martyrdom about 304, and became a favourite saint among the sailors on the Mediterranean. His name is given to certain electrical phenomena often seen at sea and on land also.

Note 273, page 145. OTTAVIANO UBALDINI (died 1498), was the son of a famous condottiere, Bernardino Ubaldini, and Aura di Montefeltro, a sister of Duke Federico. His father having died in 1437, he was bred at the court of Urbino and became the trusted counsellor of his uncle Federico, who left to him the guardianship of the young duke Guidobaldo. To personal valour and address in statecraft he united (if we may trust the rhymed chronicle of Raphael's father) a knowledge of classic literature, and a taste for music and the other fine arts. He is known to have been a zealous cultivator of astrology. By some writers Duke Federico (the circumstances of whose birth were not free from mystery) was believed to have been an Ubaldini, and this Ottaviano was openly regarded as his brother.

Note 274, page 145. ANTONELLO DA FORLI was a soldier of fortune who died before May 1488, and of whom little seems to be known apart from this anecdote. It is found also in two other books, where the witty Florentine is named as Cosimo de' Medici.

Note 275, page 145. San Leo was a fortress perched on an almost inaccessible crag eighteen miles north-west of Urbino. It is mentioned by Dante (*Purgatorio*, iv, 25) and also by Machiavelli (Art of War, iv) as a place of great natural strength. When in the spring of 1502 Cesare Borgia disclosed his hostile designs against Duke Guidobaldo, the latter, knowing that he could not hold out at Urbino, retired to San Leo, but soon afterwards fled in the garb of a peasant, and the castle was surrendered. In the same year, however, it was recaptured by stratagem. In the spring of 1503 it was besieged by the adherents of Borgia, and bravely defended for six months by Ottaviano Fregoso and the castellan Lattanzio da Bergamo (referred to in the text), in the hope of succour from Guidobaldo, who had taken refuge at Venice. Cian says that the place at last fell and was not again recovered by Guidobaldo until after the death of Alexander VI. On the other hand Dennistoun (ii, 13) asserts that by a reinforcement of twenty-five men the castle was enabled to hold out until Guidobaldo's restoration; he assigns the incident in the text to the first capture (1502), gives the name of the castellan as Scarmiglione da Foglino, and affirms that the surrender was treacherous.

⁄⁄⁄⁄⁄⁄⁄⁄⁄⁄⁄⁄⁄⁄⁄⁄⁄⁄⁄⁄⁄⁄⁄⁄⁄⁄⁄⁄⁄⁄⁄⁄⁄⁄⁄⁄⁄⁄⁄⁄⁄⁄⁄⁄⁄⁄⁄⁄⁄⁄⁄⁄⁄⁄⁄⁄⁄⁄

Note 276, page 145. DUKE VALENTINO, i.e. Cesare Borgia, Duke of Valentinois (born 1478; died 1507), was an openly acknowledged son of Cardinal Roderigo Borgia (afterwards Alexander VI) by Rosa Vanozza, who was the mother also of Cesare's sister Lucrezia. Created a cardinal on his father's accession, he procured the murder of his brother Giovanni in 1497, resigned his cardinalate the same year, was given the French duchy of Valentinois in 1498, and married Charlotte d'Albret, daughter of the King of Navarre, in 1499. Having been created Duke of Romagna by his father in 1501, he proceeded to reduce the various fiefs comprised within his intended domain, including the duchy of Urbino. After the death of Alexander VI, Cesare was held in captivity by Julius II and by Ferdinand the Catholic, escaped to his father-in-law's court in 1506, and fell in battle the following year, the very day after the close of the Courtier dialogues. Handsome, accomplished and subtle, he was a patron of learning and an adept in the cruel and perfidious politics of his day. Upon his public career is founded the famous *Principe* of Machiavelli, who says: "If all the duke's achievements are considered, it will be found that he built up a great superstructure for his future power; nor do I know what precepts I could furnish to a prince better than such as are to be derived from his example."

Note 277, page 146. Literally: "It must be believed to have been in despair."

Note 278, page 146. PUBLIUS CORNELIUS SCIPIO NASICA (Scipio with the pointed nose), was an eminent Roman jurist who was Consul in 191 B.C., and own cousin of Scipio Africanus the Elder.

Note 279, page 146. ALONSO CARILLO is said by Cian to have been one of the many Spaniards who lived at Rome in the service of popes and cardinals belonging to that nation. The Spanish annotator Fabié identifies him as a son of Don Luis and Donna Costanza de Rivera.

Note 280, page 146. MY LADY BOADILLA. Cian's identification of this lady as Beatriz Fernandez de Bobadilla, Marchioness of Moya, is confirmed by the fact that Boscan's translation (1534) gives her name as the Marchioness of Moya instead of 'my lady Boadilla.' She and her husband are warmly mentioned in a codicil to Isabella the Catholic's will, as being among that queen's most dear and faithful friends.

Note 281, page 147. In this passage, Antonio Ciccarelli's expurgated edition (1584) substitutes "a painter of antiquity" for Raphael, "certain

Roman senators" for the two cardinals, and Romulus and Remus for St. Peter and St. Paul. The picture in question has been identified as one painted by Raphael in 1513-14 for the church of San Silvestro.

Note 282, page 147. 'Aught else . . . upon thy shoulders,' i.e. a head. The Cato referred to was probably MARCUS PORCIUS CATO UTICENSIS, (born 95 B.C., died 46 B.C.), the Roman philosopher and patriot who espoused the cause of Pompey, and committed suicide on hearing of Cæsar's victory at Thapsus.

Note 283, page 148. This queen must have been Isabella the Catholic; see note 391.

Note 284, page 148. RAFAELLO DE' PAZZI (born 1471; died 1512), was a native of Florence, but was bred away from his home, doubtless owing to the proscription of his family for participation in the Pazzi conspiracy against Lorenzo and Giuliano de' Medici. Having fought for Cesare Borgia and later for Julius II, he was captured by the French in 1511, and was slain the following year in the battle of Ravenna.

Note 285, page 148. THE PRIOR OF MESSINA is now identified by Cian as a Spanish soldier, Don Pedro de Cuña, who was killed at the battle of Ravenna in 1512.

Note 286, page 148. Of PAOLO TOLOSA nothing more is known than is contained in the text.

Note 287, page 149. Like purple in Roman times, rose was the aristocratic colour at this period. Cosimo is reported by Machiavelli (*Storia Fiorentina*, vii, 6) to have said that "two ells of rose-coloured cloth make a man of quality."

Note 288, page 149. GIANOTTO DE' PAZZI is regarded by Cian as possibly identical with a certain Florentine, Giovanni de' Pazzi, who was born in 1476 and died in 1528.

Note 289, page 149. Of ANTONIO RIZZO nothing more is known than is contained in the text.

Note 290, page 149. 'The renunciation of a benefice,' i.e. the notarial deed or testament by which a priest resigned his benefice or prebend in favour of someone else.

Note 291, page 149. ANTONIO TORELLO (died 1536), was private chamberlain to Julius II and Leo X, who conferred a canonry and several prebends upon him in 1514. In the briefs he is designated as a priest of the diocese of Foglino, and is given certain benefices there, which had fallen vacant on the death of another priest. We thus infer that Torello must have been familiar with the subject referred to in the text. He was made a Roman citizen in 1530.

Note 292, page 149. These two hunchbacks have not been identified. "The Wheel" (*la Ruota* or *Rota della Giustizia*, or simply *la Rota*) was the highest civil and criminal court of Rome prior to 1870. Its name may have originated in the circular arrangement of the judges' (auditors') seats (compare the *hemicyclium* of Cicero's time), or possibly in a wheel-shaped porphyry figure set in the pavement of the hall where they sat. The play is of course on the double meaning of the word *torto*, crooked, wrong.

Note 293, page 149. LATINO GIOVENALE DE' MANETTI (born 1486; died 1553), was a native of Rome, and a canon of St. Peter's, but being of minor rank he had a wife and children. He held various offices, including that of Commissary General of Roman Antiquities, and was employed in several papal embassies. A writer of Latin and Italian verse, he was a friend of Castiglione, Bembo and Bibbiena, and is mentioned in the autobiography of Cellini, who says that he "had a pretty big dash of the fool in him,"—apparently because he presumed to improve one of the sculptor's designs for a crucifix.

Note 294, page 149. PERALTA is regarded by Cian as probably identical with a certain Captain Luijse Galliego de Peralta, who bore a letter (1521) from Castiglione at Rome to the Marquess Federico of Mantua, then fighting against the French. In this letter Castiglione speaks of having known Peralta for years as "a man of character and a valiant." Cian regards him as identical also with a certain Colonel Peralta, whose death at the battle of Frosinone is mentioned (in a letter of 1526) among those of other Spaniards.

MOLART is identified by Cian as the French soldier of fortune, "Molard," who commanded a battalion of Gascons at the battle of Ravenna (11 April 1512), and who fell there bravely fighting by the side of Gaston de Foix.

ALDANA afterwards served under the Marquess of Mantua at Pavia in 1522, having been summoned (as was Castiglione also) from Rome at the head of his company.

Note 295, page 150. The duel in question is thus described by Branthome in his Discourse on Duels. "The Grand Master de Chaumont, the King's Lieutenant in the State of Milan, also allowed a duel to two Spaniards who had asked it of him. The name of one was Signor Peralta, who had formerly been in the King of France's service, . . . and the other Spaniard was called Captain Aldana. Their combat was on horse, *à la genette* (jennet), with rapier and dagger and three darts to each man. Peralta's second was another Spaniard, and Aldana's was the gentle Captain Molart. It had snowed so much that their encounter took place in the Piazza at Parma, from which the snow had been cleared, and there being no other barriers than the snow, each of the two combatants did his duty right well. And at last my lord de Chaumont, who had appointed the ground and was umpire, caused them to retire with equal honour."

Note 296, page 150. Cian inclines to regard this Master MARCAN-TONIO as identical with a certain eccentric physician of the same name, who lived at Urbino and was the author of a fantastic law book and a long comedy. Of BOTTONE DA CESENA nothing more is known than is contained in the text.

Note 297, page 150. 'Three sticks,' i.e. the gallows.

Note 298, page 150. Of the three persons bearing the name ANDREA COSCIA and known to have lived at this time, it is uncertain which one is here referred to.

Note 299, page 150. A MS. copy of THE COURTIER contains the following passage: "Again a Venetian (forgive me, messer Pietro), coming to visit my lady Maddalena, sister to my lady Duchess,—as soon as he was near he offered her his hand, but without removing his cap. My lady Maddalena drew back a step, and drew back her hand too, saying: 'Gentle Sir, put on your cap; cover your head.' He still advanced and offered his hand; whereupon she replied: 'I will never do it, unless you cover.' Thus the poor man was so put to shame that he at last removed his cap." Under similar circumstances Madame Bernhardt is said to have reproved Edward VII (then Prince of Wales) by feigning not to recognize him with his hat on.

Note 300, page 150. MY LORD CARDINAL, i.e. Giovanni de' Medici, afterwards Leo X (born 1475; died 1521). He was the second son of Lorenzo de' Medici and Clarice Orsini, and an elder brother of the Magnifico of THE COURTIER. Made a cardinal at the age of thirteen, and exiled from Florence with the rest of his family in 1494, he was present at the election of Alexander VI, of whose character he is said to have shown true appreciation at the time by remarking: "We are in the wolf's jaws; he will gulp us down, unless we make good our flight." During the reign of Julius II, he seems to have been subservient to that pontiff, and in 1511 was a member of the court of six cardinals which acquitted the young Duke of Urbino of the charge of murdering Cardinal Alidosi. The pontificates of Alexander and Julius had exhausted Italy with wars, and the Christian world, weary of their scandalous violence, hailed with relief the accession of the cultivated and seemingly gentle young prelate, Giovanni de' Medici. Of his reign,—so brilliant in art and letters, so disastrous to the Church,—it is enough to say that the key is found in the famous phrase with which, on his elevation to the Chair of St. Peter, he greeted his brother Giuliano: "Let us enjoy the Papacy, since God hath given it us." To him the immortality of the soul was an open topic for debate, while he regarded sound Latinity and a ready tongue as more important than true doctrine and pure living. Sincerely zealous for the diffusion of liberal knowledge, he was extravagantly munificent to artists, scholars and authors. Like all his family, after the first Cosimo, he was a poor financier, and on his sudden death he was found to have pawned the very jewels of his tiara. His reckless expenditure led to the sale of indulgences, and thus in no small degree to the progress of the Reformation.

Note 301, page 150. BIAGINO CRIVELLO was one of Duke Ludovico Sforza's captains, and is mentioned (July 1500) in a list of Sforza adherents who had rebelled against Louis XII, and whose possessions were declared forfeit. The list speaks of him as keeping himself at Mantua and in Venetian territory, and as owning no attachable property in the Milanese. In April of the same year an ineffectual demand had been made upon the Marquess of Mantua for the surrender of Crivello and other chiefs of the Sforza party.

Note 302, page 150. THE DUKE, i.e. Ludovico Sforza, "Il Moro" (born 1451; died 1508), was the fourth son of the Francesco Sforza whom Duke Federico of Urbino had helped to become Duke of Milan (and whose father, a peasant condottiere, Muzio Attendolo, became known as Sforza by reason of great personal strength),—and of Bianca Maria, a daughter of the last Visconti duke of Milan. Early noted for his physical and mental qualities, Ludovico read and wrote Latin fluently, had a tenacious memory, and was a ready speaker. He was tall and of strongly marked features. Unlike his horrible brother Galeazzo Maria, he shunned bloodshed. Banished from Milan after his brother's assassination in 1476, he returned in triumph in 1479, and assumed the guardianship of his nephew Giangaleazzo, for whom he chose as bride his sister's child, Isabella (see note 396), daughter of Alfonso II of Naples. Having first sought the hand of Isabella d'Este (see note 397),—who was already betrothed to the Marquess of Mantua,—in 1491 he married her younger sister Beatrice (see note 398), whose influence is by some said to have led him to aggravate the humiliation of his young nephew and niece, the rightful duke and duchess. Being threatened by the latter's father, the King of Naples, Ludovico invited Charles VIII to enter Italy (1494) and assert the Angevine claim to Naples. His unhappy nephew died the same year, not without suspicion of having been poisoned by the uncle's order, who thereupon assumed the title as well as the despotic power of duke. Becoming alarmed at the rapid success of the French in Italy, he joined the league formed against them, and was afterwards punished for his treachery by being expelled from Milan by Louis XII and carried to France. It is said that at the time of his capture, the only favour he asked was to be allowed the use of a volume of Dante. He died a prisoner in the Castle of Loches, where, after a vain effort to escape, he was confined in an underground dungeon. At the height of his prosperity his revenues exceeded those of any Italian state except Venice. Policy and also his natural taste for intellectual pleasures led him to copy the Medici in their patronage of art and letters. He aspired to make his capital a modern Athens, and sought to attract men of fame and talent from far and wide. Both Leonardo da Vinci and the architect Bramante were in his pay.

Note 303, page 151. Cervia is a little town on the Adriatic (between Ravenna and Rimini). A Dominican, Tommaso Cattanei, was bishop of the diocese from 1486 to 1509. The pope referred to in the text was Julius II.

Note 304, page 152. 'Montefiore Inn' was a proverbial expression for a bad hostelry. The rustic inns of Italy at this period were usually wretched and for the most part kept by Germans.

Note 305, page 153. One ANDREA CASTILLO was secretary to Leo X, and died in 1545.

Note 306, page 154. Cian identifies this CARDINAL BORGIA as the Francesco (born 1441; died 1511) who was raised to the purple by Alexander VI, and was known as a schismatic.

Note 307, page 154. The modern form of *ballatore* is *ballerino*. Although the distinction is not free from doubt, there seems to be reason for believing that *danzare* was the term applied to the more stately forms of dance, while *ballare* was reserved for more animated movements. See note 147.

Note 308, page 154. The Bergamasque was and still is regarded as the rudest and most rustic of the Italian dialects.

Note 309, page 155. Except as applied to a small Tuscan stream or torrent (flowing near Acquapendente and Orvieto, and finally tributary to the Tiber), the name Paglia does not occur in modern Italian geography. In his autobiography, Cellini mentions crossing the little stream on his first journey from Siena to Rome. Later in the 16th century, Montaigne records (in his diary of a trip into Italy) having spent the night at *"La Paille"* (Italian, *Paglia*), and describes it as "a small village of five or six houses at the foot of several barren and ill-favoured mountains."

Note 310, page 155. They seem to have been playing *primero* (the modern *primiera*), a game much in vogue at this time.

Note 311, page 156. Loreto is a small hill town near Ancona, and is celebrated for its pilgrimage shrine of the Sacred House (*Santa Casa*), which was reputed to have been the veritable dwelling of the Virgin, miraculously transported by angels from Nazareth, and set down in Italy in 1294. In 1511 and again in 1524 Castiglione wrote to his mother that he was preparing to go to Our Lady of Loreto in fulfilment of a vow. The name was said to be derived from that of the widow upon whose land the house was deposited by the angels.

Note 312, page 156. Acquapendente is the name of a small town sixty-seven miles north-west of Rome.

Note 313, page 156. MONSIGNOR OF SAN PIETRO AD VINCULA was the title of Cardinal Galeotto della Rovere; see note 189.

Note 314, page 157. MONSIGNOR OF ARAGON was the title of Cardinal Ludovico of Aragon (born 1474), a natural son of Ferdinand I of Naples, and a half-brother of Alfonso II (see note 31) and Federico III of Naples (see note 401). He was not elevated to the purple until 1519; Castiglione's mention of him as a cardinal in dialogues supposed

ナイイイイイイイイイイイイイイイイイイイイイイイイイイイイイイイイイイイイイイイイイイイイイイイイイイイイイ

to take place twelve years earlier, doubtless arose from a natural confusion between the time when and the time of which they were written

Note 315, page 157. 'The *Banchi*' (Banks) was the name of a street in Rome well known in the 15th and 16th centuries. Containing the offices of the papal Curia and magistrates, it became a preferred neighbourhood, and was enriched with fine buildings, among which was the counting-house of Julius II's finance minister, Agostino Chigi, the greatest banker of his day.

Note 316, page 157. 'The Chancery' (*Cancelleria*) was at this time used for public offices and as the residence of Cardinal Galeotto della Rovere. In the *Rassegna d'Arte*, 1902, pp. 69-71, E. Bernich discusses the question as to who was its architect.

Note 317, page 157. San Celso was the name of a street and church near the Banks. The saint (Celsus) whose memory is thus perpetuated was born at what is now Cimiez, near Nice, suffered martyrdom at Rome under Nero, and was finally put to death (together with his master, St. Nazarius) at Milan in the year 69.

Note 318, page 158. CESARE BECCADELLO is regarded by Cian as possibly identical with a certain Bolognese, who was the son of Domenico Maria Beccadello, married Landomia Fasanini, and was living at the papal court as late as 1559. The Spanish annotator Fabié suggests that he was the father (1502) of the author Ludovico Beccadello, who was a follower of Bembo and wrote biographies of Petrarch and others.

Note 319, page 159. These are characters occurring in the third, sixth and ninth tales of the Eighth Day, and in the fifth tale of the Ninth Day.

Note 320, page 159. This knavish student seems to be identical with a certain CAIO CALORIA PONZIO, who was born at Messina. Of his life little more is known than that he studied law at Padua between 1479 and 1488, and, after residing two years at Venice, returned to Sicily. For an account of a short poem by him in praise of Venice, and of his dialect comedy dedicated to the Marquess of Mantua, see Vittorio Rossi's *Caio Caloria Ponzio, e la poesia volgare letteraria di Sicilia nel Secolo XV*, reprinted (Palermo, 1893) from the *Archivio Storico Siciliano*, N. S., A., xviii.

ʃʃʃʃʃʃʃʃʃʃʃʃʃʃʃʃʃʃʃʃʃʃʃʃʃʃʃʃʃʃʃʃʃʃʃʃʃʃʃʃʃʃʃʃʃʃʃʃʃʃ

Note 321, page 159. The only belfry at Padua answering to this description is said to be that of San Giacomo.

Note 322, page 159. GONNELLA. This name was borne by two famous jesters employed by the d'Este family. The one here referred to was probably the later of the two, who lived at the courts of Dukes Niccolò III and Borso, was the son of a Florentine glover Bernardo Gonnella, and married one Checca Lapi. The next buffoon referred to was probably LUDOVICO MELIOLO, who acted as steward to the court of Mantua about 1500, and was a brother of the goldsmith and sculptor Bartolommeo Meliolo (1448-1514). He was called "the father of jests."

Note 323, page 160. This is an instance of the use of the word *calunnia* (rendered 'imputation') in its primitive sense of malicious accusation without reference to truth or falsity.

Note 324, page 161. These characters occur in the sixth tale of the Third Day, and in the seventh and eighth tales of the Seventh Day of Boccaccio's "Decameron."

Note 325, page 162. The queen here mentioned is of course Isabella the Catholic; see note 391.

Note 326, page 162. Fabié says that this COUNTESS OF CASTAGNETA was Brazaida de Almada, daughter of a Portuguese cavalier Juan Baez de Almada and Violante de Castro (of the same nation). She was a lady-in-waiting to Queen Isabella, and her husband Don Garci Fernandez Manrique (third Count of Castagneta and first Marquess of Aguilar) took part in the conquest of Granada.

Note 327, page 164. If unconvinced by the "Decameron," readers of the *Corbaccio* will surely be persuaded of the justice of this opinion.

Note 328, page 165. According to one form of the legend of Orpheus, his grief at the final loss of his wife Eurydice, when his lyre had all but enabled him to recover her from Hades, led him to treat contemptuously the Thracian women, who avenged the insult by tearing him to pieces under the excitement of their Bacchanalian orgies.

Note 329, page 165. 'Braccesque leave' (*una licentia bracciesca* in the Aldine folio of 1528, and *una licentia Bracciesca* in the more correctly printed Aldine folio of 1545) is a phrase derived from the name

↗↗↗↗↗↗↗↗↗↗↗↗↗↗↗↗↗↗↗↗↗↗↗↗↗↗↗↗↗↗↗↗↗↗↗↗↗↗↗↗↗↗↗↗↗↗↗↗↗↗↗↗↗

of Braccio Fortebracci, a captain who was famous for his violence to friend and foe, and whose followers were called Bracceschi. To give a man Braccesque leave meant to dismiss him with blows.

Note 330, page 166. Although in this and a few other passages, Castiglione uses *virtù* in the sense of our "virtue," he more often gives it its etymological meaning of "manliness," which the present translator has generally rendered by "worth." In considering a word like this, we must take into account the character of him who uses it. To Machiavelli, as no doubt to most of his contemporaries in Italy, *virtù* meant simply that combination of strength, courage, tenacity and cunning that enables a man to achieve his ends,—whether good or bad.

# NOTES TO THE THIRD BOOK OF THE COURTIER

Note 331, page 169. Achaia, here used as synonymous with Greece, was the name given to that country when conquered by the Romans and made a province. Olympia was not in Achaia proper, but in the adjoining district of Elis, some forty miles south of the modern Patras. The site has been thoroughly excavated by German archæologists, the most noted discovery being that of the "Hermes" of Praxiteles and the "Victory" of Pæonius.

Note 332, page 170. That is to say, nude. According to the familiar Greek myth, Eris (goddess of discord), to avenge her exclusion from the nuptials of Peleus and Thetis, threw among the wedding guests a golden apple inscribed "To the Fairest." A dispute arising between Aphrodite, Hera and Athena concerning the apple, Zeus appointed the shepherd Paris to decide their claims. The prize having been awarded to Aphrodite, she aided Paris to carry off the beautiful Helen of Sparta, and thus gave rise to the Trojan War.

Note 333, page 171. The Order of St. Michael was instituted in August 1469, by Louis XI of France, and was highly esteemed down to Castiglione's time, but later suffered in estimation, owing to the freedom with which membership was bestowed. Francis I wore the insignia of the order at the battle of Pavia, 1525.

Note 334, page 171. The Order of the Garter was instituted by Edward III of England in 1344. He assigned to its use the chapel (at Windsor) of St. George, who was its patron saint. Duke Guidobaldo of Urbino having, like his father, been made a knight of the order, Castiglione went to England in 1506 to receive the insignia on the duke's behalf.

Note 335, page 171. The Order of the Golden Fleece was instituted by Duke Philip the Good of Burgundy (paternal grandfather of Charles V's paternal grandmother) in 1429 in honour of his third marriage, to Elizabeth of Portugal. Its badge, a golden ram, is shown in the portraits of Charles V and Maximilian I, given in the first (1901) edition of this translation.

Note 336, page 171. The king of Persia at this time was Ismail Sufi I (born 1480; died 1524). He was descended from a family of noted piety, whose peculiar beliefs became the origin of the national Persian faith. Having been proclaimed shah in 1499, after nearly a century of disorderly government by the successors of Timur the Tartar, he spent most of his reign in enlarging and assuring his dominions, and founded the dynasty that was to rule Persia until 1736. He waged an unsuccessful war with Selim I of Turkey, the son and successor of Bajazet II, and died while on a pilgrimage to his own father's tomb. His subjects revered him as a saint.

Note 337, page 172. The 'Lady whom I know' is of course the Duchess.

Note 338, page 173. PYGMALION will be remembered as the legendary sculptor-king of Cyprus, who fell in love with an ivory statue that he had made of a beautiful girl, and prayed to Aphrodite to breathe life into it. His prayer being granted, he married the girl, who was called Galatea.

Note 339, page 179. The opinions here ascribed to Plato, are found in the Fifth Book of his "Republic," but seem to have undergone serious change when he wrote his "Laws."

Note 340, page 180. The comparative merits of man and woman were much discussed in Greek antiquity and during the Renaissance, and form the subject of a copious literature in which Castiglione's contribution occupies no unimportant place.

Note 341, page 182. The reference here is to a fragment of the so-called Orphic Hymns, beginning: "Jove the End, Jove the Beginning, Jove the Middle, all things are of Jove: Jove Male, Immortal Virgin Jove." In this and other respects the theogony to which the name of Orpheus is attached, is closely related to the most ancient religious systems of India.

Note 342, page 183. The author probably refers to Aristotle's Tenth Problem.

Note 343, page 186. The reference here is doubtless to Jerome's 54th Epistle (on Widowhood), and to his first tract against Jovinianus, both written about 394 A.D. He was born in what is now the Hungarian town of Stridon about 340, and died in a monastery at Bethlehem 420 A.D. Perhaps his best remembered work is the Vulgate or Latin translation of the Bible.

Note 344, page 187. "If not chastely, then discreetly."

Note 345, page 188. OCTAVIA (born 70; died 11 B.C.), was a great-niece of Julius Cæsar, and became the second wife of the triumvir Mark Antony for the purpose (ultimately vain) of cementing the alliance between him and her brother Augustus. Her beauty, accomplishments and virtues proved unavailing against the wiles of Cleopatra, who induced Antony to divorce her. After Antony's death, she remained true to the interests of his children, including those by his first wife and by Cleopatra. Through the two daughters that she bore to Antony, she became the grandmother of the Emperor Claudius, and great-grandmother of his predecessor Caligula and of his successor Nero.

Note 346, page 188. PORCIA's first husband was Marcus Bibulus, who was Consul with Cæsar in 59 B.C. She inherited her father's republican principles, courage and firm will, and was her second husband Brutus's confidante in the conspiracy against Cæsar. On his death at Philippi in 42 B.C., she put an end to her life.

Note 347, page 188. CAIA CÆCILIA TANAQUIL appears in Roman legend as the second wife of King Tarquinius Priscus, endowed with prophetic powers, closely connected with the worship of the hearth-deity, expert in healing, and a model of domestic virtues. The traditional date of her husband's reign is 616-578 B.C.

Note 348, page 188. CORNELIA, the mother of the Gracchi (born about 189 B.C.; died about 110 B.C.), wrote letters that had survived in Cicero's day and were prized for their style. Even in her own lifetime the Romans erected a statue in honour of her virtues. Left a widow with twelve young children, she devoted herself wholly to their training, and rejected all offers of marriage, including that of Ptolemy.

Note 349, page 183. Plutarch (from whose history the narrative in the text is a paraphrase) describes ALEXANDRA as being actuated in her regency solely by ambitious motives. Her husband, Alexander Jannæus, was the son of Johannes Hyrcanus and brother of Aristobulus I, whom he succeeded as second King of the Jews after the Babylonish Captivity. His reign (104-78 B.C.) was marked by atrocities.

Note 350, page 189. The reference here is to MITHRIDATES VI, Eupator, King (120-63 B.C.) of Pontus on the southern shore of the Black Sea. In the Life of Lucullus, Plutarch relates that having been utterly defeated by the Romans in 72 B.C., Mithridates gave order to have his wives Bernice and Monima put to death together with his sisters Statira and Roxana, in order to prevent them from falling into the hands of the enemy,—while he himself took refuge with his son-in-law. Statira is described by Plutarch as grateful to her brother for not forgetting her amid his own anxieties, and for providing her the means of an honourable death.

Note 351, page 189. This HASDRUBAL was the general of the Carthaginians in their last struggle with Rome. When Scipio captured Carthage in 146 B.C., Hasdrubal surrendered, while it is said that his wife, after upbraiding him for his weakness, flung herself and her children into the flames of the burning temple in which they had sought shelter.

Note 352, page 189. In fact, HARMONIA was Hiero's granddaughter, and the wife of a Syracusan named Themistus, who (after the death of Hiero in 215 B.C.) was chosen one of the leaders of the commonwealth and afterwards perished in a fresh revolution. Death was then decreed against all surviving members of Hiero's family, and Harmonia was slain together with her aunts, Demarata and Heraclea.

Note 353, page 189. The reference is of course to the familiar story of the obstinate dame who persisted in declaring that a certain rent had been made with scissors, and whose husband vainly tried to change her mind by plunging her in a pond. Each time she came to the surface, she cried "Scissors," until, unable to speak from strangulation, she stretched forth her hand and made the sign of the instrument with two fingers. In a coarser form, the story was current in Italy even before Castiglione's time.

Note 354, page 190. The conspiracy in question was discovered in 65 A.D. Tacitus relates that EPICHARIS strangled herself with her girdle while on the way to be tortured a second time.

Note 355, page 190. LEÆNA was an Athenian *hetaira* beloved by Aristogeiton. When he and Harmodius had slain the tyrant Hipparchus in 514 B.C., she was supposed to be privy to their plan, and died under torture. The statue in question is mentioned by Pausanias and said by Plutarch (in his essay on Garrulity) to have been placed "upon the gates of the Acropolis." Recent archæologists identify its site as being on the level of the Acropolis, near the southern inner corner of the Propylæa.

Note 356, page 190. Massilia became the modern Marseilles.

Note 357, page 190. This story is taken from the "Memorable Doings and Sayings" of Valerius Maximus (*flor*. 25 A.D.), in which Castiglione mistranslates the Latin word *publicè* (at the public charge) as *publicamente* (publicly).

Note 358, page 190. Of several persons of this name, the one here referred to was probably the Roman Consul (14 A.D.),—a patron of literature and a friend of Ovid. Had the Magnifico been allowed to finish his sentence, he would (following the narrative of Valerius Maximus) have doubtless added the name of a town in Asia Minor, Julida.

Note 359, page 193. This story (which was used by Tennyson for his play of "The Cup") is found in Plutarch's tract "Concerning Women's Virtue," where the scene is placed in Galatia, in Asia Minor.

Note 360, page 195. The number of the Sibyls is usually reckoned as ten: Persian (or Babylonian), Libyan, Phrygian, Delphian, Cimmerian, Erythræan, Samian, Trojan, Tiburtine, and Cumæan,—of which the last was the most famous.

Note 361, page 195. ASPASIA (*flor*. 440 B.C.), was born at Miletus in Asia Minor, but in her youth removed to Athens, where she was celebrated for her talents and beauty, and became the mistress of Pericles, one of whose orations she is said by Plato to have composed. Her house was the centre of intellectual society, and was even frequented by Athenian matrons and their husbands.

Note 362, page 195. DIOTIMA was a probably fictitious priestess of Mantinea in the Peloponnesus, reputed to have been the instructress of Socrates. Her supposed opinions as to the origin, nature and objects of life, form the subject of Plato's "Symposium."

Note 363, page 195. NICOSTRATE or Carmenta was a prophetic and healing divinity, supposed to be of Greek origin. Having tried to persuade her son Evander to kill his father Hermes, she fled with the boy to Italy, where she was said to have given the Roman form to the fifteen characters of the Greek alphabet that Evander introduced into Latium.

Note 364, page 195. This 'preceptress . . . to Pindar' was MYRTIS, a lyric poetess of the 6th century B.C. She is mentioned in a fragment by Corinna as having competed with Pindar. Statues were erected to her in various parts of Greece, and she was counted among the nine lyric muses.

Note 365, page 195. Of PINDAR's life little more is known than that he resided chiefly at Thebes, and that the dates of his birth and death were about 522 and 443 B.C. respectively. Practically all his extant poems are odes in commemoration of victories in the public games.

Note 366, page 195. The Greek poetess CORINNA (5th century B.C.) was a native of Tanagra in Bœotia. She is said to have won prizes five times in competition with Pindar. Only a few fragments of her verse remain.

Note 367, page 195. SAPPHO flourished about 600 B.C., and seems to have been born and to have lived chiefly at Mitylene. She enjoyed unique renown among the ancients: on hearing one of her poems, Solon prayed that he might not see death before he had learned it; Plato called her the Tenth Muse; and Aristotle placed her on a par with Homer. For a recently discovered and interesting fragment of her verse, see the Egypt Exploration Fund's "Oxyrhynchus Papyri," Part I, p. 11.

Note 368, page 196. Castiglione here follows Plutarch. Pliny, on the other hand, affirms that Roman women were obliged to kiss their male relatives, in order that it might be known whether they had transgressed the law forbidding them to drink wine.

Note 369, page 196. This paragraph is taken almost literally from Livy, excepting the incident of the babies borne in arms, which Castiglione seems to have invented.

Note 370, page 197. TITUS TATIUS was the legendary king of the Sabines. His forces were so strong that Romulus was driven back to the Saturnian Hill, which had previously been fortified and which became the site of the Capitol. The familiar story is to the effect that Tarpeia (daughter to the captain of the fortress), being dazzled by the Sabines'

*ffffffffffffffffffffffffffffffffffffffffffffffffffffffffff*
golden bracelets, promised to betray the hill to them if they would give
her the ornaments on their left arms. Accordingly she admitted the enemy
at night, but when she claimed her reward, they threw down upon her
the shields that they wore on the left arm, and thus crushed her to death.
Her infamy is preserved in the name of the neighbouring Tarpeian Rock,
from which traitors were flung down.

Note 371, page 197. There is said to be no historical mention of any
Roman temple to *Venus Armata*. Castiglione may have had in mind a
passage in the "Christian Cicero" (Lactantius Firmianus, who wrote about
300 A.D.), recording the dedication by the Spartans of a temple and
statue to the Armed Venus in memory of their women's brave repulse of
a sudden attack by the Messenians during the absence of the Spartan army.

Note 372, page 197. *Calva* (bald) was one of the Roman Venus's
most ancient epithets, under which she had two temples near the Capitol.
Of the several explanations of this appellation, Castiglione seems to refer
to the one which interprets it as the memorial of the Roman women's
heroism in cutting off their hair to make bow-strings for the men during
a siege by the Gauls.

Note 373, page 197. In his life of Camillus (died 365 B.C.),
Plutarch gives a legendary account of the origin of the Handmaidens'
Festival. At a time when the Romans were ill prepared for war, the
Latins sent to demand of them a number of free-born maidens in marriage. This was suspected as a trick to obtain hostages, but no method of
foiling it was devised until Tutula, a slave girl, advised the magistrates
to send her to the Latin camp along with some of the most beautiful
handmaidens in rich attire. This was done, and at night, when her companions had stolen away the enemies' weapons, Tutula displayed a signal
torch agreed on with the Romans, who at once sallied forth, easily captured the Latin camp, and put most of the enemy to the sword.

Note 374, page 197. The Romans are said to have wearied of
Cicero's self-praise for his suppression of the Catiline conspiracy (63
B.C.). The woman in question was a Roman patrician, Fulvia by name,
who was the mistress of one of the conspirators and divulged the plot
to Cicero.

Note 375, page 198. This DEMETRIUS (II) was grandson to the
Demetrius I already mentioned (see note 136), and ruled over Macedonia from about 239 to about 229 B.C. His son, PHILIP V (237-179

B.C.), joined Hannibal in a war against Rome, which finally ended in the downfall of the Macedonian monarchy and the captivity of his son **and** successor Perseus (167 B.C.). The incident mentioned in the text is narrated by Plutarch in his work on "Women's Virtue," as also is the instance next cited by Castiglione, who however reverses the order of events.

Note 376, page 198. Erythræ was an important city on the west coast of Asia Minor opposite Chios. The nearest approach to 'Leuconia' in ancient geography is the distant town Leuconum in what is now Slavonia, between the Danube and the Save.

Note 377, page 198. Plutarch's version of this story adds that in honour of the Persian women's bravery on this occasion, Cyrus (559-529 B.C.) decreed that whenever the king returned from a long journey, each woman should receive a ring of gold.

Note 378, page 199. One of Plutarch's minor works is entitled "Apothegms and Famous Sayings of Spartan Women," and Castiglione's contemporary Marcantonio Casanova wrote two Latin distiches on "The Spartan Mother Slaying Her Son."

Note 379, page 199. Saguntum, the modern Murviedro, was a city of Greek origin on the eastern coast of Spain. After a desperate siege of nearly eight months, it was captured by Hannibal in 219 B.C.

Note 380, page 199. The reference here is to the victory, at Vercelli near Milan, by which the Roman general CAIUS MARIUS repelled the advance of the Cimbri into Italy, 101 B.C. The sacred fire (supposed to have been brought from Troy by Æneas as the symbol of Vesta, the hearth deity) was kept alive at Rome by six virgins.

Note 381, page 199. AMALASONTHA (498-535 A.D.), was the daughter of Theodoric the Great, and regent of the East Gothic kingdom from his death in 526 until her own. After a prosperous reign she is said to have been strangled by her cousin and second husband Theodatus, at the instigation of the Empress Theodora, the wife of Justinian.

Note 382, page 199. THEODOLINDA, daughter of Duke Garibald of Bavaria, married (589 A.D.) Autharis, King of the Lombards, and on his death in the following year, she married Duke Agilulph of Turin, who was proclaimed king in 591. She died in 625, after exercising the regency in the name of her son. Her virtue, wisdom and beauty were extolled; she was active in her labours on behalf of Christianity; and she carried on a correspondence with St. Gregory, who was pope from 590 to 604.

Note 383, page 199. The THEODORA here referred to is doubtless the wife, not of Justinian, but of Theophilus, Emperor of Constantinople 829-842. She died in 867, and was canonized by the Greek Church.

Note 384, page 199. COUNTESS MATILDA (1046-1115), one of the most famous heroines of the Middle Ages, was the daughter of Duke Boniface of Tuscany and Beatrice of Lorraine. She ruled over Tuscany and a large part of northern Italy, espoused the papal cause against the Emperor, and exercised an important influence upon the politics of her time. She was noted also for her religious zeal, energy, and austere yet gentle and cultivated life. Count Ludovico's supposed descent from her paternal uncle Conrad is now regarded as doubtful.

Note 385, page 200. Among the eminent women here referred to, we may note: Duke Guidobaldo's grandfather's wife, Caterina Colonna, (died 1438), who was a great-aunt of Vittoria Colonna, and was praised as "noble, beautiful, discreet, charming, gentle and generous;" his great-aunt Battista di Montefeltro, (died 1450), who, having been deserted by her worthless Malatesta husband, wrote moral essays and poetry, and was celebrated for her piety and mental gifts, as well as for her learning and literary accomplishments; his aunt, Brigida Sueva di Montefeltro, (born 1428), who, after enduring for twelve years the brutalities of her Sforza husband, became an abbess and ultimately received the honour of beatification,—her remains being revered as a sacred relic; another aunt of his, Violante di Montefeltro, (born 1430), who was famous for her talents and beauty; his maternal grandmother, Costanza da Varano, (born 1428), was a granddaughter of the Battista above mentioned, inherited much of that lady's taste for learning, became the associate of scholars and philosophers, wrote Latin orations, epistles and poems, and (by her marriage to a brother of the first Sforza duke of Milan) became the mother of Duke Guidobaldo's own mother, Battista Sforza, (born 1446), who rivalled her ancestresses' attainments, administered her husband's government judiciously during his frequent absences, and was regarded as beautiful, although tiny in person.

Note 386, page 200. Perhaps the most famous woman of the Gonzaga family was "my lady Duchess's" great-aunt, Cecilia Gonzaga, (born

1415), who shared with her four brothers the tuition of the celebrated Vittorino da Feltre, wrote Greek with remarkable purity at the age of ten, became a nun at nineteen, devoted her life to religious and literary exercises, and was regarded as one of the most learned women of her time. Her niece (?), Barbara Gonzaga, (born about 1455), was educated with especial care, became Duchess of Würtemberg, induced her husband to found the University of Tübingen, and ruled the duchy as regent after his death.

Of the Este family, two aunts (Ginevra, born 1419, and Bianca Maria, born 1440) of Isabella and Beatrice d'Este (see notes 397 and 398), were famous for their knowledge of Latin and Greek, in which languages the younger wrote both prose and verse, besides being an accomplished musician, dancer and needlewoman.

Of the Pio family, Castiglione doubtless had in mind the celebrated Alda Pia da Carpi, who was a sister of Aldus's pupil and patron Alberto Pio, aunt of Count Ludovico Pio of THE COURTIER (see note 46), and mother of the still more celebrated poetess Veronica Gambara, (born 1485).

Note 387, page 200. ANNE DE BRETAGNE (born 1476; died 1514), was the daughter and heiress of Duke Francis II of Brittany, which became permanently united to the crown of France through her marriages to Charles VIII (1492) and Louis XII (1499). Castiglione's praise of her seems to have been in the main justified. Although sometimes vindictive, she was generous, virtuous beyond the standard of her time, and carried cultivation to the verge of pedantry. She surrounded herself with artists, historians, minstrels and poets, and formed a collection of MSS. and other precious objects, largely the spoils of her husbands' Italian campaigns. Branthôme called her "the worthiest and most honourable queen that has been since Queen Blanche, mother of the king St. Louis, and so wise and virtuous."

Note 388, page 200. CHARLES VIII (born 1470; died 1498), was the son of Louis XI and Charlotte of Savoy. Having succeeded his father in 1483, and assumed royal power in 1491, he married Anne of Brittany and soon set about enforcing his pretensions to the crown of Naples, transmitted to him through his father and cousin from René of Provence, to whom the last Angevine ruler had devised the kingdom in 1435. As we have seen, the immediate cause of the invasion of Italy (1494) was a request from Duke Ludovico Sforza of Milan and Pope Alexander VI. Although the expedition was undertaken without adequate preparation and conducted with incredible foolhardiness,—continuous good fortune together with the mutual jealousies of Italian princes and the decadence of Italian military power enabled Charles to enter Milan, Florence and Rome without hindrance, to seize Naples almost unopposed, and (when threatened by a powerful league formed against him) to retire northwards, to defeat the Italians at Fornovo, and finally to reach France in safety, October 1495. His garrisons were driven from Naples in the following year, but his foray had the immediate result of expelling the Medici from Florence, and the far more important consequence of revealing to the rest of Europe the wealth and helplessness of Italy,—thus paving the way for the subsequent invasions with which the peninsula was scourged during the 16th century. The remainder of Charles's life was given up to inglorious ease and pleasure. A son of the painter Mantegna thus describes him: "A very ill-favoured face, with great goggle eyes, an aquiline nose offensively large, and a head disfigured by a few sparse hairs;" while Duke Ludovico Sforza said of him: "The man is young, and his conduct meagre, nor has he any form or method of council." His own ambassador, Commines, wrote: "He was little in stature and of small sense, very timid in speech, owing to the way in which he had been treated as a child, and as feeble in mind as he was in body, but the kindest and gentlest creature alive."

Note 389, page 200. MARGARITA OF AUSTRIA (born 1480; died 1530), was the daughter of the Emperor Maximilian I and Mary of Burgundy, and a native of Brussels. Having been betrothed to the Dauphin Charles (VIII) and then rejected by that prince in favour of Anne of Brittany, she married (1497) the Infant Juan of Castile, but soon lost both husband and child. In 1501 she married Duke Filiberto of Savoy, and after four years of happiness again became a widow. In 1507 she was entrusted by her father with the government of the Low Countries and the care of her nephew Charles (see note 462). She did much to further the progress of agriculture and commerce in her dominions, and besides showing a lofty spirit and no little political sagacity, she was a patroness of art and letters, and composed a great number of poems in French, most of which are said to be lost. Her correspondence with her father has been published.

Note 390, page 200. MAXIMILIAN I, Emperor of Germany (born 1459; died 1519), was the son of the Emperor Frederick III of Hapsburg and Eleanora of Portugal. In 1477 he married Charles the Bold's daughter and heiress, Mary of Burgundy, who bore him five children and died in 1482. On the death of his father in 1493, he was elected Emperor, and soon afterwards married Bianca Maria, niece of Duke Ludovico Sforza of Milan. He was a member of the league that forced Charles VIII to retire from Italy (1495), of the League of Cambray against Venice (1508), and of the Holy League (1511) for the expulsion of Louis XII from Italy. Although deriving little profit or honour from these and other foreign enterprises, he contrived by prudent marriages to add Bohemia and Hungary to his empire and to make Spain a possession of his family. He also effected many reforms in his government, and even founded several important institutions, such as a postal service and a permanent militia. From his youth he showed a taste for study, became a patron of scholars, poets and artists, and enriched the Universities of Vienna and Ingolstadt. Besides being an accomplished if not very successful soldier, he was the author of works on gardening, hunting and agriculture, as well as on military science.

Note 391, page 200. ISABELLA THE CATHOLIC (born 1451; died 1504), was the daughter and heiress of Juan II of Castile. Having been trained in retirement of habits of religious devotion, she married (1469) Ferdinand of Aragon, with whom she succeeded jointly to her father's crown in 1474, but was able to gain complete possession of her dominions only in 1479, the same year in which her husband succeeded his father as King of Aragon. Under her rule the Inquisition was established in Castile (1480), but she recoiled before its horrors and was reconciled to its continuance only by the direct assurance of Pope Sixtus IV. In 1481 began the long war, which (largely owing to her energy and perseverance) resulted in the expulsion of the Moors from Spain, and in which she is said to have organized the earliest military hospitals. The story of her noble patronage of Columbus is familiar. Her later years were clouded by the loss of two of her three children, including her only son, and by the unhappy conjugal life and mental disorder of her daughter, Juana, the mother of Charles V. Castiglione's praise of Isabella's lofty qualities is not a little justified by the facts of her life. In personal appearance, she is said to have been agreeable rather than handsome; her features were regular, her green eyes vivacious, her complexion olive, her hair reddish blond, and her stature above the medium.

Note 392, page 200. FERDINAND THE CATHOLIC (born 1452; died 1516), was the son of Juan II of Navarre and Aragon, and is justly regarded as the founder of the Spanish monarchy. The means employed by him in building up his power were perfidy towards other rulers and ruthless oppression of his own people. Besides the other events of his reign, noted above, mention should be made of his cruel expulsion of the Jews from Spain in 1492. These and his other persecutions, supposed at the time to be actuated by zeal for pure religion, were in fact chiefly a source of revenue, and the policy thus inaugurated,—of stifling the commerce, the industry, the free thought and the energy of the nation at the beginning of its greatness,—is now seen to have been one of the important causes of its decline.

Note 393, page 202. Of these two remarkable queens, one was doubtless Federico III's widow, the Isabella del Balzo who is mentioned below (see note 400). The other may possibly have been her predecessor Joanna, the aunt and widow of Ferdinand II; or (more probably) Ippolita Maria, who was a daughter of the first Sforza duke of Milan and wife of Ferdinand II's father and predecessor Alfonso II, and of whom Dennistoun says (ii, 122): "It was for this princess that Constantine Lascaris composed the earliest Greek Grammar; and in the convent library of Sta. Croce at Rome there is a transcript by her of Cicero's *De Senectute*, followed by a juvenile collection of Latin apothegms curiously indicative of her character and studies."

Note 394, page 202. BEATRICE OF ARAGON (born 1457; died 1508), was the daughter of Ferdinand I of Naples and Isabelle de Clermont. In 1476 she married Matthias Corvinus, King of Hungary. On his death in 1490, she married Ladislas II of Bohemia, who for a time prevented the succession of Matthias's natural son John. However the youth attained the Hungarian throne with the aid of the Emperor Maximilian; whereupon Beatrice was repudiated by Ladislas and her marriage was annulled by Alexander VI. In 1501 she returned to Italy, resided at Ischia and died childless. Like her elder sister, the Duchess Eleanora of Ferrara (see note 399), she was a woman of cultivation and taste, and in spite of her political intrigues, she is praised for having done much to strengthen the intellectual bonds between Italy and Hungary, to which country she invited Italian poets, scholars and artists.

Note 395, page 202. MATTHIAS CORVINUS (born 1443; died 1490), was the son of the famous Hungarian general János Hunyadi, and in 1458 was proclaimed King of Hungary by the soldiers whom his father had so often led to victory. His life was a nearly continuous series of great enterprises, among the most noted of which were his campaigns against the Turks and his siege and capture (1485) of Vienna, where he thereafter resided chiefly and died. By no means the least part of his fame was won by the ardour with which he advanced the cause of science, art and letters in his country, and bestowed upon his people not only an enlightened code of laws but also the benefits of Renaissance culture. He introduced printing into Hungary, and was the founder of a magnificent public library at Buda Pest, containing fifty thousand volumes, for the most part MSS. which he caused to be copied in Italy and the East.

Note 396, page 202. ISABELLA OF ARAGON (born 1470; died 1524), was the daughter of Alfonso II of Naples and Ippolita Maria, daughter of the first Sforza duke of Milan. In 1489 she made a splendid entry into Milan as the bride of her own cousin Giangaleazzo Sforza, whose rights as duke were gradually usurped by his uncle Ludovico il Moro. This usurpation has been regarded as partly due to the ambition of Ludovico's young wife, Beatrice d'Este (see note 398), who could not endure the precedence rightfully belonging to Isabella. As has been seen, it was to protect himself against the wrath of Isabella's father and grandfather, that Ludovico invited Charles VIII into Italy as his ally. When Charles reached Pavia, he had to endure the pathetic spectacle of his forlorn cousin Giangaleazzo (they were sisters' sons) in prison, and to hear the piteous pleadings of the beautiful Isabella, who fell at his feet and besought him to have mercy on her husband. Her appeal was withstood, and Ludovico of course had no scruple in setting aside the rights of her infant children. Fresh trials awaited her in her native country, to which she returned in 1500, and from which her family had been expelled.

Note 397, page 202. ISABELLA D'ESTE (born 1474; died 1539), was the oldest child of Duke Ercole I of Ferrara and Eleanora of Aragon. Having had Mario Equicola as preceptor, she married the Marquess Gianfrancesco Gonzaga (see note 446) in 1490, her early betrothal to whom prevented her from becoming the wife of Ludovico Sforza, the duke of Milan, who soon afterwards married her sister Beatrice. At Mantua she continued her literary and artistic training, and her court became one of the brightest and most active centres of Italian culture. The chief poets and painters of the time laboured for her or were her friends. Being for years in her husband's service, Castiglione knew her closely, maintained a frequent exchange of letters with her, and is only one of many who praise her beauty, her intellect, and her moral qualities; she may be regarded as the most splendid incarnation of the Renaissance ideal of woman. Her long friendship with her sister-in-law, "My lady Duchess," has been already mentioned. Some interesting details have survived as to her manner of ordering a picture. Having chosen a subject, she had it set forth in writing by some humanist of her court. These specifications were then given to the painter chosen for the purpose, and he was furnished with minute directions as to the placing of the figures and the distribution of light, and required to make a preliminary sketch. As the painting was often intended for a specific space, she took great care to secure the exact dimensions desired, by providing two pieces of ribbon to show the precise height and breadth of the picture. Her career is the subject of many scholarly volumes and articles written jointly by Alessandro Luzio of Mantua and Rodolfo Renier of Turin. The material thus collected was used by Julia Cartwright (Mrs. Henry Ady) in preparing her recent interesting life of Isabella.

Note 398, page 202. BEATRICE D'ESTE (born 1475; died 1497), married Ludovico Sforza, Duke Regent of Milan, in the same year (1491) in which his niece Anna Sforza married Beatrice's brother Alfonso, the future husband of Lucrezia Borgia. Younger, apparently less beautiful, and certainly less accomplished than her sister Isabella, Beatrice encouraged her husband's patronage of art and letters, and took part in his turbid political schemes. It will perhaps never be determined precisely to what extent she was responsible for his treatment of his young nephew and of the latter's wife (see note 396), and for the disasters to Italy that ensued, but she is known to have exercised a great ascendency over her husband's mind, and he is said to have spent at her tomb the last night before his final capture and downfall. After the expulsion of the French from Italy in 1512, her sons Maximilian and Francesco Maria successively held the duchy for a time, until it passed into the hands of Spain in 1535. For an account of her life, the reader is referred to Mrs. Henry Ady's "Beatrice d'Este, Duchess of Milan; a Study of the Renaissance," which, as well as the same writer's life of Isabella, owes much to the labours of Luzio and Renier.

Note 399, page 202. ELEANORA OF ARAGON (born 1450; died 1493), was the elder sister of the Beatrice who married Matthias Corvinus of Hungary. A projected union with Ludovico Sforza (who afterwards married her daughter) having been abandoned, she became in 1473 the wife of Duke Ercole I of Ferrara, and bore him two daughters and four sons. Other contemporary accounts confirm the praise bestowed upon her by Castiglione, and show her to have been a woman of rare merit, manly courage and enlightened culture. Fond of music, herself a player upon the harp, she seems to have been a discriminating patroness of art and letters, and at the same time to have taken an active share in the serious cares of government, especially when her husband was absent or disabled. A pleasant glimpse of her character is gained from a letter written by her to the duke's treasurer on behalf of a certain Neapolitan engineer, who had rendered important services but had fallen ill and was in want. "You will see what this poor man's needs are. You know with what devotion he has served us, nor are you ignorant who sent him to us,—a circumstance worthy of consideration. It would ill become us to treat him in his sickness as to give him cause for complaint against us. You must know what his pay is. See, then, what can be done, and arrange for helping him." She did not live to witness the downfall of her family in Naples.

Note 400, page 202. ISABELLA DEL BALZO (died 1533), was a daughter of the Prince of Altamura, and the wife of Federico III of Naples (see note 401). When her husband lost his crown in 1501, she (together with the faithful Sannazaro) accompanied him to France, and shared his exile there until his death in 1504. Being, by the terms of a treaty between Louis XII and Ferdinand the Catholic, compelled to leave France, she and her four children took refuge, first with her sister Antonia at Gazzuolo, and then at Ferrara, where she was kindly treated and maintained by her husband's nephew Duke Alfonso d'Este. Here she spent the last twenty-five years of her life, but at times in such poverty that when Julius II placed Ferrara under the ban of the Church, she obtained special permission to have religious services performed in her house, on the plea that she had not the means wherewith to leave the city.

Note 401, page 202. FEDERICO III (born 1452; died 1504), was a son of Ferdinand I of Naples, a younger brother of Alfonso II, and an uncle of his immediate predecessor, Ferdinand II. Having taken part in the weak resistance offered to Charles VIII's invasion of Naples in 1494, he became king on the early death of his nephew in October 1496, and seems to have tried to keep aloof from the turbulent schemes in which Alexander VI sought to involve him. After another vain attempt to withstand the invasion of Louis XII, and having been shamefully betrayed by the Emperor Maximilian and Ferdinand the Catholic, to both of whom he had appealed for aid, he retired with his wife and children to the island of Ischia (which furnished refuge at the same time to his widowed sister Beatrice, ex-queen of Hungary, and to his widowed niece Isabella, ex-Duchess of Milan), ceded his crown to Louis XII in exchange for 30,000 ducats and the Countship of Maine, and spent the last three years of his life in France.

Note 402, page 202. Federico's eldest son Ferdinand, DUKE OF CALABRIA, was besieged in Taranto during the Franco-Spanish invasion which resulted in his father's downfall. On a sworn promise to set him free, he surrendered to the Great Captain (see note 239), but was treacherously detained and sent as a prisoner to Spain, where he was treated by Ferdinand the Catholic with almost royal honours. He continued to reside in Spain, and on the death of his mother in 1533, he was joined at Valencia by his two sisters.

Note 403, page 203. The reference here is probably to the siege of Pisa by the Florentines in 1499, which was finally abandoned owing in part at least to the bravery of the Pisan women. Castiglione himself was the author of some Latin verses celebrating an incident of the siege.

Note 404, page 203. Tomyris was in fact queen of the Massagetæ, who were a nomadic people allied to the Scythians and dwelt north-east of the Caspian Sea. Herodotus relates that Cyrus the Great sent her an offer of marriage, and on being refused, invaded her kingdom and captured her son, but was finally defeated and slain, 529 B.C. The Artemisia referred to in the text is probably not the Queen of Halicarnassus (who fought on the Persian side at Salamis in 480 B.C.), but rather the sister-consort and successor of King Mausolus of Caria, a state on the western coast of Asia Minor. On her husband's death in 352 B.C., she reigned two years until she pined away for grief. The monument, Mausoleum, erected by her to his memory at Halicarnassus, was regarded as one of the seven wonders of the world—the others being: the Egyptian pyramids, the temple of Artemis at Ephesus, the walls and hanging gardens of Babylon, Phidias's statue of Zeus at Olympia, the Colossus at Rhodes, and the lighthouse at Alexandria. Zenobia, an Arab by birth, was the second wife of Odenathus, King of Palmyra, which lay to the east of Syria. On the death of her husband, about 266 A.D., she acted as regent for her sons and seems to have shown great talent for war as well as for the arts of wise administration; but in her effort to extend her sway over the entire East, she was defeated by the Emperor Aurelian, and adorned his triumph in golden chains at Rome. She was allowed to spend the remainder of her life in dignified retirement at Tibur (Tivoli). Semiramis was the legendary daughter of the Syrian goddess Derketo, and with her husband Ninus was regarded as the founder of Nineveh. On his death she assumed the government of Assyria, built the city of Babylon and its wonderful gardens, conquered Egypt, etc. To her the Greeks ascribed nearly everything marvellous in the East. Her name appears in inscriptions as that of the consort of an Assyrian ruler who reigned 811-782 B.C. Cleopatra, (69-30 B.C.), was directly descended in the eighth generation from Ptolemy I, the most noted of Alexander the Great's generals and the founder of the Egyptian dynasty that ended with her life. Her establishment as sole ruler, to the exclusion of her two brothers, was due to the favour of Julius Cæsar, who is said to have acknowledged the paternity of her son Cæsarion, ultimately put to death by order of Augustus. Her love of literature, and the refinement of her luxury, show her to have been no mere voluptuary.

Note 405, page 203. SARDANAPALUS,—Assurbanipal, the Asnapper of the Old Testament,—ruled over Assyria from 668 to 626 B.C., and was the last monarch of the empire reputed to have been founded by Ninus and Semiramis. His name became a by-word for effeminate luxury, but in recent times the discovery and study of the larger part of the tablets composing his library, prove him to have been a vigorous king and an intelligent patron of art and literature.

Note 406, page 205. In his life of Alexander, Plutarch extols the magnanimity with which the youthful monarch treated the captive mother, wife and two daughters, of Darius, the last King of Persia, whom he had utterly defeated in the battle of Arbela, 331 B.C. In furtherance of his plan of uniting his European and Asiatic subjects into one people, Alexander afterwards married Bersine, the elder of Darius's two daughters.

Note 407, page 205. This incident is narrated in Valerius Maximus's "Memorable Sayings and Doings" as having occurred in the first Spanish campaign of Scipio Africanus Maximus, 210 B.C., when that commander was in his twenty-fourth year.

Note 408, page 205. This story of the Platonist philosopher Xenocrates (396-314 B.C.) is derived from the same source last cited. His teaching was characterized by the loftiest morality, and included a declaration that it comes to the same thing whether we cast longing eyes, or set our feet, upon the property of others. The 'very beautiful woman' of the text is variously mentioned as Phryne and Laïs, rival *hetairai* said to have served as models to the painter Apelles.

Note 409, page 205. Cicero's version of this anecdote (*De Officiis*, i, 40) mentions Sophocles as the 'someone' rebuked by Pericles.

Note 410, page 207. The Italians still say:

> *Donna pregata, nega;*
> *E disprezzata, prega.*

ɟɟɟɟɟɟɟɟɟɟɟɟɟɟɟɟɟɟɟɟɟɟɟɟɟɟɟɟɟɟɟɟɟɟɟɟɟɟɟɟɟɟɟɟɟɟɟɟɟɟɟɟɟɟɟ

Note 411, page 210. The present translator prefers not to offer an English version of the following passage, but to reprint it, line for line, from the Aldine folio of 1528:

si che questo piu tosto un stratogema militare dir si poria, che pura continentia: auenga anchora che la fama di questo non sia molto sincera: perche alcuni scrittori d'authorità affermano questa giouane esser stata da Scipione goduta in amorose delicie: ma di quello che ui dico io, dubbio alcuno non è. Disse il Phrigio, Douete ha uerlo trouato ne gli euangelii. Io stesso l'ho ueduto rispose M. Ces. & però n'ho molto maggior certezza, che non potete hauer, ne uoi, ne altri che Alcibiade si leuasse dal letto di Socrate non altriměti, che si facciano i figlioli dal letto de i padri: che pur strano loco, e tempo era il letto, & la notte, per contemplar quella pura bellezza: laqual si dice che amaua Socrate senza alcun desiderio dishonesto, massimamente, amādo piu la bellezza dell'animo, che del corpo: ma ne i fanciulli & nò ne i uecchi, anchor che siano piu sauii: & certo non si potea gia trouar miglior exempio, per laudar la continentia de glihomini, che quello di Xenocrate: che essendo uersato ne gli studii, astretto, & obligato dalla profession sua, che è la philosophia, laquale consiste ne i boni costumi, & non nelle parole, uecchio, exhausto del uigor naturale, nõ potendo, ne mostrando segno di potere, s'astenne da una femina publica: laquale per questo nome solo potea uenirgli à fastidio: piu crederei che fosse sta to continente, se qualche segno de risentirsi hauesse dimostrato, & in tal termine usato la continentia: ouero astenutosi da quello, che i uecchi piu desiredano che le battaglie di Venere, cioè dal uino: ma per comprobar ben la continentia senile, scriuesi che di questo era pieno, & gra uc: & qual cosa dir si po piu aliena della continentia d'un uecchio: che la ebrietà? & se lo astenerse dalle cose ueneree in quella pigra, & fredda età merita tanta laude, quanta ne deue meritar in una tenera giouane, come quelle due di chi dianzi u'ho detto? dellequali l'una imponēdo durissime leggi à tutti i sensi suoi, non solamente à gliocchi negaua la sua luce, ma toglieua al core quei pensieri, che soli lungamēte erano sta ti dulcissimo cibo per tenerlo in uita. l'altra ardente innamorata ritrouādosi tante volte sola nelle braccia di quello, che piu assai, che tutto'l resto del mondo amaua, contra se stessa, & contra colui, che piu, che se stessa le era caro, combattendo uincea quello ardente desiderio che spes so ha uinto, & uince tanti sauii homini. Nõ ui pare hora S. Gasp. che douessino i scrittori uergognarsi di far memoria di Xenocrate in questo caso? & chiamarlo per continente? che chi potesse sapere, io metterei pegno che esso tutta quella notte sino al giorno sequēte ad hora di desinare dormi come morto sepulto nel uino: ne mai per stropicciar che gli facesse quella temina, potè aprir gliocchi, como oo fusse stato all'opia to. Quiui risero tutti glihomini & donne: & la S. Emil, pur ridēdo Ve ramente disse S. Gasp. se ui pensate un poco meglio credo che trouarete anchor qualche altro bello exempio di continentia simile à questo. Rispose M. Ces. Nō ui par Signora, che bello exempio di continentia sia quell'atro che egli ha allegato di Pericle? Marauigliomi ben chel non habbia anchor ricordato la continētia, & quel bel detto, che si scri ue di colui, à chi una donna domādò troppo gran prezzo per una notte, & esso le rispose, che non compraua cosi caro il pentirsi. Rideasi tutta aui & M. Ces. hauendo alquanto tacciuto . . . . disse:

The only other instance in which the translator has suppressed any part of the text is in line 35 of page 209, where the Italian word *ignuda* is not rendered.

Note 412, page 211. The event occurred in 1501, six years before the date of the Courtier dialogues.

Note 413, page 211. The Volturno flows through Capua.

Note 414, page 211. Gazuolo or Gazzuolo is now the name of an Italian commune, containing less than 5,000 inhabitants, and situated eleven miles west of Mantua.

Note 415, page 212. The Oglio is a river of Lombardy about 135 miles long; it traverses the Lake of Iseo, and joins the Po some ten miles south-west of Mantua.

Note 416, page 212. In two earlier MS. versions of THE COURTIER, the passage 'Now from this . . . even her name is unknown' reads: "Then messer Pietro Bembo said: 'In truth, if I knew this noble peasant girl's name, I would compose an epitaph for her.' 'Do not stop for that,' said messer Cesare; 'her name is Maddalena Biga, and if the Bishop's death had not occurred, that bank of the Oglio' " etc.

With slight variations this story is narrated as fact in a letter of Matteo Bandello (1480-1562), from whose tales Shakspere took plots for his plays. The letter gives the poor girl's name as Giulia and that of the Bishop of Mantua as Ludovico Gonzaga, and relates that, as it was unlawful to bury her remains in consecrated soil, he caused them to be deposited in the piazza, intending to place them in a bronze sarcophagus mounted on a marble column. The letter also affirms that the ravisher was one of the bishop's valets.

Note 417, page 212. This was Ludovico Gonzaga (born 1458; died 1511), a son of the Marquess Ludovico of Mantua and Barbara of Brandenburg, and a younger brother of "my lady Duchess's" father. Made BISHOP OF MANTUA in 1483, he continued to hold that office until his death, and appears from various contemporary documents to have been a liberal and wise prince. The last years of his life were spent at Gazzuolo, which he made a centre of culture, art and learning. His brother Gianfrancesco was husband of the Antonia del Balzo mentioned above, note 400. For particulars regarding him, see an article by Rossi in the *Giornale Storico della Letteratura Italiana*, xiii, 305.

Note 418, page 213. The basilica of St. Sebastian, on the Appian Way, dates from the 4th century, was built over the most famous of the catacombs, and enjoyed an exceptional veneration during the Middle Ages. The saint was a young military tribune born in Gaul, suffered martyrdom under Diocletian about the year 288, and was buried in the catacombs of Callistus. St. George and he were the favourite saints of chivalry, and may be regarded as the martial Castor and Pollux of Christian myth.

Note 419, page 213. FELICE DELLA ROVERE (died about 1536), was a natural daughter of Cardinal Giuliano della Rovere (afterwards Julius II) and a certain Lucrezia, the wife of Bernardo de Cuppis (or Coppi) da Montefolco; thus "my lord Prefect" of THE COURTIER was her own cousin. In 1506 she became the second wife of the elderly and eccentric Giangiordano Orsini, and the ancestress of the Dukes of Bracciano. Her name often occurs in contemporary documents, not only on account of her lofty position but because of her love of art and letters. Both Castiglione and Giancristoforo Romano were her friends. The incident mentioned in the text seems not to be referred to elsewhere. Savona, a seaport on the western Riviera, is near the birthplace of Felice's greatuncle, Pope Sixtus IV, who was the founder of the della Rovere family.

Note 420, page 214. Duke Guidobaldo's impotence is said to have given rise to the project of a divorce for his duchess.

Note 421, page 215. The reference here is to Ovid's *Ars Amandi*, which enjoyed an extraordinary reputation during the Renaissance, and from which this passage is largely derived.

〃〃〃〃〃〃〃〃〃〃〃〃〃〃〃〃〃〃〃〃〃〃〃〃〃〃〃〃〃〃〃〃〃〃〃〃〃〃〃〃〃〃〃〃〃〃〃〃〃〃

Note 422, page 218. The LAURA to whom Petrarch consecrated no less than three hundred and eighteen sonnets, is usually regarded as identical with Laure, the daughter of a certain knight of Avignon, Audibert de Noves. If this identification be correct, she was born in 1308, married Hughes de Sade in 1325, became the mother of eleven children, and died in 1348. In 1533 Francis I caused her reputed tomb to be opened, and found in it a small box which contained a medal bearing a woman's profile, and a parchment on which was a sonnet signed by Petrarch.

Note 423, page 218. The so-called "Song of Solomon" is now thought to be the work of a period later than Solomon's and to contain no mystic meaning.

Note 424, page 219. In the old romance, "Amadis of Gaul," Isola Ferma is an enchanted island, with a garden at the entrance to which stands an arch surmounted by the statue of a man holding a trumpet to his mouth. Whenever an unfaithful lover attempts to pass, the trumpet emits a dreadful sound with fire and smoke, and drives the culprit back; while it welcomes all true lovers with sweetest music.

Note 425, page 226. Here again the reference is of course to "my lady Duchess."

Note 426, page 233. The *Hypnerotomachia Poliphili*, first published by Aldus in 1499, was written by Francesco Colonna, a Dominican friar of Venice, who died an old man in 1527. The book is rare, and is said to be an allegorical romance full of lascivious erudition, and written in a pedantically affected mixture of Italian, Latin, and Venetian *patois*.

Note 427, page 235. *Ars Amandi*, i, 597-602.

Note 428, page 235. *Ars Amandi*, i, 569-72.

# NOTES TO THE FOURTH BOOK OF THE COURTIER

Note 429, page 240. Gaspar Pallavicino died in 1511, at the age of twenty-five.

Note 430, page 240. Cesare Gonzaga died in 1512, at about the age of thirty-seven. See note 43.

Note 431, page 241. Federico Fregoso was named Archbishop of Salerno in 1507, very soon after the date of the Courtier dialogues; see note 41.

Ludovico da Canossa became Bishop of Bayeux in 1520; see note 44.

Ottaviano Fregoso became Doge of Genoa in 1513; see note 11.

Bibbiena was made cardinal, and Bembo was appointed papal secretary, in 1513 see notes 10 and 42.

Giuliano de' Medici was created Duke of Nemours in 1515. As he died in 1516, Castiglione's use of the present tense ('that greatness where now he is') is inconsistent with the mention of Canossa as Bishop of Bayeux. See note 9.

Francesco Maria della Rovere succeeded to the dukedom in 1508; see note 3.

Note 432, page 242. ELEANORA GONZAGA (born about 1492; died 1543), was the eldest daughter of the Marquess Gianfrancesco of Mantua and Isabella d'Este. In 1505 Castiglione negotiated her union with Francesco Maria della Rovere, but the marriage did not take place until Christmas Eve 1509, upon which occasion Bembo wrote to Federico Fregoso that he had never seen a comelier, merrier or sweeter girl, and that her amiable disposition and surprisingly precocious judgment won general admiration. She seems to have maintained affectionate relations with her aunt and predecessor ("my lady Duchess" of THE COURTIER), whose fame quite outshone her own, and to have exhibited in after life no little strength of character. She is said to have excluded, and even to have expelled, great ladies of questionable morality from her court. Titian's portrait (1537) represents her in middle age, but his pictures, *La Bella* and *Das Mädchen im Pelz*, as well as several of his Venus heads, are generally regarded as idealized presentations of her more youthful face.

ノノノノノノノノノノノノノノノノノノノノノノノノノノノノノノノノノノノノノノノノノノノノノノノノノ

Note 433, page 246. The Piazza d'Agone occupied the site of the ancient *Circus Agonalis*, which derived its name from the *Agonalia*, a festival held twice a year in honour of Janus. Before, during and long after Castiglione's time, it was a centre of festivals, amusements and spectacles at the carnival season. It is now called the Piazza Navona.

Note 434, page 247. The famous Athenian commander CIMON (died 449 B.C.), was the son of the still more famous Miltiades. His victories repulsed the last Persian aggressions and consolidated the Athenian supremacy. Although an admirer of Spartan institutions, he seems to have been of a somewhat indulgent disposition. The SCIPIO here referred to, is probably Publius Cornelius Scipio the Elder, who was the victor over Hannibal and died 183 B.C. LUCULLUS is cited earlier in THE COURTIER as an instance of a soldier with studious tastes; see note 113.

Note 435, page 247. The Theban general and statesman EPAMINONDAS (died 362 B.C.), is said by Plutarch to have enjoyed the instruction of the Pythagorean philosopher LYSIS of Tarentum, who was driven out of Italy in the persecution of his sect, and found refuge at Thebes.

Note 436, page 247. AGESILAUS was King of Sparta 398-361 B.C. Although small and lame, he was the greatest Spartan commander, and became famous for his victories against the Persian and Greek enemies of his country. XENOPHON, historian, essayist and disciple of Socrates, was banished from Athens about the time of Socrates's death (399 B.C.), accompanied Agesilaus into Asia, and wrote a panegyric upon him, regarded by Cicero as more glorious than all the statues erected to kings.

The reverence and love of SCIPIO THE YOUNGER (about 185-129 B.C.) for the Rhodian Stoic philosopher PANÆTIUS (about 180-111 B.C.) is frequently mentioned by Cicero, from whose *De Oratore* Castiglione seems to have taken this whole passage.

Note 437, page 249. In Greek mythology Epimetheus (Afterthought) and Prometheus (Forethought) were sons of the Titan Iapetus and the ocean nymph Clymene. Angered by a deceit practised upon him by Prometheus, Zeus withheld from men the use of fire; but Prometheus stole fire from heaven and brought it to earth in a hollow reed. For this offence he was chained to a rock where an eagle preyed daily upon his liver (which grew again in the night), until he was finally liberated by Hercules. As compensation for the boon of fire, Zeus sent Pandora (the first woman, endowed with beauty, cunning and other attributes designed

ノノノノノノノノノノノノノノノノノノノノノノノノノノノノノノノノノノノノノノノノノノノノノノノノノノノ
to bring woe to man) to be the wife of Epimetheus. Although warned
by his brother, Epimetheus accepted her, with the result that she set free
the evils which Prometheus had concealed in a box. In a later form of the
legend, she received from the gods a box containing the blessings of life,
and on her being moved by curiosity to open the box, all of them (save
hope) escaped and were lost.

Note 438, page 260. BIAS was born at Priene in Asia Minor, and
lived in the 6th century B.C. He was celebrated for his apothegms and
reckoned among the Seven Sages of Greece,—the other six being: Thales
of Miletus, Solon of Athens, Chilon of Sparta, Cleobulus of Rhodes,
Periander of Corinth, and Pittacus of Mitylene,—all of whom flourished
about 600 B.C. The fame of these seven men rested not upon their
philosophy, as we use the word, but upon their practical wisdom—the fruit
of experience.

Note 439, page 260. CLEARCHUS (died 353 B.C.), was for twelve
years a cruel tyrant, not of Pontus, but of Heracles (the modern Eregli),
a city on the Black Sea about 140 miles east of Constantinople. He is said
to have been a pupil of both Plato and Isocrates, the latter of whom
represents him as a gentle youth.

Note 440, page 261. Of the dozen or more ancients known to have
borne the name ARISTODEMUS, none seem to fit precisely the description
given in the text, which is taken from a passage in Plutarch's "On the
Ignorant Prince." Plutarch may have had in mind a certain tyrant of
Megalopolis in the 3d century B.C.

Note 441, page 266. The reference here is to Book V of "The
Republic."

Note 442, page 267. Fregoso here declares for what has been called
"that Utopia of the 16th Century—the *Governo Misto*—a political invention which fascinated the imagination of Italian statesmen much in the
same way as the theory of perpetual motion attracted scientific minds in
the last century." (Symonds's "Renaissance in Italy," i, 306.) In this
regard the men of Castiglione's time, men like Machiavelli and Guicciar-
dini, were only following Plato and Aristotle.

Note 443, page 267. The reference here is to the *Cyropædia*, i, 6.

ℐℐℐℐℐℐℐℐℐℐℐℐℐℐℐℐℐℐℐℐℐℐℐℐℐℐℐℐℐℐℐℐℐℐℐℐℐℐℐℐℐℐℐℐℐℐℐℐℐℐℐℐℐ

Note 111, page 267. Castiglione seems to have in mind the game of *tavola reale*, which is similar to our backgammon.

Note 445, page 267. Circe's transformation of some of Ulysses's companions into swine is narrated in the tenth book of the Odyssey. In Castiglione's day the term "King of France" was used to signify the acme of royal power.

Note 446, page 271. GIANFRANCESCO—more commonly called FRANCESCO—GONZAGA (born 1466; died 1519), was the eldest son of the Marquess Federico of Mantua and Margarita of Bavaria, and a brother of "my lady Duchess." Having succeeded his father in 1484, he married (1490) Isabella d'Este, to whom he had been betrothed at the age of sixteen. Like his ancestors and most other petty Italian rulers of his time, he was at once *condottiere* and sovereign prince. He commanded the Italian troops against Charles VIII, and although with an overwhelmingly superior force he failed to block the retreat of the French at Fornovo, he treated that disgraceful affair as a glorious victory, and even caused it to be commemorated by Mantegna in a votive picture now in the Louvre. He served successively as captain of the imperial troops in Italy, as commander of Duke Ludovico Sforza's army, as viceroy of Naples under Louis XII, etc. He joined the League of Cambray and was taken prisoner by the Venetians. In the general disorders that filled the period of his reign, he and his more brilliant wife had the address to protect his dominions from the ravages of war. Although, as Castiglione's natural lord, he was asked and gave his consent to the latter's entry into the Duke of Urbino's court (1504), he seems to have continued to resent the affair until Castiglione's return (1516) to his service,—in which the author remained when this part of the text was written. Castiglione's eulogy was far from undeserved, for to the Marquess's munificence, no less than to his consort's taste and enthusiasm, must be ascribed the lustre of their provincial court. Besides being a patron of art and letters, he was also a successful breeder of horses for use both in war and in racing.

Note 447, page 271. The duke is said to have had no small share in planning the palace; his chief architect was one Luciano, a native of Laurana in Dalmatia on the eastern coast of the Adriatic. The cost of the structure was about £400,000 sterling. See, besides the authorities cited in note 28, Luzio and Renier's *Mantova e Urbino*, (Roux: Turin: 1893), p. 10, note 1.

*****************************************************

Note 448, page 271. The ancient basilica of St. Peter's had become ruinous by 1450, but little was done towards rebuilding it until 1506, when the execution of Bramante's plan was begun with the solemn laying of the first stone by Julius II on Sunday, 18 April. On the death of Bramante, Raphael was put in charge of the work in 1514, as we have seen (note 98), but, apparently owing to lack of funds, progress was slow until 1534 when Michelangelo's designs were substituted. The dome was completed in 1590, and the church dedicated in 1626.

Note 449, page 271. This 'street' was designed by Bramante to be a kind of triumphal way connecting the Vatican with the Belvedere pavilion. It was to be bordered by palaces, courts, gardens, porticoes, terraces, etc., but the death of Julius II led to the abandonment of the plan.

Note 450, page 271. Pozzuoli (the ancient Puteoli), situated seven miles west of Naples, was originally a Greek city, but became one of the chief commercial ports of the Roman Empire, and a resort of the patrician class. It is noted for its ruins, especially those of a large amphitheatre.

Baja (the ancient Baiæ), on the Gulf of Pozzuoli, was the chief Roman watering place, famous for its luxury, and containing the villas of many celebrated Romans. Its principal antiquities are ruins of baths.

Civita Vecchia lies on the coast about thirty-eight miles north-west of Rome, and was anciently known as Centum Cellæ. The Emperor Trajan (reigned 98-117 A.D.) converted it from a poor village into a great seaport, and of his monuments some remains are still extant.

Porto was a Roman city near the mouth of the Tiber. In Castiglione's time it had become a marshy island. One of the earliest Italian archæologists, Flavio Biondo, visited the site in 1451, and found there many huge marble blocks ready for building and bearing quarry marks of the imperial period. The Apollo Belvedere was discovered here in 1503.

Note 451, page 271. Almost the same phrase occurs in the well known letter which Raphael (who had been appointed guardian of antiquities) wrote to Leo X, urging the pontiff to avert the complete destruction of "that little which remains of Italian glory and greatness in proof of the worth and power of those divine minds." Castiglione was long supposed to be the author of the letter, but is now believed only to have aided Raphael in its composition.

Note 452, page 271. Alexandria was founded by the conqueror in 332 B.C.

Bucephalia (founded 327 B.C.) was situated on the river Hydaspes (the modern Jhelum), a branch of the Indus, about 120 miles north-west of Lahore, and was named in honour of Alexander's favourite horse, which died there. Bucephalus (ox-headed) is supposed to have been a name given to Thessalian horses, which were branded with a bull's head.

Note 453, page 271. Mount Athos (6780 feet high) forms the extremity of the easternmost peninsula of Chalcidice in Macedonia. During the Persian invasion of Xerxes (480 B.C.) it was temporarily converted into an island, and since the Middle Ages has been noted for its monasteries. Both Vitruvius and Plutarch give an account of the project mentioned in the text, and ascribe it to a Macedonian architect who appears under the names, Dinocrates, Cheirocrates, and Stasicrates,—and who also planned the city of Alexandria and was chosen to rebuild the great temple of Artemis of Ephesus. The statue was to represent Alexander, who is said to have abandoned the idea when he learned that the city to be placed in the hand of the statue would be without territory and could be provisioned only by sea,—saying that such a city would be like a child that cannot grow for failure of its nurse's milk.

Note 454, page 272. In Athenian legend PROCRUSTES was a cruel robber, who had a bed upon which he tortured captives by stretching those who were too short and by cutting off the legs of those who were too long. He was finally slain by the hero Theseus.

SCIRON was another legendary Attic robber, who compelled his victims to wash his feet on the Scironian rocks near Athens, and then kicked them into the sea where they served to fatten the turtles upon which he fed. He also was slain by Theseus, and in the same manner in which he had slain others.

In Roman myth CACUS was a gigantic son of Vulcan, living near the site of Rome. He robbed Hercules of some of the cattle stolen from the monster Geryon, and dragged them into his cave backwards, so that they could not be tracked; but Hercules discovered them by their lowing, and slew the thief.

DIOMED (not the Argive prince of the Iliad, but Ares's mythical son, who was king over the Bistones in Thrace) was slain by Hercules because he was accustomed to feed his mares on human flesh.

ANTÆUS a fabulous and gigantic wrestler of Libya, reputed to be the son of Poseidon and Gæa, the Earth goddess. Being held aloft and thus deprived of the miraculous strength derived from contact with his mother earth, he was crushed to death by Hercules.

GERYON was the mythical three-headed king of Hesperia, the theft of whose cattle constituted the tenth of the Twelve Labours of Hercules.

Note 455, page 272. "The crimes of the tyrants against their subjects and the members of their own families had produced a correlative order of crime in the people over whom they tyrannized. Cruelty was met by conspiracy. Tyrannicide became honourable; and the proverb, 'He who gives his own life can take a tyrant's,' had worked itself into the popular language." (Symonds's "Renaissance in Italy," i, 154.) "The study of the classics, especially of Plutarch, at this time as also during the French Revolution, fired the imagination of patriots." (Id., 151, note 2.)

Note 456, page 272. Similar exhortations to a fresh crusade are of frequent occurrence in Italian literature of this period, and were often used by popes and princes as a cover for their selfish designs.

Note 457, page 272. The meaning obviously is that if they had not been exiled, they never would have enjoyed their present prosperity. Plutarch tells the story in four slightly varying forms.

Note 458, page 272. MONSEIGNEUR D'ANGOULEME afterwards became Francis I (see note 111). Even stronger evidence of the author's admiration than this and another passage (see page 56), is afforded by the Proem with which he originally intended to preface the dialogues, but for which he seems to have been led by political considerations to substitute the introduction finally printed.

Note 459, page 272. HENRY, PRINCE OF WALES, afterwards Henry VIII (born 1491; died 1547), was the younger son of Henry VII and Elizabeth of York, and was educated for the church. Having succeeded his father in 1509, he married (in accordance with his parents' wish) his elder brother Arthur's widow, Catherine, the youngest child of Ferdinand and Isabella the Catholic. His accession was hailed with enthusiasm. Left rich through his father's avarice, he was generous, frank, handsome, exceptionally robust, and an accomplished athlete and scholar. Good men were delighted with the purity of his life, his gaiety pleased the courtiers, and sober statesmen found in him a singular capacity for business. Besides being a musician, he spoke Latin, French and Spanish, and was very devout,—usually attending mass five times daily. Even as late as 1521 he dedicated to the pope an anti-Lutheran tract on the Seven Sacraments, and in return received the title of Defender of the Faith. As an offset to the enormities of his later life, it is only just to remember that he raised

England to the rank of a great European power, and that for twenty years he did nothing to mar the harmony of his reign.

Note 460, page 272. 'His great father,' i.e. Henry VII (born 1457; died 1509), was the son of Edmund Tudor, Earl of Richmond, (a son of Henry V's widow Catherine), and Margaret Beaufort, whose paternal grandfather was an illegitimate half-brother of Henry IV. After the downfall of the House of Lancaster and the death of the young York princes, Henry succeeded in gathering a strong party, landed in England and wrested the crown from Richard III, 1485. Soon afterwards, by his marriage to Edward IV's daughter Elizabeth of York, he united the hostile factions that had so long harassed the kingdom. As a ruler he was avaricious, calculating, and far from popular. He is said to have left a treasure of £2,000,000 sterling. The marriage of his daughter Margaret to James IV of Scotland finally led (on the failure of his son's issue) to the accession of the Stuarts in the person of her grandson, James I.

Note 461, page 273. This is consistent with the earlier passage (see page 3) where Castiglione pretends to have been absent in England at the date of the Courtier dialogues. An earlier MS. version here reads: "as we are told by our friend Castiglione, who has just returned from England," which accords with what we have seen (note 23) to be the fact.

Note 462, page 273. DON CARLOS, afterwards the Emperor Charles V (born 1500; died 1558), was the son of the Emperor Maximilian's son Philip of Austria, and of Juana, daughter of Ferdinand and Isabella the Catholic. Born and bred in the Low Countries, and educated at least partly under the care of the future pope Adrian VI, he is said to have shown less taste for study than for military exercises, and on his accession to the Spanish throne in 1516, he was ignorant of the Spanish language. By right of his grandmother Mary of Burgundy, he already held the Netherlands. As representative of the house of Aragon, he was king of Naples and Sicily. On the death of his grandfather Maximilian in 1519, he inherited Austria, and (in spite of the rivalry of Francis I and the intrigues of Leo X) was elected Emperor;—thus achieving, without a blow, a dominion vaster than any in Europe since the time of Charlemagne.

In an earlier MS. version the text here reads: "Then messer Bernardo Bibbiena said: 'I do not think that any of those present, except myself, have seen the prince Don Carlos, who, having recently lost such a father as the king Don Philip was, has shown such courage and wisdom in this great bereavement, that although he has not reached the tenth year of his age, we may nevertheless regard him as competent to rule over all his hereditary possessions, vast though they be,—and that the Empire of Christendom (which men think will be in his hands) must grow not a little in power and dignity.' "

Note 463, page 276. FEDERICO GONZAGA, the first Duke of Mantua (born 1500; died 1450), was the son of the Marquess Gianfrancesco Gonzaga and Isabella d'Este. At the age of ten he spent some time as the hostage-guest of Julius II at Rome, where he seems to have been generally caressed. Raphael is known to have introduced the boy's face into one of the Vatican frescoes, and a little later to have painted his portrait. Having succeeded his father as marquess in 1519, he waged war for Leo X against the French. In 1527 he joined the league of Italian princes against Charles V, but went over to the Emperor's side two years later, and was created Duke of Mantua. In 1531 he married Margarita Paleologus. Both Giulio Romano and Benvenuto Cellini were in his employ.

Note 464, page 277. These lines were written after Ottaviano Fregoso's election as Doge of Genoa; see note 11.

Note 465, page 278. In an earlier MS. version, my lady Emilia continues: " 'And even if it were so, I do not see how he is on that account set above the Court Lady.' The Magnifico Giuliano said: 'We regard the Lady as the equal of the Courtier, and according to my lord Ottaviano, the Courtier is superior to the Prince; therefore the Court Lady comes to be superior to the Prince.' "

Note 466, page 281. Phœnix appears in the Iliad as appointed by Peleus to superintend the education of the latter's son Achilles.

Note 467, page 281. ARISTOTLE was summoned (342 B.C.) to undertake the education of Alexander, who was then thirteen years old, and whom no one had thus far been able to control. The philosopher's training continued uninterruptedly for four years, included instruction in poetry, rhetoric, philosophy, physics and medicine,—and is said to have had beneficial effect upon the future conqueror's character.

Note 468, page 281. Stagira lay on the easterly side of the Chalcidic peninsula. Philip had destroyed it in his Olynthian campaign of 348 B.C., but rebuilt it at Aristotle's request and caused a gymnasium to be erected there, in a shady grove, for use of the philosopher and his pupils, among whom was Alexander.

Note 469, page 281. Plutarch expressly affirms that Alexander's policy, of uniting all the nations under his sway into a single people, was not founded on Aristotle's advice, as indeed an examination of the latter's political theories would seem to prove.

Note 470, page 281. The Bactrians were an Aryan people dwelling on the upper Oxus, in what is now Afghanistan. They were conquered in 327 B.C. by Alexander, who married Roxana, the daughter of one of their princes. In ancient times the inhabitants of northern and eastern Europe and Asia were called Scythians.

Note 471, page 281. CALLISTHENES was a cousin and fellow pupil of Alexander's. On Aristotle's recommendation, Alexander took Callisthenes with him on his Asiatic expedition of 334 B.C., but, exasperated by his young kinsman's plain-spoken disapproval of his conduct, had Callisthenes put to death.

Note 472, page 282. DIO (born about 408; died about 354 B.C.), was an austere Syracusan philosopher who became an ardent disciple of Plato on the occasion of the latter's short residence at the court of Dionysius the Elder, and later induced the younger DIONYSIUS also to invite Plato to Syracuse, where, however, the philosopher was unable to check the tyrant's profligacy.

Note 473, page 284. Bembo was thirty-six years old at the date of the Courtier dialogues.

Note 474, page 285. In Book III of Bembo's *Gli Asolani* (1505) a hermit discourses to Lavinello on the beauty of mystical Christian love. Bembo had a villa called Lavinello, near Padua.

Note 475, page 285. Much of the following disquisition seems to be drawn from Plato and from Bembo's *Gli Asolani*. As Bembo is known to have revised THE COURTIER before publication, we may assume that he was content with the form and substance of the discourse here attributed to him.

*ffffffffffffffffffffffffffffffffffffffffffffffffffffff*

Note 476, page 294. STESICHORUS was a Greek lyric poet who lived about 630-550 B.C., and was supposed to have been miraculously stricken blind after writing an attack upon Helen of Troy. His true name is said to have been Tisias, and to have been changed to Stesichorus because he was the first to establish a chorus for singing to the harp. Fragments of his verse have survived.

Note 477, page 291. These 'five other stars' are of course the five planets then known (Mercury, Venus, Mars, Jupiter and Saturn), in addition to the Sun and Moon, which were until long afterwards regarded as planets. "The sun, the moon and the five planets were always to be found within a region of the sky extending about 8° on each side of the ecliptic. This strip of the celestial sphere was called the Zodiac, because the constellations in it were (with one exception) named after living things (Greek ξῷον, an animal); it was divided into twelve equal parts, the Signs of the Zodiac, through one of which the sun passed eevry month, so that the position of the sun at any time could be roughly described by stating in what 'sign' it was." Arthur Berry's "Short History of Astronomy" (London, 1898), p. 13.

Note 478, page 302. Castiglione here follows that version of the Hercules myth which represents the hero, tormented by the poisoned shirt sent him by the jealous Deianeira, as throwing himself upon a burning pyre on Mount Œta, whence he was caught up to heaven in a cloud.

Note 479, page 302. Compare: Exodus, iii, 2; Acts, ii, 1-4; and II Kings, ii, 11-12.

Note 480, page 303. This dialogue is by some represented as having actually taken place in the presence of Raphael.

Note 481, page 304. PLOTINUS was born in Egypt about 204 A.D., and taught philosophy at Rome. He lived so exclusively the life of speculation that he seemed ashamed of bodily existence, and concealed his parentage, birthplace and age.

Note 482, page 304. ST. FRANCIS (Gianfrancesco Bernardone, 1182-1226), was born and died at Assisi near Perugia, and was canonized in 1288.

Note 483, page 305. II Corinthians, xii, 2-4.

Note 484, page 305. Acts, vii, 54-60.

Note 485, page 305. St. Luke, vii, 37.

Note 486, page 305. Mount Catria lies less than twenty miles to the southward of Urbino, between Pergola and Gubbio, and rises a little more than a mile above the sea level. It is mentioned by Dante in the *Paradiso* (xxi, 109).

# LIST OF EDITIONS OF THE BOOK OF THE COURTIER

## COMPILED FROM THE FOLLOWING SOURCES:

Copy in the Library of the Spanish Academy at Madrid, . . . . . . . . . . . ace
Copy in the Alessandrina Library at Rome, . . . . . . . . . . . . . . . . . . . ala
Copy in the Ambrosiana Library at Milan, . . . . . . . . . . . . . . . . . . . . amb
Copy in the Angelica Library at Rome, . . . . . . . . . . . . . . . . . . . . . . ang
Copy in the National Library at Madrid, . . . . . . . . . . . . . . . . . . . . . bnm
Copy in the National Library at Paris, . . . . . . . . . . . . . . . . . . . . . . . bnp
Brunet's *Manuel du Libraire* (Paris: 1860-65), . . . . . . . . . . . . . . . . bnt
Copy in the Braidense Library at Milan, . . . . . . . . . . . . . . . . . . . . . bra
Copy in the British Museum, . . . . . . . . . . . . . . . . . . . . . . . . . . . . . brm
Brunet's *Manuel du Libraire, Supplément* (Paris: 1878), . . . . . . . . . bts
Copy in the Casanatense Library at Rome, . . . . . . . . . . . . . . . . . . . . cas
Copy in the Cavriani Library at Mantua, . . . . . . . . . . . . . . . . . . . . . cav
Copy in the Chigiana Library at Rome, . . . . . . . . . . . . . . . . . . . . . . chi
Copy in the Corsiniana Library at Rome, . . . . . . . . . . . . . . . . . . . . . cor
MS. bibliographical notes by the late Count D'Arco, at Mantua, . . . . . . d'a
Copy examined by the translator in the National Library at Paris, . . . . exd
List of editions appended to Fabié's (1873) edition of Boscan's
   Spanish translation, . . . . . . . . . . . . . . . . . . . . . . . . . . . . . . . . . . fab
Copy in the University Library at Jena, . . . . . . . . . . . . . . . . . . . . . . jen
List of editions appended to Aristide Joly's *De Balthassaris Castil-
lionis opere cui titulus "Il Libro del Cortegiano," etc.* (Caen:
   1856), . . . . . . . . . . . . . . . . . . . . . . . . . . . . . . . . . . . . . . . . . . . . jol
List of editions appended to Count Mazzuchelli's Life of Casti-
glione (Rome: 1879), . . . . . . . . . . . . . . . . . . . . . . . . . . . . . . . . . maz
Copy in the New York Public Library, . . . . . . . . . . . . . . . . . . . . . . . nyp
Card Catalogue of the antiquarian bookseller Olschki, at Florence, . . . ols
Copy owned by the translator, . . . . . . . . . . . . . . . . . . . . . . . . . . . . opd
Giambattista Passano's *I Novellieri Italiani* (Turin: 1878), . . . . . . . . pas
Article by Reinhardstöttner in *Jahrb. f. Münchner Gesch.* (1888,
   pp. 494-9), . . . . . . . . . . . . . . . . . . . . . . . . . . . . . . . . . . . . . . . . . . rei
Copy in the Marciana Library at Venice, . . . . . . . . . . . . . . . . . . . . . stm
Copy in the Vatican Library at Rome, . . . . . . . . . . . . . . . . . . . . . . . vat
Copy in the Vittorio Emanuele Library at Rome, . . . . . . . . . . . . . . . . vel
List of editions appended to Count Carlo Baudi di Vesme's (1854)
   edition of THE COURTIER, . . . . . . . . . . . . . . . . . . . . . . . . . . . . . ves

# LIST OF EDITIONS

THE LANGUAGE IS ITALIAN UNLESS OTHERWISE INDICATED
DATES AND NAMES ENCLOSED IN PARENTHESES ARE NOT FREE
FROM DOUBT

| | | | |
|---|---|---|---|
| 1528 | Venice | Aldine Press: fol.: April: | opd |
| 1528 | Florence | The heirs of Filippo di Giunta: 8vo: October: | opd |
| (1529) | Tusculano | Alessandro Paganino: 12mo: | stm |
| 1529 | Florence | The heirs of Filippo di Giunta: 8vo: | opd |
| 1530 | Parma | Antonio di Viotti: 8vo: | opd |
| 1531 | Florence | Benedetto Giunti: 8vo: | opd |
| 1531 | Parma | Antonio di Viotti: 8vo: | ves |
| 1532 | Parma | Antonio di Viotti: 8vo: | stm |
| 1533 | Venice | Aldine Press: 8vo: with a few poems by Castiglione: | exd |
| 1534 | Barcelona | Pedro Monpezat: fol.: Spanish version by Juan Boscan Almogaver: | fab |
| 1537 | Florence | Benedetto Giunti: 8vo: | brm |
| 1537 | Paris | For Jean Longis and Vincent Sertenas: 8vo: French version by Jacques Colin: | exd |
| (1537) | Lyons | Denys de Harsy: 8vo: Colin's French version: | opd |
| 1538 | Venice | Vettor de' Rabani and associates: 8vo: | stm |
| 1538 | Venice | Giovanni Padovano for Federico Torresano d'Asola: 8vo: | exd |
| 1538 | Venice | Curzio Navò and brothers: 8vo: | cor |
| 1538 | Lyons | Françoys Juste: 8vo: Colin's French version revised by Estienne Dolet: | exd |
| 1539 | Venice | Curzio Navò for Alvise Tortis: 8vo: | stm |
| 1539 | s. l. | Printer not mentioned: 8vo: abbreviation by Scipio Claudio: | maz |
| 1539 | Toledo | Printer not mentioned: 4to: Boscan's Spanish version: | fab |
| 1540 | Salamanca | Pedro Touans for Guillermo de Milles: 4to: Boscan's Spanish version: | ace |
| 1540 | Paris | Printer not mentioned: 8vo: (Colin's) French version: | ala |

////////////////////////////////////////////////////////////

| | | | |
|---|---|---|---|
| 1541 | Venice | Aldine Press: 8vo: | opd |
| 1541 | Venice | Gabriel Giolito de' Ferrari: 12mo: | stm |
| (1541) | s. l. | "T-A": 4to: Boscan's Spanish version: | fab |
| 1542 | Medina | Printer not mentioned: 4to: Boscan's Spanish version: | brm |
| (1542) | s. l. | Printer not mentioned: 4to: Boscan's Spanish version: | bnm |
| 1543 | Venice | Gabriel Giolito de' Ferrari: 8vo: | pas |
| 1544 | Venice | Gabriel Giolito de' Ferrari: 8vo: | opd |
| 1544 | Venice | Alvise de Tortis: 8vo: | chi |
| 1544 | Antwerp | Martin Nucio: 8vo: Boscan's Spanish version: | fab |
| 1544 | s. l. | Printer not mentioned: 8vo: | maz |
| 1545 | Venice | Aldine Press: fol.: | opd |
| 1545 | Paris | Printer not mentioned: 12mo: (Colin's) French version: | brm |
| 1546 | Venice | Gabriel Giolito de' Ferrari: 8vo: | exd |
| 1546 | Paris | For Arnoul l'Angelier: 12mo: Colin's French version: | opd |
| 1547 | Venice | Aldine Press: 8vo: | opd |
| 1547 | Venice | Gabriel Giolito de' Ferrari: 8vo: | maz |
| 1549 | Venice | Gabriel Giolito de' Ferrari: 12mo: | chi |
| 1549 | Venice | Alvise de Tortis: 8vo: | vel |
| 1549 | Paris | Gelles Corrozet: ——: (Colin's) French version: | bnt |
| 1549 | Paris | Jean Lor—: 16mo: (Colin's) French version: | vel |
| 1549 | s. l. | Printer not mentioned: 4to: Boscan's Spanish version: | ves |
| 1550 | Lyons | Gulielmo Rovillio: 16mo: | opd |
| 1551 | Venice | Gabriel Giolito de' Ferrari and brothers: 12mo: | stm |
| 1552 | Venice | Gabriel Giolito de' Ferrari and brothers: 8vo: text revised by Ludovico Dolce: | exd |
| 1552 | Venice | Domenico Giglio: 12mo: | opd |
| 1553 | Lyons | Gulielmo Rovillio: 12mo: | brm |
| 1553 | Saragossa | For Miguel de Capila: 8vo: Boscan's Spanish version: | fab |
| 1554 | Florence | The heirs of Bernardo Giunti: 16mo: | stm |
| 1556 | Venice | Girolamo Scoto: 8vo: Dolce's text: | cav |
| 1556 | Venice | Gabriel Giolito de' Ferrari: 8vo: Dolce's text: | stm |

*1111111111111111111111111111111111111111111111111111*

| 1550 | Venice | Simbeni for Bernardin Fagiani: 8vo: with Paolo Giovio's Life of Castiglione:......cav |
| 1559 | Venice | Gabriel Giolito de' Ferrari: 8vo: Dolce's text:.brm |
| 1559 | Toledo | Printer not mentioned: 4to: Boscan's Spanish version:......................maz |
| 1560 | Venice | Gabriel Giolito de' Ferrari: 8vo: Dolce's text: ......................brm |
| 1561 | London | William Seres: 4to: English version by Thomas Hoby:..................brm |
| 1561 | Antwerp | The widow of Martin Nutio: 8vo: Boscan's Spanish version:................ala |
| 1561 | Wittenberg | Johannes Crato: 4to: Latin version by Hieronymus Turler:.................jen |
| 1562 | Venice | Francesco Rampazzetto: 12mo:...........cav |
| 1562 | Venice | Printer not mentioned: 8vo: with Giovio's Life: .............................opd |
| 1562 | Lyons | Gulielmo Rovillio: 12mo: Dolce's text:.....opd |
| 1562 | Venice | Gabriel Giolito de' Ferrari: 12mo:........ang |
| 1563 | Venice | Same edition as the last, with change of date on title-page:..................maz |
| 1564 | Venice | Same edition as the last, with change of date on title-page:..................stm |
| 1564 | s. l. | Printer not mentioned: 8vo: edition erroneously dated "MDXLIV":..............ves |
| 1565 | Venice | Gerolamo Cavalcalovo: 12mo: Dolce's text:..stm |
| 1566 | Munich | Adam Berg: 8vo: German version by Lorenz Kratzer:.....................vat |
| 1568 | Venice | Domenico: 12mo:....................brm |
| 1569 | Venice | Gabriel Giolito de' Ferrari: 12mo:........vel |
| 1569 | Wittenberg | (Johannes Crato): 8vo: Turler's Latin version: ........................maz |
| 1569 | Valladolid | Francesco Fernandez de Cordoba: 8vo: Boscan's Spanish version expurgated:.....brm |
| 1571 | London | John Day: 8vo: Latin version by Bartholomew Clerke:..................brm |
| 1573 | Venice | Comin da Trino: 8vo: with Giovio's Life:...opd |
| 1574 | Venice | Gabriel Giolito de Ferrari: 8vo:..........maz |
| 1574 | Venice | Comin da Trino: 8vo:.................maz |
| 1574 | Venice | Domenico Fari: 12mo: Dolce's text:.......exd |
| 1574 | Antwerp | Philippo Nucio: 8vo: Boscan's Spanish version: ...............................exd |

ィィィィィィィィィィィィィィィィィィィィィィィィィィィィィィィィィィィィィィィィィィィィィィ

| 1577 | Antwerp | Philippo Nucio: 8vo: Boscan's Spanish version: .............................. bts |
| 1577 | Strasbourg | Bernhardus Jobinus: 8vo: Latin version of Book I by Johannes Ritius: ............. ves |
| 1577 | London | Henry Bynneman: 8vo: Clerke's Latin version: ............................. exd |
| 1577 | London | Henry Denham: 4to: Hoby's English version: ............................. brm |
| (1577) | Paris | Pierre Gaultier: 16mo: Colin's French version: ............................. opd |
| 1580 | Lyons | Thibauld Ancelin for Loys Cloquemin: 8vo: French version by Gabriel Chapuis with text: ........................... stm |
| 1581 | Salamanca | Pedro Lasso: 8vo: Boscan's Spanish version: .. ols |
| 1584 | Venice | Bernardo Basa: 8vo: text expurgated by Ciccarelli, with Life by Marliani: ....... stm |
| 1584 | Frankfort | Bernhardus Jobinus: 8vo: Latin version by Johannes Ritius: .................... ala |
| 1585 | London | Thomas Dauson: 8vo: Clerke's Latin version: ............................. brm |
| 1585 | Lyons | Claude Bourcidan for Jean Huguetan: 8vo: Chapuis' French version with text:... vel |
| 1585 | Paris | Nicholas Bonfons: 8vo: Chapuis' French version with text: .................... exd |
| 1585 | Paris | Georges l'Oyselet for Cl. Micard: 8vo: Chapuis' French version: .............. exd |
| 1587 | Venice | Curzio Navò and brothers: 8vo: .......... d'a |
| 1587 | Venice | Domenico Giglio: 12mo: ................ exd |
| 1588 | London | John Wolfe: 8vo: Hoby's English version revised, with text and Chapuis' French version: ........................... opd |
| 1592 | Paris | Nicholas Bonfons for Abel l'Angelier: 8vo: Chapuis' French version with text:... exd |
| 1593 | Venice | La Miniana Compagnia: 8vo: Ciccarelli's expurgation: ....................... stm |
| 1593 | London | George Bishop: 8vo: Clerke's Latin version: ............................. exd |
| 1593 | Dilingen | Johann Mayer: 8vo: German version by Johann Engelbert Noyse: ............. ang |
| 1599 | Venice | Paulo Ugolini: 16mo: Ciccarelli's expurgation, with Marliani's Life: .......... ang |

| | | |
|---|---|---|
| 1599 | Antwerp | Philippo Nucio: 8vo: Boscan's Spanish version expurgated:.....................maz |
| s. d. | s. l. | Printer not mentioned: 4to: Boscan's Spanish version: ........................bnm |
| 1600 | Florence | (The heirs of Filippo di Giunta): 4to:......d'a |
| 1601 | Venice | Giovanni Alberti: ——:..................jol |
| 1603 | London | T. Creede: 4to: Hoby's English version:....brm |
| 1603 | London | George Bishop: 8vo: Clerke's Latin version:.brm |
| 1606 | Venice | Giovanni Alberti: 8vo:...................ves |
| 1606 | Frankfort | Lazarus Zetzner: 8vo: Clerke's Latin version: ............................amb |
| 1612 | London | Thomas Adams: 8vo: Clerke's Latin version: ............................brm |
| 1619 | Strasbourg | Bernhardus Jobinus: 8vo: Ritius's Latin version: .........................cas |
| 1619 | Strasbourg | The heirs of Lazarus Zetzner: 8vo: Clerke's Latin version:...............brm |
| 1663 | Strasbourg | For Simon Paullus: 8vo: Clerke's Latin version: .........................exd |
| 1667 | Strasbourg | Bernhardus Jobinus: 8vo: Ritius's Latin version: .........................maz |
| 1668 | Zürich | Printer not mentioned: 8vo: Ritius's Latin version: .........................maz |
| 1684 | Frankfort | For Carl Schaeffer: ——: German version by "J. C. L. L. J.":.................rei |
| 1690 | Paris | Estienne Massot for Estienne Loyson: 12mo: French version by (L'Abbé Duhamel): ...........................exd |
| 1713 | Cambridge | William Innys: 8vo: Clerke's Latin version revised by S. Drake:..................exd |
| 1724 | London | A. Battesworth and others: 8vo: English version by Robert Samber:............nyp |
| 1727 | London | W. Bowyer: 4to: English version by A. P. Castiglione, with Life and text:.........opd |
| 1729 | London | E. Curll: 8vo: Samber's English version:....brm |
| 1733 | Padua | Giuseppe Comino: 4to: Volpi edition, with other works by Castiglione and Marliani's Life: ........................opd |
| 1737 | London | Olive Payne: identical with edition of 1727, title-page changed:.............opd |
| 1742 | London | H. Slater and others: identical with edition of 1727, title-page changed:..........opd |

| | | |
|---|---|---|
| 1766 | Padua | Giuseppe Comino: 4to: Volpi edition, with Life by Pierantonio Serassi:.............opd |
| 1771 | Vicenza | Giambattista Vendramini Mosca: 8vo: 2 volumes, with Serassi's Life:..........opd |
| (1772) | s. l. | Printer not mentioned: 8vo: 2 volumes:.....d'a |
| 1799 | Bassano | Remondini: 8vo: 3 volumes, including other works by Castiglione:............'.d'a |
| 1803 | Milan | La Tipografia dei Classici Italiani: 8vo:.....bnp |
| 1822 | Milan | Giovanni Silvestri: 8vo: with Serassi's Life:..brm |
| 1828 | Bergamo | Mazzoleni: 12mo: 2 volumes:............bra |
| 1831 | Milan | Niccolò Bettoni and the brothers Ubicini: 4to: .............................amb |
| 1842 | Venice | Girolamo Tasso: 8vo: 2 volumes, expurgated, with Serassi's Life:.............opd |
| 1844 | Parma | Fiaccadori: 16mo: expurgated edition:......amb |
| 1848 | Copenhagen | Schultz: 4to: early French version of Book III, edited by N. C. L. Abrahams:.......exd |
| 1854 | Florence | Felice Lemonnier: 8vo: annotated by Count Carlo Baudi di Vesme:................opd |
| 1873 | Madrid | Rivadeneyra for Alfonso Durán: 8vo: Boscan's version annoted by A. M. Fabié:.opd |
| 1884 | Turin | Libreria Salesiana: 16mo:................vel |
| 1884 | Florence | P. Metastasio for G. C. Sansoni: 16mo: with preface by Giulio Salvadori:........opd |
| 1889 | Florence | Gaspare Barbèra: 8vo: expurgated and annotated by Giuseppe Rigutini:..........opd |
| 1890 | Milan | Edoardo Sonzogno: 8vo: with preface by Lodovico Corio:.....................opd |
| 1892 | Florence | Same edition as that of 1889, with changed date on title-page:....................opd |
| 1894 | Florence | Carnesecchi for G. C. Sansoni: 8vo: annotated by Vittorio Cian:................opd |
| 1900 | London | Constable for David Nutt: 8vo: Hoby's English version edited by Walter Raleigh:.opd |
| 1900 | London | Edward Arnold (Essex House Press): 8vo: Hoby's English version edited by Janet E. Ashbee, with woodcut ornaments by C. R. Ashbee:...............opd |
| 1901 | New York | De Vinne for Charles Scribner's Sons: 4to: English version by L. E. Opdycke, with notes, seventy-one portraits, etc.:........nyp |

## NOTE

Professor Cian has for several years had in preparation a second and elaborately revised issue of his edition of 1894. The present translator was, in 1901, given access to the MS. notes then collected by the professor, and now begs to acknowledge the use that he was kindly allowed to make of them.

# INDEX